Europe as Empire

Europe as Empire

The Nature of the Enlarged European Union

Jan Zielonka

OXFORD
UNIVERSITY PRESS

OXFORD

UNIVERSITY PRESS

Great Clarendon Street, Oxford OX2 6DP

Oxford University Press is a department of the University of Oxford.
It furthers the University's objective of excellence in research, scholarship,
and education by publishing worldwide in

Oxford New York

Auckland Cape Town Dar es Salaam Hong Kong Karachi
Kuala Lumpur Madrid Melbourne Mexico City Nairobi
New Delhi Shanghai Taipei Toronto

With offices in

Argentina Austria Brazil Chile Czech Republic France Greece
Guatemala Hungary Italy Japan Poland Portugal Singapore
South Korea Switzerland Thailand Turkey Ukraine Vietnam

Oxford is a registered trade mark of Oxford University Press
in the UK and in certain other countries

Published in the United States
by Oxford University Press Inc., New York

British Library Cataloguing in Publication Data

Data available

Library of Congress Cataloging in Publication Data

Data available

Typeset by SPI Publisher Services, Pondicherry, India.
Printed in Great Britain
on acid-free paper by
Biddles Ltd., King's Lynn,
Norfolk

ISBN 0-19-929221-3   978-0- 19-929221-9

1 3 5 7 9 10 8 6 4 2

Preface

This book tries to comprehend the evolving nature of the European Union following the fall of the Berlin Wall in 1989. Its major focus is the last wave of enlargement that has profoundly transformed the EU. Although there are many parallels between the European integration process and the state-building process, the end product of the former is anything but a Westphalian superstate. The new emerging polity resembles a kind of neo-medieval empire, and this book tries to spell out the origin, the shape, and the implications of this empire.

Enlargement is not the only factor frustrating the Westphalian scenario. Now that French and Dutch voters have delivered a negative verdict on the European constitutional treaty, the most appropriate slogan might well be: *The European state is dead, long live the European empire!* The constitutional project was seen by many as a decisive breakthrough in the European state-building process, but the French and Dutch voters have called the bluff of those in favour of a European superstate. As always occurs in referenda, voters were guided by a range of concerns but the result made it clear that the idea of a European state is effectively dead. The question now emerges: what next? This book offers a straightforward answer: the Union is on its way to becoming a kind of neo-medieval empire with a polycentric system of government, multiple and overlapping jurisdictions, striking cultural and economic heterogeneity, fuzzy borders, and divided sovereignty.

This book sets forth a novel way of thinking about the EU and the process of European integration. It shows 'two Europes' coming together following the end of the cold war. It proposes a system of economic and democratic governance that meets the ever greater challenges of modernization, interdependence, and globalization. It also suggests the most plausible ways of promoting peaceful change in Europe and beyond. The book argues that mainstream thinking about European integration is based on mistaken conceptual assumptions and it spells out more effective and legitimate ways of governing Europe than through the adoption of a

European Constitution, the creation of a European army, or the introduction of a European social model.

The book covers many fields from politics and economics to foreign affairs and security. It gives ample space to both theoretical and empirical considerations. It analyses developments in both Eastern and Western Europe. It also tries to talk about the EU in an unconventional manner. It is therefore clear that I would not have been able to write this book without the help and encouragement of my students and colleagues. My gratitude goes first to those who read early drafts of individual chapters and offered me their insightful advice. I am especially indebted to Timothy Garton Ash, Grzegorz Ekiert, Christopher Hill, Charles S. Maier, Walter Mattli, Alexander J. Motyl, Jan-Werner Muller, Adam Roberts, Wojciech Sadurski, Andre Sapir, Gwendolyn Sasse, and Helen Wallace. Three anonymous reviewers have also been extremely generous and helpful. I also received many inspiring comments from my students at the University of Oxford and the European University Institute in Florence. Lars Hoffmann and Anna Sobczak have assembled a vast body of valuable empirical and bibliographical data for this book. Further assistance was provided by Nora Fisher and Stefan Szwed. Dominic Byatt from Oxford University Press has steered this project with extraordinary tact and care. My special thanks go to Ania Krok-Paszkowska who not only helped me to spell out some key arguments, but also to edit the entire work.

Oxford
15 October 2005

Contents

Introduction: The Neo-medieval Paradigm

What is the nature of the enlarged European Union (EU)? The Union is larger and more diversified than ever but this is where clarity and consensus end. Neither official documents nor the academic literature are able to describe the enlarged EU in any straightforward and commonly agreed manner. The dominant paradigm is state-centric: the EU is on its way to becoming a kind of Westphalian federation with a central government in charge of a given territory. However, this book will try to show that the enlarged EU increasingly resembles a neo-medieval empire rather than a classical Westphalian type of (federal) state. In the enlarged Union we are likely to see interpenetration of various types of political units operating in a system without a clear power centre and hierarchy. Socio-economic discrepancies are likely to increase without consistent patterns. The enlarged EU is likely to have soft borders in flux rather than hard and fixed external borders. Multilevel and multicentred governance in concentric circles will be the norm. Pan-European identity will be blurred and fragile with no truly European demos. In short, enlargement will change the Union beyond recognition, even though other structural factors such as modernization or globalization are also at play here.

The Union will resemble an empire, but this is not the type of empire the Euro-sceptics have feared so much.[1] The EU is not becoming a superstate projecting its ever greater power all over Europe and beyond. It is becoming a polycentric polity penetrating rather than controlling its environment. A multiplicity of various overlapping military and police institutions is likely to remain the norm. The contrast between the EU and the imperial might of the contemporary United States or nineteenth-century Britain is enormous.[2] This is because the EU resembles an empire we know from many centuries earlier. Its multilevel governance system of concentric circles, fuzzy borders, and soft forms of external power projection resemble the system we knew in the Middle Ages, before the rise of nation states, democracy, and capitalism. The book tries to grasp the nature of this new emerging polity and assess its implications.

Genesis of the book

The book is written as a polemical response to the mainstream literature on European integration. There are two features of this literature that I find particularly striking. First, most of the literature applies statist analogies and terms when writing about the EU. Second, the EU's eastward enlargement is often treated as a routine institutional operation that is unlikely to change the course and nature of European integration.

Although hardly any work explicitly claims that the Union is a state in the making, the European integration process is described as the kind of state-building process that followed the 1648 Peace of Westphalia. The Union is said to be gradually acquiring the major characteristics of a state: central government, external borders, common currency, citizenship, constitution, and even a surrogate for a European army. And these state-like institutions are always at the centre of the European debate rather than cultures, societies, nations, markets, or politics proper. The last wave of enlargement is said to change little here because students of European integration tend to treat it as if it were merely a diplomatic or bureaucratic exercise. Today, most textbooks on the EU contain one chapter on enlargement, but enlargement hardly impinges on the contents of other chapters dealing with what the authors and editors consider as core European issues.

This book is guided by an entirely opposed rationale. I look at this last wave of enlargement as part of an unprecedented historical process generated by the fall of Communism and the East–West division of Europe. The last wave of enlargement represents an enormous import of diversity that can hardly be addressed by the new members' formal adoption of the entire body of European laws and regulations: the famous (or infamous) *acquis communautaire*. I also believe that the last wave of enlargement has opened the door to further EU accessions on strategic rather than strict economic, legal, or cultural grounds. The decision to open accession negotiations with Turkey is a clear manifestation of this, and Ukraine may require a similar solution in the not-too-distant future. In other words, this particular wave of enlargement has dramatically and irreversibly transformed the nature of the Union, and we need to come to grips with this transformation.

Moreover, the use of statist terms and analogies is quite misleading because the Union is anything but a state. It has no effective monopoly over the legitimate means of coercion. It has no clearly defined centre of authority. Its territory is not fixed. Its geographical, administrative,

2

economic, and cultural borders diverge. And the Union is a very different kind of international actor than any of the states we know from history. The last wave of enlargement has not made the Union look more like a state. On the contrary, enlargement has resulted in more layers of authority, more cultural, legal, and political pluralism, more diversified and cross-cutting institutional arrangements. As mentioned earlier, enlargement is not the only factor generating changes in the Union. Nevertheless, enlargement understood in broader historical, economic, and cultural terms is a clearly identifiable and powerful variable behind the current changes and it cannot be treated as a footnote to the study of European integration. In other words, enlargement calls for a change of paradigms guiding the European integration process. An extra chapter on enlargement in the books on European integration is not sufficient. Enlargement demands a change in the entire set of arguments contained in these books or else makes them largely inadequate and outdated.

I realized that a new paradigm for the study of European integration is badly needed only a few years ago when I tried to understand the evolving nature of borders in Europe following the eastern enlargement.[3] Borders are not simply lines on maps where one jurisdiction ends and another begins. Borders are complex institutions shaping the nature of polities they demarcate and to which they belong. Different units usually have different kinds of borders. Westphalian states have relatively fixed and hard borders. Moreover, their geographical and functional borders usually overlap, that is, there is no disjunction between administrative boundaries, military frontiers, cultural traits, and market transaction fringes. However, my study revealed that the Union is unlikely to achieve all that. Enlargement implies an enormous import of diversity that will prevent the Union from overcoming the already existing discrepancy between its functional and territorial boundaries.

Moreover, the EU is unlikely to have fixed, relatively hard, and centrally governed borders. Although new communitarian solutions for organizing the EU's borders are being introduced, the British, Irish, and Danish opt-outs negotiated in Amsterdam show their limits.[4] Although European leaders by and large support the hard border regime envisaged by the system of Schengen, a growing body of evidence suggests that the system is unduly harsh, impractical, and at odds with the Union's main foreign policy objectives. In the era of cascading interdependence it is difficult to seal any borders, but especially those that are in constant flux due to successive waves of enlargement. A hard border regime does not necessarily mitigate concerns about terrorism, cross-border crime, and migration.[5]

At the same time, hard borders hamper profitable trade, alienate the EU's current and future neighbours, and jeopardize the existing Western system of civic rights and freedom. Some of the new member states from Eastern Europe are particularly unhappy about the Schengen *acquis* because it frustrates cross-border human links of their respective nationals, curbs flourishing economic relations resulting from these links, and even causes some legal problems.[6]

Indeed, the Union is likely to end up with soft border zones in flux rather than with hard and fixed external borderlines as envisaged by Schengen. Not a 'fortress Europe', but a 'maze Europe' is likely to emerge as a consequence.[7] In such a 'maze Europe' different legal, economic, security, and cultural spaces are likely to be bound separately, cross-border multiple cooperation will flourish, and the inside/outside divide will be blurred. In due time, the EU's borders will probably be less territorial, less physical, and less visible.[8] They will not look like fortified lines on the ground, but like zones where people and their identities mingle. In this sense, they will resemble the borders of a neo-medieval Europe rather than the borders of a Westphalian Europe. The linear concept of the border was not known in the Middle Ages; borders were treated more like geographical zones than lines and were fairly open. Moreover, there was hardly any overlap between administrative, economic, military, and cultural borders at the time. And so I decided to explore the medieval paradigm somewhat further and contrast it with the Westphalian paradigm dominating the literature on European integration. This story explains the genesis of this book.

Unidentified political object

Jacques Delors once called the EU an 'unidentified political object' and the term has frequently been used since.[9] The term suggests that the Union is quite mysterious and largely unexplainable. And in fact, the very purpose and character of the EU has always been a highly controversial, if not enigmatic topic. From the very start of the European integration project, ambiguity, double language, and contesting sets of underlying principles have been the norm not only in the political, but also in the legal domain. Successive generations of European leaders were faced with multiple and ever-changing agendas for which there were no ready-made solutions. They wanted to provide growth, peace, and cultural satisfaction for their constituencies, but different decades demanded different policies, and none of the envisaged set of policies could equally suit the very diversified and broad set of objectives. It would be wrong to assume that the leaders always knew what the best course of action would be, and if some thought that they knew, they usually were unable to agree on carrying it out. Persistent differences among European actors concerned the very nature of integration (federalism versus intergovernmentalism), the functional scope of integration (high politics versus low politics), and there were competing national agendas on nearly every question. In this situation pragmatism, incrementalism, and vagueness were the only ways to make any progress. It has been evident from the very beginning of European integration that ambitious and straightforward cooperative projects have a fairly good chance of being shot down. A good example is the story of the European Defence Community (EDC) project launched by the French government in the early 1950s and voted down in the French parliament largely because it did not try to conceal its federalist design.[10] In other words, European policy-makers were faced with a choice: integration in disguise or no integration. The language of successive cooperative arrangements had to be vague at times, and no specific destination point for the European project could ever be officially proclaimed. In fact, students of the early stages of European integration show that Jean Monnet and his supporters were fully aware of this problem and consciously tried to defer conflicts and reduce to a minimum the likelihood of an inflammatory public debate on any of their proposals.[11]

This ambiguity and vagueness of successive cooperative arrangements has solved some problems, but at a certain price. Efficiency requires that policies are geared towards achieving a limited number of specified objectives by the use of certain clearly defined means. This has always proved difficult in the history of European integration. The frequently deplored 'democratic deficit' of the Union is also in part the result of the unclear arrangements. The European electorate can hardly execute democratic control over EU decision-makers if it does not really know what exact choices are being made by them. And there are also numerous practical problems in interpreting the depth and course of integration. For instance, the set of gradually accumulated European laws containing quite complex if not mysterious formulations confront European actors with an ever greater challenge of comprehension and interpretation. The recently undertaken efforts to simplify the European treaty system in the form of a new constitution represent a response to this increasingly untenable situation.[12]

Lack of clarity and straightforwardness was also causing problems for students of European integration. The so-called 'dependent variable problem' is especially evident.[13] What is it exactly that we are trying to explain? How does one accurately establish what a successful prediction might be, given the problematic notion of the final condition of integration? Are we not trying to explain something that does not yet exist and whose existence can only be postulated? 'At best we have a putative dependent variable', admitted Ernst B. Haas and, he argued, this may render the entire theory of European integration 'obsolescent'.[14]

In the absence of any commonly agreed description or definition, academics have often resorted to the use of metaphors to help us comprehend the very nature of the Union. In the early 1970s, for instance, Donald J. Puchala compared the integration project to an elephant that 'blind' academics could visualize only through touching its various peculiar parts. 'Alas', admits Puchala, 'the elephant grew in size and changed in form at the very moment that the blind men sought to grasp it!'[15]

Two decades later Helen Wallace and William Wallace sought to describe the EU by using a metaphor of flying geese:

Geese fly in formation, mostly in V shape when they know in which direction they are traveling, sometimes in 'huddles', when their destination is unclear. The formation is functional in terms of aerodynamics, configured to provide lift and to maintain speed as efficiently as possible over long distances, as well as to defray the impact of turbulence as far as possible.... Within the broad formation—'skein'— geese apparently fly in family groups, eating together when the skein takes breaks on the journey, each skein composed of several families. The stronger or 'dominant birds' take responsibility for 'signaling' to the others and lead the take-offs as the birds enter flight.[16]

The flying-geese metaphor was especially helpful for comprehending a purposeful movement by a diversified group of actors under rotating leadership. However, the authors were quick to admit that the EU is probably composed of different kinds of birds: 'some eagles, some sparrows, even some chickens that cannot actually fly.'[17]

Architectural metaphors have been even more popular than zoological ones. Many authors have compared the integration project to the construction of a house or a group of houses. But such analogies assume a well-thought-out architectural design which is not only functional, but also visually attractive. In fact, the European construction resembles certain districts of Tokyo or Manhattan where one building is built next to or even on top of another without any clear architectural let alone aesthetic pattern. Beautiful new skyscrapers mix with ugly ruins. Sometimes a façade exists stranded without a building behind it; other times every available square metre is used efficiently.

Some authors have borrowed terms from geometry or physics to describe the European construction. The most popular terms were ones such as concentric circles, variable geometry, or multispeed Europe. These terms proved useful in describing individual features of the integration project, but were unable to grasp the full and complex picture in its historical dimension.

Philippe C. Schmitter, who in the 1960s and 1970s used complicated models to describe the nature of European integration, changed his attitude in the 1990s and suggested the use of Latin terms when imagining the future of the Euro-polity.[18] The problem was that these Latin terms—*condominio, consortio, confederatio,* and *stato/federatio*—strikingly resembled the statist terms that Schmitter himself found misleading and wrong for talking about the EU.

This leads us to the key problem in conceptualizing the past, current, and future EU. We need a complex and sophisticated paradigm and not just an inspiring metaphor or a fancy term to comprehend the Union. And the most relevant, insightful, and in fact dominant paradigm is the statist one. The state paradigm grasps both functional and territorial features of politics and government. It is not abstract, but has clear sociological, economic, and cultural dimensions. And it is also historically rooted in the sense that it emerged in the late Middle Ages and has continued its existence in different forms and places up to the present. No wonder therefore that nearly all theorists and practitioners refer to the state paradigm in one way or another when analysing European integration and trying to conceptualize its future destination. 'The perseverance of the "touch of stateness" is quite impressive in the context of European integration studies', confirmed Jo Shaw and Antje Wiener, for example.[19] And Schmitter added: 'our language for discussing politics is indelibly impregnated with assumptions about state.'[20] In short, it is difficult, if not impossible to discuss the future shape of the enlarged EU without referring to the notion of a state. The state must therefore represent the port of departure for our discussion, the major reference point, and the key analytical benchmark.

Should Europe become a state?

Walter Hallstein, the first head of the European Commission, is quoted as saying: 'Let us create the European State—or is Europe finally to abdicate?'[21] Several decades later the German Minister of Foreign Affairs,

Joschka Fischer, bluntly called for creation of a 'European Federation' in his speech at Humboldt University.[22] However, the idea of a European (super) state has never been popular among the European electorate, and therefore support for it usually comes in an indirect, if not entirely concealed manner.[23] Friends of a European (super) state do not usually advocate the creation of a European 'nation writ large' or a kind of 'United States of Europe'.[24] However, they see a state in its variety of shapes and forms as the superior historical formation able to assert efficient and legitimate control over a given territory.[25] Many of them believe that the Union should resemble some kind of a state or else it will perish. How then does a concealed statism reveal itself? What are the basic features of the statist argument? Let me identify three of them.

First, and most obviously, the state-centred argument always emphasizes the state and its institutional structures rather than the nation, politics, or markets. 'Institutions govern relationships between people. They are the real pillars of civilization', is reported to have been the favourite motto of Jean Monnet.[26] Institutional engineering rather than cultural and economic factors should therefore be given priority, according to the statists. For instance, the democratic deficit is to be tackled by reorganizing the European parliamentary system rather than by creating a truly European demos. Peace and security are to be assured by setting up intergovernmental institutions rather than through balance-of-power politics or by mitigating cultural prejudices and historical fears. Trade is more about central regulations (positive and negative alike) than about spontaneous exchanges between economic actors. The underlying assumption behind this argument is that it is easier to engineer or manipulate state institutions rather than culture, politics, or economic markets. One can probably envisage the creation of a European state, but not a European nation, for instance. Moreover, according to statists, it would be wrong to endorse any cultural or economic determinism: does history not show us that states can function in different kinds of economic and cultural settings?

Second, the state-centred argument proposes giving the Union more and more responsibility for market, money, security, and solidarity in member states. Ultimately, the Union should have a single central government in charge of a given territory with clear-cut borders, a common European army and police force, a single European citizenship, a common market, and a common social policy. The government may well have a federative rather than unitary nature, but it will basically resemble a modern version of the sovereign, territorial state that emerged in Europe following the 1648 Peace of Westphalia. When the Union's efforts to acquire all these functions and powers falter, the friends of a European state talk about a dangerous stalemate in the process of European integration, as if no other more flexible solutions could suit the purpose of integration. In other words, statists believe that European integration is making progress only when the Union is gradually acquiring all the major prerogatives of a Westphalian type of state.

Third, the state-centred argument would like the Union to provide an overlap between its functional and geographical borders. If one looks at the historical process of state formation following the Peace of Westphalia, success has largely been determined by the degree to which states were able to assure overlap between administrative borders, military frontiers, cultural traits, and market fringes. So the friends of a European state oppose a Union which is made up of concentric circles or variable geometric patterns resulting from various opt-outs negotiated by individual member states in the areas of foreign, monetary, or social policy. They believe that European integration should be about increased convergence across various functional fields and within a given territory. Since such convergence is unlikely in a broader European setting, the idea of a 'core group' has been launched in various forms and shapes by the statists.

There is no doubt that the aforementioned kind of argument is always present in the discourse concerning European integration, even if it is explicitly denied that the ultimate objective is a European (super) state. In other words, a kind of European state is a crucial proposition in both theoretical and practical terms. We now should ask whether the creation of a European state is a visible prospect and if not, what is a possible alternative. The major objective of this book is to show that enlargement renders the rise of a European state impossible. The enlarged Union will look more like a kind of medieval empire than a Westphalian type of state. Let us now see what are the major features of these two systems.

The neo-medieval alternative

The state has evolved in many different shapes and forms since the Middle Ages. One can hardly compare such diverse notions of a state as absolutist, (neo)liberal, totalitarian, welfare, regulatory, or postmodern. For most analysts the Westphalian notion of a state represents a way to group all the major characteristics of different states within one coherent paradigm.[27] The Westphalian state formally has absolute sovereignty over its territory. Its borders are fixed and hard, its socio-economic system is relatively homogeneous, and one single (national) culture predominates. The Westphalian state also has a clear hierarchical governmental structure with one centre of authority. There is a high degree of overlap between the legal, administrative, economic, and military regimes within it. The systems of legal justice and financial redistribution are unified and the notion of citizenship is simple and exclusive. The Westphalian state also has a single and centralized police force and army.

Historians point out that some of these characteristics were acquired much later than the Peace of Westphalia. According to Charles Maier, for instance, modern territoriality and the modern nation state depend upon 'the material possibilities for controlling large regions of the earth' and these arrived only in the mid-nineteenth century with the advent of electricity, steel, and steam.[28] Political scientists argue that some crucial notions of a Westphalian state such as sovereignty are merely a theoretical abstraction, or a kind of 'organized hypocrisy' as Stephen Krasner put it.[29] Sociologists point to the existence of decentralized multinational states or even states with large city regions that undermine the Westphalian notion of centralism, hierarchy, and homogeneity.[30] That said, the Westphalian paradigm represents a fairly coherent and empirically verified way of organizing territorial authority. Authority was organized quite differently before the late Middle Ages. In fact, as Jean Dunbabin argued: 'It was not until the end of the fifteenth century that *status* (i.e. state) was first used with its modern connotation.'[31]

How did the medieval system differ from the Westphalian one and can the former ever re-emerge? First of all, authority in the medieval system was shared and spread; it was neither unified nor exclusive. As John Gerard Ruggie put it, the medieval system of rule reflected 'a patchwork of overlapping and incomplete rights of government', which were 'inextricably superimposed and tangled', and in which 'different juridical instances were geographically interwoven and stratified, and plural allegiances, asymmetrical suzerainties and anomalous enclaves abounded.'[32]

Instead of the hierarchy of powers there was a 'criss-crossing pattern of competing networks of clients'.[33] Public authority was fragmented and 'privatized'. Each lord used to have more than one vassal. One man could become the vassal of more than one lord. These lord–vassal relations were very complex and confusing. Multiple allegiances were the norm and they were usually asymmetrical. Jurisdictions over feudal lands were plural and overlapping. Unlike in a Westphalian state, there was no monopoly of law-making. Nor were all 'citizens' subject to the single law of their land. In fact, sharp, impenetrable border lines were unknown in the Middle Ages. Instead there were much looser concepts such as *limes* and *marches*.[34] Needless to say, there was little overlap between geographical and functional borders of authority. The rise of autonomous towns and cities with strong guilds multiplied the government even further.[35] Sovereignty in the Middle Ages was not seen as an absolute concept. Alongside territorial sovereignty the universal sovereignty of the emperor or pope was usually recognized.[36] Internal and external security was also 'privatized' and linked to the complex set of relations between lords and vassals. Plurality of government was linked to cultural diversity. Nations in the modern sense of the word did not exist in the Middle Ages, and cultural identity was weakly connected to the network of authority.[37]

The Westphalian state was often seen as a 'machine propelled by energy and directed by information flowing from a single center in the service of a plurality of coordinated tasks'.[38] Medieval writers, on the other hand, described a social order functionally divided like the individual. The Westphalian paradigm was positivist, the state being a purposefully constructed formal structure for the performance of basic public tasks. The medieval paradigm was naturalistic and spiritual: authority should reflect natural harmony and justice under God.

Of course, it would be rather naive to claim that the earlier described medieval system could ever be recreated. But it is certainly legitimate to ask whether a kind of 'postmodern' equivalent of medievalism could represent a workable alternative to a Westphalian type of state in the contemporary European context. Table 0.1 presents two such contrasting models of organizing government and politics.

Two types of empire

My use of the term empire requires special justification and explanation. The term empire has been used to describe many different political actors. Alexander Motyl has pointed to the fact that Amazon lists no less than 10,513 books with empire in the title on its website; Barnes and Noble lists 10,210.[39] Most of these books assume that empire is about control by the metropolis of various peripheral actors through formal annexation or various forms of economic and political domination.[40] However, here the consensus ends. Control can be exercised through various combinations of

Table 0.1. Two contrasting models of the future EU system

Westphalian superstate	Neo-medieval empire
Hard and fixed external border lines	Soft-border zones in flux
Relatively high socio-economic homogeneity	Socio-economic discrepancies persist without consistent patterns
A pan-European cultural identity prevails	Multiple cultural identities coexist1
Overlap between legal, administrative, economic, and military regimes	Disassociation between authoritative allocations, functional competencies, and territorial constituencies
A clear hierarchical structure with one centre of authority	Interpenetration of various types of political units and loyalties
Distinction between EU members and non-members is sharp and important	Distinction between the European centre and periphery is most crucial, but blurred
Redistribution centrally regulated within a closed EU system	Redistribution based on different types of solidarity between various transnational networks
One single type of citizenship	Diversified types of citizenship with different sets of rights and duties
A single European army and police force	Multiplicity of various overlapping military and police institutions
Absolute sovereignty regained	Divided sovereignty along different functional and territorial lines

military, economic, and cultural means. It can be formal or informal to various degrees. It can be based on coercion or incentives or a combination of both. The periphery status within the empire can also differ. Some actors are given access to the metropolis decision-making and resources, while others are kept at a distance or even subject to open discrimination and exploitation.

The nature of both metropolis and peripheral actors can also differ. In most cases the metropolis has a centralized government, differentiated economies, and shared political loyalties, while the 'imperializable peripheries', to use Michael W. Doyle's term, have weak government, undifferentiated economies, and highly divided political loyalties.[41] However, the imperial metropolis can also have a relatively weak, limited, and decentralized government, inefficient economic system, and multiple cultural identities. In particular medieval empires were known for having limited and decentralized government performing only a few basic governmental functions.[42] They were ridden by internal conflicts between a king or emperor and the lower aristocracy, whether feudal or bureaucratic, while the persistent divergence of local cultures, religions, and traditions implied a highly divided political loyalty.[43]

Empires also differ in their degree of 'completeness, self-absorption, and universalism', and whether they form a hierarchy from a 'central Cosmos to a peripheral Chaos', to use Ole Wæver's expressions.[44] Some empires are tight and hierarchic, while others are organized in concentric circles or even form quite loose multiple independencies.[45]

The metropolis does not always have a master plan of imperial conquest. States can become empires by default because they try to bring some order to unstable neighbours or try to convert barbarians into 'good' citizens or Christians. Likewise, an empire does not need to arise via outright aggression. Some empires rose quietly or even surreptitiously through uneven modernization and social differentiation. As Alexander Motyl puts it: 'Empires can emerge silently—without noisy campaigns or bombastic proclamations of manifest destiny.'[46]

The current literature usually focuses on empires of the two last centuries such as the British, Russian, and increasingly also the American one.[47] We can call them Westphalian empires, that is, Westphalian centralized states turned empires through military conquests, territorial annexations, or international economic exploitation. As mentioned earlier, my use of the term empire has nothing to do with these characteristics.[48] The EU is not a Westphalian centralized state; it is a sort of civilian rather than military power and offers economic help to its peripheries rather than trying to exploit them. Yet, when we look at the ever-further extension of EU borders and at the 'aggressive' export of EU rules to its neighbours we cannot but conclude that the EU is (or is becoming) an empire of some sort.[49] In fact, the latest EU enlargement looks like a prototype of imperial politics. In essence it was about asserting the EU's political and economic control over the unstable and impoverished eastern part of the continent through skilful use of political and economic conditionality. True, the post-Communist countries were not 'conquered' but invited to join the EU, and they did so quite eagerly. Moreover, at the end of the accession process they were offered access to the EU's decision-making instruments and resources. Nevertheless, the discrepancy of power between the EU and the candidate states was enormous and one wonders how much actual freedom the candidate countries could ever have had in the accession negotiation process. In fact, the Union has from the start made it clear that the candidate countries must adopt the entire body of European law before entering the Union. Of course, their compliance with EU laws was often more apparent than real, but cheating is the essence of imperial relations characterized by structural asymmetries. The fact is, however, that within empires the peripheral states operate under de facto (if not *de jure*) constrained sovereignty. This is also the case when we look at the set of relations between the EU and its new members and would-be members. Table 0.2 contrasts these two basic modes of imperial politics: the neo-Westphalian empire and what I call a neo-medieval one.

It should be reiterated that this is an ideal model and not a description of any such historical entity. For instance, there was a great deal of decentralized layering and soft power extension in the Middle Ages, but never before did so many sovereign powers decide to pull their various resources together and form an imperial centre.[50] My use of ideal types and models therefore requires further explanation.

Uses and abuses of models

European integration is a very complex process, but the way political scientists cope with this complexity is through the use of certain paradigms, and models pointing to ongoing trends.[51] These models can also show which future options for the EU are more probable than others and explain why this is so. In this book I distinguish between only two possible models indicating contrasting options for the future course of European integration. Each of these models represents a conceptually possible expression of political authority organized at the national and transnational level.[52] One

Table 0.2. Two contrasting types of empire

Major features	Neo-Westphalian empire	Neo-medieval empire
Mode of territorial acquisition	Conquest	Invitation
Governance structure	Centralized	Polycentric
Type of control	Coercion and bribes	Incentives or their denial
Means of control	Military and political	Economic and bureaucratic
Borders between metropolis and periphery	Clear and sharp	Fuzzy
Power relations between metropolis and periphery	Perpetual asymmetry and hierarchy	Periphery gradually gains access to decision-making of the metropolis
Degree of universalism	High	Low
Sovereignty in the periphery	Constrained or denied altogether	Constrained through sharing

points in the direction of a Westphalian type of state, and the other in the opposite direction of a neo-medieval empire. The former is about concentration of power, hierarchy, sovereignty, and clear-cut identity. The latter is about overlapping authorities, divided sovereignty, diversified institutional arrangements, and multiple identities. The former is about fixed and relatively hard external borderlines, while the latter is about soft-border zones that undergo regular adjustments. The former is about military impositions and containment, the latter about export of laws and modes of governance. This dichotomy will be spelled out in more detail in the successive chapters focusing on individual functional fields. Despite this effort, nevertheless, both the Westphalian and medieval models merely represent theoretical benchmarks rather than the exact approximation of the course of history. They both ought to be treated as analytical paradigms indicating different ways of exercising political authority rather than empirical blueprints.[53] The purpose is to identify two possible options for the Union's future, and to examine which option is more probable and why. The purpose is to stimulate new thinking about the European project that corresponds better with the evolving reality.

The exercise is not entirely abstract, because the current EU in fact contains elements of both these models. On the one hand, there are reasons to believe that the Union is anything but a Westphalian type of (super) state. Several member states do not want see the Union in charge of their foreign, monetary, or social policy, for instance. The Union lacks a strong and coherent sense of cultural identity, much less a European demos or *patria*. Globalization with its massive labour and capital flows makes it difficult for the Union (or in fact for any other actor) to maintain a minimum degree of sovereignty, hierarchy, and order. On the other hand, however, the Union is trying hard on behalf of its member states to regain a degree of control over the forces of globalization and to assert its sovereignty within its borders. In spite of all the resistance detailed here, it is gradually introducing some forms of central European government not only in the field of foreign, monetary, and social policy, but even in the areas of defence and justice and home affairs. The Union is also trying to improve its democratic credentials and enhance a common European cultural identity, for instance through the European citizenship project.

According to official rhetoric, enlargement is not going to reverse this latter trend; and as Joschka Fischer argued, it even reinforces the determination to accomplish the construction of a European federal state.[54] The official EU policy is that widening the Union goes hand in hand with its deepening.[55] The enlargement process has been accompanied by efforts to deepen EU integration through the expansion of the *acquis communautaire*, the creation of a single market, and the imposition of a strict external border regime. New countries can join the EU, but only after meeting an ever-growing list of conditions which would make them compatible with current members and allow for their adaptation to the existing system. Those who are not yet EU members are supposed to be kept at bay through custom quotas and tariffs and the Schengen regime. But this is not what we see on the ground. For instance, Norway and Iceland are part of Schengen while EU members such as Poland, Ireland, and Slovenia are not, albeit for different reasons. Will it ever be possible for the enlarging Union to secure a strong overlap of various cultural traits, market transaction fringes, and administrative boundaries? And if not, how much internal diversity can the Union withstand without compromising efficiency and legitimacy? Can a single authority be in charge of jurisdiction, taxation, and social questions in a Union increasingly acting in concentric circles? Today these are the most hotly debated questions and the answers to these questions do not necessarily suggest a Westphalian superstate in the making. This book will address these kinds of questions and assess their broader systemic implications.

My exercise is anything but perfect, however, and some words of caution are due before I proceed further. To start with, models cannot but simplify complex processes and structures. This concerns models focusing both on history and on the future of Europe. As mentioned earlier, various studies showed that the Peace of Westphalia did not instantly and directly produce a new political order.[56] War can start or end on a certain day but political systems and their characteristics evolve over time. Major concepts associated with the Westphalian order can also be questioned. Andreas Osiander has pointed out, for instance, that the term 'sovereignty' was hardly even mentioned in the Peace Treaties of 1648.[57] It is obviously not my intention to entertain either the myth of Westphalia or the myth of Copenhagen. (The latest accession treaty was signed in Copenhagen in 2003 and the original set of accession criteria was also elaborated in Copenhagen a decade earlier.) My aim is to explain the ongoing changes with the help of two contrasting models, however imperfect.

The Westphalian model may well be controversial, but it is widely recognized and referred to. The medieval model is more difficult to justify.[58] There was hardly any democracy in the Middle Ages even though it is hard to ignore the importance of Roman and Canonic law across the continent. Can one talk about a market economy in the Middle Ages even though there was a 'transactional' trading and banking system of some sorts? There was at the time a Holy Roman Empire, but students of the Middle Ages argue that it was neither Roman, nor holy, nor even an empire. And most importantly, one could hardly talk in the Middle Ages about 'sovereign nation states' that are so vivid at present. So, why use the term neo-medieval empire? As mentioned earlier, I find the alternative terms currently used to describe the EU to be rather inadequate. To start with, mysterious terms such as 'unidentified political object' or 'postmodern polity' do not allow us to compare the Union to any other types of polities we know from history.[59] I use the term 'neo-medieval empire' exactly to emphasize that the EU's ways of organizing governance and projecting power abroad are not unique, but have been tried in previous stages of European history, even though in an entirely different sociopolitical context. Of course, simple historical analogies never work, and I do not attempt to apply them. That said, utilizing historical comparisons can be helpful in identifying basic analytical benchmarks. They also represent a rich source of inspiration.[60] In fact, there is a growing body of literature using medieval and imperial metaphors and this literature will be drawn upon throughout the book.[61]

Although I have chosen to work with only two abstract models, various in-between solutions can also be envisaged. In fact, Helen Wallace has pointed out to me that in her view neither of my contrasting models is in the making, but a compromise between the two exemplified by the Roman empire: a loose governmental arrangement, but with a common currency and army, as well as some sort of common citizenship and language, may well be emerging.[62] It is also possible to conceive of more than two models. For instance, James A. Caporaso distinguished between three models for the evolving EU: the Westphalian, Regulatory, and Postmodern.[63] As mentioned earlier, Schmitter envisaged four models for the evolving Union: *condominio*, *consortio*, *confederatio*, and *stato/federatio*.[64] My own study on Europe's future borders also distinguished between four rather than only two basic types of regimes: liberal internationalism, imperial neo-medievalism, parochial nationalism, and Westphalian superstatism.[65] The use of only two models increases the risk of error and oversimplification, but it also allows for sharper contrasts and clearer argument. Moreover, the main aim of this book is to show that the Westphalian model is not in the making as suggested (implicitly or explicitly) by many students of European integration, and I offer a relatively straightforward alternative. Here I follow Giovanni Sartori's recommendation to use contrary or opposite concepts and models in describing any reality.[66] The neo-medieval and the neo-Westphalian models contrast with each other very well: the Westphalian system is what the medieval model is not, like democracy and autocracy for instance.[67]

Of course, critics can still insist that too much complex reality is squeezed into my models. They may also point out that some of the features I attribute to either the Westphalian or the medieval model have no historical precedence. They can argue that I am creating a straw man and projecting an artificial reality. If one applies absolute criteria of judgement I have no grounds to refute this criticism. However, applying absolute criteria of judgement would discredit most of social science and leave us at the mercy of astrologers and fortune tellers. Like all other social scientists I have had to perform a difficult balancing act while choosing between clarity and ambiguity, simplicity and confusion, dogmatism and relativism. I do not claim that my choices are perfect. But those who believe that I have created a straw man should be able to answer one basic question: if the enlarged EU does neither resemble a Westphalian state nor a medieval empire, what does it resemble? Do they have a more plausible model or paradigm to describe the emerging polity? An anything-goes approach to European integration is not enough, I would argue.

This book looks at the existing empirical evidence and tries to establish whether it fits in the neo-Westphalian or neo-medieval model. My findings suggest that the enlarged EU increasingly resembles a neo-medieval empire, but do not tell us with precision whether this is good or bad news for Europe. Neo-medievalism is not a synonym of anarchy and chaos. Indeed I would argue that diversity, called by another name, 'pluralism', is Europe's greatest historical and cultural treasure. Diversity is also a prerequisite of modernity, in the sense that only highly diversified and pluralistic societies acting in a complex web of institutional arrangements are able to succeed in conditions of modern competition. However, there are some obvious problems arising from neo-medievalism, especially in the field of democracy, culture, and social justice. Democracy could hardly work in a complicated if not impenetrable system of multilayered and multispeed arrangements run by an ever-changing group of unidentified and unaccountable people. The minimum degree of political trust, loyalty, and solidarity requires a certain sense of cultural identity, and this can hardly develop in a complex system of open-ended arrangements, with fluid membership, variable purpose, and a net of concentric functional frames of cooperation. In a Europe with fuzzy borders and polycentric governance it would be difficult to distribute public goods in any organized manner, let alone pursue any vision of social justice. The implications of the neo-medieval scenario will be discussed in more depth at the end of the book, but I must confess that I am not yet able to grasp the variety of possible implications of the emerging reality. My aim in this book is to show that mainstream thinking on the process of European integration is based on incorrect conceptual assumptions. Without a change of paradigm we will be unable to comprehend the ongoing developments, assess their implications, and identify proper solutions for addressing these implications. Even now, we are trying to apply Westphalian solutions to a largely neo-medieval Europe, and are surprised that these solutions do not work. But I hope that this book will inspire us to search for more effective ways of governing the EU than through adoption of a European Constitution, strengthening the powers of the European parliament, creating a European army, or introducing a central redistribution and taxation system via Brussels. I also hope to stimulate the necessary imagination for comprehending the evolving nature of the Euro-polity and identifying proper solutions for coping with it.

Although this book does not try to develop or test any particular theory, I hope that my findings suggest a different way of looking at the European integration process or even at some broader issues such as state-building and interstate relations.[68] I try to learn from various empirical studies and from diverse theoretical analyses, but I also try to explore a new conceptual and analytical terrain for understanding change in Europe, however risky. I deplore the tendency among fellow social scientists to cling to inadequate or obsolete concepts in describing these processes in Europe. My critique is especially directed at the misguided or confusing use of such terms as state, empire, sovereignty, convergence, or democratic representation in the study of integration. I find some of the empirical evidence in the field patchy, if not misleading altogether. Consider, for instance, the very inconclusive set of evidence showing the impact of the EU on its member states or the results of public opinion surveys (such as Eurobarometer) on attitudes to various European projects.[69] I do not think that any of the existing theories of political science in general and European integration in particular can on their own explain (let alone predict) all important European developments. In fact, I find most of these theories complementary to a large degree and I suggest that they should be mixed together in a creative manner. For instance, one can be a liberal–constructivist–realist regardless of what the guardians of individual theoretical temples may think.[70] Analyses integrating external and internal factors offer a better understanding of the European project than those exclusively focusing on only one internal or external dimension.[71] I also try to show that political scientists may make better use of other disciplines such as law, philosophy, and history rather than trying to contradict them.[72] In short, this book is not only about the enlarged EU, but also about a way of studying some broader political processes in Europe and beyond.

Structure of the book

The first three chapters show what the inclusion of several new countries from Eastern Europe implies for the government and politics of the EU. Is enlargement the decisive factor changing the nature of the EU and if so, how? In Chapter 1, I will try to trace the initial gap between the current and the new member states. How great was this gap and in which fields was it particularly striking? I will also try to establish to what degree various domestic reforms undertaken by individual post-Communist countries have been successful in making them more compatible with the former EU-15 (EU with fifteen member states).

The way the EU accession process contributed to greater convergence across the old East–West divide will be examined in Chapter 2. What was the purpose of the accession process, how was it designed and implemented, and what has been achieved in practice? I will argue in Chapter 2 that the eastern enlargement was an impressive exercise in empire-building. The Union tried to assert political and economic control over that unstable and impoverished neighbourhood. But this imperial exercise lacked a broader strategic vision, it was prone to parochial pressures, and its implementation was fairly benign. The countries of Eastern Europe had to comply with an ever-growing list of conditions, but they were given access to the EU's decision-making and resources at the end of the accession process.

In Chapter 3, I will assess the process of mutual adaptation between the two parts of Europe. I will also try to rethink the role and meaning of divergence in the process of European integration and search for the best way to handle it. I will argue that it would be difficult for the Union to acquire the basic features of a Westphalian state due to persistent divergence across various functional and geographical fields. However, the dividing lines do not necessarily run across the former East–West divide. Moreover, if one abandons the Westphalian paradigm, divergence may be seen as an asset rather than only as a liability for the future EU. Looser and less-integrated systems can cope well with diversity, and even profit from it. Besides, divergence is subject to political engineering with enlargement being a powerful tool for remedying the existing gaps in Europe.

The next three chapters will examine the functioning of the enlarged EU in three crucial fields: economics, democracy, and foreign affairs. In all these fields the Union seems to be making progress in constructing a typical Westphalian state. It consolidated the single economic market and introduced its own common currency, the euro. The European parliament was given enhanced powers. Internal borders are gradually being abolished, while the external borders of the EU are being tightened. The Union is also in the process of acquiring a surrogate of its own army together with an institutional framework for implementing a common defence policy.

That said this book provides evidence suggesting that a neo-medieval rather than a Westphalian pattern is in the making. Chapter 4 examines how the enlarged EU is likely to respond to the major economic challenges. Will the enlarged EU attempt to bridge the internal development gaps by flexible policies stimulating growth or by central redistribution from Brussels? Will the enlarged EU cope with the challenge of global economic competition by opting for more institutional differentiation or central regulation? Will it try to insulate itself from poor and unstable neighbours or try to govern them? In all three cases I found the enlarged EU more likely to embrace what I have identified as the neo-medieval rather than the neo-Westphalian alternative.

In Chapter 5 major challenges to democratic governance are examined and again I find the enlarged EU more likely to opt for neo-medieval than neo-Westphalian solutions. I show that the Union is likely to have an ever more multilayered and multicentred governance structure. Various non-majoritarian institutions are likely to dominate a weak European parliament(s). And we are likely to see neither the assertion of a European demos nor consolidation of a European public space.

Chapter 6 focuses on various aspects of 'external' affairs in Europe. It first shows that the Union is not on its way to becoming a Westphalian type of international actor. Foreign and security policy is still largely in the hands of member states and not the Union. Moreover, these member states are often hopelessly divided and eager to use various non-European institutional tools for their foreign and defence policies. The emerging international system in Europe also looks more medieval than Westphalian. The system is not anarchic, and collective bargaining over laws and procedures rather than balancing and ganging up over territorial gains is the essence of interstate politics at present.

It is one thing to identify the emerging European system; it is quite another to find solutions for coping with this system. The implications of neo-medievalism are anything but clear and it is highly uncertain whether a neo-medieval Europe will be a better place than the Europe of today. The concluding chapter will try to identify the implications of neo-medievalism for the Union's geostrategic position, its governance capacity, and its political legitimacy. It will also try to establish how to handle the emerging neo-medieval empire in Europe. Does the EU's new geographic reach demand a new type of geopolitics? Can the process of integration be maintained within a broader and more diversified setting? Can the EU system of governance be made more democratic and legitimate? There is a case for optimism, I argue. Although a neo-medieval empire would cause many problems and difficulties, it would also have some important advantages. A flexible neo-medieval empire in concentric circles would be in a better position than a European state to cope with the pressures of modernization and globalization. It would also be in a better position to compete with other great powers by pulling together vast European resources, but without eliminating Europe's greatest strength: its pluralism and diversity. A neo-medieval empire would also be well suited to provide conflict prevention in its neighbourhood by shaping countries' behaviour through the mechanism of EU membership conditionality. A neo-medieval empire might even be in a good position to be seen as democratically legitimate by bringing governance structures closer to the citizens, and making the system more transparent and open.

1
Return to Europe

It is often asserted that the last round of EU enlargement is not fundamentally different from the previous ones. In macroeconomic terms, for instance, the size of eight new member states from Eastern Europe vis-à-vis the EU-15 is broadly equivalent to the size of Greece, Portugal, and Spain vis-à-vis the EC-9 (the initial nine member states of the European Communities) in the 1980s. In 2002, the population of the eight eastern newcomers amounted to 19 per cent of the EU-15, whereas in 1980 the population of the three southern newcomers amounted to 22 per cent of the EC-9.[1] The gross domestic product (GDP) of the three southern candidates was equivalent to about 10 per cent of the EC-9, while the GDP size of the eight amounts to about 9 per cent of the EU-15.[2] Moreover, accession negotiations between the current twelve candidates closely resembled the pattern of previous enlargements. Not only procedures were similar, but also the substance of these negotiations. Consider the issue of agriculture that was the most controversial issue in the case of both the southern and the eastern enlargements.

However, these comparisons miss or underplay one fundamental point: the new member states from Eastern Europe are all post-Communist states. Before 1989 crossing the East–West divide was like entering a totally alien, if not hostile empire with different laws, economy, education, ideology, and culture.[3] True, from a broader historical perspective Eastern and Western Europe share some important characteristics, but under Communist rule Eastern Europe was a vivid antithesis of what the EU was about.[4] The question raised by this chapter is whether new member states from Eastern Europe were able to dispose of the Communist legacy within the past fifteen years and complete their 'return to Europe', to use their favourite expression.[5]

The major issue here is not so much the ability of Eastern Europe to catch up with Western Europe in terms of economy, law, and administration.

This issue will be tackled in Chapter 3. In this chapter I want to examine whether the ten Eastern European states aspiring to the Union were able to secure peace and build democracy and a free market on the ashes of Communism. I will look at the scope and form of reforms in Eastern European countries since 1989 and assess their relative success (or failure) in the context of European integration.

Of course, the Eastern European 'return to [the] Europe' of democratic and prosperous states is one thing; EU membership is another. However, there was little possibility of enlargement taking place before Eastern Europe had secured peace, democracy, and free markets. In fact it is quite plausible to believe that the main rationale behind enlargement was to secure these conditions rather than merely making Eastern Europe fully compatible with the EU regulatory framework. This chapter will therefore argue that it is crucial to go beyond a narrow institutional perspective when looking at the enlargement process and keep in mind the broader strategic considerations behind this process.

Moreover, the results of this enquiry reveal many features of the emerging Euro-polity. They tell us whether enlargement is likely to produce sharp or fuzzy cultural, economic, and political borders between the enlarged Union and its new neighbours further east and south-east. They tell us whether the enlarged EU faces internal or largely external security problems. They tell us whether enlargement is likely or unlikely to produce economic chaos and illiberal democratic practices. They tell us whether the Communist legacy is likely to form a fundamental obstacle for the smooth adoption and implementation of European laws, procedures, and institutions in new member states. Indeed, one can hardly comprehend the nature of the enlarged EU without a closer look at the new member states. We need to know their political and ideological backgrounds, the scope and forms of their respective transitions, and their present economic, democratic, and cultural characteristics. This chapter offers such background information.

This chapter also helps us to understand the question analysed in more depth in Chapter 2: why has the EU decided to extend membership to post-Communist countries? And it will also help to compare the old and new members of the EU, a topic covered in Chapter 3.

In the conclusion of this chapter I argue that the overall success of the reform process is beyond any doubt in all eight countries that joined the Union in 2004 and even in the so-called 'pre-ins': Romania and Bulgaria. However, this conclusion does not refute the initial assertion about the neo-medieval nature of the enlarged Euro-polity. Although new members have made considerable progress in securing peace and building democracy and free markets, their progress is uneven across individual fields and countries. This cannot but increase diversity within the EU as a result of enlargement. Although the achievements of the new members are clearly greater than those of other post-Communist countries, a sharp cultural, democratic, and economic border can hardly be established. The Union would therefore find it hard to provide a significant degree of overlap between its geographical and functional borders and to assure a Westphalian type of European governance.

Assessing Eastern European progress

The enlargement discourse tends to draw a negative picture of the new members. They are regularly accused of failing to implement some of the 80,000 detailed regulations falling under the *acquis communautaire*. We are told that their accession to the Union is going to paralyse its institutions and water down the process of integration. Eastern European citizens are often portrayed as a threat to Western European jobs, to the principle of rule of law, to cultural habits, and to national identities. Of course, some of the specific criticisms and concerns are justified, but these are 'luxury' problems when one looks at these countries from a broader historical and political perspective. Even staunch supporters of a European state must acknowledge that peace, prosperity, and democracy in the region are of truly prime importance for both Western and Eastern Europe. And, if one looks at the new members from this broader historical and political perspective the picture is anything but negative. In fact, the achievements of these countries amount to a historical 'miracle' in both absolute and relative terms.

When Communism fell, it was highly uncertain whether the countries considered here would ever be able to secure peace, prosperity, and democracy. In fact, a plethora of academics and media commentators argued that transition would lead to economic chaos, social upheaval, praetorian politics, and possibly foreign intervention.[6] Today most of these countries enjoy higher economic growth than the EU average. The security of none of them is seriously challenged and democracy is firmly established. Although progress has not always been even across individual countries and sectors, it is difficult to question their extraordinary successes. It is enough to consider post-1989 developments in Yugoslavia, Belarus, or even Russia to see how painful the exit from Communism can be. When

25

we later point to various problems and gaps between the old and new EU members it is always crucial to contrast the bad news with the good and assess its relative value. Convergence between Europe's west and east is important for more ambitious integrative projects, but the absence of major instability in Central and Eastern Europe is even more crucial and should never be taken for granted.

This leads me to the factors behind this extraordinary success in the region. Academics have identified a variety of important factors shaping post-Communist trajectories such as initial conditions, institutional choices, timing and sequencing of reforms, learning and quality of policies, the strength of a state apparatus, ethnic composition, geographic proximity to the West, and external support.[7] They all refuted the kind of optimistic determinism suggesting that the collapse of Communism and the victory of Western liberalism would make a swift convergence between the east and west of Europe the most natural development.[8] Nevertheless, they failed to establish a plausible set of casual relations between these factors. Moreover, individual factors' contribution to the successes and failures are also unclear and hotly contested.[9] In other words, the political engineering of domestic actors mattered, but so did cultural and historical legacies as well as external pressures, transnational and international alike. The single-factor theories have clearly failed to explain the successes and failures in the region and we must struggle with complex and often conflicting evidence explaining the scope and paths of reforms there.

Assessing the impact of single factors is also tricky because the single factors behind Eastern European transitions can usually be further disaggregated. For instance, most students of the region emphasize the importance of the constitutional process following the fall of the Communist regime. But what was more important: the constitution-making process itself or the end product of this process?[10] Have popular referenda enhanced the legitimacy of the adopted constitutions?[11] Does the choice of parliamentary or presidential system matter, and if so where and how?[12] Have some constitutional models improved democracy in Eastern Europe more than others?[13] In my own study of Eastern European constitutions I observed that different historical contexts generated different constitutional preoccupations.[14] For instance, constitutions have provided Baltic countries with the symbolic opportunity to express popular aspirations for free, democratic, and sovereign statehood. But in countries such as Russia, Ukraine, or even Poland new constitutions were largely about fixing the rules of the institutional power struggle which was tremendously detrimental to government stability and threatened local elites with political extinction. I found that some institutional choices clearly matter. For example, the choice of a strongly proportional (PR) electoral system in the region implied parliamentary fragmentation, undermining the efficiency of democratic work, while the choice of a weak PR system left many voters with no parliamentary representation. But I also found that institutional choices are largely a matter of complex political bargaining and the final product of this bargaining tends to resemble a hybrid that only partially corresponds with an original institutional design or model. Although some institutional solutions proved to work better than others, they were not necessarily the product of institutional or constitutional engineering, but resulted from cultural, economic, and social factors characteristic of a given country at a given time.

The external impact on transitions in the post-Communist space has also been found to be extremely important, but at the same time difficult to assess. Has transition been shaped by external actors such the EU, the United States, Russia, and the International Monetary Fund (IMF) or by broader historical processes such as the collapse of the Soviet empire, ethnic conflicts, waves of migration, capital flows, and the rise and fall of various ideological doctrines?[15] What was more influential: carefully designed strategies of external actors or the informal diffusion of norms and practices as well as the demonstration effect?[16] Can we say that the external impact on economic and democratic transitions was positive only? After all, some authors have argued that the EU exported its democratic deficit to Eastern Europe and prevented rapid economic growth there.[17] And can we talk in black-and-white terms about the impact of various external factors in view of a very mixed set of empirical evidence? For instance, as Frank Schimmelfenning's study showed, EU democratic conditionality has had uneven impact on individual post-Communist states.[18] This impact was easy to detect in countries with mixed party systems and shifting political patterns, but not in either the most liberal or the most illiberal states. In other words, there is a high degree of interplay between internal and external factors affecting transitions in Eastern Europe.[19] We should keep in mind all this complexity when judging the progress of individual states under consideration.

Another major problem in making any assessments concerns the grouping of countries under simple labels. The usual labels such as Central or South-eastern European are vague while labels such as post-Communist or Balkan are not only vague but also controversial. How long does it take to get rid of the post-Communist stigma, ask many scholars in the region? Others hasten to add that not all countries belonging to the Balkans manifest the 'Balkan syndrome' associated with war and ethnic cleansing.[20] Grouping countries according to cultural or religious characteristics is even more controversial. In particular, there is hardly any evidence confirming the alleged 'civilization border' between the Catholic and Orthodox parts of Europe (that also runs across individual countries such as Romania). Nor can we prove that countries belonging to the former Habsburg Empire share different values and attitudes than countries formerly belonging to the Ottoman Empire. As Alina Mungiu-Pippidi and Denisa Mindruta show, political attitudes in former Habsburg and Catholic Slovakia are similar to former Ottoman and Orthodox Christian Romania and Bulgaria.[21] This is not to deny the importance of cultural legacies, but to show that different legacies have been at work in countries discussed here.[22] For instance, in some cases Communist institutions modified pre-Communist patterns more than in other cases. Besides, cultural legacies are only one of the many variables shaping the post-Communist environment.

In this chapter (and in the book as such) I focus on those Central and Eastern European countries that joined the Union in 2004, plus Romania and Bulgaria. This excludes Cyprus and Malta who joined the Union in the same year. It also excludes Croatia, even though in June 2004 Croatia was moved from the status of applicant to candidate country for EU membership and some of its economic indicators are more impressive than those of the new EU members. The case of Croatia not only shows that the formal distance to EU membership is not directly related to statistical progress; it also shows that history moves fast in this region, albeit unevenly. Croatia, unlike Serbia, was able to overcome the legacy of war fairly quickly and displayed remarkable progress in various fields. Despite global economic slowdown, Croatia reached and maintained a relatively high rate of economic growth in the first years of this decade and attracted a considerable amount of foreign direct investment (FDI).[23] The results of the 2002 parliamentary and presidential elections in particular, signalled a major positive change in Croatia's political orientation and the beginning of its closer regional and international integration. This was instantly noticed and rewarded by the Union, but as this book goes to print, Croatia still has a different type of relationship with the Union than even Romania and Bulgaria, and it is therefore grouped in a different category.

The group of ten countries singled out in this book includes three post-Soviet republics (Estonia, Latvia, and Lithuania), and three Balkan countries (Slovenia, Bulgaria, and Romania).[24] Countries like Poland or Hungary are fairly 'old' nation states, but their territory has shifted (and shrunk) over decades. Countries like Slovenia, Slovakia, and the Baltic states have only recently 'fled' from larger federal units, and their national identity is still a sensitive question. Romania and Poland are relatively large in terms of territory and population, while most other states in the group are relatively small. Despite all these differences the countries did better on average than other countries in the former Communist space and their closeness to the Union is therefore not accidental. Both quantitative and qualitative evidence is used to assess their progress. Such progress is evaluated in historical and comparative terms. I first examine how much has changed since 1989, and how these countries are currently performing in light of initial expectations. This is followed by a detailed comparison of the countries across the entire post-Communist region. Who are the champions and the laggards in the post-Communist transformation? Can we draw a map for the region that shows progress both in terms of time and geographic space? Moreover, the analysis cannot but be multi-dimensional. After all, a successful 'return to Europe' would require significant progress in many different fields ranging from security to democracy, civil society, and economy. However, these are very different fields and progress in one of them is not necessarily conducive to progress in another. For instance, it has been argued that democracy makes it more rather than less difficult for the government to introduce painful economic adjustments.[25] Moreover, reforms in the individual fields have different time schedules. As Ralf Dahrendorf rightly argued on the eve of post-Communist transition, constitutional changes can be introduced in a matter of months and it takes several years to accomplish market reforms, but the development of a viable civil society requires some sixty years or at least two generations.[26]

Market reforms and social peace

One of the greatest positive surprises of the post-Communist history in the ten countries concerned has been the virtual absence of any dangerous political and social instability following the introduction of extremely painful economic adjustments. Such instability had been widely expected by social scientists anticipating fierce public resistance to macroeconomic stabilization and introduction of a free market.[27] And all the countries in question had to climb out of a very steep 'valley of tears', to use Ralf Dahrendorf's expression.[28] The drastic fall in production was devastating throughout the entire region. It was partly due to the collapse of the Council for Mutual Economic Assistance (COMECON) markets, and partly due to price liberalization and very tight fiscal and monetary policies. In the first two years of transition output fell by around 20–40 per cent in all countries in the region. (The fall was even more dramatic if we take into consideration industrial output.)

The sharp fall in production led to an immediate surge in unemployment which, except in the Czech Republic, rose in less than three years from virtually zero in 1990 to double-digit levels.[29] Economic stabilization programmes also led to a sharp fall in living standards. Wages fell by around 26 per cent in Hungary, 17–22 per cent in Poland, Romania, Slovenia, and Slovakia, and 45–65 per cent in the Baltic states and Bulgaria.[30] A dramatic growth of poverty and an unprecedented increase in social differentiation followed. By the mid-1990s, more than 50 per cent of Romanian citizens were found to be living below the subsistence minimum and even in such relatively prosperous countries as Hungary and Poland, one-third of the population was living below the poverty line. Life expectancy also fell. In Hungary, for instance, the life expectancy of males had fallen to nearly eight years below the EU average.

All this painful readjustment could not but produce public frustration and even depression. For instance, in 1992 only 11 per cent of interviewed Poles believed that their country was going in the right direction, while 74 per cent held the opposite view. Also, 48 per cent of respondents described the situation of their own household as bad, while only 11 per cent described it as good.[31] So, why did the Poles not rebel once again? And why was there relative social peace in other Central and Eastern European states? True, there were sporadic strikes and other forms of industrial action undertaken in various countries. Successive government coalitions have usually been voted out of office after only one parliamentary term or put under political pressure to step down even earlier. But no widespread public rebellion against the programme of economic transformation took place in any of the ten countries.

One possible explanation is that the cited statistics paint a too negative, if not a misleading picture. For instance, although unemployment has indeed risen sharply since the beginning of transition, its current rate is comparable with the one prevailing in the EU. (In fact, the level of unemployment in such countries as Hungary and Slovenia for 2001 was 5.7 per cent, and thus much below the EU-15 average of 7.4 per cent[32]). Moreover, most statistics do not take into account the sizeable unregistered 'second' or 'shadow' economy in the region and its impact on individual welfare. In Hungary, for instance, it has been calculated that the shadow economy generates nearly half of the country's GDP. (Public opinion data may also exaggerate the level of frustration and unhappiness among Eastern Europeans.)

Another explanation has been offered by Elena A. Iankova in *Eastern European Capitalism in Making*.[33] Iankova has showed that successive governments and industrial actors have worked hard to maintain social peace by skilful institutional engineering in the form of tripartism. In other words, the main political and industrial actors reached various corporatist types of agreement not to exploit the economic pains of transition for their short-term gains. They were, of course, involved in hard industrial bargaining but they chose to conduct this bargaining via an institutional process of negotiations between the government, employers, and employees.[34] This institutional form of bargaining aimed at a fairer distribution of the burdens and rewards of economic transition. It included multiple participants at not only national, but also local levels of governance and production. As a result of successive compromises, the costs of transition have been spread over time and between different groups of the population thus preventing uncontrolled and widespread forms of industrial protest. For instance, the painful reforms of national health and welfare programmes have been postponed in most of the countries.

Another explanation has been offered by Béla Greskovits. In *The Political Economy of Protest and Patience* he argued that social peace could be maintained because of the emergence of a 'low-level equilibrium' between the economic and the political sphere.[35] Democracy and market economy could be simultaneously introduced only because neither was fully implemented. Democracy could only stabilize at the price of some of its qualitative aspects due to the economic crisis and economic transformation. Economic transformation, in turn, remained feasible only at the cost of its speed and radicalism. The economic and political systems reached equilibrium, but at a lower level than in developed Western market democracies.

However, the positive impact of external actors is the most frequently cited explanation for relative social peace in the region.[36] Economic stabilization programmes and market reforms, however painful, were required by Western financial institutions as a precondition of any financial or technical aid. These reforms were also needed to make the countries eligible for EU membership. Moreover, the general public could plainly see the advantages of a capitalist economy over a Soviet-type economy in terms of growth and welfare. The demonstration effect of the successful economic story in Western Europe was clearly powerful in all post-Communist countries under consideration and it was reinforced by the progressive diffusion of Western practices following the fall of the Iron Curtain.[37] This made sacrifices easier to bear, at least for a limited period of time.

Public patience and a general endorsement of economic restructuring by Central and Eastern European populations paid off in the end. Since 1989 GDP has increased by more than 48 per cent in Poland, 32 per cent in Hungary, and 20 per cent in Slovenia.[38] Those who were late in introducing macroeconomic readjustments and structural reforms had to wait somewhat longer for positive growth. Bulgaria and Lithuania did not register positive growth until 1998 and Romania only in the year 2000. Moreover, high growth in some countries has been followed by a drastic, although temporary crisis. The most striking example is the case of Poland that in 2000 registered growth of 4 per cent followed by only 1.1 per cent growth in 2001. (The EU average growth was 1.5 per cent that year[39]). There is no doubt, however, that the ten countries in question managed to jump the first and most important economic hurdle with relative success, largely thanks to public patience and cooperation (see Fig. 1.1).

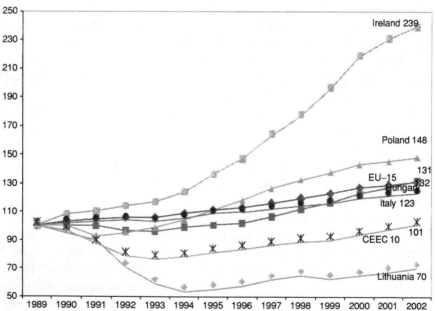

Figure 1.1 Cumulative GDP growth 1989–2002 in selected countries of the EU-25
Source: OECD 2002; EBRD 2002

Constitutional liberalism or praetorianism?

It is difficult to install workable democracy amidst deep economic crisis and rapid social change: this was the message conveyed by social scientists on the eve of the Eastern European transition.[40] Many feared that new forms of bureaucratic, populist, paramilitary, or nationalistic dictatorship would rise from the ashes of Communism. A scenario of uncontrolled and unmediated political mobilization that would overflow institutional channels was frequently envisaged. Experts feared that praetorian politics of military coups, student riots, workers' strikes, and mob rule would bypass the work of representative institutions, if not abolish them altogether.[41] How could one build a workable democracy without the basis of civil society, which was virtually destroyed during the Communist period? Could democracy emerge without strong parties able to aggregate and articulate major policy options and provide communication between the elite and citizens? Moreover, could either former Communists or their nationalist counterparts act as unbiased crafters of democracy? At the early stages of transition it would have been difficult to give any positive answers to these kinds of questions. In fact, there were at the time many noisy populist politicians in the region promoting the politics of mass mobilization over the politics of the ballot box, claiming that economic miracles would require dictatorial rather than democratic forms of government, and believing that nationalism rather than common democratic experience would represent the best solution for regional integration.

However, from the perspective of a decade or so we can confidently prove the sceptics wrong. In all ten countries under consideration democracy is firmly established. Communist constitutions have been revised and put into practice throughout the region. Elections are free and fair. Institutions of parliamentary representation are working relatively smoothly despite mounting pressure for systemic reform from above and below. (Consider, for instance, the task of adjusting the respective legislation of individual countries in anticipation of EU membership.) True, illiberal governmental practices have been only recently abandoned in countries such as Bulgaria, Romania, and Slovakia. Political parties are still relatively weak across the region. Parliaments score badly in successive rankings of public approval. The civil society network is still underdeveloped despite considerable internal and external efforts to foster its growth. And it is clear that certain features of the Western system are sometimes weakly connected to cultural reality in the region.[42] One should therefore be cautious in evaluating Eastern European progress and not expect all new democracies to look like the most advanced old democracies within a few short years.

However, despite such problems and qualifications, the countries in question have managed to construct a fairly workable system of liberal constitutionalism.[43] They have done this by introducing the balance-of-power principle and guaranteeing basic civic and human rights. Their newly adopted constitutions impose a tight corset on the citizenry, taking away some power from the people and putting it into the hands of constitutional framers and courts. The populist slogan 'all power to the soviets' has not returned to political rhetoric. Democracy has become a matter of rules, procedures, and institutions. This has made their democracies 'deliberative' rather than 'voluntaristic'.[44] This made it more difficult for the majority of the day to manipulate the democratic system to its own partisan advantage. This enabled democracy to function reasonably effectively rather than fall prey to paralysis and chaos. This, in short, has made the praetorian type of politics highly unlikely in the region, despite the numerous challenges.

Certainly, the successful Western experience played a role in the ten countries' decisions to opt for constitutional liberalism. Despite its restrictive features, liberal constitutionalism secured rather than undermined democracy in Western Europe and there was clearly no appetite in Eastern Europe for democratic experiments. However, it is also clear that constitutional liberalism proved useful for local actors uncertain of their political futures and afraid of taking political strife away from parliaments and constitutional courts onto the streets.

Flash points that never flashed

At the early stage of transition security was probably the greatest concern of all students of Central and Eastern Europe.[45] The Soviet Union was still there and some even feared a resurgence of German hegemony in the region. But an eruption of local conflicts on territorial, ethnic, or economic grounds was feared even more than a hypothetical return to imperial practices on the part of regional powers. All over Central and Eastern Europe there were large groups of people who believed that they were living on the wrong side of existing borders. Would they not reach for arms to remedy what they saw as historic injustice? Would not outstanding territorial disputes re-emerge? Could newly created states consolidate their political systems without large-scale violence? And how were the emerging economic conflicts after the collapse of the COMECON order to be handled? Were not chaos, uncertainty, and renationalization of defence postures to be expected? Were we not heading for a long period of local violence and pan-European instability?

These were all very difficult questions and it is not surprising that pointing to possible 'flash points' in the region became the favourite occupation of security studies specialists. In fact, the inter-war history of Central and Eastern Europe illustrates how populism, xenophobia, and personality cults stimulate international adventurism and domestic op-pression. For instance, in the aftermath of the 1938 Munich Agreement, Polish nationalists ordered military intervention in Czechoslovakia in order to regain the disputed region of Cieszyñ, and Slovak populists proceeded to make themselves the only legal party in Slovakia and to organize a clerico-fascist regime there. With the help of Hitler, Magyar revisionists regained some of Hungary's former territories from Czecho-slovakia and Romania. German aggression against Yugoslavia in 1941 was immediately followed by Hungarian aggression in order to regain further territories.[46]

However, after the fall of the Berlin Wall and the Soviet system no such problems returned to the ten countries discussed herein. Vicious violence erupted in the Balkans bringing about death and misery. There was also indiscriminate use of violence in Russia and in the Caucasus. But the ten Central and Eastern European countries remained an oasis of peace and stability, if one discounts the very short-lived Yugoslav army intervention in Slovenia. In some cases this looks like a virtual miracle. Consider, for instance, the potential for ethnic violence in the region. In Latvia, most notably, 48 per cent of the population was non-Latvian and the authorities were encountering serious difficulties in creating a loyal and cohesive citizenry from a multinational population with divergent political views and allegiances. The fact that 34 per cent of the population was Russian added a special security dimension to the Latvian minority problem. But even in countries with minority populations that did not exceed 10 per cent of the total population (Poland, the Czech Republic, Slovenia, and Hungary), the potential for ethnic violence was ever present. Hungary, for instance, is ethnically homogenous, but the 3.5 million Magyars who live outside Hungary's borders have often been victims of persecution and discrimination by local authorities in Romania, Slovakia, Ukraine, and Serbia. Even relatively stable and prosperous Czechoslovakia underwent a split along ethnic lines with potentially destabilizing consequences, especially for Slovakia.

How was it possible to avoid cross-border violence and major inter-national conflict? Certainly the restraint of major regional powers, most notably Russia, greatly contributed to stability in the region. Russia decided not to use force as an instrument of foreign policy even when faced with the assertive minority policies of Estonia and Latvia.[47] The terrifying picture of devastating violence in the Balkans also acted as a powerful deterring factor for all would-be warlords in the region. In other words, local actors in the ten countries under consideration deemed the price of reaching for arms to remedy perceived injustice to be too high. At the same time, the opportun-ity to improve one's own lot through peaceful economic and democratic reforms seemed to be a realistic option after the fall of the Soviet system. In fact, the fall of the Soviet system clearly showed that a country's power and well-being is affected more by the state of its economy and 'human capital' than by territorial conquest, international ganging-up, or other forms of military adventurism. And finally Western promotion of numerous secur-ity cooperation frameworks played a role in preventing the outbreak of a major conflict at the centre of Europe. The North Atlantic Treaty Organization (NATO) was the quickest to move in the region through the all-embracing Partnership for Peace programme and membership for democratic champions in the region.[48] The EU also induced individual governments to settle their border disputes by signing the EU's Pact for Stability as a precondition of EU membership.[49] As generals, defence min-isters, and ordinary soldiers began to meet and train together, exchange intelligence, and buy each other's military equipment, confidence grew and historic suspicion faded. Potential flash points have never flashed.

Comparison with other post-Communist states

The achievements of the ten countries aspiring to the EU can only be fully appreciated when compared with the developments in other countries of the former Soviet space and the Balkans. In Chapter 3 we will see how the ten were able (or unable) to catch up with the Western part of the contin-ent. In this section we examine of how they performed in comparison to the eastern and south-eastern part of the continent. Only through this double-track comparative enquiry, can we make a proper judgement about the degree of their success and failure.

Our data point to a considerable gap between the ten and the rest of post-Communist Europe in nearly all fields. However, the gap is not as sharp as the 'clash of civilizations' theory would suggest, and it is hardly along strict religious lines. Moreover, history moves fast in this region and past trends can hardly be taken for granted. For instance, on the eve of the new millennium Russia recorded significant growth after some years of recession and chaos. As the 2001 European Bank for Reconstruction and Development (EBRD) Report put it:

Russia has reached a critical juncture in its transition and is now facing a historic opportunity. The economy has rebounded strongly from the August 1998 crisis spurred by strong real exchange rate depreciation and high commodity prices. Political and economic conditions have created an unusual window of opportunity to implement many reforms: strengthening the federal system, improving governance through key structural reforms and creating a more effective social safety net, the fight against pervasive corruption.[50]

As mentioned earlier, Croatia also registered impressive economic progress in recent years and public support for Victor Yushchenko in the 2004 presidential elections gives hope that Ukraine may also embark on the road of serious economic restructuring and growth.

Of course, some statistics can be misleading. For instance, in the mid-1990s Albania was praised for its growth and economic discipline by many international institutions: its growth was reaching 10 per cent, inflation fell to single digits, and external imbalances were reduced sharply. However, the collapse of the pyramid scheme revealed the weakness of Albania's financial institutions and the fragility of government's political authority. Albania plunged into anarchy that left some 2,000 people dead and produced a sharp economic decline (7 per cent GDP decline in 1997).[51] In other words, progress can never be taken for granted, and one needs to look at various indicators in different fields to assess individual countries' abilities to secure durable prosperity, democracy, and peace.

The gap between the ten and the rest of Eastern and South-eastern Europe is most evident in the economic field. Other Eastern European countries, in particular Belarus, Ukraine, and Russia, are not only poorer then most of the ten, but also experienced much longer and deeper economic recession following the collapse of Communism in the region. Although some of them have recently registered notable economic growth, they still attract relatively little foreign investment and score very badly on the 'country risk classification' index. Their macro- and microeconomic policies are considered poor in comparison with the ten, their privatization programmes are lagging behind, and levels of corruption are much higher.[52] Differences are particularly striking when one looks at the banking system and financial markets. In the ten countries in question, financial markets are increasingly important and banking competition is largely open (although Slovenia has resisted pressure to open its banking sector to foreign competition for a long time). In other post-Communist countries a competitive banking system, though formally introduced, does not exist in practice, and small investments are usually autofinanced from retained earnings.[53]

However, as Table 1.1 shows, comparison of individual countries reveals a more complex picture. While the gap in GDP per capita between the Eastern European laggard, Ukraine, and the champion among the ten, Slovenia, is enormous (US$781 and US$9,416 respectively in 2001), the gap between other individual countries from the two groups is not always so evident. Most notably, in 2001 Russia's GDP per capita was higher than the Romanian and Bulgarian figures. Croatia's GDP per capita is also higher than GDP per capita in several Central and Eastern European countries. While Russia and Ukraine are having problems in collecting tax revenues and balancing their state budgets, Belarus is doing as well in this respect as some prosperous market economies of the ten.[54] Ukraine and Belarus also have low rates of unemployment as compared to other countries, but the official statistics probably ignore so-called 'hidden' unemployment in redundant state-owned industrial and agricultural sectors. There is also no doubt that countries such as Russia, Belarus, Ukraine, and Albania lack a wide and stable social consensus on the need to continue market reforms that would eradicate the remnants of the Soviet-type economy. In this respect the situation in the eight countries that joined the Union (plus Romania and Bulgaria) is entirely different. And it is important to keep in mind that economic fortunes had an impact on various other fields. For instance, countries with better economic outcomes also displayed more favourable health conditions (see e.g. life-expectancy differentials)[55]. Earnings inequality also increased faster in countries with poorer economic performance.

Gaps between the ten and other post-Communist countries are also evident in the field of democracy. The ten manifested a greater ability to secure law and order within their respective territories, their constitutions observe the balance-of-power principles and guarantee a wide range of citizens' rights and freedoms, their media are not under direct governmental control, and their opposition political parties and trade unions are recognized and tolerated. In short, their democratic systems are already consolidated, with strong liberal features built in. The same is often not the case in other Eastern and South-eastern European countries. Belarus with its autocratic regime of President Lukashenka is obviously the most striking

Table 1.1. The economic map of Eastern Europe

Country	GDP growth 1989*	GDP growth 2002†	Cumulative change in GDP 1989–2002 (1989 = 100)	GDP per capita in 2001 (US$)	Years of GDP decline 1989–2001	FDI—inflows per capita 2000 (US$)*	Unemployment 2001†	Country risk classification‡ 1 = the lowest; 7 = the highest	Corruption perception index§ 0 = highly corrupt; 10 = highly clean	Economic liberalization score** 1 = the highest; 7 = the lowest
Bulgaria	0.5	4.0	77	1,619	6	123	19.9	5	4.1	2.25
Czech Republic	1.4	3.4	105	5,473	6	434	8.0	2	4.2	2.08
Estonia	8.1	4.0	90	3,786	6	226	12.4	3	6.0	1.92
Hungary	0.7	3.5	132	5,121	4	116	5.7	2	4.8	2.00
Latvia	6.8	5.0	72	3,249	4	168	13.1	4	4.0	2.33
Lithuania	1.5	4.0	70	3,249	6	102	16.5	4	4.6	2.42
Poland	0.2	1.4	148	4,654	2	240	18.4	2	3.5	1.92
Romania	−5.8	4.2	83	1,743	7	45	6.6	6	2.9	3.92
Slovak Republic	1.4	3.6	109	3,668	4	381	19.4	3	4.0	2.33
Slovenia	−1.8	3.1	120	9,416	4	55	5.7	2	6.0	2.17
average CEEC10	**1.3**	**3.6**	**101**	**4198**	**4.9**	**189**	**12.6**	**3.3**	**4.4**	**2.33**
Albania	9.8	6.0	103	1,225	4	41	19.0	7	2.5	3.75
Belarus	8.0	2.0	85	1,096	6	9	2.2	7	3.3	6.25
Croatia	−1.6	3.5	80	4,548	6	182	15.3	4	3.5	3.50
Russia	0.0	3.5	63	2,136	8	−2	9.0	5	2.8	3.92
Ukraine	4.0	4.0	42	781	10	12	3.7	7	2.2	4.42
average EU15	**3.6**	**1.5**	**131**	**20,700**	**0**	**n.a.**	**7.9**	**n.a.**	**7.7**	**n.a.**

source: ^EBRD 2001, ^^EBRD update 2002, *OECD 2002, **Transparency International 2004, ***Freedom House 2002.

example. However, most other countries of Eastern and South-eastern Europe are classified as only 'partially free' and having merely an 'electoral' form of democracy.[56] In other words, their democratic systems are far from being consolidated (see Table 1.2).

In fact, it is not only the ruling elite that is responsible for lower democratic standards in these countries. As Dieter Fuchs and Hans-Dieter Klingemann's complex data on citizens' values show, there are no more than 25 per cent of 'solid democrats' in such countries as Albania, Moldova, Belarus, Ukraine, and Russia.[57] At the same time, the level of law abidingness and confidence in governmental institutions is below average, while wide strata of the public find violence legitimate. In these countries there is also much higher support for the restoration of the Communist system. For instance, as late as 1998, 51 per cent of Ukrainian respondents thought that it would be better to restore the former Communist regime, while only 19 per cent of Romanians agreed with this statement and the figure in countries such as Poland, the Czech Republic, Slovenia, and Croatia was even lower.[58]

Civil society institutions are also more developed in the ten countries aspiring to the EU than in the rest of the post-Communist space. For instance, in the Czech Republic with a population of about 10 million inhabitants there are 44,000 registered non-profit organizations, whereas in Ukraine, with an almost five times greater number of inhabitants, there are approximately 30,000 registered non-governmental organizations (NGOs).[59] This comes as no surprise when one considers public opinion data on civic values such as self-responsibility, solidarity, trust in others, work ethic, ethnic tolerance, political motivation, and civic engagement. For instance, according to the 1995–9 World Values Survey, ethnic tolerance in Russia and Ukraine is merely 3 per cent compared to 30 per cent in the Czech Republic, 20 per cent in Slovenia, and 14 per cent in Bulgaria. The data showing citizens' self-responsibility also reveal considerable gaps between the ten and the rest: Ukraine 14 per cent, Russia 16 per cent, Poland 36 per cent, Romania 31 per cent, and Lithuania 24 per cent. However, the pattern is not consistent. The Hungarian self-responsibility index is only 12 per cent, for instance.

One can hardly expect the successful completion of democratic and economic reforms in Eastern and South-eastern Europe without consolidation of the respective state structures. The central government of Serbia and Montenegro in Belgrade has little control over the policies of some of its parts, such as Kosovo and Montenegro. Russia is able to control some of its territory, such as Chechnya, only by the massive and often brutal use of

Table 1.2. The democratic map of Eastern Europe

Country	Citizen support for different types of democratic community*					Independent evaluation of democratization progress			NGOs membership density per milion of population§	Life expectancy at birth**
	Support for democratic rule	Support for autocratic rule	Law abidingness	Ethic tolerance	Civic engagement	Democrati-zation score†	Rule of law score†	Press freedom index		
	(in per cent positive support)					1 = the highest level / 7 = the lowest level		0–30 = Free / 31–60 = Partly free / 61–100 = Not free		
Bulgaria	80	19	96	14	2	3.00	4.00	29	282.9	70.9
Czech Republic	88	4	86	30	7	2.13	3.13	25	323.6	75.3
Estonia	85	6	91	5	3	1.94	2.13	18	1111.1	71.6
Hungary	83	5	89	13	9	1.94	2.50	23	350.4	71.7
Latvia	79	8	83	8	5	1.94	2.88	19	571.7	70.9
Lithuania	87	15	90	3	2	1.88	2.88	19	414.9	72.5
Poland	n.a.	n.a.	n.a.	5	0	1.50	1.88	18	94.3	73.8
Romania	89	22	94	6	9	3.31	4.50	35	108.9	70.5
Slovak Republic	88	4	82	17	6	1.94	2.63	22	390.4	70.5
Slovenia	82	6	85	20	8	1.81	1.88	20	1053.3	76.2
Albania	98	65	92	2	7	3.94	4.88	48	223.4	73.6
Belarus	75	17	80	4	1	6.56	6.00	82	75.5	69.9
Croatia	95	13	74	22	13	3.25	4.13	33	445.7	74.1
Russia	51	20	85	3	3	4.81	5.38	60	21.6	66.7
Ukraine	75	17	81	3	1	4.69	5.38	60	33.6	69.5

source: *Fuchs D., Klingemann H-D., in Mair, P., Zielonka, J., (2002) ''The enlarged European Union; Diversity and adaptation''; **Freedom House 2002; ***Press Freedom 2002; ^Union of International Associations, (2002) ''Yearbook of International Organisations: Guide to Civil Society Networks''; ^^ UNDP (2004) ''Human Development Report 2004'' force. Ethnic division also makes it difficult for the governments of Ukraine and Macedonia to apply their authority throughout the entire territory of the country. Belarus may be a strong state but it is a weak nation state. In fact, the weakness of a national identity in Belarus is often considered the main factor underpinning popular support for the autocratic regime of President Lukashenka.[60]

Conclusions

There are clearly some systemic differences between the eight countries that joined the Union (plus Romania and Bulgaria) and other countries in the former Communist space. However, it is difficult to identify a sharp threshold that would allow drawing a clear and plausible cultural, economic, and democratic border of Europe. Instead there is a continuous decline of a democratic community and economic efficiency travelling east and south-east, with many exceptions and paradoxes present. Besides, the ten can easily be divided into different groups. Romania and Bulgaria form a less developed and culturally somewhat different group than the countries more in the centre of Europe such as Poland, the Czech Republic, and Hungary. The Baltic states also have their peculiar characteristics. Similarly, there are large gaps and differences within individual states. Consider the economic, political, and cultural gap between the western and eastern parts of Poland or between Transylvania and the rest of Romania. However, these differences should not be overstated. As mentioned earlier, there is hardly any evidence confirming the alleged 'civilization border' between the Catholic and Orthodox part of Romania. Likewise, religious cleavages are only partly responsible for the ongoing conflict between the eastern and western parts of Ukraine.[61] Cultural legacies are only one of the many variables shaping the post-Communist environment. For instance, war in the Balkans is largely responsible for different economic and political paths in this region, regardless of different cultural legacies.

One conclusion is straightforward and evident, however. The eight countries that joined the Union (plus Romania and Bulgaria) have made remarkable progress since the fall of Communism in all fields considered. This was never taken for granted in the first decade following the fall, and pushed the EU towards embracing the new democracies in a serious manner. As we will see in Chapter 2, this led to a decision to embark on the enlargement process with the hope of stimulating pan-

European convergence which was seen as a remedy for the perceived threats. Today, when moving from Western Europe further east and south-east, one still can encounter many differences in terms of democracy, economics, and culture. However, one no longer feels like entering a different, hostile empire. The ten may not look exactly like the 'old' EU-15 member states, but they clearly belong to the same broad category of states, economies, and societies. Their accession to the EU increases the EU's diversity, but it will not import insecurity, produce economic chaos, introduce dramatically different democratic practices, or confront the current member states with an alien culture. The eight have entered the Union as confident and secured states with uncontested borders, consolidated democracy, ever stronger economic markets, and mainstream European culture. (Probably, the same will soon apply to Romania and Bulgaria.) Their neighbours further south and east are clearly less stable, less economically developed, and less democratic, but the gap between the ten and the rest of the post-Communist Europe is neither sharp nor consistent, and as such it is subject to engineering. Moreover, there are many economic, social, and cultural bridges between these countries. This means that introducing any hard functional borders between the enlarged EU and its new neighbours is not an easy, let alone sensible proposition. The enlarged EU will be open-ended, diversified, pluralistic, and polycentric. It will resemble more a neo-medieval empire than a Westphalian superstate. However, this empire is likely to be fairly democratic, and stable in economic and security terms.

2

European Power Politics

In the final stages of EU accession negotiations one had the impression that the entire process was chiefly about dimes. The member states and the applicant countries argued fiercely about the level and scope of funds to be contributed and distributed in the enlarged EU. The member states, especially those contributing most to the EU budget, feared that enlargement would cost them too much. The applicant states feared that the new member states would get relatively less from the EU budget than the old ones. In the end, one can argue, the accession took place because the dimes on offer for Eastern European states were rather insignificant for Western European states, but sufficiently significant for the Eastern European ones.[1] After all, the combined economic potential of new members was relatively small: the equivalent of a medium-large Western European state such as the Netherlands. This economic discrepancy implied that the same amount of money had a different meaning for the member states and the applicant states and it proved to be a major factor facilitating enlargement.[2] This is quite paradoxical if one considers that initially many students feared that economic discrepancies would be a major factor preventing rather than facilitating enlargement.

However, this story about dimes shows only a small part of a much broader picture. Enlargement was a complex and quite sophisticated response to a plethora of challenges and problems facing Europe since the end of the cold war, and in this sense it was primarily about paradigms rather than dimes. It was also about interests and power. As I argue in this chapter this particular wave of enlargement was, in fact, an impressive exercise in empire building. The Union tried to assert political and economic control over the unstable and impoverished eastern part of the continent. This enlargement was thus about filling in an unprecedented power vacuum in the northern, eastern, and southern parts of the continent. It was about conquering, reforming, and regulating new emerging markets. In essence it was about securing peace and prosperity in the future Europe through the skilful use of EU membership conditionality.

The amount of dimes involved in this enlargement may have been relatively low, but one should not forget that the real prize was not financial but political. Through enlargement the Union was giving the candidate states access to its decision-making. Moreover, the depth and scope of this enlargement is likely to change the very nature of Europe and European integration. Enlargement creates pressure for introducing far-reaching reforms of the Union's institutional structure. It produces winners and losers among vast social groups within and across individual countries. It determines Europe's position in world affairs.

The truly historical dimension of this particular enlargement was frequently emphasized by Western and Eastern European politicians, but in the end they could not escape a public quarrel about dimes and some rather trivial issues such as milk quotas.[3] How was this possible? Were all strategic objectives behind enlargement abandoned? Who were the most important actors and what interests did they bring to the table? And how have policies of the two sides gradually evolved in practice? These are the major questions discussed in this chapter.

Enlargement policy evolved over a period of fifteen years. The earliest calls for embracing Eastern European countries by the Union were raised immediately after the fall of the first Communist regimes in 1989.[4] The first eight of these countries formally joined the Union on 1 May 2004. Table 2.1 shows the chronology of major events leading to enlargement. This chronology does not reveal anything in particular. The entire process evolved gradually over time and the formal accession negotiations were completed in a period similar to the previous cases of enlargement.[5] There were many dramatic moments during this enlargement process, but one should keep in mind that none of the previous enlargements was ever smooth and painless.[6]

Despite the similarities, however, I again try to argue that this enlargement was very special. None of the previous cases of enlargement involved such a striking projection of the EU's political and economic power upon the applicant states. In the past, the EU conditionality package had never been so extensive or intrusive. The asymmetry of power between the two 'negotiating' partners had never been so striking. And the geopolitical considerations behind enlargement had never been so salient. In other words, the Union not only started to organize its internal political space

Table 2.1. Calendar of events, 1989–2005

1989	
June	In partly democratic elections, Solidarity wins a landslide victory in Poland; Tadeusz Mazowiecki becomes the first non-Communist prime minister.
July	The Western Economic Summit is held in Paris. It asks the European Commission to coordinate the necessary measures to assist economic restructuring in Poland and Hungary (so-called Phare programme, later extended to other countries in the region).
November	The Berlin Wall collapses. The German Democratic Republic opens its borders.
1990	
April	A Special European Council in Dublin agrees on a common approach on German unification and on Community relations with Central and Eastern European countries.
May	The Agreement establishing the European Bank for Reconstruction and Development (EBRD) to provide financial support to Central and Eastern Europe countries is signed in Paris.
July	Cyprus and Malta apply for EU membership.
October	Germany is unified, and the *Länder* of the former East Germany become part of the EU.
1991	
February	Representatives of Czechoslovakia, Hungary, and Poland meet in the Hungarian town of Visegrad and adopt the 'Declaration on cooperation between the Republic of Poland, the Czechoslovak Federal Republic, and the Republic of Hungary on the path for advancing towards European integration'.
June	Croatia and Slovenia declare their independence, which is followed by the outbreak of armed conflict in the Balkans.
December	Gorbachev announces his resignation and the Soviet Union ceases to exist.
December	The Europe Agreements on political dialogue and economic cooperation are signed with Poland, Hungary, and Czechoslovakia.
1992	
November	The break-up of Czechoslovakia and the establishment of two separate states: Slovakia and the Czech Republic.
December	The Central European Free Trade Agreement (CEFTA) is signed in Krakow, Poland. All the signatories had previously signed association agreements with the EU, which is why CEFTA functions as a preparation for full EU membership.
1993	
March	The French minister Edouard Balladur launches the idea of a Pact for Stability in Europe.
June	European Council in Copenhagen approves EU enlargement for countries of Central and Eastern Europe, and defines political and economic criteria for membership.
November	Maastricht Treaty comes into force. European Community becomes the European Union.
1994	
March	Hungary applies for EU membership, followed by other post-Communist countries the next two years.
December	European Council in Essen proposes a 'strategy of preparations for membership' (pre-accession strategy) to candidate countries.
1995	
May	The Commission adopts a White Paper on preparing the associated countries of Central and Eastern Europe for integration into the EU internal market.
June	Europe Association Agreements on political dialogue and economic cooperation are signed with Estonia, Latvia, and Lithuania.
December	EU Summit in Madrid, the EU member states endorse a preliminary enlargement calendar.

Table 2.1. (*Continued*)

1997	
July	The Commission presents 'Agenda 2000—for a stronger and wider Europe' with opinions on the applications of ten Central and Eastern European countries.
December	The European Council in Luxembourg takes the decision to open negotiations with the first six candidates (Cyprus, the Czech Republic, Estonia, Hungary, Poland, and Slovenia) that were judged capable of meeting the Copenhagen criteria.
1998	
March	Cyprus, the Czech Republic, Estonia, Hungary, Poland, and Slovenia begin accession negotiations with the EU.
November	The Commission adopts the first reports assessing progress of countries applying for accession. Ministerial-level accession conferences start with Cyprus, the Czech Republic, Estonia, Hungary, Poland, and Slovenia.
1999	
March	The Czech Republic, Hungary, and Poland become NATO members.
March	Berlin European Council agrees on financial perspectives 2000–6.
May	The Treaty of Amsterdam enters into force.
December	European Council in Helsinki decides to open accession negotiations with Bulgaria, Latvia, Lithuania, Malta, Romania, and Slovakia and to recognize Turkey as an applicant country.
2000	
February	The accession negotiations with Bulgaria and Ranania are opened.
2001	
December	European Council in Laeken takes the decision to conclude negotiations by the end of 2002 with the candidate countries ready for accession so that they can take part in the European Parliament elections in 2004.
2002	
October	The European Commission recommends the conclusion of accession negotiations by the end of 2002 with the following countries: Cyprus, the Czech Republic, Estonia, Hungary, Latvia, Lithuania, Malta, Poland, the Slovak Republic, and Slovenia. The Commission considers that these countries will be ready for EU membership from the beginning of 2004.
December	European Council in Copenhagen officially concludes accession negotiations with ten countries.
2003	
February	Treaty of Nice comes into force.
March	First referenda on EU accession are held in Malta and Slovenia with a majority of voters in favour of accession. Like referenda are held in other candidate countries throughout 2003 with similarly positive outcomes.
April	The European Parliament endorses the next wave of enlargement.
April	The Treaty of Accession between the EU and Cyprus, the Czech Republic, Estonia, Hungary, Latvia, Lithuania, Malta, Poland, Slovakia, and Slovenia is signed in Athens, Greece.
2004	
May	Bulgaria, Estonia, Latvia, Lithuania, Romania, Slovakia, and Slovenia join NATO.
May	Cyprus, the Czech Republic, Estonia, Hungary, Latvia, Lithuania, Malta, Poland, Slovakia, and Slovenia become EU members.
December	Croatia and Turkey are invited to start accession negotiations in 2005 subject to certain conditions.
2005	
April	The Treaty of Accession with Bulgaria and Romania is signed in Luxembourg, Paving the way for their membership of the Union on 1 January 2007.
May	French referendum on EU Constitution is held. Anxiety over the EU's enlargement to the east and over Turkish candidacy are cited as reasons for a 'no' vote.

Table 2.1. (*Continued*)

June	Dutch reiterate French sentiment with 'no' vote rendering moribund the Constitution that had been previously ratified by nine member states.
October	European Council decides to open membership negotiations with Croatia and Turkey and to start association talks with Serbia-Mantenegro.

along an imperial pattern; it also started to behave towards its neighbours in a truly imperial fashion.[7]

However, I argue that the Union's neo-medieval nature produced external policies that were different from the imperial policies of Westphalian actors of the nineteenth and twentieth century. The EU's imperial policy was quite benign and incentive driven. The final objective was not the conquest of Eastern Europe, but the establishment of peace, democracy, and prosperity in the region. The EU's means were civilian rather than military. The Union tried to export its institutions, norms, and practices in the hope that this would help these countries to maintain economic growth, stabilize their political order, and secure their borders. Integration had helped Western Europe to achieve all this in the post-1945 period and the same recipe was used for Eastern Europe in the post-1989 period. I argue that narrowly defined material considerations, despite the usual national and sectoral pressures, seemed secondary in this particular case of enlargement. Moreover, and by extension, this enlargement was less about institutional and financial bargaining and more about power politics old-style. The Union embarked on this imperial policy primarily for its own benefit, but the candidate countries were also benefiting. Eastern Europeans looked at enlargement as a means to move from Europe's periphery to its centre. They also viewed the EU's membership conditions as largely in line with their strategy of modernization and democratization.

This chapter first scrutinizes in greater detail the purpose behind this wave of enlargement. It then looks at the design and implementation of the EU's enlargement policy. Why was the conditionality blueprint so intrusive, but its application so benign and ambiguous? The final section examines how the Union was able to resist various parochial pressures from potential losers and successfully to conclude the accession negotiations. Finally I point to the implications of this peculiar application of imperial policy for the Union's internal structure and for relations with its future neighbours.

The purpose of accession

Why did member states and applicant states begin and successfully accomplish accession negotiations? Why did the Eastern European states apply for membership and why did the Western European states decide to admit them? One can look at the objectives of actors involved in the enlargement process either in power terms or in functional terms.[8] In the latter case one tries to establish what kind of Europe the member states and the applicant states are striving for through the entire process of accession in terms of security, economics, and culture. In the former case one tries to establish how the member and applicant states try to gain or maintain power through the process of accession. The key terms here are control and access. The member states are trying to assert control over the candidate states, and the latter in turn try to gain access to the Union's resources and decision-making. Functional objectives in terms of security, economics, and culture have been spelled out on many occasions by various negotiating actors. This hardly ever happened with power objectives. In fact, the very term 'power' is totally absent in the European discourse and we have to rely on suppositions and abstract analyses of interests.

Functional and power objectives may well be of a different nature, but they are closely related. For instance, economic gains derived from enlargement not only improve the general well-being of Europe's citizens, they also enhance the power position of the Union and its individual member states. Similarly, if enlargement brings stability to the new member states, this enhances the Union's power position vis-à-vis other international actors. One can multiply similar examples. Let us first scrutinize the functional objectives, and focus on power objectives in the next section.

Most states in Eastern Europe already expressed their desire to enter the EU in the early days of independence, and their motivations were quite straightforward. They wanted to join a club of secure, prosperous, democratic, and relatively well-governed countries. They saw themselves as naturally belonging to Europe, but deprived of the opportunity to enjoy democracy and the free market by Soviet hegemony and Western European acquiescence to that state of affairs. With the fall of Communism this historical injustice had to be remedied, and accession to the EU was to make their return to Europe complete. As Vaclav Havel put it in his speech to the European Parliament:

Europe is one political entity whose security is indivisible. The idea that there could forever be two Europes—a democratic, stable and prosperous Europe engaged in integration and a less democratic, less stable and less prosperous Europe—is, in my opinion, totally mistaken. It resembles a belief that one half of a room could be heated and the other half kept unheated at the same time. There is only one Europe, despite its diversity, and any weightier occurrence anywhere in this area will have consequences and repercussions throughout the rest of the continent.[9]

The official motivations of the EU member states were similar to the ones expressed by the applicant states, although in Western Europe the emphasis was less on historical justice and more on tangible common interests. The main argument was that security, prosperity, and democracy in Europe require opening to the countries further north, south, and east. As Tony Blair put it in November 2002: 'Enlargement will extend Europe's area of peace, democracy and prosperity. We will also be safer and more secure through better co-operation on border controls, asylum and immigration, joint efforts to tackle cross-border crime, and shared environmental standards.'[10] The President of the European Commission, Romano Prodi, argued in a similar vein: 'Enlargement is the fulfillment of the European project. This project has given us half a century of peace and prosperity, and it should be extended to the whole continent.... Enlargement is also a terrific opportunity to redefine our role in the world.'[11] The public seemed to share these objectives. According to a December 2002 poll conducted by the EU among its fifteen member states, 84 per cent thought that enlargement would open up new markets for local products, 78 per cent believed that the EU would be culturally richer after enlargement, and 69 per cent said that enlargement would reduce risks of war and conflicts in Europe.[12]

However, the problem was that EU states created the impression that all the aforementioned noble objectives count for little when it comes to practice. In other words, throughout the entire accession process the Union and its leaders acted as if enlargement were a problem rather than an opportunity and that as such it could better be postponed if not avoided altogether. In the first years after the fall of the Berlin Wall the EU refused officially to endorse even the very idea of EU membership for the new democracies. Instead individual Western European leaders tried to articulate various alternative solutions to full-fledged membership for these countries. The most well known among them was President Mitterrand's proposal to create a loose 'European Confederation' as an alternative to enlargement, at least in the short and medium term.[13] Under mounting pressure of events in the entire post-Communist space, the Eastern European bid for membership was officially recognized by the

1993 European Council in Copenhagen, but the Union, nevertheless, refused to commit itself to any scope or timetable for the first post-Communist accession.[14] Ambiguous and vague rhetoric concerning enlargement was the norm throughout the following decade, and accession negotiations were dominated by technical and financial details, both trivial and local. For instance, how could one treat seriously the proclaimed strategic aims of enlargement when member states quarrelled about importing two extra lorry loads of Bulgarian strawberry jam and an extra 12 kilos of Slovak ham per member state per day?[15]

This situation led many to believe that the Union in fact had no interest in enlargement, but found itself in a situation of 'rhetorical entrapment', to use Frank Schimmelfennig's expression.[16] Enlargement did not take place because of 'the constellation of power and interests' among member states, Schimmelfennig argued, but because member states fell victim to their vague rhetoric promising to overcome the continent's division by bringing under one institutional roof all European countries sharing their liberal values. Those who resisted enlargement were 'shamed' and compelled to follow policies that were consistent with their rhetoric about norms and values rather than with the rational calculation of their interests.[17]

My own interpretation is somewhat different. I would argue that most EU leaders have been fully aware of political, security, and economic benefits resulting from enlargement. In other words, these interests, however vague, were important and real and they were seen as such not only by leaders, but also the public at large. A union of democratic European states trying to create lasting peace among them and able to resist any form of authoritarianism is not just a 'founding myth of European integration', as Schimmelfennig seems to argue.[18] It is the very rationale for European integration. The fact that member states spend most of their time arguing about agricultural subsidies and competition laws does not mean that they were paying only lip service to peace, liberal economics, and democracy.[19] The preservation of these very norms and values was always said to represent the key pillars of national and European interests. There is no reason to believe that these were only rhetorical statements with little practical meaning.

Of course, politicians need to balance many different interests, and they usually pursue a policy à la carte, constantly switching gears from worthy pan-European schemes to narrow national agendas. This was also the case with this enlargement. Germany, most notably, had to balance its policy of enlargement with the imperative of its fresh and costly reunification.

Each Western European country had to cope with its own corporate pressures, especially in sectors exposed to Eastern European competition such as agriculture, textiles, and steel. There was also a ballot box factor that had to take into account voters' anxiety about opening EU borders to the goods, labour, and culture of Eastern European countries.[20] Nevertheless, all this does not imply that peace, prosperity, and democracy in Europe were not seen as the basic purpose behind the member states' policies. In fact, there was overwhelming agreement that under the new circumstances following the fall of Communism and the end of the cold war, enlargement would be the most suitable means of securing peace, prosperity, and democracy on the continent.

Wim Kok was Prime Minister of the Netherlands and member of the European Council between 1994 and 2002, the crucial years leading to eastward enlargement of the EU. His view on the purpose of enlargement is therefore very telling. In 2003 he wrote:

Throughout my life, I have been a convinced European. From my youth I remember the last world war, and I know the value of the peace, stability and prosperity which we have today. I understand how much we have gained from the process of European integration in the past half-century. The wars and atrocities in former Yugoslavia have demonstrated what Europeans can do to each other when forces of disintegration are allowed to overtake the wish for unity. The enlargement of the European Union to me, therefore, is the fulfillment of a vision—a vision that is too easily forgotten in times when security and prosperity within Europe are taken for granted. But if we pause to reflect, we see that this vision is what the EU and its enlargement are really about: the reunification of Europe's peoples in a constitutional framework that encourages them to work in peace and stability.[21]

It would be difficult to provide evidence showing that other Western European leaders ever disagreed with this statement.[22] One should add that the objectives of Western and Eastern European elites clearly converged when seen from this perspective.

The question, however, is why the Union's policies seemed only weakly to reflect this set of basic interests? Why was its enlargement policy so ambiguous, exposed to parochial pressures, and subject to delays? To answer this question one needs to look at the very nature of the Union as a political actor: its neo-medieval 'internal' nature results in a peculiar way of making foreign policy. I offer some tentative observations on the EU as an international actor before offering a more in-depth analysis in Chapter 6.[23]

The Union always tends to act along institutional rather than strategic logic and it often uses a technical and procedural approach in meeting its objectives. This is basically so because the EU is not a typical state able to identify its 'national' interest and act accordingly. The EU is a complex international institution in search of purpose, workable procedures, and legitimacy. This has several implications for the way its policies evolve. First, the Union has always had difficulties in formulating its broader strategic purpose because of the persistent differences within Europe concerning the very nature of integration and competing national agendas. This does not mean that the Union's policies are not interest based, but only that these interests are not openly and clearly defined and not always implemented in a straightforward (or if you wish, strategic) manner. In fact, the Union was never even able to spell out the very purpose of European integration and of its own existence. No wonder that statements about the purpose of enlargement were also ambiguous and vague. Integration by disguise was followed by enlargement in disguise, it may be argued.[24] Second, the Union's policies towards the outside world have always been determined by its internal rather than external agenda. The need and readiness to search for internal compromise, if not consensus, has been one of the Union's prime characteristics, and it has usually required side payments to obstructionist countries and the application of the lowest common denominator. This has created in our case an impression that the Union negotiated more with itself than with the applicant countries throughout the entire process of accession. Third, the Union's policies are procedural rather than substantively guided. Given the lack of a clear strategic purpose and the threat of vetoes, the Union must rely on certain procedures, that is, on the community method of enlargement. So it acts according to a plan and agreed rules that prevent flexibility and adjustment to external shocks and pressures. This has created an impression that the enlargement process was more about technical and procedural issues than about implementation of the EU's vital interests.

In conclusion, the Union enlarged not because it was rhetorically trapped, but because enlargement was a tool of meeting the most vital interests of its member states. The Union's accession policies were ambiguous and prone to local pressures, but these were always characteristic features of its external policies. The Union is not a state-like actor able to pursue a coherent and determined strategy. Most nation states have fewer problems in bridging the gap between their rhetoric and action. They can more easily resist corporate sectoral pressures hampering their broader long-term objectives. And their policies are more concerned with developments on the ground rather than merely with institutional cohesion and procedural correctness. However, this does not imply that enlargement was not in the Union's interest. Western European leaders have always claimed that enlargement is about securing peace, prosperity, and democracy in the new European setting, and there is no reason to question this claim. I argue in the next section that this set of basic economic and political interests required application of the EU's power vis-à-vis the post-Communist states. Enlargement policy was a clever way to acquire control over developments in the post-Communist space in a carefully orchestrated, comprehensive, and largely friendly manner.

Imperial design and the process of accession

The fall of the Soviet empire produced a huge power vacuum in Central and Eastern Europe. Although individual countries became formally independent, a vast political and economic space emerged that was open for the contest of ideas and profits. Democracy and free markets have been proclaimed as objectives throughout the entire region, but as we showed in Chapter 1 it was far from certain whether these countries would be able to meet these objectives. In fact, in many cases anarchy rather than democracy become the order of the day. Economic structures became hostage to vested interests or even criminal mafias. The borders of newly 'liberated' states were questioned and ethnic tensions turned violent in some places. Even in relatively stable countries it was not clear which institutional solutions and regulatory frameworks would be adopted, who would conquer the emerging markets, and what kind of military alliances would emerge.

When Communism fell, the EU was obviously one of the most powerful actors in this region, and it is clear that it could not but try to fill the power vacuum emerging on its borders. Enlargement emerged in due time as the Union's prime instrument of gradually acquiring control over the former Communist space. The promise of EU accession persuaded states in Eastern Europe to adopt EU laws and regulations, to open markets for EU goods and services, and to settle internal and external disputes in a peaceful manner. This was power politics at its best, even though the term 'power' was never mentioned in the official enlargement discourse. The Union was acquiring control over the post-Communist space by promising access to its decision-making and resources. The compliance of candidate states was largely voluntary, and mostly based on incentives rather than punishments. Moreover the Union demanded from candidate states a lot of noble things such as democracy, rule of law, and friendly relations with their neighbours. That said, however, the design was truly imperialist, to use Robert Cooper's expression. Enlargement was about building a new type of 'cooperative and voluntary empire' in order to fill a power vacuum that emerged on the ashes of the repressive Soviet empire.[25] The key instrument used in this endeavour was the policy of conditionality.

The policy of linking aid and other forms of benefits to certain conditions has been widely used by many international actors since at least the 1980s (albeit often under different names such as the policy of leverage, linkage, or economic statecraft).[26] However, the EU policy of conditionality vis-à-vis the countries of Eastern Europe gradually evolved into the most ambitious project ever practised in the modern history of international relations. First of all, on offer was not just financial aid or political support, but something much more precious: membership of this most exclusive European club. Membership represented not only access to EU funds and decision-making; it also provided these states with a special kind of economic credibility and political legitimacy. In fact, these rewards were already available in the advanced stages of the pre-accession process. The candidate countries were receiving substantial economic assistance in making their economies more compatible with the EU and they were offered a political platform for regular consultations with EU leaders via the so-called 'structured dialogue'. The sequence of 'structured dialogue' meetings proved to be a rather symbolic exercise, but the enlargement financial package was substantial—75 billion euros proudly compared to the Marshall Plan by the President of the European Commission.[27] The demonstration effect of belonging to an exclusive European club was also present already in the pre-accession stage. For instance, the three Baltic candidate states were not hit by the 1998 Russian financial crush proportionally to their level of economic interdependence with Russia. Foreign investors apparently concluded that the Baltic states were already under the EU financial umbrella.[28]

The second unique feature of EU conditionality policy was its enormous scope. A similar blueprint was applied to several different countries and across various functional fields. The agenda for Eastern European adjustment required by the EU was extremely broad and ranged from free elections and property rights to export quotas and unified standards for the production of the most trivial items. The basic conditions for enlargement were spelled out in Copenhagen in 1993 and subsequently specified in the Agenda 2000.[29] The adoption of the *acquis communitaire* by the applicants has been one of the clearly stated conditions for accession.

And the *acquis* is made up of some 20,000 laws, decisions, and regulations, spanning nearly 80,000 pages and still growing.[30]

The third unique feature of EU conditionality policy was its intrusiveness. The EU not only told Eastern European applicants what they should do—in terms of, say, new legislation or administrative reform—but also sent representatives to specific ministries there to make sure that the changes were being made as prescribed through its 'twinning' programme. The whole process of readjustment was being carefully monitored. At every stage, the champions and laggards among the applicant countries were identified at regular review sessions. The key terms of the conditionality policy were safeguards, benchmarks, guidance, and screening. The EU discourse was very much inflexible and hierarchical, leaving little space for negotiations. Indeed, when a group of scholars analysed the language of the European Commission's regular reports on the candidate countries they concluded: 'The idea of an inferior Eastern Europe, counterpoised to the dominant Western Europe, is embedded in the discourse between the EU and the applicant Eastern European states.... In its discourse, the EU appropriates discursive power over eastern applicants.'[31]

Of course, there was more than only discursive power behind the EU policy of conditionality. The structural discrepancies between the EU and the candidate states from Eastern Europe were indeed enormous, and they concerned both material and normative aspects of power. In economic terms the size of all the applicants from Eastern Europe was not greater than that of a medium-size EU country such as the Netherlands. About 70 per cent of the candidate states' exports went to the EU and only 4 per cent of EU exports went the other way (2002 data).[32] Moreover, the EU negotiated with individual applicants as a bloc and the adopted 'regatta' system of negotiations forced the applicants to compete with each other in meeting EU demands.[33]

The normative power of the EU should also be taken into consideration. EU fundamental norms of democracy, market economy, human rights, and social justice were seen as an example to follow by all applicant states. Moreover, the EU was in a position to provide authoritative interpretations of these norms, to accord or deny international recognition of certain policies, and to confer international legitimacy upon applicant states' behaviour.

In view of the enormous scope and density of EU intervention in the domestic affairs of the applicant countries, scholars began to talk about 'EU governance' in these states.[34] However, it is hard to resist the impression that the type of this governance was indeed imperial. The EU was providing decisions and expected compliance and obedience from the applicant states. The Union was providing models and the applicant states were supposed to copy or imitate them. It was offering teaching and training, and the applicant states were expected to socialize and learn. The EU proposals and solutions were to be taken over by virtue of their place of origin and not necessarily by virtue of their substance. The applicant states' compliance was voluntary only in theory. In practice, these states could not afford to turn their backs to the EU's demands and expectations. This asymmetrical structure in both material and ideational terms allowed the Union to exercise a remarkable degree of control over Eastern Europe without resort to economic punishments, let alone physical violence.[35] As Melinda Kovács and Peter Kabachnik argued: 'Eastern enlargement involves the construction of an empire that grows by willing dependencies, not by force. The illusion of self-determination by the applicants allows them to make application their own decision, since there is no direct coercion or military aggression.'[36]

Benign empire in action

EU structural dominance over Eastern European applicants was thus enormous, allowing the Union to put in place a very broad, detailed, and intrusive package of conditionality. This was combined by an upbeat and at times quite arrogant rhetoric on the part of various EU officials. If one believed this language the EU accession process looked like the most advanced example of institutional engineering or even the apogee of a modernist dream. The EU presented itself as an agent of rational scientific policies which drastically reshaped the European landscape in a planned, effective, and controlled manner. The agenda for readjustment was elaborated in great detail covering nearly every sphere of human life. A complex system of incentives and disincentives was installed and the whole process of readjustment was carefully monitored along a complex set of criteria. After the fall of the Berlin Wall it seemed that there would be no limits to the EU's ability to reshape continental Europe for the benefit of its citizens. Subsequently, EU officials promised to create a new order (if not a new man) on the ashes of Communism. However, these modernist pretensions proved largely utopian.

The EU has indeed put in place a very complex system of conditional accession, but its application was never very purposeful, consistent, or assertive. In fact, there are at least five good reasons to conclude that the imperial policy of EU was relatively benign, and slightly detached.[37]

First, at the end of the accession process the candidate countries from Eastern Europe were getting seats at the EU's 'table'. The structural inequality was thus not to be perpetuated indefinitely. Moreover, and because of this, the EU old member states could not afford to antagonize the future member states too much because when admitted these states would be in a position to take 'revenge' for bad treatment in the pre-accession period.[38]

Second, the asymmetry between the EU and applicant states allowed the EU to turn a blind eye to Eastern European non-compliance. Of course, non-compliance in certain fields could complicate EU internal functioning after the enlargement. However, in the pre-accession stage the EU's overall pre-eminence made it less sensitive and vulnerable to Eastern European disobedience.

Third, the EU conditionality package was not straightforward, but rather highly ambiguous. This created a margin of flexibility in complying with EU conditions for accession. For instance, there was no single model of democracy, administration, or social policy that the EU expected the candidate states to adopt. Different EU member states tried to export their own national solutions, but candidate states had ample opportunity to pick and choose among the different solutions offered and mix them with home-made ones.[39] Indeed Eastern European politicians tended to apply EU conditionality in a way that suited their own partisan aims, effectively blurring the intended effect.

Fourth, the EU monitoring and 'screening' of the candidates' progress was often superficial and inconsistent. This was partly due to the vagueness of many conditions, and partly due to their contradictory nature.[40] Moreover, there were simply too many and highly diversified conditions to be met by the candidate countries, and the Union repeatedly failed to provide a sound system of weighting of individual criteria and of judging their importance. This made it difficult for the European Commission to report in any depth on the implementation of all these conditions.[41]

Finally, EU policies towards Eastern Europe evolved more by default than by design. The Union has never articulated the vision of Europe for which it is striving and its policies have been guided by an accidental combination of internal and external pressures rather than broader strategic considerations. As explained earlier, the Union is not a state-like actor able to pursue a coherent and determined strategy. Its policies are procedure rather than substance guided, and they are often dominated by local agendas. The lack of a clear European strategy made it difficult for the Union to select its main objectives and match them with adequate instruments. It also created communication problems and made individual policies inconsistent with each other. As a result, the accession process has time and again fallen victim to manipulation by various sectarian groups within the EU and candidate states.

To sum up, behind the façade of the carefully engineered project there was a great deal of chaos and vagueness. The ultra-modernist pretensions were largely utopian. Liberal rhetoric could not hide the power game evolving across the old East–West divide. Under careful scrutiny the accession process looks rather like an imperial exercise of asserting political and economic control over an unstable and underdeveloped neighbourhood. Of course, the level of institutionalization is much higher today than ever in the past and the Union has been using chequebooks rather than swords as leverage. Nevertheless, the substance of its policies has been similar to many previous imperial exercises: export of laws, economic transactions, administrative systems, and social habits. The Union did not attempt to conquer and subjugate Eastern European countries; it tried to make them look more like its old member states and in the end it has allowed them access to common decision-making. Moreover, the Union's policies have not been carefully engineered by a powerful governmental centre in Brussels. Although the European Commission has been one of the most important actors behind the accession process, many other power centres and groups of organized interests were able to have their share of influence. This last point requires more detailed elaboration because so far I have treated the negotiating partners as largely unified and autonomous actors. The reality is more complex, however, especially on the Union's side.

Agents behind the accession

The term 'empire' has often been associated with the absolute sovereignty of a single individual.[42] Empire without an emperor is an odd concept, one might say.[43] Obviously, the EU does not have any emperor. In fact, it does not even have a single centre of government. The European Council, the highest power centre within the Union, is composed of the heads of sovereign states who are able to veto collective decisions in many important areas. When analysing the European system of government, scholars talk about a multilevel government or even about a government by net-works.[44] I deal in more detail with the EU governance system later in the book.[45] Here, however, it is important to address one fundamental question: if so many different actors have formally (and of course informally) shaped the accession process, how was it possible to arrive at the point of accession without any major political turbulence? Even if one assumes that most actors saw the enlargement as a useful means of securing peace and prosperity in Europe, this does not necessarily guarantee smooth completion of the accession process. What is good for Europe as such is not necessarily good for a particular constituency, and one can hardly expect that loyalty to Europe will always prevail. Moreover, individual actors can fundamentally differ about the most appropriate scope, form, and time-frame of enlargement. In fact, the propagated myth that enlargement was a win–win process has time and again been challenged by potential losers. So why have these potential losers failed to prevent enlargement?

First of all the foes of enlargement formed a large, but very diversified group that was unable to build and sustain a common front of opposition. Various side payments and other forms of concessions to potential losers further mellowed the resistance. Moreover, enlargement was strongly supported by important external actors, such as the United States. And last but not least, the European Commission proved to be a powerful actor committed to the successful completion of the project it effectively ran.

Some groups opposed enlargement on ideological grounds. In Western Europe it was often argued that widening was largely incompatible with deepening and so enlargement would undermine the Union's federalist aspirations.[46] In Eastern Europe it was often argued that EU accession would erode newly regained independence and lead to moral relativism if not decadence.[47] Some other groups opposed enlargement because it was likely to affect their material interests. In Western Europe enlargement was feared especially by farmers and those industrial sectors in which Eastern Europe had a competitive advantage (steel, basic chemicals, textiles, and certain other low-value-added products). In Eastern Europe enlargement was feared by older and uneducated people living in small towns and rural villages. Those employed in redundant heavy industries or within the huge but non-competitive agricultural sector also feared being on the losing side after their countries' accession to the Union.[48]

On the nation state level cost–benefit calculations looked much more complex, however. The German case is very illustrative in this context. On one hand, Germany as the EU 'front-line' country had a strategic interest in pushing EU borders further east, and German firms were expected to earn the greatest amount of money as a result of enlargement. Yet Germany was also host to the highest number of Eastern European migrants and many of its firms were particularly exposed to competition from Eastern European firms, especially in such sectors as steel and the construction industry. Subsequently, the public fear that enlargement would bring about more crime, unemployment, and the erosion of cultural identity was stronger in Germany than in countries which were expected to benefit less from the enlargement such as Ireland, Spain, or Italy. For instance, according to the November 2002 Eurobarometer, 73 per cent of Spaniards were in favour of enlargement and only 8 per cent were against. In Germany the figures were 64 per cent in favour and as much as 27 per cent against. Not surprisingly therefore the German government's support for enlargement was anything but unconditional.

This leads me to another important factor in securing the successful completion of the accession process: the opponents of enlargement were often appeased if not bribed. Germany wholeheartedly endorsed enlargement only after securing restrictions on the movement of workers from the new members for a period of up to seven years, a clear breach of the single market arrangement with free movement as one of its basic principles. Those member states that feared that enlargement would reduce their benefits from the Common Agricultural Policy and the structural funds were also appeased. New member states were offered only 137 euros per head of population in the field of regional policy, compared with 231 euros per head for Greece, Spain, and Portugal.[49] Direct payments to Eastern European farmers were to commence in 2004 at 25 per cent only, rising to 100 per cent over a period of ten years. Critics of enlargement in the Union have also been pleased by the decision to include so-called 'safeguards clauses' in the Accession Treaty that are of wider and longer duration than in previous enlargements.[50]

There is indeed no doubt that the Union has been more generous to its own foes of enlargement than to those from the applicant states. In fact, at the final stage of negotiations it looked like some of the new member states were to become net payers rather than net beneficiaries from the EU budget, especially in the first years after accession.[51] Nevertheless, some concessions have also been made to satisfy Eastern European opponents of enlargement.[52] For instance, several applicant states were granted restrictions on the purchase of their agricultural property for up to twelve years.[53] The 'topping-up' of the direct payments in agriculture was raised to 55 per cent in the first year. Some additional (but small) financial concessions were made at the last moment before signing the accession deal (especially in the case of Poland). A total of 322 'transitional measures' had been agreed in seventeen of the thirty-one negotiating chapters. Although most of them were sought by the applicant states, it is worth noting that concessions have usually been made in those sectors that were effectively under the control of EU firms operating in the applicant countries.

All this complex balancing of various claims, interests, and norms could not have been done without the skilful performance of the European Commission.[54] Although the Commission was not *de jure* an independent actor, it was de facto setting the agenda of negotiations with the candidates, monitoring the implementation of EU entrance conditions, and providing direction to deliberations within the European Council. As Ulrich Sedelmeier and Helen Wallace put it:

A team of policy advocates formed inside the Commission, and ensured that policy moved from the Europe Agreements to Copenhagen and the pre-accession strategy. They used the consensus among the macro-policymakers about the inappropriateness of defensive opposition to enlargement to move policy forward incrementally. They made effective use of agenda-setting power and successfully forged alliances.[55]

The completion of the accession negotiations was clearly in the interest of the European Commission. The Commission was handling all the details of the accession process and the successful completion of this process was bound to highlight its utility for any major European endeavour. Of course, the Commission was not necessarily interested in a speedy political deal between the EU and the applicant countries, something that was advocated by many commentators throughout 1990s. On the contrary, the Commission was largely responsible for putting in place a Byzantine structure of conditions, guidance, and screening that made the entire process look like an endless technical exercise unable to grasp the historical momentum created by the fall of Communism. Nevertheless, the failure of the enlargement process would have been a blow to the Commission's authority, and therefore the Commission always insisted on moving forward with accession.[56] There was hardly any resistance to its exercise of 'leadership in disguise' on the part of the European Council. Unlike in the fields of taxation or institutional reforms the European Council has never vetoed any proposal made by the Commission in the field of enlargement.[57] Of course, for successive proposals the Commission consulted with crucial actors involved in the accession process. But in view of all the conflicting demands and interests, it was impossible to please them all, and so the Commission was forced to take a bold stance on several occasions.[58] The so-called 'road map' elaborated by the Commission in November 2000 proved particularly effective in mobilizing the successive four EU presidencies (not all of them very fond of enlargement) to stick to the envisaged timetable of negotiations as a criterion for their success.[59]

Finally, we need to mention the role of external actors pressing for a speedy and fair enlargement of the Union. Most notably, the United States has been an enthusiastic supporter of the EU enlargement process, even though the US clearly preferred geographic widening over functional deepening of the EU. Numerous international organizations (governmental and non-governmental) have also developed a range of policies to complement the EU enlargement process.[60] And one should keep in mind that many business firms were multinational rather than national or European and many of them have been pressing the candidate states to adopt the *acquis communautaire* more vigorously than the European Commission itself, for largely commercial and not political reasons, of course.

Conclusions

It was often argued that the Union is an economic giant but a political dwarf. It was lamented that it is unable to project its power abroad in a decisive and purposeful manner. The Union was said to be a master at multiplying various institutional and regulatory frames, but unable to develop a sound foreign and security policy. These claims were certainly justified when the Union was faced with outbreaks of violence (such as in the Balkans) or a decision to go to a war (twice against Iraq). However, the last wave of enlargement has also shown that the Union is able to apply its power and leverage abroad in a purposeful and effective manner. Enlargement has shown that export of institutions and regulatory frames can be an efficient instrument of foreign policy. The Union has proved that it can act as a true political giant if not like a true empire when it comes to stabilizing its external environment. In short, enlargement was a quintessential foreign policy act and it represented the best quality of power politics in contemporary Europe.[61]

It would be utterly wrong to describe enlargement as merely a rhetorical or normative exercise. The interests behind enlargement were very real, and could not be reduced to some small material gains. At stake were peace, democracy, and the prosperity of Europe as a whole. EU leaders did not, and could not, specify possible threats or come forward with a plausible worst case scenario. Nevertheless, time and again they made clear that they were not about to take the risk of abandoning the project that they thought would make Europe more prosperous and secure. The project was highly complex and time consuming and as such prone to various local pressures. Vague and chaotic declarations, inconsistent moves, and even open contradictions between individual policies were quite frequent during the accession process. Yet, the Union has proved to be good at a certain type of imperial power politics based on political negotiations, legal regulations, and economic leverage. The project also allowed a leading role for the European Commission, which was crucial in setting the path of deliberations, negotiations, and decisions. The Commission was thus able to resist parochial pressures aimed at hijacking or frustrating the entire process, and managed to steer it towards successful completion.

Of course, this chapter has pointed out several weaknesses in the EU's approach. The Union never spelled out clearly the vision of Europe for which it was striving. Its policies were overly procedural and failed to appeal to broader public.[62] The search for internal consensus resulted in many side payments to powerful interests within the Union which are likely to cause numerous problems in the future, especially for the new members. And the Union lacked imagination and determination in reforming its own institutions prior to enlargement. We can therefore expect that the enlarged EU will see a multiplication of various functional and institutional arrangements resembling the medieval imperial pattern. But we can also expect that the success of this enlargement will encourage the Union to act towards its new neighbours in an equally imperial fashion. Countries such as Turkey, Serbia, Ukraine, Belarus, and Russia would obviously represent an even greater challenge, but then the interests at stake are also greater.[63] This last wave of enlargement has proved that the Union is quite skilful and determined when it comes to protecting its most vital interests.

3
Diversity and Adaptation

Securing peace and prosperity in Eastern Europe is certainly important for the EU, but even more important is maintaining peace and prosperity within the Union itself. The two projects may be in harmony, but they may also be in conflict. Much depends on whether the enlargement is designed and implemented in a way that strengthens rather than weakens the process of European integration. The reverse is also true: not all visions of European integration are compatible with a workable enlargement. The problem is not only that widening makes deepening more difficult. The danger is that poorly designed and implemented enlargement may para-lyse European institutions, erode Western democratic standards, produce economic chaos, and even undermine Europe's security. The architects of enlargement always argued that the project is about exporting Western peace, democracy, and prosperity to Eastern Europe. But it is easy to envisage the opposite scenario, namely that various Eastern European 'diseases' will be imported into Western Europe through enlargement. Even a short visit to some large German or Austrian cities clearly shows that embracing Eastern Europe also has many negative aspects.[1] The question is: what is the balance of costs and benefits and how can enlarge-ment be made to work in tandem with European integration?

In Chapter 1, I argued that the new member states from Eastern Europe have made enormous progress in stabilizing their political order, installing democratic institutions, and creating market economies. Was this all enough to make them fit for membership in this exclusive European club? Since this wave of enlargement was guided largely by political considerations can one truly believe that the tough legal and economic criteria for EU entrance have been met in practice? It took the current member states several decades to arrive at common practices across vari-ous functional fields. How can one expect the new member states from

Eastern Europe to do the same within a few short years? What about the welfare gap between the old and new members? What about problems of national minorities in Eastern Europe? Do not communist habits persist behind the facades of democratic and market institutions? Are not the new members supporters of American rather than European foreign policy? In short, will enlargement not end in failure despite all good intentions? Has the price of enlargement been too high, after all? Does enlargement herald the weakening if not the demise of European integration? Of course, these are not just rhetorical questions and they were frequently raised in the political and academic discourse on enlargement (although usually in a more politically correct manner).[2]

At the centre of these anxieties is the perceived level of diversity between the old and new EU members. The fear is that despite the intensive process of mutual adaptation the post-Communist states from Eastern Europe are not yet truly compatible with Western European ones. They are much poorer than West European states. Their democracy and in some cases even their statehood is newly established and presumably more fragile. Their economic, legal, and administrative structures are less developed. They also have their own distinct histories, societies, and cultures. They have different foreign and security preoccupations. Although they all share the aspiration to join the Union, their visions, interests, and priorities do not necessarily converge with one another nor with those of long-standing EU members. In fact, in view of the numerous structural differences between the new and old EU member states, it is difficult to expect there to be a major and durable alignment of their respective political preferences and behaviour. The EU will thus be a much more diversified entity following this particular wave of enlargement. This is not good news for the friends of the European state because Westphalian states are known to be relatively homogeneous. In fact, it is often said that their major achievement was to suppress the diversity that existed in the Middle Ages. And so the friends of the European state ask themselves: how much diversity can the Union withstand without falling prey to stagnation or even serious crisis? Should not the Union try to suppress this neo-medieval feature?

This chapter will try to show that the map of unity and diversity in the enlarged EU is extremely complex, and does not simply correspond to the old East–West divide. Moreover, the division lines themselves are constantly changing, with the enlargement process itself constituting an important factor forcing adaptation and serving to push individual states into a single regulatory framework, if not necessarily in a common political direction. However, the European effect works unevenly in different functional areas and territories. There are other 'unifying' factors at play, with globalization (or perhaps simply Americanization) in particular producing different models and loyalties than Europeanization as such.[3] In addition, there are also centrifugal forces within the new member states that continue to generate diversity rather than unity across Europe.

A certain degree of diversity is thus unavoidable, but I argue that there is no need to demonize it. The diverse nature of the Union of fifteen member states did not cause any dramatic developments. In fact, we learned that not all types of diversity need prove detrimental to the process of European integration. Diversity can have either positive or negative connotations, depending on context and objectives, and much of its effect clearly depends on what is being sought, in which field, and under what particular set of circumstances. A more diversified Union will look more like a neo-medieval empire than a neo-Westphalian state, but this does not necessarily imply a demise of European integration. Much depends on whether the Union will find effective and legitimate ways to manage the ever greater diversity.

This chapter first attempts to conceptualize the impact of diversity on the process of European integration.[4] It seeks, in particular, to establish whether the increased level of diversity is a bane or a blessing for the enlarged Union. Will diversity lead to actual divergence in structure and policy?[5] Need we fear a possible paralysis of European institutions after the enlargement? The chapter then examines in more depth the evolving map of divergence in Europe, first by looking at macroeconomic indicators, and later at democracy and civil society. In the conclusions, it points to major characteristics of the enlarged Euro-polity which are caused by its new scope, form, and meaning of diversity.

Diversity and European integration

Diversity is a normal state of affairs in complex polities and various academic disciplines have quite a relaxed attitude towards the phenomenon. Democracy studies, for instance, see diversity, or as they call it, pluralism, as a pillar of democratic order. Economic studies look at diversity as an engine of development and innovation. However, studies of European integration tend to view diversity with suspicion. For many students and practitioners, the progress of European integration is simply measured by the degree to which the Union is able to achieve greater cohesion. The failure of European integration, on the other hand, is illustrated by examples of persisting and irreconcilable differences among individual member states. In the literature on European integration concepts of fusion, convergence, cohesion, and integration are often used as synonyms,[6] and this inevitably leads to a tendency to demonize any sort of diversity. But why is diversity seen as so problematic in this particular field?

The reasons for criticizing diversity are many. One is a misguided perception of the ultimate aim of integration. If European unity is the aim of integration, differences in structure and behaviour are seen as something to be overcome or even as something fundamentally undesirable. But unity as such was never the ultimate aim of integration.[7] In the extreme, of course, such an aim could lead to the creation of an Orwellian-like state that is not only totalitarian, but also inefficient,[8] a scenario that is of particular relevance in the context of eastward enlargement. Moreover, homogenizing tendencies in the process of European integration have also made it necessary for the Union to develop and 'legalize' the concepts of subsidiarity and flexibility,[9] although, interestingly enough, such subsidiarity discourse has scarcely been applied to the issue of eastward enlargement, with the applicant states being denied the opportunity for the various opt-outs that have already been negotiated by some current member states in the areas of foreign, monetary, social, or border-related policy (e.g. the Schengen *acquis*). In fact, an insistence on total alignment with EU norms and regulations always remained the prevailing discourse in the process of enlargement, not only for tactical but also for strategic considerations.

This uneven treatment of current and prospective EU members suggests a resistance to accept the unknown 'other' as a partner in a well-established project—and this is yet another reason for demonizing diversity. This is a quite natural psychological reaction to change and has been experienced in previous cases of enlargement. When Greece, Spain, and Portugal attempted to join the then European Communities, for instance, fears of migratory flows and the import of lax Mediterranean legal culture were quite widespread.[10] Identity formation involves a distinction being made between the 'self' and the 'other', and despite their persisting European quest, the countries behind the Iron Curtain have long been stigmatized as an 'other'. As Giuliano Amato and Judy Batt have observed:

The division of Europe has left its mark on perceptions in the West, reinforcing long-standing prejudices about the East as 'backward' and less 'civilized' than the

West, not fully 'part of Europe'. The prospect of enlargement to the East has brought these prejudices to the fore, further contributing to the tendency to portray the increasing diversity that it entails as a new and uniquely threatening challenge for the EU.[11]

As stated earlier, for the applicant states enlargement represented the 'return to Europe' after many years of Soviet domination.[12] For many of the current member states, on the other hand, enlargement looked more like a missionary crusade, in which the applicant countries were sometimes treated as an equivalent of medieval barbarians that needed to be taught the superior Western ways of doing business and politics.[13] In other words, the view was that they should resemble EU prototypes or otherwise be kept at bay with the use of export quotas and Schengen. At the same time, however, it is evident that no single EU prototype actually exists.[14] The fifteen EU members were themselves very diversified and one can argue that the *acquis communautaire* contains rules that are technical rather than normative, and which, as such, can hardly represent a serious factor in identity formation. In fact, EU identity is closely linked to a pan-European culture and history of which the new member states are an incontestable part. To put it another way, it is evident that European identity can hardly remain the exclusive commodity of an organized group of the powerful and the rich.

Another reason for attacking diversity emerges from the positivist predilection for social and institutional engineering that is widespread among both social democratic and Christian democratic political parties. The Union is seen as a means of controlling the very complex and diversified European environment through the use of communitarian solutions.[15] While the liberal approach tolerates and even praises diversity of structure and action, the positivist approach is about disciplined crafting aimed at curbing various forms of diversity, especially those that might lead to a durable divergence. This requires a careful selection of targets (agenda setting), elaboration of conditions, safeguards and timetables, active guidance, and regular screening.[16] Failure to meet certain targets or deviation from the envisaged route is evaluated in a very negative way. As pointed out in Chapter 2, the EU policy of enlargement was very much concerned with engineering and crafting. The applicant states were confronted with the requirement of implementing a set of conditions that was aimed at making them EU compatible. Their progress in meeting these conditions was subject to regular screening. Accession was meant to take place only once the applicants had met the envisaged targets.

But can crafting and engineering ever succeed in a complex European environment? After all so many of the existing European arrangements have developed in such an ambiguous and paradoxical manner. Chapter 2 has also shown that the last wave of enlargement evolved very much by default, despite the often pompous rhetoric of engineering and crafting. This is because EU accession conditions were often imprecise, impractical, and contradictory. The screening process was superficial and subject to discretionary interpretations. And the successive decisions taken within the process of enlargement resulted from hard and largely unpredictable political bargaining that did not resemble any carefully crafted blueprint. Moreover, the Western European experience shows that engineering does not eliminate diversity, only modifies it. As one comprehensive study of the impact of EU policies and legislation on the member states suggested:

The process patterns and policy outcomes of Europeanization have not been uniform across the member states, and do not reflect either the well defined will of a 'unified supranational actor' or a pervasive problem-solving rationality which imposes itself 'automatically' as to increase the overall efficiency of European policy decisions in the context of a transnational interdependence of policy problems. Instead, the political reality of European policy-making is 'messy' insofar as it is uneven across policy areas and member states, institutionally cumbersome, and subject to the dynamics of domestic politics each with its own particular logic. As a consequence, the outcomes of European policy-making tend to be much more diverse than one would expect and preclude any simplistic explanation of Europe-induced changes.[17]

In other words, despite crafting and engineering, diversity already appears as a normal state of affairs within the EU, and in this regard eastward enlargement will change little. The Union will have more countries, but there will still be large and small countries in the Union, there will be the rich and the poor, the original six and latecomers, the Protestant and the Catholic, those obsessed with American power and those allied with it, those with socialist governments and those with conservative ones, as well as unitary nation states and states with powerful regions. Each EU country will belong to several groups at the same time, opposing some countries on some issues and joining them on other issues. Similarities will go hand in hand with dissimilarities, and some countries will not easily fit into any of the aforementioned categories. European integration will be still about reconciling and accommodating these multiple differences, but it will, as always in the past, fall short of securing any considerable degree of convergence and unity across EU borders.

Diversity and European institutions

Fears that enlargement may destroy the existing delicate balance of power in the Union also prompt criticism of diversity. It is especially feared that new member states from Eastern Europe will opt for looser forms of European cooperation and this in turn will reinforce calls for more advanced forms of integration within a smaller and more convergent European core.[18] Of course, the creation of such a core might have serious negative implications for the entire process of European integration. Most crucially, it would imply abandoning of the so-called community model in which all member states are treated on an equal basis, undertaking the same mutual obligations, and following the same rules. The *acquis communautaire* represents the essence of this model and it is for this reason that the applicant states were denied opt-outs from its components.[19]

The import of additional diversity from Eastern Europe may indeed result in a more intergovernmental rather than federative mode of European cooperation, but the institutional positions of the new members cannot be seen as fixed at this stage. Especially some smaller Eastern European countries may soon find that communitarian solutions serve their interests quite well, because they protect them from domination by large member states. New communitarian solutions may also flourish because they will offer the Union more problem-solving capacity in various functional fields. In fact, this is also the lesson of European integration history. Although each previous wave of enlargement led to a certain increase in diversity, communitarian solutions nevertheless gradually became the norm in many new fields. In short, a mixture of communitarian and intergovernmental modes of European cooperation is likely to characterize the Union in the wake of this enlargement.

Nor should one fear that enlargement will necessarily lead to the creation of a strong European core. The idea of a core Europe has been raised many times in the history of European integration, but it has nevertheless not been implemented. Instead the Union has developed more modest forms of diversification in the form of temporary or permanent opt-outs, subsidiarity, and flexibility. The core would add an extra layer of institutional cooperation without abandoning existing layers within the EU itself, and its creation could even lead to serious conflicts. Some of the member states would be worried about being excluded from the core, while others would fear that joining the core would subject them to domination by other core members. Not all these fears need be realized, but it is even difficult to envisage which countries could possibly form a European core. France is no longer seen as the engine behind the European integration project after the 'no' vote in the 2005 referendum on the European Constitution, and Germany would probably be unwilling to push for a core on its own.

Although creation of a tight European core is unlikely, enlargement will increase variable geometry within the Union. For instance, there are currently three geometric objects in the monetary union: members of the euro-zone (twelve), members of the New Exchange Rate Mechanism (ERM II) (one), and members with floating exchange rates (two). With the eastward enlargement we are likely to have a fourth geometric object: members with currency boards (currently Estonia and Bulgaria have currency boards). A Union with more variable geometry will, of course, be more complex, but this does not mean that it will function less efficiently. In fact, one can argue the opposite, namely that an EU presenting a single geometric object would be too rigid to respond to a variety of economic and political pressures confronting individual member states and the Union.[20]

However, increased diversity, it is argued, carries the risk of decision-making paralysis. It was already difficult to get fifteen states in line, and adding extra states to the list may well prevent the emergence of any meaningful consensus in the future. Moreover, the accession negotiations resulted in no less than 322 transitional measures that are bound to complicate decision-making even further. Again, however, this does not need to be the case. Decision-making deadlock might have already been anticipated in a union of fifteen diverse member states, and yet it was often avoided through the escape routes devised by the actors involved.[21] Indeed, according to Adrienne Héritier, it is precisely this 'logic of diversity' which may spur European policy-making on at least two grounds. First, although decision-making under conditions of diversity may indeed run into stalemate this is usually not the end of the story. There is ample evidence that European actors (the Commission and the member states) are very resourceful in finding ways out of and around deadlock situations, finding 'escape routes' in order to develop these policies even after they have seemingly failed. Typical modes of circumventing deadlocks applied especially by the European Commission involve the creation of vague, innocuous-looking framework legislation which unfolds its detailed binding power only much later (e.g. industrial emission into air); shifting arenas to find new political allies and new issue linkage possibilities (e.g. public services); changing legal frameworks in order to avoid demanding decision-making rules (e.g. social policy); relabelling or reframing policies in order to create a larger supportive basis (e.g. poverty policy), to name only a few.[22] Second, under conditions of diversity a dynamic of 'political regulatory competition' comes into play among members, with each member state trying to 'upload' its policy practices onto the European level.[23] If a member state is successful in incorporating them into the European agenda, it can subsequently save policy adjustment costs at the domestic level. Hence, the policy diversity of member states is an important source of the acceleration of policy production at the European level and it is by no means the Commission which is always the one to launch new policy ideas to avoid a decision-making deadlock.[24] According to Héritier, it is arguably simpler to accommodate more rather than less diverse member state interests within one polity: in the heterogeneous polity, accommodation and compromise-seeking becomes the cardinal feature of decision-making.[25] Similar conclusions have been reached by Lisa Martin, who argues that a diversity (or as she puts it, a heterogeneity) of interests creates opportunities for trade-offs among actors and so increases the likelihood of agreement rather than stalemate.[26] True, diversity combined with the consensus-based decision-making system can sometimes lead to paralysis. But this is more likely to be the fault of the consensus-based decision-making apparatus than of the diversity as such.[27] Nor is diversity necessarily inimical to the democratic system. On the contrary, diversity, albeit under the name pluralism, is more commonly seen as indispensable to democracy.

In conclusion, it can be argued that there is little reason to fear the various kinds of diversity in the Union which enlargement brings. While diversity can at times jeopardize certain forms of cooperation, it can also facilitate cooperation and hence foster further integration. Diversity teaches adaptation, bargaining, and accommodation. It is a source of competition, self-improvement, and innovation. Thus, it may also prove to be not only an important prerequisite of democracy, but also of efficiency, in that it may be argued that it is only highly diversified and pluralistic societies acting in a complex web of institutional arrangements that are able to succeed in conditions of modern competition.

Is it possible to distinguish between 'good' and 'bad' types of diversity?[28] Yes, but only in a very abstract and normative manner. In reality whether diversity is beneficial or problematic depends on the particular context and set of objectives. Those who would like to see the construction of a Westphalian European federation would probably view diversity with suspicion, but this does not necessarily mean that diversity is bad for Europe and the process of European integration. But the opposite does not always hold true either. Diversity in certain forms and under certain circumstances can also cause problems in a neo-medieval setting. Students of European integration have no reason to demonize diversity, but they have all kinds of reasons to study the evolving lines of diversity and assess their possible implications in various fields and in the context of individual integrative projects. Let us try to see what kind of diversity patterns are emerging in an enlarged EU. The existing literature on enlargement usually views diversity in the fields of economics, democracy, and foreign policy as being the most problematic. The countries of Eastern Europe may well find themselves within EU borders, but a clear East–West divide is said to persist in all three functional fields. Is this the case? Can one argue that economic, political, and cultural maps of the enlarged EU show clear differences between the old and new members? And if the picture is more complex, what should we make of it?

Economic 'fault lines' in the enlarged EU

Analysts usually point to gaps in the economic size and wealth between the old and new member states. In this sense all agree that this enlargement is indeed very special. The total GDP at market prices and current exchange rates of new members is less than 5 per cent of the GDP of the EU comprising fifteen states. Moreover, the new members have an average GDP per capita of only 40 per cent of the existing members (at purchasing power parity). When Spain and Portugal joined the European Communities in 1986 they had an average per capita GDP of 70 per cent of the existing EU. From this vantage point economic disparities are said to create pressure for large financial transfers from rich to poor member states, prevent the new members from fully implementing the existing *acquis*, and disrupt the smooth functioning of the Economic and Monetary Union (EMU) and the single market.[29]

The welfare gap between the old and new EU members is indeed significant.[30] Nevertheless, one wonders whether wealth is the best indicator to help us understand the economic functioning of the enlarged EU. One can argue that health (potential growth) rather than wealth (income) is a much better indicator. Moreover, significant economic gaps also existed between the fifteen member states without causing major economic problems. And it would also be wrong to portray this enlargement as an act of charity by the richer European states.

Let us start with the assertion that accession of poor countries from Eastern Europe will create serious economic problems. When one looks at the experience of previous waves of enlargement, problems were usually caused by richer member states such as Belgium rather than by poorer, more dynamic states such as Portugal or Ireland. As Jean-Luc Dehaene and Ania Krok-Paszkowska forcefully argued:

Health, not wealth is the key factor determining whether an economy will be able to meet the objectives of achieving increasing convergence of economic performance and greater social and economic cohesion within the EU. Most Central and Eastern European Countries (CEECs) are now small, dynamic economies with institutional frameworks, and financial sectors that are adequate, and in some cases even better than could be expected for their level of development.[31]

As shown in the Table 3.1, growth rates are generally higher in the states which have recently acceded to the EU than in the old member states, and in the future they are expected to get even higher.[32] Experience with previous enlargements shows that EU membership is a powerful factor fostering growth rates in new members, and this in turn helps to achieve convergence in income. Ireland is a very good example (although the example of Greece is less encouraging). Today Ireland has one of the highest incomes per capita in the entire EU (although EU membership was only one among many different factors behind Ireland's success). Of course, most new members from Eastern Europe would have to bridge a much greater initial gap in welfare than Ireland did, but then few had expected the Irish economy to grow so quickly from the moment of accession.[33] Besides, countries such as Slovenia already have an income per capita comparable with Greece and Portugal (although Slovenia has the highest propositional rural population among all new members). This brings me to another important point. Welfare gaps existed within the EU-15 and they caused few economic problems. As the Table 3.1 shows, for instance, Austria's gross national income (GNI) per capita is more than double that of Portugal. The gap between Sweden and Greece is even greater. And Luxembourg's GNI per capita is nearly twice as high as that of Sweden or Austria. Accession of Eastern European states will make differences in welfare more visible, more striking, and probably more challenging, but the Union is quite accustomed to living with such differences.

Differences in overall economic potential between the old and new members are also striking, but they are hardly problematic for the smooth functioning of the Union. For instance, the experience of a crisis by small-sized economies from Eastern Europe is not likely to cause any serious disruptions to the economic condition of the EU as such. By comparison, if Germany or France with their huge economic potential experiences a

Table 3.1. The economic map of the EU-25

Country	GDP growth 1992*	GDP growth 2002*	Cumulative change in GDP 1992–2002 (1992=100)	GNI per capita in USD 2001†	Years of GDP decline 1992–2002	Unemployment 2002*	Corruption perception index‡ 0=highly corrupt 10=highly clean	Monthly minimum wage in PPS, January 2003§	FDI inward flows* in EUR Million	Rural population† as % of total
Cyprus	n.a.	2.2	146	12,320	0	5.3	5.4	n.a.	419	n.a.
Czech Republic	−0.5	3.4	120	5,250	4	7.3	4.2	389	5,489	25
Estonia	−14.2	4.0	130	3,580	4	9.1	6.0	264	603	31
Hungary	−3.1	3.5	137	4,710	2	5.6	4.8	384	2,730	35
Latvia	−34.9	5.0	119	2,910	3	12.9	4.0	239	497	40
Lithuania	−21.3	4.0	100	2,930	4	13.1	4.6	252	198	31
Malta	4.7	2.8	149	9,210	1	7.5	6.8	752	350	n.a.
Poland	2.6	1.4	155	4,190	0	20.0	3.5	351	6,377	37
Slovak Republic	−6.5	3.6	141	3,700	2	19.4	4.0	265	486	42
Slovenia	−5.5	3.1	147	10,050	1	6.0	6.0	668	1,647	51
average AC10	**−8.7**	**3.3**	**134**	**5,885**	**2**	**10.6**	**4.9**	**396**	**1,880**	**37**
average EU15	**1.2**	**1.9**	**135**	**23,583**	**1**	**6.4**	**7.7**	**949**	**5,008**	**24**
Austria	2.3	1.5	122	25,220	0	3.6	8.4	n.a.	956	33
Belgium	1.6	1.4	122	24,540	1	7.3	7.5	1162	6,211	3
Denmark	0.6	1.3	127	32,280	1	4.5	9.5	n.a.	2,692	15
Finland	−3.3	1.2	139	25,130	2	9.1	9.7	n.a.	307	41
France	1.3	1.6	121	24,090	1	8.7	7.1	1150	11,893	24
Germany	2.2	1.0	114	25,120	1	8.2	8.2	n.a.	4,930	12
Greece	0.7	4.0	131	11,960	1	10.3	4.3	617	53	40
Ireland	3.3	3.7	209	22,660	0	4.4	7.5	910	942	41
Italy	0.8	1.2	118	20,160	1	9.1	4.8	n.a.	3,345	33
Luxembourg	4.5	3.4	172	39,840	0	2.4	8.4	1338	26,648	n.a.
Netherlands	2.0	1.6	131	24,970	0	2.6	8.7	1225	6,331	10
Portugal	2.5	1.8	129	11,120	1	5.0	6.3	543	508	34
Spain	0.9	2.0	132	15,080	1	11.4	7.1	617	2,447	22
Sweden	−1.7	1.6	126	27,140	2	4.9	9.2	n.a.	2,955	17
UK	0.2	1.7	132	24,430	0	5.1	8.6	983	4,909	10

source: *EUROSTAT 2003, **World Bank 2003, ***Transparency International 2004

†the minimum wage is indicated only for 9 countries of the EU15

^^ in calculation of the cumulative change in GDP and years of GDP decline, for Cyprus year 1993 was taken into consideration serious economic crisis this would have a much greater negative impact on other members. As pointed out earlier, the small economic size of the new members also facilitates economic transfers. Even a tiny sacrifice by the old richer members means a great deal for the new poorer members. Besides, as we have seen in Chapter 2, the Union was able to keep financial transfers under control. Subsidies to new member states are not to exceed a certain percentage of their national GDP and are to be matched by domestic funds. In this way, the contributions by individual member states to the EU budget do not have to be increased and the EU budget itself will remain balanced.

Moreover, most transfers should not be seen as charitable gifts. For instance, the EU cohesion funds were initially envisaged as a means by which weaker economies could be compensated for opening their markets.[34] It was forcefully argued at the time that without cohesion funds integration would be likely to benefit primarily the rich, rather than poor and peripheral countries.[35] Other studies pointed out that moving production from the old to the new member states allows the latter to match competitive pressures from low-labour-cost countries in the Third World. As a group of Italian experts argued in their study of trade competition and delocalization of production in the context of the EU enlargement: 'The body of research presented here rejects the notion that enlargement be characterized as "taking on board the poor". Rather, enlargement is a way to new gains in competitiveness and welfare, the source for such gains being an enhanced, more efficient international division of labor.'[36]

Poor members from Eastern Europe have indeed found it difficult to implement some 'expensive' elements of the *acquis communautaire*. For instance, it is estimated that the implementation of the environmental dimension of the *acquis* will cost the new member states as much as 120 billion euros.[37] However, one should ask whether keeping these states outside the EU would address the environmental concerns of the Union any better? After all, even a hard border under the Schengen regime cannot prevent Eastern European pollution from entering the EU, although it could well prevent Eastern European migrants from entering the Western European labour market. Nevertheless, as I will argue later, such migration is not likely to rise dramatically with enlargement, despite the existing welfare gaps and higher unemployment rates in the new members.[38] Besides, and more crucially in this context, such migration would by and large be economically beneficial for the old members and the Union as such.[39]

Poor members from Eastern Europe are also said to be unable to implement the so-called 'social *acquis*', and are prone to be accused of 'social dumping'.[40] This seems unfair. The EU's 'hard' *acquis* on social policy is very thin. It consists of only seventy directives relating to such issues as free movement of workers, equal opportunities, labour regulations, and health and safety at work. It was the EU and not the Eastern European states that temporarily suspended the introduction of some of these arrangements (namely the free movement of workers from the new members). Other arrangements in the field of social policy concerning such issues as employment and the fight against social exclusion represent only 'soft' *acquis*. Soft *acquis* consists of recommendations and desires rather than formal obligations.[41] Consequently, one cannot talk about 'social dumping.'

Of course, there are also economic differences between the old and new member states that are more problematic. However, in my view, they largely concern economic institutions rather than macroeconomic indicators. As Laszlo Bruszt put it:

The emerging capitalism in CEE countries looks like an institutional desert, at least in comparison to the form(s) of capitalism evolving within the European Union. Institutions that would improve the market power of the different categories of economic actors and allow for the emergence of 'win–win' forms of cooperation among them are lacking.[42]

One may also add cultural factors that underpin the working of not only economic, but also political institutions. Cultural factors are seen, for instance, as an important factor behind much higher levels of corruption in the new member states.[43] This leads to the next major issue determining differences between the old and new member states: democracy and political culture.

Diversity in democracy and political culture

It is more difficult to establish a clear pattern of divergence and convergence within the enlarged EU in the field of democracy and political culture than in the economic field. (And it is not that easy to establish which differences are really problematic.)[44] When we look at democratic institutions across the enlarged EU there is no clear East–West divide, at least from the formal point of view. All new members are either parliamentary or semi-presidential republics. (There are no monarchies among them, at least not yet.) They all have constitutions providing checks and balances between different branches of power. Citizens' basic rights and freedoms are guaranteed by law. True, laws on the media in the new member states are in constant flux, with government officials trying to manipulate television broadcasting in particular. However, in this sense the situation is not as bad as in some old EU member states such as Italy.[45] The party systems in the new member states are also in constant flux, but currently this is also true in some old member states.[46] The non-governmental organizations (NGOs) of civil society are said to be underdeveloped in the new member states, but when we look at Table 3.2 NGO membership density per million of population is sometimes lower in Western European states than in Eastern European ones.

Legal treatment of ethnic minorities that do not have citizenship of the country they live in is often quoted as a major distinguishing feature of some of the new member states. The problem concerns especially many Russians in Latvia and Estonia and the Roma population in such countries as Romania, the Czech Republic, and Hungary.[47] That said, the situation for Roma is not much better in some Western European countries such as Spain.[48] Moreover, it is not entirely clear whether one can differentiate between the East European treatment of the 'old' minorities, and the West European treatment of the 'new' minorities (i.e. foreign migrants that are also deprived of some basic civic rights).[49] In other words, Eastern Europe does not dramatically differ from Western Europe in its treatment of non-citizens.

In sum, a comparison of formal laws and institutions does not reveal any particular pattern of divergence between old and new EU members. Nor is there a striking East–West divide when we look at independent evaluations of democracy, rights, and freedoms. Bulgaria and Romania usually score badly here, but this is one of the main reasons why they were not admitted to the Union together with other post-Communist states. Those admitted, however, usually score well in various evaluations. For instance, according to the Freedom House rating cited in Table 3.2, not only Greece, but also France offers fewer political rights than any of the new members. Other Freedom House data show that Italy (together with Greece) has a lower democracy ranking than, for instance, Slovenia or Lithuania.[50]

Comparative studies of political values and behaviour produce similar results: no sharp threshold can be identified between West and East; instead, there is a continuous decline in the extent of a democratic community further east and south beyond the EU's new borders. This does not imply that a wholly homogenous political culture exists within the

Table 3.2. The democratic map of the EU-25

Country	Independent evaluation of democratization					Citizen support of different types of democratic community^^			
	Press Freedom Index* 0–30=Free 31–60=Partly free 61–100=Not free	Political rights score* 1=The most free 7=The least free	Civil liberties score* 1=The most free 7=The least free	Freedom rating* 1=Free 2=Partly free 3=Not free	NGO membership density per million of population‡	Support for democratic rule	Support for autocratic rule	Law abidingness	Ethnic tolerance
						(in per cent positive support)			
Bulgaria	29	1	3	1.5	282.9	80	19	96	14
Czech Republic	25	1	2	1.5	323.6	88	4	86	30
Estonia	18	1	2	1.5	1,111.1	85	6	91	5
Hungary	23	1	2	1.5	350.4	83	5	89	13
Latvia	19	1	2	1.5	571.7	79	8	83	8
Lithuania	19	1	2	1.5	414.9	87	15	90	3
Poland	18	1	2	1.5	94.3	n.a.	n.a.	n.a.	5
Romania	35	2	2	2.0	108.9	89	22	94	6
Slovak Republic	22	1	2	1.5	390.4	88	4	82	17
Slovenia	20	1	2	1.0	1053.3	82	6	85	20
average CEEC10	**23**	**1.1**	**2.1**	**1.5**	**355.4**	**85**	**10**	**88**	**12**
average EU15	**16**	**1.2**	**1.5**	**1.0**	**732.2**	**88**	**6**	**93**	**32**
Austria	24	1	1	1.0	560.7	n.a.	n.a.	n.a.	n.a.
Belgium	9	1	2	1.0	558.7	n.a.	n.a.	n.a.	n.a.
Denmark	9	1	1	1.0	909.1	n.a.	n.a.	n.a.	n.a.
Finland	10	1	1	1.0	885.9	75	10	94	20
France	17	2	2	1.0	98.3	n.a.	n.a.	n.a.	n.a.
Germany	15	1	2	1.0	73.1	93	1	88	45
Greece	30	3	3	1.5	350.3	n.a.	n.a.	n.a.	n.a.
Ireland	16	1	1	1.0	945.4	n.a.	n.a.	n.a.	n.a.
Italy	27	1	2	1.0	102.2	n.a.	n.a.	n.a.	n.a.

Table 3.2. (Continued)

Country	Independent evaluation of democratization					Citizen support of different types of democratic community[^^]			
	Press Freedom Index* 0–30=Free 31–60=Partly free 61–100=Not free	Political rights score* 1=The most free 7=The least free	Civil liberties score*	Freedom rating* 1=Free 2=Partly free 3=Not free	NGO membership density per million of population‡	Support for democratic rule	Support for autocratic rule	Law abidingness	Ethnic tolerance
						(in per cent positive support)			
Luxembourg	14	1	1	1.0	4,732.8	n.a.	n.a.	n.a.	n.a.
Netherlands	15	1	1	1.0	364.4	n.a.	n.a.	n.a.	n.a.
Portugal	15	1	1	1.0	404.1	n.a.	n.a.	n.a.	n.a.
Spain	18	1	2	1.0	140.0	92	8	97	23
Sweden	8	1	1	1.0	757.6	93	5	93	40
UK	18	1	2	1.0	100.3	n.a.	n.a.	n.a.	n.a.

source: *Press Freedom 2002, **Freedom House 2002, ^Union of International Associations (2002), ‡Union of International Organisations: Guide to Civil Society Networks'', ^^Fuchs D., Klingemann H-D., in Mair, P., Zielonka, J., (2002) ''The enlarged European Union; Diversity and adaptation''.

enlarged EU. As a study by Fuchs and Klingemann shows, levels of self-responsibility differ markedly between Sweden and Spain, for example, and a number of Central and Eastern Europeans already approximate the Spanish pattern.[51] In addition, while per capita GDP in Slovenia may well be close to Western levels, its citizens nevertheless reveal a much lower level of civic engagement and social trust. Table 3.2 also shows that Finland has lower support for democratic rule than any of the new member states, while Spain has higher support for autocratic rule than most of the new member states.

Studies focusing on language configuration, religious beliefs, and popular culture also confirm that there is no clear-cut cleavage between the new and old member states. For instance, David D. Laitin showed evidence of a pan-European culture that is rapidly infusing countries of Eastern Europe.[52] This transcendent European culture exists in conjunction with national cultures, which remain vibrant in both the West and the East. More to the point, the differences among national cultures within the old EU member states are considerable, and the national cultures of the new member states fall well within the extremes set by these old member states. In fact, Laitin argues that the cultural practices of the new member states from Eastern Europe are more proximate to the cultural practices of the original six EC members than are the cultural practices of the later entrants. New peripheral member states often have more motivation to assimilate into the norms of the centre than is the case for populations closer to the centre.

Despite all the previously cited evidence some scholars still insist that communist legacies persist in the new member states despite all reforms and adjustments. As Vladimir Tismaneanu argues:

East European political cultures remain heavily indebted to the ideological age: symbols, myths, rationalized miracles, liturgist nationalisms and teleological pretence have developed after the short-lived 'postmodern' interlude of the revolutions of 1989. And with them, the politics of emotion, unreason, hostility, anger and unavowed, unbearable shame. This is indeed the politics of rancorous marginality, 'cultural despair' and convulsive impotence that the nascent democratic (dis)order can barely contain.[53]

However, Tismaneanu acknowledges that his evaluation applies more to countries such as Russia, Ukraine, or Romania rather than the new EU entrants. He also points to the rise of populist politics based on symbols, myths, and nationalism in some Western European states such as Austria.

Students of legacies and culture usually focus on discourse and narratives that are difficult to compare across various countries.[54] Nevertheless, comparative empirical analyses also confirm that a history of communist rule accounts for a significant share of the cross-cultural variance in democratic values. At the same time they show that religious traditions of the new member states from Eastern Europe set them on distinct trajectories that were not erased by communism.[55] In other words, Catholic and Protestant traditions make the new EU members more similar to the old ones despite their legacy of communism.

The EU accession process is usually seen as an important factor consolidating new democracies in Eastern Europe which can be interpreted as another impetus for fostering compatibility if not homogeneity between the old and new EU members.[56] However, it has also been pointed out that the practice of EU democracy often works against transparency, accountability, and active popular participation.[57] Indeed, in the pre-accession period there were numerous examples of the EU urging Eastern European states to adopt various solutions without public deliberation and parliamentary control.[58] This shows that the Union's homogenizing pressure can be a mixed blessing for both the new member states and the EU itself. I will return to this issue in Chapter 5.

The American bias

The new member states from Eastern Europe have been described as an 'American Trojan Horse' within the Union.[59] This accusation primarily concerned the openly pro-American foreign policy of the new member states. The issue became highly politicized in early 2003 after the heads of several Eastern European states signed an open letter supporting the American iron fist policy towards Iraq.[60] Moreover, it has been argued that their economic reforms opt for American-inspired neo-liberal solutions that are insensitive to social justice. Eastern Europeans are also seen as susceptible to American cultural trends and consumption patterns. And they are supposed to share the American rather than the European value system concerning politics and society.[61] In short, new EU members differ from the old ones by acting and looking like the United States of America, and as such are unlikely partners in developing some common European projects, especially those that are distinct from if not in opposition to American ones.

This argument seems wrong to me on two accounts, one conceptual and another empirical. First, it assumes that it is possible to construct two distinct American and European models of politics, economics, and society. However, this has never been accomplished in any systematic and widely accepted manner.[62] The existing literature usually operates with models, categories, and classifications built around factors that are easier to operationalize and measure than a vague American–Western European dichotomy. In some of these categories or models the United States finds itself in the company of some Western (and Eastern) European states, but the company changes depending on the field under consideration. Second, if one insists on the American and the (old) EU dichotomy, the existing empirical evidence clearly shows that the new member states from Eastern Europe are closer to the Western European structure and behaviour than the American model. Let me develop these points somewhat further.

When one examines economic literature it is hard to find studies that would build their argument along the American–Western European dichotomy. For instance, Hamden-Turner and Trompenaars distinguished between seven cultures of capitalism, that of Britain, the United States, Germany, Sweden, France, the Netherlands, and Japan.[63] When analysts operate with dichotomies they usually do not draw a clear line between the EU and the United States, but focus on other differentiating factors such as hierarchy or intervention in the market. For instance, a popular distinction is made between a liberal and an interventionist economic model. This dichotomy is based on the role of the state across national economic systems. Interventionists hold the view that national competitiveness is based on a well-established structural role of the state carried out via industrial policy, whereas liberals rely primarily on the free interplay of market forces (via functioning competition policy), a stable legal/macroeconomic environment, and justify state intervention only in the case of actual or potential market failure. The line is usually drawn between the Anglo-Saxon and continental European economic systems, but in reality the 'old' EU had at least five states that could be labelled liberal (together with the United States): Britain, the Netherlands, Denmark, Finland, and Ireland.[64] In Eastern Europe the state no longer has an economic monopoly, but it would be wrong to assume that its role is minimal compared to Western European states. On the contrary, economic reports from the region often talk about lagging privatization, over-regulation, and arbitrary state intervention.[65] In short, despite great progress in trimming the economic role of the state in Eastern Europe, most countries can still be described as interventionist rather than liberal.

One should add that behind the pressure to trim down the role of the state in Eastern Europe were primarily forces of globalization that imposed on these states the iron laws of economic competition. If one wants to identify a single international actor behind Eastern European liberal reforms one needs to point to the special role of the EU rather than that of the United States. After all, the EU is their largest trading partner and a major part of the EU *acquis* that these states were asked to adopt was about deregulation, competition policy, and creation of a legal system that allows economic actors to act in a liberal fashion.

One would expect Eastern European states to opt for social policy solutions that are closer to the American rather than Western European standards and patterns. After all, these countries are relatively poor and can little afford expensive welfare provisions. Moreover, the EU's *acquis communautaire* in this field is quite thin. And Eastern European governments have encountered much less resistance from entrenched interests when seeking to implement radical social reforms than is the case in Western Europe. Nevertheless, all these countries attempted to combine economic growth with social protection rather than relying largely on neo-liberal solutions. As János Mátyás Kovács argued in his comparative study of Eastern European welfare systems:

'Americanization' of the welfare regimes has remained a rhetorical exercise rather than a powerful economic strategy.... Although occasionally Eastern European social reformers may make bolder experiments than their West European colleagues in marketizing/privatizing certain welfare schemes, these experiments are far from being irresistible under the pressure of the social legacies of communism, the daily challenges of the transformation, new statism/conservatism and the requirements of European integration; and similar reforms have been initiated (also with mixed results) by a few Western European welfare states as well.[66]

Trying to fit Eastern European countries into the American–Western Europe dichotomy in the field of democracy seems to me an even more futile exercise. Literature usually talks about such types of democracy as majoritarian, plebiscitarian, consociational, deliberative, postmodern, liberal, or postnational. Britain, France, and Germany are treated as separate if not unique cases, and so is democracy in the United States. One may argue that some new democracies in Eastern Europe more closely resemble the French or the German democratic model; although a single Western European model of democracy does not exist. Moreover, none of the Eastern European democracies resemble the American model.

When we look at the system of values the story is more or less the same. Data from the World Values Survey allow us to distinguish between an Anglo-Saxon (or English-speaking) group of countries whose values are

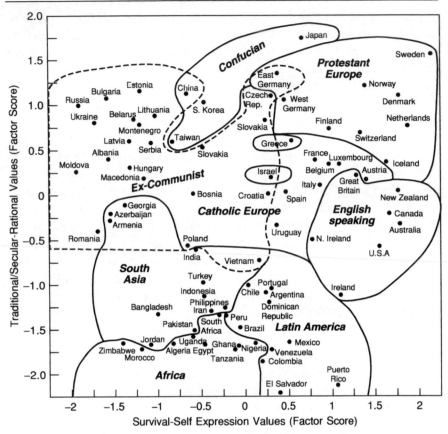

Figure 3.1 Central and East European values in global perspective

Source: Ronald Inglehart, 'East European Value Systems in Global Perspective', in *Democracy and Political Culture in Eastern Europe*, Hans-Dieter Klingemann, Dieter Fuchs, and Jan Zielonka (eds.) (London: Routledge, 2006).

distinct from those of either Protestant or Catholic Western Europe. Ex-Communist countries form a distinct group with new EU members situated close to Protestant and Catholic Western Europe, but still at a fair distance from English-speaking countries, including the United States.

A more sharp and clear distinction between Western Europe and the United States has recently been proposed in the field of foreign and security policy. According to Robert Kagan, American and European perspectives are diverging on the all-important questions of power—the efficacy of power, the morality of power, the desirability of power, and military power per se:

Europe is turning away from power, or to put it a little differently, it is moving beyond power into a self contained world of laws and rules and transnational negotiation and cooperation. It is entering a post-historical paradise of peace and relative prosperity, the realization of Immanuel Kant's 'perpetual peace'. Meanwhile, the United States remains mired in history, exercising power in an anarchic Hobbesian world where international laws and rules are unreliable, and where true security and the defense and promotion of a liberal order still depend on the possession and use of military might.[67]

The problem with Kagan's analysis is not only that it idealizes the United States and caricatures Western Europe, but in our context, the problem is that it ignores considerable heterogeneity within Western Europe itself. On the one hand, we have in Western Europe countries such as Britain and France which frequently apply their military might in various parts of the world. (The former is a close ally of the United States, of course, while the latter is usually in opposition to it.) On the other hand, there are countries such as Finland, Sweden, Austria, and Ireland that stick to their formal neutrality and political non-alignment. In between there is a variety of countries, some of them with sizeable military potential while others have no potential whatsoever. Some of them are interventionist while others are reluctant to engage in any conflicts. Some of them are traditional friends of the United States, while others keep the United States at a distance. New member states from Eastern Europe represent a very similar picture. True, they all signed a letter supporting American policy towards Iraq, leaving in limbo those Western European states that fervently opposed this policy. However, the *Wall Street Journal* letter was drafted by the office of the Spanish prime minister, and the collection of signatures was coordinated at 10 Downing Street in London.[68] The original letter of eight was signed by three Eastern European leaders (Vaclav Havel, Peter Medgyessy, and Leszek Miller) together with five Western European ones (Jose Maria Aznar, Silvio Berlusconi, Tony Blair, Jose-Manuel Durão, and Anders Fogh Rasmussen).[69] The list of less outspoken but quite genuine supporters of American policy in Western Europe is in fact much longer, especially when it comes to less sensitive issues.[70] True, public opinion in such states as Spain or Italy has been quite negative about American policy towards Iraq. But so was the public in new member states from Eastern Europe. For instance, 70 per cent of Czech citizens were against the attack on Iraq and only 16 per cent supported the American intervention in Iraq without a United Nations (UN) mandate[71]. In Poland, which is considered pro-American, 62 per cent of Poles believed that Poland should not support the American intervention in Iraq, with only

29 per cent expressing the view that Poland should support the United States.[72] Even if sanctioned by the UN, the war on Iraq was supported only by 28 per cent in Bulgaria and 20 per cent in Estonia.[73]

Of course, it would be wrong to assume that there are absolutely no differences in attitudes and policies between Western and Eastern European elites and public. For historical reasons the public and elites in post-Communist countries are probably more sensitive to possible security threats than public and elites in the western part of Europe. In this sense Eastern European publics share more security perceptions with the American public.[74] Successive governments in Poland, in particular, have seen the alliance with the United States as a means of escaping centuries of domination by Germany and Russia. However, it would be wrong to conclude that there is a clear and consistent cleavage between old and new EU members when it comes to the United States. Americans might well recognize their own foreign-policy designs when looking at such countries as Italy or Poland, but when it comes to democratic practices, social systems, or cultural habits they will see a more complex picture across the entire enlarged EU. Part of this picture might resemble the United States, but another part would not. Some policies of European states will be to the American liking, but others may well be disliked, depending on the issue and political circumstances. The United States has always been part of European politics, economics, and culture, admired by some and contested by other European actors.[75] Enlargement will change little in this respect. If the EU is indeed faced with a new type of American challenge, this is not due to enlargement but to major historical shocks like the fall of the Soviet Union or the 9/11 terrorist attack.

Conclusions

The eastern enlargement is often seen as a threat to the entire integration project. Indeed, for some Euro-sceptics, this is part of the appeal of enlargement. Among those committed to the Union, however, there are many voices expressing fear that increasing diversity and differentiation will preclude more advanced forms of European integration. Enlargement would indeed produce more diversity, but as I have tried to show in this chapter there are no reasons to demonize this increased diversity. Diversity has always existed within the Union and the current line between unity and diversity does not follow the East–West border that existed during the cold war. Moreover, it has been the end of the cold war rather than the prospect of enlargement that has forced the EU to rethink and readjust the integration project. Enlargement is a response to the new post-cold war developments. It is not in itself the source of the difficulties. The fact that the long-standing ideological and military East–West divide no longer exists cannot but affect the shape and ambition of European integration, and those who seek to proceed with integration as if nothing had happened in Europe in the late 1980s risk acting like homeowners who insist on running an air conditioning system in a house that no longer has any walls.[76] In short, it is the European integration project that needs to be adjusted to enlargement, and not the other way around. In the first instance, we would have to comprehend that a more diversified Union resembles a neo-medieval empire and then we must search for new ways of organizing our political, cultural, and economic life within it. Not every kind of diversity has to be endorsed, but we need to learn how to cope with diversity in a more creative, pragmatic, and relaxed manner. We also need to adjust our ambitions, much to the disappointment of those who are still dreaming about a European super-state able to compete with the United States. But the diversified European empire does not need to be a lame duck in international politics and an inefficient entity in the field of economics. The history of world politics shows that both empires and superstates have their distinct assets and liabilities. In economics, too, diversity can be a recipe for chaos, but also for coping with complex problems in a sophisticated and innovative manner. The same can be said for democracy: diversity under the name of pluralism is the essence of democratic order, although certain types of diversity can also produce democratic deadlocks if not anarchy. Moreover, it is important to note that the first year of an enlarged EU-25 produced few signs of new members paralysing the European decision-making apparatus. Poland (together with Spain) initially resisted the new system of voting rights envisaged by the draft of the European Constitution but in the end a compromise was reached. It was the French and the Dutch 'no' vote on this constitution that in fact caused some degree of paralysis, albeit more of a political rather than of an institutional nature.

The following chapters will try to examine how an enlarged, more diversified, and neo-medieval EU is going to perform in various functional fields. What are the major challenges facing this neo-medieval empire, and what solutions can make it easier for the Union to cope with these challenges? Before embarking on this discussion, however, it is important to keep one major finding of this chapter in mind. The scope of diversity as such does not need to represent a problem provided that the Union is able to find some effective and legitimate ways of governing the increased diversity. Westphalian modes of governance will be found to be inappropriate for handling the neo-medieval setting of today. This applies to all major fields, from economics and democracy to foreign affairs. This also applies to the ways the Union tries to form its core political and cultural identity. I will consider the most appropriate ways of handing the increased diversity in the ever larger Europe later in the book.

4

Economic Governance

The enlarged EU is the biggest economic bloc in the world with the largest single market. Its population exceeds the combined population of the three North American Free Trade Agreement (NAFTA) states (the United States, Mexico, and Canada), and the combined population of the two largest economies, the United States and Japan. The twenty-five member states generate about a quarter of world GDP and more than a fifth of global trade. There can be no doubt that the Union is an economic giant able to shape the world's product and capital markets.

That said, the last wave of enlargement has not necessarily enhanced the Union's economic fortunes. The absolute size of the EU economy is larger, but its GDP per capita is lower than before enlargement. New members are growing faster than the old ones, but they have larger (and rather backward) agricultural sectors and higher rates of unemployment. The Union no longer needs to spend enormous amount of money to defend itself, but it has acquired rather porous borders with unstable and underdeveloped countries in Eastern and South-eastern Europe. Some of the challenges caused by enlargement are not new. For instance, the Union already had serious immigration problems, especially from the Maghreb countries. However, this is hardly a consolation as the new challenges of enlargement are likely to reinforce some old challenges such as structural unemployment, the burden of pensions, the technological gap, and indeed migration.

Moreover, developments within the enlarged Union should be seen in a global economic context. The economy of the Union is not autarkic, but rather is linked to the outside world by a dense web of laws and transactions. These transactions are made by many and various actors, public and private, local and global, national and multinational. In short, the EU economy is highly interdependent and exposed to developments outside its borders. The picture is quite complex, which means that the implications of enlargement can hardly be grasped simply by looking at some basic macroeconomic indicators. The new diversified European economic space will require new modes of economic governance that may transform the Union beyond recognition.[1] As the economic space of the Union enlarges together with the intensity and patterns of economic transactions, one ought to try to envisage how European institutions responsible for the delivery of public goods are likely to react. How will they try to interact with the enlarged market or even try to shape it? Will we see in this enlarged and more diversified Union more effort to impose standardization and harmonization from the top? Or are we likely to see more devolution and flexibility allowing 'multiple speeds', 'variable membership', and 'overlapping jurisdictions'?

This chapter identifies three major economic challenges facing the enlarged EU and the most likely modes of economic governance to address them.[2] First, the Union is facing the challenge of internal coherence and adjustment. Will the enlarged EU attempt to bridge the internal development gaps by flexible policies stimulating growth or by central redistribution from Brussels? Second, the Union has tough competition from the United States and rapidly growing economies in Asia. Will the enlarged EU cope with this challenge by opting for more institutional differentiation or central regulation? Third, there is the challenge of economic instability caused by poverty and conflicts in the EU's immediate neighbours to the south and east. Will the enlarged EU try to insulate itself from its neighbours or try to govern them? In my view, one of the basic choices facing the Union is between the neo-medieval and Westphalian modes of economic governance. Of course, in fast-moving fields such as economics it is always risky to apply historical labels such as medieval and Westphalian. Nevertheless, the choices facing European decision-makers can well be reduced to our original dichotomy presented in the introductory chapter. The EU can cope with the three types of economic challenges either by opting for a clearer hierarchical structure of economic decision-making or by allowing or even stimulating interpenetration of various economic and administrative units through shared ownership and institutional differentiation. Internal development gaps can be tackled either by strengthening the centralized system of European redistribution or by relying on spontaneous market adjustments resulting from greater liberalization and devolution. The Union can either try to seal its borders and aim at providing a greater overlap between its legal, administrative, and economic regimes, or it can soften its borders and opt for greater disassociation between authoritative allocations, functional competencies, and territorial constituencies. The latter solution would blur the distinction between EU members and non-members, while the former would make it sharper.

In this chapter I will try to show that the choice facing the enlarged EU is not simply between so-called continental and Anglo-Saxon solutions. Nor is the choice necessarily between interventionist and neo-liberal economics. The choice is also between a neo-medieval and neo-Westphalian economic mode of governance. Table 4.1 identifies these two contrasting models of economic governance in the future Union.

Of course, it should again be stressed that this simple dichotomy is not able to grasp the entire complex set of economic interactions confronting the enlarged EU. Moreover, enlargement is only one of many factors prompting the Union to adopt a certain mode of economic governance. Modernization, globalization, and various ideological trends also lie behind the EU's choices.[3] Nevertheless, I hope that this dichotomy helps us to comprehend the evolving nature of the enlarged EU even in the rapidly moving and complex field of economics.

This chapter shows that more flexible and more diversified modes of economic governance resembling a neo-medieval pattern are best suited to coping with this triple challenge of internal cohesion, global competition, and cross-border interdependence. Statist solutions relying on central, hierarchical government and one-size-fits-all rules have often proved unworkable in the history of European integration. However, this chapter

Table 4.1. Two contrasting models of economic governance

Economic challenges	Neo-Westphalian responses	Neo-medieval responses
Coherence	Increased European budget centrally distributed to poor countries, regions, and social groups such as farmers	Increased liberalization and devolution stimulating growth. EU assistance is scarce and aimed at promoting efficiency rather than equality
Competition	Clear hierarchical institutional structure supported by a rigid legal and regulatory frame, centralized competencies, and regular screening	Institutional differentiation through delegation, devolution, and decentralized experimentation reflecting shared (administrative) ownership
Instability	Containment of and insulation from unstable neighbours through hard borders for goods and labour. Mutual relations are centralized and incentives are in the form of development aid	Export of European laws and regulations to neighbours leading to a gradual geographic extension of European economic governance. Mutual relations are decentralized and aimed at facilitating movement of goods and labour

will argue that these statist solutions are even more unrealistic and ill-adapted for the enlarged EU. The new member states from Eastern Europe are likely to support the neo-medieval option with only minor qualifications.

These findings are not surprising for the students of economic geography, public finance, and international trade.[4] They have long argued that the integration of markets does not necessarily lead to the harmonization of societies' institutions. Especially when markets became larger, multiple jurisdictions are both possible and desirable. This is because the increased heterogeneity in preferences over public goods which accompanies different economic roles, development levels, and cultures creates pressures for more complex structures of administrative responsibility. It is important to let the borders of jurisdictions change endogenously. An effective economic regime must allow individuals and member states to organize themselves into a pattern of overlapping jurisdictions, with each jurisdiction responsible for the provision of a specific class of public goods. Optimal 'club size' for individual public goods differs and so does the optimal membership for individual jurisdictions. The efficiency predicament requires that there is a gradual move away from a static hierarchical system where government functions are ordered according to pyramidal organization among jurisdictions. Instead flexible forms of cooperation are required within an ever more decentralized system of intersecting alliances.[5] The term 'neo-feudalism' has even been used to describe this process of interaction between the markets and jurisdictions, and it is in line with my neo-medieval argument.[6]

The challenge of internal cohesion

Chapter 3 described the scope and depth of economic gaps between the old and new EU members. The welfare gap is clearly the most striking: the new members have an average GDP per capita only 40 per cent of that of the existing members (at purchasing power parity).[7] I argued that enlargement may be the most efficient way of helping the new members to catch up. I also pointed out that although the size of the current gap between the old and new members is quite unprecedented, the Union is quite accustomed to coping with different levels of wealth, institutional frameworks, and economic cultures. In short, economic gaps between old and new members do not need to be dramatized. The question remains nevertheless: how will the new gaps be addressed by the Union in practice? In the context of our discussion one should ask, in particular, whether enlargement will induce more central redistribution or decentralized self-help based on growth-promoting policies?

There are reasons to believe that the new member states will push for the former option, but I will try to show that the latter option might in fact be more beneficial to them in the long run and that this can be reflected in policies of at least some of the new members.[8] Moreover, those insisting on a greater redistribution are likely anyway to fail. The majority of the old member states are likely to resist pressure for any increased financial transfers to poorer members, especially through the central bureaucracy in Brussels.

As mentioned earlier, the accession negotiations have been dominated by the issue of agricultural subsidies and structural and cohesion funds. Eastern Europeans demanded financial transfers similar to the ones existing among the EU-15. In the end they have got much less than they wanted, but many vowed to argue the case further after accession.[9] Direct transfers from the central EU budget have also been stressed in the political campaigns preceding accession referenda in all would-be member states. Eastern European governments tried to convince their somewhat Euro-sceptic public that joining the Union would imply significant net payments, thus making up for some of the constraints on their formal sovereignty as well as for economic and cultural pressures from the more affluent part of Europe. When later the European Commission proposed shifting some money from the Structural and Cohesion Funds to the Lisbon Agenda aimed at improving the Union's competitive edge, the new members rang the alarm. 'The Union cuts on the poor' was the headline in the largest Eastern European newspaper, *Gazeta Wyborcza*.[10] Can governments in Eastern Europe be expected to switch gears and become relaxed about financial transfers from Brussels?

Of course, the policies of the new members are guided not only by economic, but also by political considerations. Behind the insistence on direct transfers are various vocal and rather selfish pressure groups such as farmers. Nevertheless, one may argue that various kinds of direct transfer are quite legitimate when one considers the preconditions of economic growth, let alone economic fairness. New member states may well need some injection of economic assistance to grow quickly without major disturbances. This is needed if only their weak producers are asked to open their markets to goods and services from much stronger (and often more generously subsidized) economic actors from the old members. The creation of the Cohesion Funds was in fact guided by that kind of rationale and the new intra-EU economic gaps are much greater than those created by the southern enlargement in the 1980s. Has not enlargement made it plainly clear that the Union can no longer avoid serious taxation and redistribution?[11] How can any political and economic unit function properly without a fair degree of extraction and expenditure allocation? Even the most 'minimalist' nation states have a budget of at least 15 per cent of the GDP.[12] The EU's current budget is merely 1.27 per cent of its combined GDP and even this low ceiling has never been reached in practice. If the Union wants to resemble a modern Westphalian state it needs to raise its revenues quite substantially and distribute them in a centralized, purposeful manner.

All this is easier said than done. Major contributors to the EU budget such as Britain, France, Germany, Austria, Sweden, and the Netherlands fiercely resist any increase in the common budget. They want the budget to be capped at 1 per cent of GDP instead of being allowed to rise to the 1.24 per cent that had previously been agreed in anticipation of enlargement.[13] It is hard to see any dramatic shift in their policies and despite the federalist ambitions pronounced in some of these states.[14]

Moreover, it is not clear whether increased reliance on net payments from Brussels would indeed enhance Eastern European economic fortunes and turn them into more equal EU partners. As the case of Greece has already shown, EU financial transfers do not by themselves guarantee significant economic growth.[15] Nor do they ensure macroeconomic stability, market integration, and innovation. Indeed, transfers may produce lethargy, aid dependence, and even corruption.

The new members might not be very familiar with the case of Greece, but they know well the East German case where enormous subsidies (around 170 billion euros per year) have strangled rather than promoted local incentives and created a structurally dependent economy.[16] And there is little evidence to suggest that people living in East Germany believe that the generous West German transfers satisfied their quest for equality and justice. The case of the Italian *Mezzogiorno* is another warning.[17]

The conclusion drawn from these experiences suggests that central redistribution from Brussels might be more a curse than a blessing for the new members and as such should not be seen as the main rationale for joining the EU.[18] The new members' ability to catch up with the old will depend primarily on factors other than financial transfers.

Most economists argue that the surest way to enhance growth is through credible market and policy institutions. The new members need EU policies that stimulate innovation, competition, and deregulation. They need more FDI and subcontracting. They need help in enhancing marketization and professionalization. They need entrepreneurship education and greater affiliation with corporate ethics and culture. They need help in learning how to apply modern technologies and improve the quality of their goods and services. They need rules facilitating mobility and promoting flexibility. They need a system that lowers the barriers to market entrance and exit (the latter through a sound bankruptcy law, for instance). In short, they need stimuli to continue the economic regime change rather than merely obtaining EU financial transfers. Centrally distributed net transfers do not teach them how to reduce economic costs or to improve the quality of supplier networks. They do not teach them how to sell products in tough markets or to enhance labour productivity. Transfers induce complacency vis-à-vis the sponsors and are at odds with the logic of competitive exposure stimulating growth, efficiency, and creativity.

The aforementioned arguments ought to be comprehended not only by the new members, but also by the old members and central authorities in Brussels. The EU governance system is too rigid and hierarchical for coping with the new economic gaps in Europe. Although the Common Agricultural Policy is widely seen as the most inefficient if not corruption-prone system of direct transfers, the EU is unable to abolish it.[19] Labour mobility between the old and new members has been frozen for several years to come, and many hidden protectionist rules are likely to continue discriminating against Eastern European producers and exporters.[20]

New member states have been particularly worried about the EU's plans to impose high social and environmental standards on their producers because this would effectively impede their competitive edge.[21] As the Czech President, Vaclav Klaus put it: 'The claims for quasi-universal social rights are disguised . . . attempts to protect high-cost producers in highly regulated countries, with unsustainable welfare standards, against cheaper labor in more productive countries.'[22]

The new members also worry about possible efforts to limit tax competition by the EU because they need to continue offering better conditions to investors if they are to catch up with the more developed members. After all, Ireland's successful growth promotion policy included serious tax cuts. For instance, Ireland's top marginal tax rate fell from 80 per cent in 1975 to 44 per cent in 2001.[23]

The new members also worry that the convergence criteria required by the Maastricht Treaty will prevent any fast growth and by the same token frustrate their efforts to catch up with the old members. This is because fast growth in their case would imply much higher rates of inflation and public deficit than allowed by Maastricht. For instance, the new members are sorely dependent on investments in infrastructure in order to implement the necessary structural adjustments and fulfil the objectives of real (rather than merely nominal) convergence.[24]

Harmonization of trade rules for all EU members has meant that some new members, such as Estonia, have had to increase their external tariffs and non-tariff barriers (e.g. subsidies, quotas, and anti-dumping duties) with regard to low-cost locations outside the EU. This is another factor frustrating the process of catching up, at least in this particular case.[25]

The Union is therefore faced with a difficult dilemma: should divergence between old and new members be tackled by more regulation, harmonization, and centralized distribution from Brussels? Or should the Union foster deregulation, flexibility, devolution, and other growth promoting policies? Of course, the two options are not totally exclusive. Some type of harmonization and regulation might promote rather than just hamper growth and competition. Moreover, some type of selective central redistribution can also be helpful in promoting growth.[26] But the earlier arguments clearly show that net transfers are not the only, let alone the most efficient way of fostering convergence between the old and new members. In fact, there are good reasons to believe that the new members would be better off with more devolution, deregulation, and competition—stimulating growth—even at the expense of some net transfers from Brussels.[27] In other words, a neo-medieval rather than neo-Westphalian way of tackling the new level of economic divergence would be more plausible and a more realistic prospect for enhancing growth.

Of course, the neo-medieval option is not entirely cost free. Growth-promoting policies based on competition, devolution, and deregulation would leave certain segments of the economy and population disadvantaged. The older generation in the new member states working in the inefficient agricultural or industrial sectors will find it particularly hard to adjust to a new competitive environment, and it is unclear how these people could be taken care of within the neo-medieval setting. Systemic transition has created large segments of poor people already. The situation is particularly worrying in Bulgaria where a recent report found more than 50 per cent of the population living below the national poverty line.[28] But even in much more developed countries such as Hungary the percentage of those living below the subsistence minimum or poverty line has tripled since 1992. True, these worrying statistics have been questioned on several grounds.[29] Nevertheless, there is no doubt that greater devolution, flexibility, and deregulation will leave some people disadvantaged.

However, in the field of social policy a neo-medieval setting is also emerging. In Eastern Europe the state is no longer the sole provider of social benefits. Instead we observe a growing pluralization of welfare supply systems. Some of them are now in private hands and ruled by the laws of global economic markets. (Pensions by private insurance companies depend on the rate of return on investments.) Some are still in the hands of the state, while yet others are linked to the European redistribution system through agricultural and cohesion funds. Rapid privatization of social policy in Eastern Europe has not necessarily been dictated by any ideological fanaticism or by powerful external actors like the World Bank or the United States. The Eastern European public has been reluctant to entrust and empower their extremely costly, unprofessional, and corrupt state and corporatist bureaucracies.[30] In effect, privatization was not only rapid, but reached all sectors including health care, social care, education, housing, pensions, and employment services. In the Czech Republic, for instance, funding of the universal health insurance scheme has been left to a new compulsory health insurance system, with private companies offering insurance and collective contributions from employers, employees, and the state. Although they remain semi-public in nature, and the health insurance scheme continues to be guaranteed by the state, this has led to a proliferation of insurance companies. These companies are profit-oriented and offer services for fees, while the contributions from the state to this health insurance system have been progressively reduced.[31]

Similar trends are also being observed in the western part of Europe, although in some cases at a slower pace. As Tony Blair, the British Prime Minister, has put it:

The way to provide social protection today is not more and more regulation or high business costs and taxes, it is through making our workforce highly adaptable, more employable and better skilled, through encouraging the development of technology; promoting small business; and making welfare systems help people off benefit and into work, with specific measures to combat exclusion. We need a new social model for a new European reality.[32]

This new European reality in the social protection field is thus far from the centralized, hierarchical, and highly regulated system of a Westphalian state. Rather, it resembles a complex neo-medieval system with a multiplicity of actors and an increased diversification of normative and institutional instruments, as well as spaces for industrial bargaining. The EU does (and will) represent only one link in such a multilevel and multiactor system of social policy governance, setting some limited regulatory standards and providing some limited social benefits.[33] But the gross of social policy effort would be in various different hands: private, public, and semi-public. The role of municipalities, charitable institutions, and welfare associations is also likely to increase. After all, before the rise of the Westphalian state social policy was largely handled by town councils, fraternities, and guilds. (Another important social policy actor was the Church.) According to Anthony Black, the volume of social legislation, control, and provision in the Middle Ages invites 'comparison with modern welfare socialism'.[34] Hospitals, almshouses, and old people's homes were either sponsored or run by town governments. The medieval fraternities provided the 'obligatory assistance' to their members and generated funds out of subscriptions and voluntary donations aimed at helping the poor and hospitals.[35]

Obviously, the usual warning about applying historical analogies applies. The neo-medieval system of governance would have to be conceptualized much more seriously before it is allowed to evolve in practice. The Union would have to make sure that devolution, flexibility, and deregulation does not leave large segments of the population in poverty and without any workable system of social protection.[36] In time, such a situation would surely lead to major social conflicts. Nevertheless, the trend towards neo-medievalism is clearly on the rise in Europe, especially when it comes to convergence-oriented policies, and it is further reinforced by the pressure of external competition coming from non-European actors. This leads us to the next major challenge confronting the enlarged EU: how to maintain a competitive edge in a globalized economy?

The global competition challenge

Western Europe began to lose its competitive edge in the 1970s after three decades of high growth and stability. Two successive oil shocks are often seen as a direct cause of this downturn, but policy mistakes and more general global trends in the field of trade, technology, and demography should also be considered here. In recent years the Union has managed to reinstate a fair degree of macroeconomic stability with inflation well under control. Nevertheless, growth in Europe is still lower than in the United States, while unemployment much higher. The most worrying trend is the widening gap in productivity growth between the EU and the United States. Empirical evidence indicates that roughly two-thirds of the gap in EU GDP per capita relative to the United States can be attributed to lower labour utilization, while lower average labour productivity accounts for the remaining third.[37] The problem of weak productivity growth in the EU is particularly acute in the service sector, that accounts for some 70 per cent of all jobs and GDP in the EU.[38] Table 4.2 compares European and American economic performance over years.

Productivity is crucial because the more workers can produce in a given time, the more the economy can grow without shortages and inflation. And sustained non-inflationary growth provides the resources for redistribution, research, education, and development. In the current EU there is a negative spiral at work: lower GDP growth and employment rates push for increased public spending. But higher taxation further undermines the competitiveness of EU firms. If the economies within the EU fail to stimulate further growth, it will be impossible to maintain

Table 4.2. USA and EU 25 compared

Indicators		EU-25	USA
GDP	billion EUR	9,613	11,084
GDP per capita in PPP	EU15 =100	91	137
Corruption Perception Index*	0=highly corrupt 10=highly clean	6.6	7.5
Annual inflation	in %	2.0	2.3
Unemployment rate	in %	9.0	5.7
Labour productivity per person employed	EU15=100	92.7	122.0
Gross domestic expenditure on R&D	as % of GDP	1.91	2.74
General government debt	as % of GDP	63.2	61.1
Total population	million	454.9	291.4
Fertility rate	births per woman	1.5	2.1
Life expectancy at birth (in years)	men	74.8	73.8
	women	81.3	79.4
Structure of the population by age	% aged <15	16.8	21.4
	% aged15-64	67.2	66.2
	% aged>65	16.0	12.4
Population with completed higher education	% 25-64 years	20.4	26.7
Number of personal computers	per 100 inhabitants	31	66

source: EUROSTAT 2004, *Transparency International 2004

existing levels of social spending—and this would have all sorts of negative economic, social, and political implications.

The problem is aggravated by quite dramatic demographic changes.
Over the next fifty years, the EU will witness the ageing of the large postwar generation, while at the same time fertility rates are low. (The demographic situation in the new member states is only slightly better than in
the old ones.) Growing life expectancy will decrease the size of the
working-age population and increase the number of pensioners. This
may increase age-related public expenditure (notably pensions, health
care, and long-term care) by between 3 and 7 percentage points of GDP
by 2050, with the effects taking hold from 2010.[39] The European
Commission estimates that in a scenario of no policy changes, EU growth
might fall from the present underlying rate of 2 to 2.5 per cent to around
1.25 per cent over the period 2000–50. This translates into a reduction of
per capita GDP growth in the EU by about 0.4 per cent on average per
year.[40] Since the United States is not likely to experience a similar problem,
the EU economy is likely to find itself in a very difficult position. The
present EU share of 18 per cent of world production is likely to fall to 10
per cent in 2050, while that of the United States could continue to rise
from 23 per cent in 2000 to 26 per cent in 2050.[41]

True, some European economies perform very well even compared to the
United States. For instance, in the 2003 Growth Competitiveness Index
prepared by the World Economic Forum, Finland supplanted the United
States as the most competitive economy in the world.[42] However, the
performance of some large EU economies like Italy and France is much
worse and this drags down the EU's average competitive position.[43]

It is also true that the American economy has its own problems that might
in due course affect its currently superior productivity growth rates. For
instance, corporate and private debts appear rather large in the United States
and the American current account deficit is rapidly growing. However, in
the past the United States has always manifested a remarkable capacity to
finance its current account deficits easily and cheaply and it is far from
certain whether the euro will eventually undermine this capacity.[44] Moreover, any serious economic problem in the United States is likely to affect
Europe. For instance, with the American current account deficit becoming
harder to finance there is concern that a sharp fall in the American dollar
could bring deflationary pressures to other countries.

Finally, it would be wrong to assume that Europe must resemble the
United States in order to be able to remain competitive.[45] For instance, the
level of redistribution in Europe is higher than in the United States

because the Union tries to spread its growth more fairly.[46] European labour does not produce less per hour than American labour, but it works much less per year due to longer holidays and various other social rights and entitlements.[47] Generous social provisions do not necessarily represent an economic liability. After all Sweden, Finland, and Denmark with their high levels of welfare spending score as well as the United States on the Global Competitiveness Index. What might be responsible for a low competitive edge in some European countries is the rigidity of their welfare systems and the failure of welfare reforms.

With all these qualifications, however, it is hard not to conclude that the EU must increase its growth rate and improve its overall competitive position. In fact, at the 2000 Lisbon European Council the Union set itself an ambitious strategic goal 'to become the most competitive and dynamic knowledge based economy in the world' within a decade.[48] This is easier said than done, of course.[49] Nevertheless, the Lisbon Agenda and various economic analyses point to the desired direction: the EU needs less vertically integrated firms, greater mobility within and across firms, greater flexibility of labour markets, greater reliance on market finances, and higher investment in both research and development (R&D) and higher education.[50] The Lisbon Agenda does not call for abandoning Europe's social concerns, but it calls for a more effective system of economic governance.

A typical Westphalian response to external competitive pressures would be to strengthen the state's institutional structure by further centralization, regulation, and hierarchical control. The economic governance system would become more orderly, transparent, and just, in the sense that free riding would not be permitted. However, such a system could not but become more bureaucratic and rigid, preventing spontaneous cross-border exchanges and leaving little room for grass-roots initiatives.

From time to time the Union manifests that kind of Westphalian reflex. The fairly rigid macroeconomic criteria of the Stability Pact are a good example. Nevertheless, neo-medieval types of response to competitive pressures seem to prevail. In fact, the 2004 Ecofin decision to allow Germany and France to bend the Stability Pact rules represented a triumph of flexibility over the rigidity in the Union's approach to economic governance, despite the economic and political arguments against this decision. So let us try to spell out what a neo-medieval response to competitive pressures would amount to.

The neo-medieval response would stimulate investment, innovation, and entrepreneurship through greater flexibility and decentralization.

Devolution and delegation would be used as a means of creating incentives for local dynamics and decentralized experimentation. Diffusion-oriented policies would aim at stimulating learning processes and improving the capacity for change.[51] The Union would not try to strengthen its grip on various policy areas, but instead promote a sense of shared ownership and partnership with various economic actors. EU institutions would not try to have the final say on all decisions, but instead would act as facilitators, mediators, and coordinators. The European Commission, in particular, would not always try to act as a chief rule-maker, policy-maker, supervisor, and regulator, but would let various national and local actors act in the way they found most efficient and legitimate. Moreover, a greater use would be made of various autonomous bodies carrying out collective tasks on behalf of the Union as a whole, especially in the fields of funding and regulation. This would require changes in the current treaty, but the examples of the European Investment Bank and the European Central Bank are quite encouraging.

A neo-medieval type of government would allow a multiplication of various steered networks, and hybrid arrangements with little hierarchy and enforced participation. Vertical interactions among European governments would increasingly take the form of mutual adjustments, intergovernmental negotiations, and joint decision-making.[52] The dominant governing principle would not be a centralization of power in the Commission, but delegation by both the Commission and member states to specialized autonomous bodies operating with different degrees of centralization.[53] The Commission and the Council would only perform some strategic tasks aimed at creating incentives for innovation and adaptation. They would not insist on having a single institutional solution for individual functional problems, but instead allow institutional flexibility and differentiation. They would not insist on the creation of a simple hierarchical structure, but instead allow a variable geometry with an extensive overlap between the EU and the national or subnational domains. They would not insist on a single way of implementing EU laws and regulations, but instead allow decentralized and creative implementation of these laws and regulations. They would not insist on accumulating central powers and cataloguing their own competences, but on spelling out and promoting innovative organizational principles and governance practices. Decisions on the appropriate assignment (to European, national, or local level) would depend on a trade-off between many different factors such as the intensity of external pressures or the degree of heterogeneity of preferences and needs. The impact of these factors evolves over time and depends on the intensity, scope, and structure of economic integration.[54]

That kind of system of economic governance does not seem to be better equipped for coping only with global competition, but also with the enlarged and more diversified European economic space. As mentioned earlier, new members are keen to see the Union acting in a flexible rather than rigid manner because their own peculiar economic situation is ill suited for one-size-fits-all rules. They are keen to see further liberalization rather than harmonization because they think that the former would help them to enter the competitive markets of the old members while the latter would hamper this. They are keen to see more devolution and decentralization in the EU's economic governance because they doubt Brussels' ability to comprehend, let alone properly address, their current economic problems.[55]

In an enlarged Union, variable geometry is likely to become a natural response to differences of situation or preference. Increasing heterogeneity will make uniform general rules inappropriate if not altogether counterproductive. (It is already clear that uniform EMU's fiscal rules make no sense for the enlarged EU, for instance.) Insistence on keeping the entire *acquis* untouched if not 'holy' risks creating rigidities that impede devolution and responsiveness to changing economic circumstances. In short, enlargement will only enhance the neo-medieval type of responses to external competitive pressure at the expense of Westphalian solutions.

The neo-medieval type of response to global competitive pressures is clearly in the spirit of the Lisbon Agenda, but documents like that are hardly ever able to inject the necessary momentum of dynamism and change. Any significant change in the European governance system is more likely to result from external pressures and shocks. Enlargement and global competitive pressures represent a powerful incentive for change in the neo-medieval direction. But any major economic instability right across the EU's borders could represent a real shock rather than merely pressure.[56] Let us examine how the EU tries to prevent such a shock.

The cross-border interdependence challenge

The EU's new neighbourhood is extremely diversified. However, if one excludes the four small European Free Trade Association (EFTA) countries (Iceland, Norway, Switzerland, and Liechtenstein), EU neighbours all have relatively backward economies, young, growing, but poor populations, and shaky political systems. The Union is already confronted with economic migrants and in some cases also criminals and terrorists coming from these countries. If there is no improvement in current trends in these countries, the Union is likely to be confronted with serious political, economic, or even security shocks with spillover effects that will be difficult to contain on its borders. Table 4.3 shows the gravity of the cross-border interdependence challenge.

The table shows that the situation is particularly alarming in the EU's Mediterranean neighbours. Over the past several decades these countries have not only witnessed a surge in political violence, but also experienced very poor growth rates. Egypt and Tunisia are the only countries to have exceeded 2 per cent growth since 1975, while Algeria, for example, shows a small negative growth.[57] Most countries in the region have a GNI not exceeding US$2000 per capita. (Israel with its steady growth and US$16,020 GNI per capita is obviously a different case in this region. Note also a relatively high GNI per capita in Lebanon.) Thirty per cent of the population in the Mediterranean region lives on less than US$2 per day and illiteracy rates remain high. Only 0.6 per cent of population use the Internet and only 1.2 per cent have access to a computer.[58] Although some of these countries have developed close trade ties with the EU, they still attract minimal foreign investment.

The economic situation in the EU's new eastern neighbours is less gloomy, but difficult nevertheless. The economies of the former Soviet Union that are now part of the Commonwealth of Independent States (CIS) began to grow at a relatively rapid pace following the 1998 financial crisis. Russia has done particularly well at attracting a lot of foreign investment and registering rapid economic growth, reaching 6.2 per cent in 2003. However this impressive growth has been largely based on favourable commodity prices, in particular for oil and gas.[59] Although current growth in Russia is higher than in the new EU members, its GNI per capita is only half of that in the new EU members, and a quarter of that of the old ones. That said, Russia with its GNI of US$2,130 per capita scores much better than Ukraine and Belarus (US$780 and 1,360, respectively). Moldova with its GNI per capita of US$460 is the region's poorest country. Of course, Moldova's sovereignty is constrained by the presence of Russian troops, but there is also a lack of basic economic infrastructure combined with poor economic management. In Belarus the government is firmly in charge of its territory, but entertains old Soviet practices that make it difficult to register any sound economic progress. It must be said, nevertheless, that Belarus was able to avoid the successive waves of economic chaos

Table 4.3. EU 25 and its neighbourhood

	Population in million	Area in thousand sq. km	Gross National Income per capita 2002 USD	Rural population % of total	Old-age dependency ratio (65+/15–64) (%)	Human Development Index (HDI) 2001[*] 0=lowest 1=highest	FDI inflows[**] 2002 in million USD	Corruption Perception Index 2003[**] 0=highly corrupt 10=highly clean	Adult illiteracy rate 2001[*] % age 15 and above	Population below income poverty line[*] in %	Internet users 2001[*] per 1,000 people
EU25	454	3,990	16,504	29	22	0.897	395,906	6.6	n.a.	n.a.	268.8
Southern Europe											
Albania	3	29	1,450	57	11	0.735	213	2.5	n.a.	n.a.	2.5
Bosnia Herzegovina	4	51	1,310	57	14	0.777	321	3.3	n.a.	n.a.	11.1
Bulgaria	8	111	1,770	33	24	0.795	479	3.9	n.a.	n.a.	74.6
Croatia	4	57	4,540	42	22	0.811	981	3.7	n.a.	n.a.	111.3
Macedonia, FYR	2	26	1,710	41	15	0.784	77	2.3	n.a.	n.a.	34.2
Romania	22	238	1,870	45	20	0.773	1,106	2.8	n.a.	23^	44.7
Serbia and Montenegro	8	102	1,400	48	21	n.a.	475	2.3	n.a.	n.a.	n.a.
Eastern Europe											
Belarus	10	208	1,360	30	20	0.804	227	4.2	n.a.	n.a.	42.4
Moldova	4	34	460	58	16	0.700	111	2.4	n.a.	82^	13.7
Russia	144	17,075	2,130	27	18	0.799	2,421	2.7	n.a.	53^	29.3
Ukraine	49	604	780	32	21	0.722	77	2.3	n.a.	25^	11.9
Mediterranean											
Algeria	31	2,382	1,720	42	6	0.704	n.a.	n.a.	32.2	15.1^^	6.5
Egypt	66	1,001	1,470	57	7	0.648	n.a.	n.a.	43.9	43.9^^	9.3
Israel	7	21	16,020	8	15	0.905	n.a.	7.0	n.a.	n.a.	276.6
Jordan	5	89	1,760	21	5	0.743	n.a.	n.a.	9.7	7.4^^	45.2
Lebanon	4	10	3,990	10	9	0.752	n.a.	4.6	13.5	n.a.	77.6
Libya	5	1,760	n.a.	n.a.	n.a.	n.a.	n.a.	n.a.	n.a.	n.a.	n.a.
Morocco	29	447	1,170	44	7	0.606	n.a.	n.a.	50.2	14.3^^	13.7

Table 4.3. (*Continued*)

	Population in million	Area in thousand sq. km	Gross National Income 2002 per capita USD	Rural population % of total	Old-age dependency ratio (65+/15-64) (%)	Human Development Index (HDI) 2001* 0=lowest 1=highest	FDI inflows* 2002 in million USD	Corruption Perception Index 2003* 0=highly corrupt 10=highly clean	Adult illiteracy rate 2001* % age 15 and above	Population below income poverty line* in %	Internet users 2001* per 1,000 people
West Bank and Gaza	3	n.a.	1,110	n.a.	n.a.	n.a.	n.a.	n.a.	n.a.	n.a.	n.a.
Syria	17	185	1,130	48	5	0.685	n.a.	n.a.	24.7	n.a.	3.6
Tunisia	10	164	1,990	34	9	0.740	n.a.	4.9	27.9	6.6^^	41.2
Turkey	69	775	2,490	34	9	0.734	1,037	3.1	14.5	10.3^^	60.4
Asia											
China	1,280	9,598	960	63	10	0.721	52,700	3.4	14.2	46.7^^	25.7
India	1,048	3,287	470	72	8	0.590	3,449	2.8	42.0	79.9^^	6.8
Japan	127	378	34,010	21	26	0.932	9,326	7.0	n.a.	n.a.	448.9

source: all data World Bank, except * UNDP, **UNSTAD, ***Transparency International
^USD 4 a day 1996-1999 ^^USD 2 a day, 1990-2002

experienced by more democratic, but highly unstable Ukraine.[60] However, it is hoped that the election of Viktor Yushchenko as Ukraine's president following the 2005 'Orange Revolution' will bring greater economic stability and progress.

In the western Balkans the enlarged EU needs to cope with Albania and several states which broke away from the former Yugoslavia. Some of the latter are not even proper states, but semi-protectorates effectively run by the international community. This especially applies to Kosovo, but also to Bosnia-Hercegovina. The statehood of Serbia and Montenegro is also in flux, and the same may soon also apply to Macedonia (officially called the Former Yugoslav Republic of Macedonia). All this has adversely affected the economic situation of these countries. Although in recent years they all embarked on various economic reforms and registered respectable growth rates, their fortunes are still haunted by the legacy of war, opaque state structures, and foreign dependence.[61] High fiscal deficits persist in the region, combined with high unemployment rates, widespread corruption, and crime. Unemployment in Serbia and Macedonia is about 30 per cent; in Bosnia-Hercegovina it is 40 per cent; and in Kosovo it even reaches 60 per cent. According to the European Commission, the percentage of firms bribing frequently was estimated in 2002 at 36 per cent in Albania, 23 per cent in Macedonia, 22 per cent in Bosnia-Hercegovina, and 16 per cent in Serbia and Montenegro.[62] The only country in the region that is clearly making rapid economic and political progress is Croatia. Its GDP per capita is higher than the average in the new EU members, its annual growth in recent years is also higher and more stable than in the new EU members, and it has even registered remarkable progress in aligning itself with the European system of laws. By 2003 Croatia had adopted more than 50 per cent of the existing *acquis communautaire*.[63]

Croatia submitted its official membership application to the EU in February 2003 and hopes to join the Union together with Romania and Bulgaria in 2007. This outcome is not certain, but is quite likely[64]. The same cannot be said about another official candidate to the EU: Turkey. A neo-medieval scenario for the enlarged EU may make EU membership for Turkey a realistic option. In fact, in October 2005 the EU opened accession negotiations with Turkey. However, these negotiations are expected to take many years and their outcome is anything but certain. It would therefore be safe to assume that for the next decade Turkey will remain an EU neighbour rather than member.[65] (The reverse assumption would imply that the immediate neighbour of the EU is Iraq and this would, of course, make considerations even more complex.)

Turkey is a large country with a relatively unstable political and economic system. Many of its 69 million inhabitants have low living standards—the monthly average salary in Turkey is only 362 euros per capita.[66] Inflation was high for decades (averaging at 69.9 per cent during the period 1997–2001, but stabilizing at single-digit rates since 2003) and foreign investment is low (only 0.5 per cent of GDP in the period 1996–2001). Public debt is very high and the trade balance is negative. About 40 per cent of the population works in agriculture, but produces only a small share of the total GDP (about 13 per cent). Structural economic adjustments are being attempted, but at a slow pace and not always with success. The macroeconomic situation of Turkey is not as dramatic as in some other EU neighbours. However, given the size of the country, its sensitive geopolitical location, and its proclaimed but contested (both internally and externally) European aspirations, Turkey certainly will continue to represent a formidable challenge for the Union.

There is a tendency to view relations with neighbours in terms of foreign and security policy. This, in my view, is largely wrong because in the case of the EU relations with neighbours are largely about economic policy or more precisely about economic governance. Of course, many economic problems in the EU's immediate neighbourhood require diplomatic, political, or even military solutions, but in the final analysis a broadly understood economic policy is arguably the most crucial. This is for at least three basic reasons. First, the EU's most powerful instruments of pressure are in the field of economics rather than foreign and security policy proper. Second, in the past the Union has proved more eager to apply its economic rather than military instruments on its neighbours and nothing is likely to change in this respect. Moreover, and more crucially, the application of political leverage by the EU has proved most efficient when backed by a skilful application of economic sticks and carrots. Third, potential instability outside the EU's borders is likely to have primarily economic rather than security implications for the EU. The EU does not fear a military invasion of its territory, but it does fear a dramatic rise in migration due to war or poverty in the neighbourhood. After all, the war in the Balkans has already confronted the Union with many new migrants.[67] The Union also fears a possible energy crisis caused by instability in some of its new neighbours. The EU-25 consume about twice as much energy as their neighbours, but produce four times less oil. Moreover, most of the world's oil production takes place in countries that are directly contiguous with the EU's neighbours.

There is also a tendency to view EU relations with neighbours in traditional Westphalian terms, namely as centrally steered interactions between sovereign entities separated by hard borders.[68] In fact, these kinds of relations were practised during the cold war even in the period of détente and regardless of increased openness and interdependence elsewhere in the world. However, today it is by and large acknowledged that the Union should have a different kind of policy towards neighbours despite its effort to seal the external border in line with the Schengen blueprint.[69]

In recent years various European institutions adopted documents dealing with the EU's neighbourhood. A single strategic goal is emerging from all these documents: the EU needs to export various forms of its governance into neighbouring states. The traditional policy of aid and trade has been found to be insufficient. The neighbouring countries are asked to 'approximate their legislation to that of the Internal Market' and in exchange they are offered 'further integration and liberalization to promote the free movement of persons, goods, services and capital (four freedoms)'.[70] The European Commission believes that 'interdependence—political and economic—with the Union's neighborhood is already a reality' and the European Council adds that 'geographical proximity will generate converging interests and increase the importance of working together to address common challenges'.[71] The Council stressed that enlargement should enhance rather than hamper the EU's relations with its neighbours and expressed determination to avoid drawing new dividing lines in Europe and to promote stability and prosperity within and beyond the new borders of the Union.[72] In this spirit the Commission declared its will to 'ensure continuing social cohesion and economic dynamism' in the neighbouring states through 'regional and sub-regional cooperation and integration', seen as preconditions for 'stability, economic development and the reduction of poverty and social division in our shared environment'.[73]

The EU's aim is not separation from or containment of troublesome neighbours as envisaged by the Westphalian paradigm. Its aim is creation of 'a zone of prosperity and a friendly neighborhood'.[74] The proposed means of action are not limited to diplomacy, trade, and defence but are aimed at building a common infrastructure, joint border management, interconnected transport, energy, and telecommunication networks, cross-border cultural links, and mutual tackling of security and environmental threats. The Commission believes that the establishment at a pan-European level of an open and integrated market functioning on the basis of compatible or harmonized rules and further liberalization would bring significant economic and other benefits to both the EU and its neighbour- hood. It hopes that a political, regulatory, and trading framework, which enhances economic stability and institutionalizes the rule of law, will increase the attractiveness of the EU neighbours to investors and reduce vulnerability to external shocks. It argues that the EU *acquis* offers a well- established model with which to establish functioning markets and com- mon standards for industrial products, services, transport, energy, and telecommunications networks, environmental and consumer protection, health, labour, and minimum quality requirements. The strategy is to bring the neighbours as close to the Union as they can be without being a member. It is hard not to conclude that were this strategy to succeed the distinction between EU members and non-members would become blurred and the Union would shape economic transactions and legal rules on the territory of its neighbours.

This is quite an ambitious programme drafted in a truly neo-medieval spirit. And one should keep in mind that it is primarily directed to the most unlikely candidates for membership among the neighbours: Algeria, Egypt, Israel, Jordan, Lebanon, Libya, Morocco, the Palestinian Authority, Syria, Tunisia, Ukraine, Moldova, and Belarus.[75] The official candidates to the EU—Turkey, Croatia, Romania, and Bulgaria—and potential other candi- dates from the western Balkans are offered even more advanced (and intrusive) forms of cooperation envisaged by the accession package. These countries are asked to adopt the entire set of European laws and integrate their economies fully with the EU economic space. The conditionality principle towards these countries is applied across various fields and in a quite assertive manner. In fact, there is sufficient evidence to argue that these countries are being subject to even greater scrutiny than the countries that joined the EU in 2004. After all they are more dependent on the EU and have more problems in aligning themselves with the EU's standards.

This last observation applies most vividly to Kosovo and Bosnia- Hercegovina. None of these entities are able to carry out reforms demanded by the Union, so the Union is trying to implement these reforms itself, often with only nominal approval from local actors. Kosovo and Bosnia-Hercegovina are de facto semi-protectorates governed by Euro- pean officials under the formal auspices of the United Nations. European institutions and members are by far the largest donors to these countries. They have their peacekeepers on the ground and Since 2003 also their police forces. The majority of the various civilian foreign personnel (governmental and non-governmental) come also from the EU. The High

Representatives in both countries are European. Their policies reflect a set of goals and measures elaborated by various EU documents. For instance, in 2000 the EU adopted the so-called 'road map' for Bosnia-Hercegovina that envisaged a detailed package of eighteen major reforms to be implemented in this country. In 2002 the European Commission went a step further and spelled out an elaborate procedure of monitoring, evaluating, and conditioning these reforms.

This self-proclaimed task is enormous. Consider, for instance, the scope of the envisaged custom and tax reforms in Bosnia. The Union set for itself an objective to create and maintain efficient and effective customs controls and to support reform of the taxation system, in particular the introduction of value-added tax (VAT). Technical assistance and training of Bosnian custom officials by EU member state officials was programmed together with modernization of the Bosnian Custom Services' IT resources. The EU also envisaged technical assistance and training of Bosnian tax officials accompanied by investment to strengthen tax compliance and enforcement capacities, in particular by establishing and consolidating control, tax fraud investigation, and debt management departments. A detailed plan to support the introduction in Bosnia of the necessary legislation based on the EU's *acquis* was also envisaged.[76] The High Commissioner subsequently established a 'Bulldozer Committee' to push through simplification of tax codes and boost public revenues with a country VAT.[77] The Committee also promised to demolish barriers to trade and investment by eliminating contradictory legislation and forcing through basic economic reforms.

The Kosovo economy is formally under the trusteeship of the EU Pillar of the United Nations Mission in Kosovo (UNMIK). This gives the Union an even greater degree of discretion in shaping economic life than is the case in Bosnia. Under European leadership the UNMIK has not only imposed laws and reforms, it even made itself responsible as trustee and administrator for a vast amount of state and socially owned property across Kosovo, including some 370 socially owned enterprises.[78]

It is often assumed that the use of vast external emergency powers is due to the peculiar security situation in the western Balkans. This was certainly true some years ago, but what is at stake today in the western Balkans is primarily the issue of economic governance. As Gerald Knaus and Felix Martin have observed:

When the High Representative [in Bosnia-Hercegovina] speaks of emergency today, he refers not to bulletins broadcast on the public radio station inciting violence against peace-keeping troops, but to an inefficient tax system in need of reform, the over-regulation of private business, or specific technical features rendering the judicial system less than efficient. When he speaks of enemies of the Bosnian state he means not armed paramilitaries committing premeditated arson, but business evading sales taxes or politicians implied in procurement scandals.[79]

The Union is certainly concerned about a possible resurgence of a violent inter-ethnic conflict in the western Balkans, and the violent clashes between ethnic Serbs and Albanians in Kosovo in the Spring of 2004 have demonstrated that security in the region cannot be taken for granted. Nevertheless, the Union's major preoccupation these days is to make the economy of these countries work. As we have seen, the Union tries to address the problem by exporting (or even imposing) its own model of economic governance.

The case of the western Balkans might be extreme, but we have seen that the pattern of dealing with poor and unstable neighbours of the EU is similar in each case. The Union tries to make these countries look more like itself. Neighbours are asked to adopt European laws and administrative solutions in exchange for aid, liberalization of mutual exchanges, and integration. The process has a long time-span; it is gradual and conditional. The more certain countries manage to become compatible with the Union, the more they are integrated in various (but not all) functional fields. The distinction between EU members and non-members is becoming increasingly blurred. There is progressive interpenetration of various types of economic and political units. Sovereignty is more divided than ever and redistribution is no longer confined to countries within the EU. In fact, the external borders of the Union are increasingly fuzzy despite the rhetoric and practice of Schengen.[80] This kind of policy clearly resembles a neo-medieval rather than a Westphalian pattern in the sense that the Union tries to extend its governance onto the neighbours rather than insulate itself from them. Of course, in the case of protectorates such as Kosovo and Bosnia the Union effectively imposes many rules and policies. Nevertheless, the governance network there is still quite multilayered and the Union insists on strengthening the principle of shared ownership. Of course, Westphalian and neo-medieval actors tend to have a different set of policies towards their internal and external environment. Chapter 5 will examine this differentiation in more detail.

Conclusions

Poor neighbours confront the Union with different problems than the most dynamic economic competitors. The challenges of the internal cohesion following enlargement are of yet a different nature. Nevertheless, in all three cases the Union opts for what we call neo-medieval rather than neo-Westphalian solutions. As borders of economic governance become extended, they also become fuzzier. The Union finds it increasingly difficult to assert central, hierarchical control over its ever-expanding territory and multiplicity of different economic actors. Flexibility, devolution, delegation, and decentralization seem therefore the most natural kinds of response for coping with an enlarged and highly diversified economic space with fuzzy borders. The structure of economic governance increasingly resembles complex variable geometry rather than a simple overarching framework. The role of European institutions is becoming more about facilitating, mediating, networking, coordinating, and promoting good economic practices than about adopting and enforcing rigid rules and laws. This kind of governance is not only a question of necessity; according to a growing body of experts it also represents the most effective way of stimulating cohesive growth and addressing economic shocks. They argue that the best type of governance is gardening rather than engineering.[81] They show that overlapping, polycentric jurisdictions work better than monopolistic, territorially fixed, and nested ones.[82] They show that multi-level governance in concentric circles can be more responsive to local constituencies, more open to experimentation and innovation, and more reliable in meeting undertaken commitments than centralized, hierarchical governance.[83] Their ideas are increasingly being embraced by the EU itself. As Romano Prodi, former President of the European Commission put it: 'The way to achieve real dynamism, creativity and democratic legitimacy in the European Union is to free the potential that exists in multi-layered levels of governance.'[84] This chapter has shown that the new EU members from Eastern Europe are also likely to endorse this type of governance. They by and large endorse policies stimulating further growth through liberalization, flexibility, and decentralization. They are reluctant to concentrate most economic powers in a single European centre. They are also likely to support active policies aimed at extending the European system of governance beyond the EU's borders, although their prime interests are in East and South-eastern Europe, not in the Mediterranean.

However, the emerging neo-medieval type of economic governance in Europe is not entirely unproblematic. The Union must find a proper balance between hierarchy and anarchy. It has to ensure that flexibility, delegation, and decentralization do not create 'authority holes', leaving certain firms and stockholders without jurisdiction and protection. It also has to find ways to provide a minimum degree of accountability of various governance networks. Basic principles of democracy and social organization may also clash with the aforementioned outlined principles of governance. For instance, how is social solidarity (let alone unity) to be sustained in a polity governed by the principles of freedom and competition? How are the existing forms of democratic representation to be combined with multilevel economic governance in concentric circles? And how is the new system to be prevented from being prone to interest group capture and corruption? The exact shape of the emerging system of governance can also differ depending on choices and circumstances. As Liesbet Hooghe and Gary Marks pointed out, different types of multilevel governance generate different solutions and problems.[85] For instance, it makes a difference whether individual layers of governance are designed around particular communities or around particular problems. It also makes a difference whether we have a fixed or fluid number of governance layers. The mechanism of coordination and competition between different governance layers is also important. These kinds of questions have to be addressed in more detail by European analysts and decision-makers. This chapter has merely tried to show that a neo-medieval rather than neo-Westphalian type of economic governance is indeed in the making.

5

Democratic Governance

The European Union has ever more powers, and is expected to exercise these powers in a democratic manner.[1] True, the core of EU activity and its strongest constitutional prerogatives still lie in the field of economics. Education and cultural policies are largely excluded from the Union's competence, as are defence and police powers. Moreover, such crucial aspects of economic policies as taxation or social welfare are still firmly in the hands of the member states.[2] Nevertheless, the Union enjoys powers unparalleled by any other transnational organization and these powers affect the fortunes of millions of European citizens.[3] Moreover, the way the Union is governed affects, and some would say perverts, the democratic system of its member states.[4] Today, the European, national, and local governance systems are increasingly enmeshed, producing a very complex, ambiguous, and novel *polity*.[5] The question is: what kind of democracy can possibly work in such a polity? Does enlargement change the nature of democratic governance in Europe, and if so, how? This chapter will try to show that enlargement reinforces the neo-medieval mode of democratic governance in Europe. The enlarged EU will be a more multilayered and multicentred polity than a typical Westphalian state, with non-majoritarian institutions in charge of a weak and culturally segmented European public space.[6] We are unlikely to see convergence of democratic cultures across the continent that would fit in the Westphalian scenario. It would therefore not be easy to establish the purpose of democratic policies in this complex and segmented cultural setting, and the Union would have to find new ways to articulate and aggregate public preferences. New ways would also need to be found to assure transparency, responsiveness, and compliance from public institutions.

Whether the evolving European governance system can still be called 'democratic' is a matter of debate. This debate is partly about the definition of democracy, but it is also about the very nature of the unit that is either conducive or detrimental to democratic governance.[7] It is often argued that democracy can only work in a typical Westphalian state. As Ralf Dahrendorf bluntly put it: 'Apart from nation-states, we shall never find appropriate institutions for democracy.'[8] But does this mean that any kind of democracy on the European level is doomed to failure? Or should we rather try to make sure that the Union resembles a Westphalian state? Those who advocate ever further powers for the European Parliament eventually leading to a Westphalian type of parliamentary representation and a pan-European majoritarian government seem to believe in the latter option. They usually acknowledge that democracy can hardly come about through the process of institutional and legal engineering only. They also know that at present there is no such thing as a European 'people' who could constitute a European state. Yet as Jürgen Habermas forcefully argued:

Peoples emerge only with the constitutions of their states. Democracy itself is a legally mediated form of political integration. It is a form that depends, to be sure, on a political culture shared by all citizens. But if we consider the process by which European states of the nineteenth century gradually *created* national consciousness and civic solidarity—the earliest modern form of collective identity—with the help of national historiography, mass communications, and military duty, there is no cause for defeatism.[9]

Is it true that democracy can only function in a kind of Westphalian (nation) state? After all, such leading experts as Robert Dahl, among others, wrote about democracy in Greek and Roman city states.[10] When the city state found itself in trouble, largely because of external pressures, democracy was transferred to a larger unit better suited to cope with these pressures: the nation state. The EU is also seen as a response to global pressures that undermine the functioning of Westphalian nation states. Will the Union become a new democratic unit?[11] And how will democracy look after the shift?

The latter question focuses our attention on the evolving nature of democracy in different times and under different circumstances. When democracy moved from city states to nation states it became representative democracy rather than the assembly democracy known at the level of the city state. Democracy continued to change shape at different historical stages of Westphalian nation states. On the eve of the twentieth century many parliamentary governments in Europe were still dependent on their local monarchs, elections were hardly free, and secret and electoral rights were severely restricted. For instance, in France and Belgium women were allowed to vote in parliamentary elections only after the Second World War.[12] Significant changes have also occurred in recent years. More and more decisions affecting respective national electorates are now being taken by various supranational bodies or worse, by quite mysterious global economic, regulatory, or even judicial networks.[13] Within nation states more and more powers are being shifted to non-majoritarian institutions such as constitutional courts and central banks. At the same time and somewhat contradictorily, calls for plebiscitarian solutions have also intensified leading to more frequent use of popular referenda. Public spaces in nation states are becoming more pluralistic, multicultural, and complex, with mass media rather than parties shaping political agendas. Output rather than input type of legitimacy is more in use than ever, but the existing democratic institutions clearly have problems in coping with the cultural change that has reshaped public expectations of this output. As Jacques Thomassen put it:

> What can we say about a democracy in which individual liberty prevails to the extent that the role of the government and institutionalized politics is increasingly questioned, where a pluralist process of decision-making leaves little room for an impartial interpretation of the general interest, where political participation seems to be directed to individual and private ends at the expense of the recognition and pursuit of the public good?[14]

This chapter will examine whether enlargement weakens or reinforces some of these overall democratic trends in Europe. As in the previous chapters I work with a simple neo-medieval and neo-Westphalian dichotomy. Again, the use of 'neo' makes clear that I am talking about abstract models without any intention of drawing a historic analogy. (In fact, one can hardly find examples of democratic governance in medieval Europe even if one applied the most flexible definition of democracy.) Table 5.1 shows two contrasting models of democratic governance that are seen as possible in the enlarged EU. I focus on three basic components of the emerging democratic order and argue that in each case enlargement renders the neo-medieval model a more realistic option.

I try to avoid normative judgements about the emerging Euro-democracy in this particular chapter.[15] However, it will soon be obvious that the emerging governance model can hardly be called 'democratic' in traditional Westphalian terms. This does not necessarily mean that neo-medievalism offers no effective means for political participation, representation, and accountability. However, participation, representation, and accountability would work differently in a neo-medieval Europe

119

Table 5.1. Two contrasting models of democratic governance

Major features	Neo-Westphalian model	Neo-medieval model
Structure	Coherent system of nested governments, stretching up to a unified and encompassing European level	Multilevel and multicentred governance in concentric circles
Representation	Parliamentary representation is dominant, but constrained by constitutional provisions	Non-majoritarian institutions dominate over a weak parliament(s)
Identity	An easily identified demos based on ethnic and civic ties and operating within a rich and compact public space	Multiplicity of distinct demoi operating in a segmented public space; pan-European identity is blurred and weak

and so, by extension, democracy would also assume a different meaning. Whether the new meaning and features of democracy are likely to be seen as legitimate is another matter. I will deal with these issues in more depth at the end of this book. But first let us examine how enlargement is likely to shape the nature of democratic governance in Europe.

Governance structure

At the early stage of European integration it was unclear whether major governmental powers would rest with the member states or would be transferred to the emerging European polity. The basic assumption always was that power should lie at one level or another, that functional boundaries should correspond with territorial ones, and that a viable government requires a clear centre, hierarchy, and competence allocation.[16] Today the structure of European governance operates at several different levels. Authority is shared and dispersed among various governmental centres. These centres often have different sites, different geographic reach, and operate in different functional fields. The system is not only multilayered, multicentred, and heterogeneous, but also lacks a clear allocation of competence and straightforward hierarchy. Competencies of various governmental agencies are overlapping and blurred. Dispersion of jurisdiction across different levels and the splitting of decision-making into multiple arenas is pronounced.[17]

All this variable geometry with multiple centres of authority and overlapping competencies makes one think of medieval Europe. The medieval ruling structure was, to use Anderson's description, 'an inextricably super-imposed and tangled one, in which different juridical instances were geographically interwoven and stratified and plural allegiances, asymmetrical suzerainties and anomalous enclaves abounded'.[18] Daniel Philpott added: 'Feudal lines of obligation resembled a system of arteries in a body, not a pyramid with an apex.'[19] Today, EU institutions are said to look and function like a 'junction box': a concentrated point of intersection, inter-action, and filtering between country-based institutions and processes and the wider international context.[20] The EU's organizational structure is said to resemble a 'garbage can' with different cross-cutting policy networks operating without a straightforward division of power and hierarchy.[21] Instead of a single continent-wide jurisdiction, authority is said to be 'spliced into multiple, functionally-specific, policy regimes with overlap-ping national memberships'[22].

The terms used to describe the medieval governance structure are some-what different from the terms used to describe governance in the contem-porary EU. Nevertheless, the resemblance is striking. In any case, it is evident that the current EU structure bears little resemblance to ones that function in Westphalian states. The question is, however, whether this hybrid multilevel European governance in concentric circles can last. Maybe we are simply confronted with a transitory arrangement that is unworkable in the long run, especially in view of the last wave of enlarge-ment. Perhaps it is time to consolidate a single European centre of gov-ernment. Indeed, does enlargement call for a simpler structure, separation of powers, and straightforward division of competencies? In the Union of six or even fifteen West European countries it was often possible to avoid decision-making deadlocks. But is not a Union of twenty-five diverse countries condemned to paralysis? Since the late 1990s there has been mounting evidence that European leaders are indeed afraid that enlarge-ment is going to paralyse the EU institutional structure.[23] This is why the Union embarked on a major institutional reform prior to eastern enlargement. And when one scrutinizes the substance of calls for deepen-ing European integration, one realizes that deepening was largely about state-building.

After the disappointing results of the EU treaty revision completed in 1999 in Nice, European leaders opted for a spectacular institutional 'big bang': a new European constitution.[24] The new constitution was asked to respond to two major requests elaborated by the European Councils in Nice and Laeken: 'the request for the European system to be clarified and simplified; and the creation of new tools for going in the direction of "more Europe".'[25] The only way to implement such a mandate was to reform the EU governance structure along the Westphalian pattern by enhancing the powers of the European centre, reducing the ever greater legal and institutional plurality and giving the Union the means for taming political divergence. This proved to be wishful thinking, however. The adopted constitutional treaty has clearly fallen short of the Westphalian expectations.[26] Let me explain.

Even assuming that this treaty will ever became law, it is hard to see it as a *Constitutio Westphalica*, to use Stéphane Beulac's terminology.[27] The treaty does not create a centralized European structure with horizontal and vertical hierarchy, even though the treaty 'gives' the European Council its 'president' and 'minister for foreign affairs'. The treaty does not eliminate concentric circles and different layers of European governance. On the contrary, it creates more opportunities for member states to create inner circles of cooperation and contains various provisions for opting in or out of these circles. The treaty simplifies decision-making procedures in some respects by, for example, adopting a new voting system, but it also complicates them in other respects by, for instance, introducing various 'emergency breaks', 'safeguards', or 'accelerators'. The treaty makes an effort to set out the EU's competencies more clearly, but still contains many vague and ambiguous arrangements.[28] Moreover, and quite naturally, shared competencies between EU and member states still abound.[29] Commenting on this constitutional treaty the Centre for European Reform concluded:

The new treaty makes it clear that the EU is not a state. The Union lacks most of the administrative and coercive powers that characterize sovereign countries.... Under the constitutional treaty the EU will be far more diverse and flexible than it is now. Different groups of Member-states will be able to pursue integration—in defense, or criminal law or even the harmonization of tax bases—while others can choose to watch from the fringes....[The draft treaty] opens up the possibility that member-states will take a 'pick 'n' mix' approach to future integration, in line with their very different capabilities and ambitions.[30]

It is not difficult to explain why the Union failed to adopt a more Westphalian draft of a constitution. To start with, the final shape of the constitutional treaty was in the hands of the heads of the member states, and they were reluctant to delegate more powers to the European centre of authority. This is not surprising. Constitutional framers always tend to adopt constitutional solutions to suit their own institutional interests.

The Union was granted more powers in the fields of migration, asylum, and trans-border crime because the member states are clearly unable to cope with these problems on their own. But in most other fields such as defence, taxation, employment, social policy, education, and culture member states protected their sovereign powers well. They also reinforced the principle of subsidiarity which restricts the EU's ability to acquire new competences. Governments of new member states from Eastern Europe were among those most determined to prevent any decisive shift of powers to the European centre. As the Latvian president, Vaira Vike-Freiberga, put it:

Latvia sees the EU as a union of sovereign states .... We do not see the need at the moment to create a unified federal European state .... Europe's vast diversity is one of its greatest strengths. While this diversity may present challenges to consensus-building, it is a resource that must be nurtured and cherished. Every member-state of the European Union, whatever its size, has the potential to make a meaningful contribution to the organization as a whole.[31]

And Slovenia's Foreign Minister, Dimitrij Rupel, added: 'The basis of diversity management is the principle of subsidiarity. Subsidiarity can be an efficient means of avoiding unnecessary disputes.'[32]

New member states from Eastern Europe have also resisted efforts to make the European Commission a more effective centre of government by insisting that each member state will have its own commissioner with the right to vote. Likewise they insisted that the system of a rotating EU presidency will remain in place in one way or another. This system implies that the main centre of governance in the EU moves from one European capital to another on a regular basis, thus preventing the rise of a single European centre in Brussels.

Institutional history is another reason for failing to adopt a Westphalian draft. Constitutional framers did not begin their work with a blank page, but with a large body of laws shaping the EU institutional structure.[33] They could not just create a new structure from scratch. They had to work with the complex structure already in place. In fact, the drafting of the constitutional treaty was very much a 'tidying-up exercise'.[34] The aim was to simplify, consolidate, and organize the existing body of laws and present them in a more accessible manner. The aim was not, and probably could not have been, to create a totally new institutional set-up. Such a move would have affected so many different actors and their interests that it would have strangled the entire exercise. For instance, imagine that the framers had attempted to do away with the multilayered nature of European governance. They would not only have had to tackle the division of competencies between the national and European level, but also to address the problem of the intermediate level, namely cities and regions.

By now all the larger states of Europe have established forms of intermediate, regional, or 'meso' government.[35] The powers and status of this intermediate level varies greatly, from the cooperative federalism of Germany, to the asymmetrical devolution of the United Kingdom, the strong, quasi-federal system of Spain, or the largely administrative regionalism found in France, Poland, and Italy. In some cases, the European Commission has been the catalyst behind the rise of the regional level of governance, insisting that regional institutions be set up to manage the Structural Funds. (This was especially the case in the new member states from Eastern Europe, but also in Greece and Sweden.) However, in other cases the creation of a regional level of governance was a response to bottom-up pressures for the recognition of cultural and historic entities (Spain and the United Kingdom) or the management of linguistic and ethnic conflict (Belgium and Northern Ireland).

Regions may well be heterogeneous, but they are usually formidable economic and political actors operating across the entire European space and beyond.[36] Rather than performing complementary functions in a national division of labour, regions compete in global and European markets. Regional leaders often bypass their respective national governments and seek political support, economic resources, and cultural sustenance outside state boundaries. They often form strategic alliances with other regions and seek support from European institutions. The situation is further complicated by the rise of cities, which like regions have been positioning themselves in the new European and global division of labour since at least the 1980s. (Most of the population in the new member states lives in cities.)[37]

Regions (and cities) can hardly be erased from the institutional map of the Union to suit the Westphalian blueprint. Nor is it possible to establish a uniform regional level of governance across the entire EU because individual regions have different origins, functions, powers, identities, and structures. As Michael Keating put it: 'This is a complex political order, comparable, although not identical to, the pre-state European order of overlapping and underlapping sovereignties, different types of authority in the state, the economy and civil society, and competing forms of legitimacy.'[38]

This complex political order could hardly be tackled by the adoption of a Westphalian constitution. One should be realistic about the potential for constitutional engineering. The multilayered structure of European governance can hardly be 'squeezed' or 'levered' by a decree, even a constitutional one. But this is not necessarily bad news because complex, multilayered, and flexible systems are not as detrimental to the smooth functioning of the EU's governance system as is often claimed by European statists. And this is yet another reason for not adopting a Westphalian constitution.

There is a growing body of literature arguing that variable geometry and competing jurisdictions should be applied to such a complex and highly diversified environment as the enlarged EU.[39] Flexible governance arrangements and overlapping, polycentric jurisdictions are said to serve well both efficiency and redistribution. They allow decision-makers to adjust the scale of governance to reflect heterogeneity. They provide more complete information on constituents' preferences, and are more adaptive in response to changing preferences. They are also more open to experimentation and innovation, and facilitate more credible commitments. Centralized governance, on the other hand, is said to be insensitive to local demands and ill-suited to accommodating diversity.

In conclusion, enlargement is likely to reinforce the multilayered, multicentred, and heterogeneous nature of European governance. Efforts to prevent this from happening by adopting a Westphalian type of constitution have failed. They failed partly by default and partly by design. It was not at all certain whether introducing a single continent-wide jurisdiction would improve governance in a highly diversified enlarged EU. Moreover, attempted moves to a single hierarchical European structure encountered resistance from political actors active at a national and regional level. The governance structure in the enlarged EU will therefore be very complex. The question is: does it work in a democratic fashion?

Majoritarianism versus constitutionalism

One can say many negative things about Westphalian states, but when it comes to democratic governance they have a fairly good record. True, democracy arrived in these states much later than the Peace of Westphalia and some of these states experienced autocratic or even totalitarian order in their history.[40] Nevertheless, democracy is basically associated with the existence of Westphalian states. As Juan J. Linz and

Alfred Stepan bluntly put it: 'Without a state, no modern democracy is possible.'[41]

The key pillar of this democracy is parliamentary representation. People elect their representatives to a parliament and this parliament adopts laws and usually also decides about the composition of the executive. Political parties are primarily organized with the aim of winning elections.[42] In order to gain power and implement their programmes they need to have a majority of parliamentary seats and this often requires forming coalitions with other parties. A parliamentary majority is not entirely free to have its way on all matters. It has to obey the constitution that divides power between the parliament, the executive, and the judiciary. The constitution also guards against an easy denial of certain individual or territorial rights. In other words, the majoritarian principle is only one pillar of democracy in Westphalian states; the other is constitutionalism with its emphasis on bills of rights, territorial or functional devolution of power, the independence of the judiciary, and some other institutions such as central banks and regulatory agencies.

In recent decades the constitutional elements have been strengthened in most European states. This has partly to do with disastrous experiences in the inter-war period. After all, many autocrats had come to power via democratic elections, and measures were taken to prevent the 'tyranny of majority' by introducing some tighter constitutional constraints on the respective parliamentary majorities. This implied, among others, 'judicization' of politics: parliamentary dominance was to be curbed by assigning to judges the role of constitutional review status.[43] More recently, constitutionalism has been enhanced by the complexity of modern governance that requires special 'technical' expertise in certain fields and justifies the creation of various independent regulatory agencies.[44] That said, the electorate remains an ultimate reference in all the Westphalian states of Europe, and the parliament is still the central political institution. If you want to know who holds most powers in a given state you need to look at the composition of the parliamentary majority.

In the EU the situation is very different. Here the position of the parliament is much weaker. The problem is not so much in the catalogue of formal powers bestowed on the European Parliament, but rather in the peculiar nature of the European parliamentary game. The European Parliament has no ruling majority as we know it from national systems: it has neither a governing cabinet nor a governing programme to sustain or oppose.[45] Moreover, the Parliament, the Commission, and the Council are created more or less independently, therefore the element of 'fusion' that is usually observed between cabinets and their parliamentary majority does not exist. (But as mentioned earlier, the separation of powers principle has never been implemented in the EU in the same way it has been in national democratic systems.) Cleavages within the European Parliament break more along national 'boundaries' rather than along party affiliations or ideologies. Although members of the European Parliament are now directly elected to five-year terms, these elections tend to serve as popularity contests for the ruling national governments, and as such do not help the Parliament to assert itself as a central institution in charge of the European political space. In fact, major decisions by the EU often rely on the legitimacy of national parliaments rather than the legitimacy of the European Parliament. And the Union has undertaken many steps to strengthen the formal role of these national parliaments in EU decision-making. The problem is that these national parliaments are agents of their national (and often partisan) electorates and as such are ill-suited for exercising pan-European governance.

Although the formal powers of the European Parliament have gradually been increased over the past years, the Parliament is not the principal, let alone sole legislator and its say in selecting the European executive and judiciary is very limited.[46] In the EU power is much more in the hands of non-majoritarian institutions, that is, the Commission, the European Court of Justice (ECJ), the European Central Bank, and the European Council, than is the case in member states.[47] The composition of the Council is indirectly related to electoral results in individual countries, but the complex (and still evolving) way of weighing votes in the Council leaves little space for the assertion of majoritarian politics.[48] (One should add that national executives are often able to bypass their respective parliaments by making decisions in the European Council[49]). At the same time, more powers are being shifted to the ever growing list of European (regulatory) agencies. Most of these agencies are autonomous if not independent, and their existence is often justified by the slowness and weakness of the legislative process.[50] Table 5.2 contains a list of EU agencies and institutions. It shows that European governance is very much dispersed and heavily reliant on the technical expertise of bureaucrats and experts.

Of course, effective governance requires special skills and knowledge as well as long-term commitment—usually in short supply among members of parliament.[51] The problem is that non-majoritarian institutions are often more responsive to the wishes of narrow and partisan lobbies than to a broader European electorate.[52] Moreover, it is not easy to make

Table 5.2. European Union agencies and institutions

Name	Location	Year	Primary Function
European Parliament	Brussels, Strasbourg, Luxembourg	1950s*	Legislative
Council of the European Union	Brussels	1950s*	Legislative
European Commission	Brussels	1950s*	Executive
Court of Justice	Luxembourg	1952	Judicial
European Economic and Social Committee	Brussels	1957	Dialogue/Information
European Investment Bank	Luxembourg	1958	Regulation
Cedefop—European Centre for the Development of Vocational Training	Thessaloniki	1975	Dialogue/Information
Eurofund—European Foundation for the Improvement of Living and Working Conditions	Dublin	1975	Dialogue/Information
Court of Auditors	Luxembourg	1977	Auditorial
EEA—European Environmental Agency	Copenhagen	1990	Information
ETF—European Training Foundation	Turin	1990	Executive
European Ombudsman	Strasbourg	1992	Dialogue/Information
Europol—European Police Office	The Hague	1992	Executive
EMCDDA—European Monitoring Centre for Drugs and Drug Addiction	Lisbon	1993	Information
EMEA—European Agency for the Evaluation of Medicinal Products	London	1993	Regulation
OHIM—Office for Harmonization in the Internal Market	Alicante	1993	Regulation
Committee of the Regions	Brussels	1994	Dialogue/Information
EU OSHA—European Agency for Safety and Health at Work	Bilbao	1994	Dialogue/Information
CPCO—Community Plant Variety Office	Angers	1994	Regulation
CdT—Translation Centre for Bodies of the European Union	Luxembourg	1994	Executive
EUMC—European Monitoring Centre on Racism and Xenophobia	Vienna	1997	Information
European Central Bank	Frankfurt	1998	Regulation
EAR—European Agency for Reconstruction	Thessaloniki	2000	Executive
CEPOL—European Police College	London	2000	Pillar III/Training
European Union Institute for Security Studies	Paris	2001	Pillar II/Information
European Union Satellite Centre	Torrejón de Ardoz	2001	Pillar II/Information
European Data Protection Supervisor	Brussels	2001	Advisory/Information
EESA—European Food Safety Authority	Parma	2002	Information
Eurojust—European Body for the Enhancement of Judicial Cooperation	The Hague	2002	Pillar III/Coordination
EMSA—European Maritime Safety Agency	Lisbon	2002	Regulation
EASA—European Aviation Safety Agency	Cologne	2002	Regulation
ENISA—European Network and Information Security Agency	Heraklion	2004	Information/Dialogue
ERA—European Railway Agency	Lille/Valenciennes	2004	Information
European Centre for Disease Prevention and Control	Stockholm	2004	Information
FRONTEX—External	Warsaw	2005	Coordination Training Borders Agency

*Set up under the Founding Treaties in the 1950s

these various regulatory agencies transparent and accountable.[53] Governance in the Union is not based on the principle of parliamentary representation but resembles, to use Wallace and Smith's expression: 'enlightened administration on behalf of uninformed publics, in cooperation with affected interests and subject to the approval of national governments'.[54] Indeed, European politics is hardly shaped by the European Parliament. Non-majoritarian institutions are stronger than in typical Westphalian states. European (or even national) elections do not make a major impact on the course of European integration. Referenda on European issues in individual states are hardly a way to enhance majoritarian politics. We have already seen how a tiny minority of the European electorate in Denmark and Ireland could prevent the rest from going ahead with certain pan-European projects. In the Council majority rule applies only partially and when it is formally used it is, usually, on an issue where a consensus has been previously reached. Great care is taken to avoid confrontation with what the governments consider are vital interests. Veto points are everywhere and there are many checks and balances. This became a major source of concern even among those who do not think that the Union suffers from a 'democratic deficit'. As Yves Mény put it: 'The growing dissatisfaction with democracy, particularly in Europe, is the result of the continuing expansion of the constitutional pillar to the detriment of the popular one.'[55] The question is: will enlargement 'bring power back to the people' and make the European Parliament the true centre of European governance?[56] Or to use our terms, will the EU chose the Westphalian democratic path towards greater parliamentary representation?

It must be noted that after the fall of Communism in Eastern Europe there was intense public pressure to let the people decide their own fate without constitutional restrictions. The belief that power should rest in the hands of voters and their parliamentary representatives was very strong. As Andrzej Rapaczyński forcefully argued on the eve of Poland's democratic transition:

Polish views usually yield to the following reasoning: all legitimate political power flows from the people. The depository and embodiment of the people's own sovereignty is the national legislature, chosen in universal, equal, direct, secret, proportional elections. Therefore, the parliament, as the most direct representative of the people, reflecting the principal voices of the nation, should be the supreme organ of the government, and determine the policy of the nation.[57]

These views became more pronounced as the membership of the Union drew nearer. As the Estonian Minister of Foreign Affairs, Toomas Ilves, put it in his 2001 lecture at Humboldt University:

The democratic nation-state that developed in most of Europe after the Enlighten-ment and the French Revolution holds that the citizen has a say in what happens in his country. It is the absence of this feeling that distinguishes undemocratic coun-tries from democratic ones, it was the failure to allow the citizen his say that led ultimately to the fall of the Berlin Wall....[But now there] is suspicion that that fundamental decisions, previously made in a transparent and legally understand-able way at the level of the democratic post-Westphalian nation state, are now being transferred to a higher body. In this body, the link between the opinions of an individual and his opportunities to express them through established means (such as through a political party or pressure on his parliament representative) is no longer clear....This I believe, is the crux of the dilemma facing the finalité of Europe.[58]

However, there is little evidence suggesting that the new member states were ever willing to put this rhetoric in practice either in their own states or in the EU. Non-majoritarian institutions and practices have spread throughout Eastern Europe over the last decade or so and they were recently also embraced in the European context. To start with, the new member states' desire to 'empower the people' after the long period of dictatorship has not deterred them from installing and empowering sev-eral non-majoritarian institutions within their own borders.[59] Consider, for instance, the spectacular rise to power of constitutional courts.[60] In-stitutions of constitutional judicial review had no precedent in these countries prior to transition, and the judicial system as a whole had no tradition of independence. At the early stage of transition, constitutional courts were composed of small groups of political appointees; and many constitutional judges fell victim to political manipulation or even tried to use the court as a springboard for their own political ambitions.[61] Yet, these courts gradually acquired binding powers and statutory independ-ence and began to take decisions on most crucial and often controversial issues. Wojciech Sadurski who studied constitutional courts in the region documented that these courts often dealt with national legislation in a manner contrary to the wishes of the parliamentary majorities and gov-ernments of the day.[62] Important aspects of laws on abortion, the death penalty, 'lustration' (screening of officials suspected of improprieties under the auspices of the ancien régime), criminal prosecution of former Communist officials responsible for crimes against the people during the Communist period, economic austerity measures, fiscal policy, citi-zenship requirements, personal identification numbers for citizens, and indexation of pensions have all been struck down.[63] Sadurski and some other observers named the Hungarian Constitutional Court 'the most activist constitutional court in the world', one that serves as the example for other courts in Eastern Europe.[64]

This unprecedented, wide-ranging activism has made the courts more rather than less popular among the respective publics. In 1995 in Hungary public support for the Constitutional Court was 58 per cent, compared to the parliament at 36 per cent and the government at 35 per cent.[65] Central banks experienced a similar rise to power across the entire region, together with many other regulatory agencies in such fields as mass media, environment, health, and safety.[66]

Of course, it is not certain whether this trust in non-majoritarian institutions will be extended to their European equivalents. However, despite some ritual complaints about Euro-bureaucracy, new member states were usually quite supportive of the European Commission which after all can be seen as a kind of independent regulatory agency in charge of the internal market.[67] It is quite likely that new member states, like the old ones, will try to manipulate rather than eliminate European regulatory agencies.[68] The new member states will probably invest more diplomatic capital in trying to get some of the new agencies on their own soil than in asserting majoritarian controls over them.

Moreover, in the debate on the European Constitution the officials from the new member states were eager to increase the role of national parliaments rather than the European Parliament.[69] Such a solution can be seen as a means of enhancing the democratic legitimacy of the Union, but hardly as a way of enhancing majoritarian politics. After all, this solution increases the opportunity for individual national parliaments to prevent majoritarian decisions taken by majorities in the Council and European Parliament (under co-decision procedures). The new members' insistence on the principle of sovereignty and equality between (large and small) states can also be seen as a kind of resistance towards fully-fledged majoritarian politics.[70] The former is basically about the option of vetoing decisions taken by the majority of states. The latter protects small states (and their small electorates) against decisions taken by large states. Nearly all new member states are quite small, if not tiny, with a history of foreign domination by larger and more powerful neighbours. They are therefore reluctant to allow large countries with large electorates to dominate European decision-making. Let us not forget also that in the history of Eastern Europe hegemonial politics have been practised not only by Russia and the Soviet Union, but also by such important

EU members as Germany, Poland, Italy, Sweden, and Austria/Hungary. Even such a large state as Poland fiercely opposed the new voting system introduced by the draft of the European Constitution because it feared a possible alliance of such large (and federalist) states like France and Germany.[71] In the recent constitutional debate most new member states also preferred to have a President of the European Commission elected by the European Council rather than the European Parliament. This has prevented the Commission from being transformed into a 'parliamentary cabinet' similar to those functioning in Westphalian states.

The European Parliament likewise has little support or recognition among the new member states' electorates. Although some of the most famous Eastern European public figures campaigned for seats (and generous European salaries) in the European Parliament, only a tiny minority of the respective electorates bothered to vote. The turnout in the new member states in the June 2004 elections to the European Parliament was dramatically low.[72] These results do not mean that the Eastern European electorate is sceptical about the European project as such because a few months earlier impressive majorities of these electorates rushed to the polls to support their countries' membership of the Union.[73] But the Eastern European electorate seems to be quite sceptical about the role and functioning of the European Parliament. In this situation it is difficult to see the Union moving towards a fully-fledged system of parliamentary representation as a result of enlargement.

In summary, enlargement is not likely to halt let alone reverse the current trend to grant more powers to non-majoritarian institutions in the Union. The new member states may not become the principal agents of non-majoritarian solutions, but they are not likely to press for more Westphalian democracy either. Nor is enlargement likely to strengthen the position of the European Parliament. This makes the European system of representation 'inferior' to the national one, but it is far from certain whether majoritarian politics embedded in a system of parliamentary representation could ever work in the Union. As Renauld Dehousse rightly argued: 'The parliamentary system with its majoritarian aspects is ill adapted to the needs of a hybrid creature like the EU, characterized by great diversity and by strong national feelings.'[74] Majoritarian politics, according to Dehousse, invites conflicts between the Union and the member states: increased parliamentary representation clashes with the member states' representation.[75] And can we talk about a European system of representation without a truly European demos? This leads me to the next great democratic dilemma for the enlarged EU: the future shape of the European public space.

Public space and democratic culture

Democracy is not only about institutions; it is also about culture under-stood in broader political, legal, and economic terms. Democratic institutions are only able to persist if they enjoy a political culture which is congruent to and supportive of its democratic structures.[76] The key terms usually used in this context are demos, ethos, and identity. The EU can hardly become a democratic polity without a distinct community sharing certain beliefs and values. In the EU case, these values and beliefs ought to be not only democratic, but also 'European', which means communitarian if not altogether supranational.[77] Of course, demos, ethos, and identity are not primordial and stable categories. They evolve over time through experiences and discourses in a certain public space. The role of political agents such as parties and civil society organizations is crucial in shaping them. Mass media also play an important role in facilitating communication.

For the last several decades Westphalian states enjoyed all of these capabilities. The demos was usually formed by a single nation that represented a closely bound if not homogenous cultural community sharing common history, habits, and language.[78] Political discourse was taking place in a clearly defined public space in which it was relatively easy to communicate and identify common public goods (or at least major competing alternatives). Parties and civil society organizations were strong and vibrant. The media system was diversified and sophisticated. The EU, on the other hand, is said to possess none of these attributes. There is no single and easily identifiable European demos for and by which European policies are being made. At best we can talk about an ever-growing plurality of European demoi with distinct histories, habits, and languages. Political discourses are largely confined to national public spaces with little sign of a truly European public space emerging with the progress of European integration.[79] Political parties are also active mainly within state boundaries and their alliances on the European level are still artificial constructs.[80] Some civil society organizations were able to cross nation state borders, but they usually see themselves as global rather than merely European movements. Even NGOs calling themselves European do not actively support the European integration project. (Of course, the European Movement represents an important exception here.) In fact, the no-global movement which gathers together some of the currently most vocal and recognized NGOs has chosen the EU as one of its major objects of gothenburg criticism. This was particularly painfully manifested on the streets of Gothenburg, during the EU summit there in

June 2001.[81] Moreover, there is no single European newspaper if one does not count some globally operating newspapers such as the *Financial Times*. And *Euro-news*, launched in 1993 after a series of failed experiments in pan-European television, has never been able to reach a broad European public.[82] We cannot but conclude that the current diversified and segmented European public space looks more medieval than Westphalian. One therefore wonders whether this does not represent a major impediment to a workable democracy at the European level. Perhaps it is difficult to enjoy a political culture congruent to democracy in a weak and open-ended public space? Maybe democracy cannot work without formation of a single demos, ethos, and identity?

Experts tell us, however, that the case does not have to be hopeless. Unlike in the Middle Ages, the European public space is filled with distinct, but nevertheless quite democratic national communities that are determined to preserve their values when engaged in European politics. Different languages and systemic fragmentation do not prevent fruitful communication if basic values are shared. Values conducive to democracy are largely of civic rather than ethnic nature, and as such are more universal.[83] In due time, various integrative projects cannot but increase cultural affinity if not convergence across the continent.[84] Consider, for instance, the homogenizing impact of the single currency or of visa-free travel. Besides, the point is not to build a European nation-writ-large but to enhance a sense of constitutional patriotism across the continent.[85] As Kalypso Nicolaïdis has rightly observed, a voluntary and differentiated 'community of project' is less demanding than a holistic 'community of identity'.[86] Indeed there is some wisdom in the European Commission's slogan promoting 'unity in diversity'. After all, identity that does not recognize pluralism, individualism, and multiculturalism can hardly be conducive to a democratic system.[87]

Thus democracy in a neo-medieval cultural setting might still be possible. But it would be a different type of democracy than the one existing in Westphalian states. The latter requires a strong if not dominant European identity and a pan-European civic culture. Such identity and culture can only develop and persist with genuine European civil society and political parties. There is also the need for a vibrant public sphere to emerge with the help of the pan-European media system. The question is: will enlargement facilitate or stall this Westphalian scenario?

It can well be argued that only with enlargement to Central and Eastern Europe can the EU finally claim to be 'European' as opposed to merely West European. Moreover, a study of various writings by Eastern European dissidents in the cold war period suggested that the idea of Europe was stronger at its periphery than at the centre. 'Indeed the periphery was the centre!', observed Jacques Rupnik.[88] But as accession to the EU came closer this seemed no longer to be the case. Individual states from Eastern Europe became more concerned with defending their unique cultural features than in embracing the pan-European ideal. The Czech Prime Minister, Václav Klaus, expressed the anxiety of millions of fellow Eastern Europeans by asking: shall we let our identity 'dissolve in Europe like a lump of sugar in a cup of coffee?'[89] This has been confirmed by opinion polls. According to the June 2004 *Eurobarometer*, the majority of those polled in the new member states consider themselves as 'their nationality only' rather than call themselves 'European to some extent'[90]. (In the old member states the result is the reverse.) Even more striking is the fact that 'European-ness' in the new member states dramatically decreased with accession to the Union. Between autumn 2003 and spring 2004 the number of those who consider themselves 'their nationality only' rose by 12 per cent, while the number of those who see themselves as 'European to some extent' declined by 7 per cent. (And one should keep in mind that according to the same poll, the level of knowledge about the EU is higher in new member states than in the old ones.)

When it comes to civic culture the picture is more complicated, in the sense that no sharp threshold can be identified between the new and old members. For instance, according to the World Survey of Values, Spain scores as badly as Lithuania in perceiving violence as illegitimate. Support for autocratic rule is higher in Finland than in Hungary, Estonia, or Slovenia. But Germany (East and West) shows even less support for autocratic rule than any of the new members. Ethnic tolerance in the Czech Republic is higher than in Spain, but Spain is much more tolerant than either the Baltic states or Hungary. And in Poland and Estonia the solidarity index is much higher than in Sweden, but still lower than in Spain.[91]

As was shown in Chapter 3, comparisons of civic culture between old and new EU members does not reveal any particular pattern of divergence. Of course, the communist legacy could not but leave some traces. For instance, people in the new member states express much less confidence in their law and law enforcement systems than is the case in old member states.[92] However, this does not necessarily imply that they have less espect for law and the police. They may simply be frustrated by the structural and financial problems that make their systems function poorly.

The conclusion that can be drawn from the analysis of these data is that enlargement will further increase the plurality of civic cultures in the Union, making it difficult to arrive at the fairly homogenous cultural pattern required by the Westphalian scenario. This conclusion is further reinforced by the fact that there are hardly any pan-European agents able to promote greater cultural homogeneity. As pointed out in Chapter 4, organizations of civil society are still underdeveloped in most new member states and this especially applies to NGOs interested in EU-related issues.[93] Parties are more developed in the new member states and some of them have joined the existing federations of parties in the European Parliament. However, it would be wrong to assume that parties in the new member states are similar to their equivalents and partners in the old member states. As Klaus von Beyme has observed: 'Party research faces the difficulty that the ideological labels developed in the West hardly fit in Eastern Europe... [Moreover], it is highly doubtful that the parties of East-Central Europe are as central in coordinating the networks of organized interests, regional units, bureaucratic experts as in the West.'[94] Party systems in the new member states are still extremely fragmented and lack programmatic structuring. Parties in Eastern Europe have far fewer members than parties in Western Europe and can count on much lower voter identification. The main competition is usually between the reformed communists and the democratic camp; neither of these two camps can easily fit into the Western European notion of left and right.[95] Even though some of these parties succeeded in securing seats in the European Parliament and their members have joined the Euro-federations, it is far from certain that they will act as agents of cultural homogenization across the Union. The 2004 European elections saw an increase in Euro-sceptic members of European Parliament (MEPs), many of them coming from the new member states of Eastern Europe.[96]

Finally, there is little reason to suggest that enlargement will stimulate development of the European public space. During accession negotiations all Eastern European governments insisted that their language became one of the official languages of the EU, thus undermining the efforts of those who would like to see fewer rather than more languages as the means of pan-European communication. (One should add that although Russian is not an official EU language, more citizens in new member states speak Russian as their first language than, for example, Estonian or Latvian.) Nor is there any evidence to suggest that enlargement will stimulate the growth of pan-European media. Although many newspapers in the new member states are now in hands of international media conglomerates, national television is still very much under the control of local governments.[97]

To summarize, progressive integration has certainly enhanced a sense of European identity, but it has not produced the European people for and by which EU decisions are being made. Moreover, the European identity has not replaced national identities, but has grown alongside these identities. The result is a complex mosaic of democratic cultures interacting with each other across the ever wider Union. Each successive enlargement has increased the cultural plurality; public space has become larger and more diversified and the Union has been confronted with new democratic habits and practices. The last wave of enlargement was no exception to this trend. Citizens in Eastern Europe cherished the European ideal when outside the Union, but they were not prepared to give up their national identity upon joining either. Their ethos and practices are by and large democratic, but they usually are somewhat different to those already present in the Union. And so we are unlikely to see convergence of democratic cultures across the continent that would fit the Westphalian scenario. In this field like in all others discussed in this book the setting will be increasingly medieval.

Conclusions

Over the last several years we have witnessed a heated debate about the alleged democratic deficit of the EU.[98] The problem with this discussion is that it chiefly relies on Westphalian criteria of judgement. But the EU is not a state and we need to find different ways to evaluate its democratic performance. As Yves Mény rightly put it:

Our challenge is to conceive something called democracy at a higher, supranational level. But it would be wrong to think that a simple transposition of our national schemes could work. We have to invent not only adequate rules but, first of all, a new concept of 'post-national democracy.'[99]

But what does this 'post-national democracy' imply? And how can one name and describe the polity in which this democracy is to function? Philippe Schmitter's description of a system that he labelled *condominio* comes close to what we have tried to suggest here.[100] Territorial as well as functional constituencies would vary in the *condominio* system, says Schmitter. Instead of a single Europe with recognized and contiguous borders, there would be many Europes: a trading Europe, an energy Europe, an environmental Europe, and so forth. Instead of one 'Eurocracy' there would be 'multiple regional institutions acting autonomously to solve common problems'.[101] We may add that majoritarian politics would not be the key democratic device in this system, and the parliament(s) would have to share powers with many powerful (sometimes more powerful) non-majoritarian institutions. The public space in this system would be fragmented and weak, and there would hardly be a single dominant identity, ethos, and demos. According to Schmitter, *condominio* resembles the 'preexisting Euro-state system', and we may add that this system is truly medieval in its nature (as suggested by its Latin name.)

This system has been on the rise in the Union for some time already, and this chapter has showed that enlargement has reinforced its foundations. The question is, nevertheless, whether this system can still be called democratic. Public representation and participation under this system are weaker than in traditional Westphalian states. Democratic controls and the accountability of European officials are also problematic. And it is difficult to establish the purpose of democratic policies in a complex and segmented cultural setting. New ways have to be envisaged to articulate and aggregate public preferences. New methods of assuring the transparency, responsiveness, and compliance of public institutions must be put in place. We still do not know what these new ways and methods should be about, but at least we know what is at stake and which ways and methods are simply inadequate. Trying to use Westphalian democratic devices to govern the neo-medieval setting seems to me a rather futile exercise, if not counterproductive altogether. Moreover, there is no reason for despair. Although the emerging democratic governance system has many weaknesses, it is probably in a better position than the Westphalian system to recognize pluralism, individualism, and multiculturalism in the wider EU. This new emerging system also seems better suited to orchestrate genuine dialogue, consent, and voluntary compliance than the centralized and hierarchical Westphalian system. This new system could also be in a better position to secure public solidarity that reaches beyond narrow ethnic ties. And one should also keep in mind that the European governance system would not be in charge of all issues across different regional levels in the way the Westphalian system is. Member states would have their own exclusive spheres of competence governed by the traditional system of parliamentary representation. Regions and cities will also try to increase their functional reach and will search for yet different modes of democratic governance that are more appropriate to their own specificity. Of course, without some basic division of competences and forms of institutional arbitration, the neo-medieval EU might fall into anarchy. This is why Europe may need some kind of constitution, provided that this not a *Constitutio Westphalica*.

I will return to these issues in the concluding chapter. It is crucial that new and effective ways of public participation in European decision-making are found for this new system to deserve the name 'democratic'. This is more likely to be done through the mechanism of public contestation rather than through representation. In other words, the capacity of citizens to contest European decisions will be more crucial in a neo-medieval setting than the functioning of institutional channels of representation.

6

Governance Beyond Borders

The current European discourse on foreign policy and defence is very much Westphalian. The Union is said to be on its way to acquiring the most typical characteristics of a Westphalian state: diplomacy, army, police, intelligence, and hard external borders. The 1992 Maastricht Treaty has established a common foreign and security policy (CFSP) to assert the Union's 'identity on the international scene' and 'covering all areas of foreign and security policy'. Then the 1999 Helsinki Declaration of the European Council created the European Security and Defence Policy (ESDP). The office of the EU High Representative for the CFSP was created in the same year and the EU is soon likely to have its own minister for foreign affairs.[1] There are currently 128 diplomatic missions of the Union all over the world (called EU delegations) and their number is growing.[2] Some 50,000 to 60,000 soldiers will soon be at the EU's disposal to perform the full range of peacekeeping and peace-enforcing tasks.[3] In addition, a special EU Military Committee (EMC) and the European Military Staff (EMS) have been set up to run the European defence policy. In 2003 the Union undertook its first military and police operations, three in the Balkans and one in the Democratic Republic of Congo. At the end of 2004, 7,000 European troops took off their badges bearing the NATO emblem and replaced them with the EU's star-spangled insignia.

With the integration of the Schengen *acquis* into the framework of the EU by the Treaty of Amsterdam, the EU has also acquired distinct external borders. The Union has even created its own institutions to fight international terrorism. A new intelligence 'clearing house' to pool information on extremists has been created, together with a special EU 'coordinator' to oversee the fields involved in the anti-terrorism fight including police and judicial work, intelligence-sharing, and cracking down on extremists' financing.

Nevertheless, I argue that this story of a Westphalian state in the making is rather biased if not altogether misleading. When it comes to diplomacy and security the Union resembles a neo-medieval empire, not a Westphalian state. Foreign and security policy is still largely in the hands of member states, and on the most crucial issues, ranging from the wars in the Balkans to the wars in Iraq, these states have found themselves hopelessly divided. Moreover, member states use the European framework as one among many institutional tools of foreign policy. They often prefer to act within the United Nations (UN) framework or via the Organization for Security and Cooperation in Europe (OSCE), Council of Europe, or NATO. Foreign and security policies are often carried out by formal or informal coalitions of the willing, contact groups or bilateral initiatives. Individual member states have a complex set of diplomatic relationships within and across EU borders and they pursue their security in a different manner depending on the case and circumstances of the day. Most notably, their loyalty is sought not only by the EU, but also by the United States. And so, like in the Middle Ages, European actors are subject to two competing universalistic claims.

Not only does the Union as such resemble a neo-medieval empire. The emerging international system in Europe looks also more medieval than Westphalian. The system is geared towards the two aforementioned power centres and is not anarchic. Collective bargaining over laws, procedures, and the empire's institutional structure is the essence of interstate politics at present. In the enlarged EU we are unlikely to see the typical Westphalian interstate politics of balancing, bandwagoning, and ganging up over territorial gains and spheres of influence. As Sebastian Princen and Michèle Knodt put it in their recent book on the Union's external relations, we have in Europe 'a polycentric system, which is split into multiple, overlapping arenas that are characterized by loose coupling'[4]. In my view, this is the essence of new medievalism.

This chapter will try to spell out all these arguments in more detail. It will first try to show what kind of international actor the EU has become, especially since the end of the cold war and the eastward enlargement. Second, it will try to scrutinize the evolving international system in Europe. How do various parts of the emerging European empire interact with each other, and how does the new pattern of interaction differ from the Westphalian pattern of interstate relations? Finally, it will try to examine how the emerging European empire copes with the contending power centre of the United States. Along which lines are political and institutional loyalties split in Europe? And how is the competition between the EU and the United States being handled?

As in of previous chapters the complex reality will be reduced to two contrasting and somewhat simplistic models and scenarios. I am perfectly aware that the legal principle of sovereignty was never fully observed in practice. (In fact, some authors argue that 'autonomy' rather than 'sovereignty' was the principle codified by the Peace of Westphalia.)[5] Westphalian politics were not always about hegemony, because some countries could still opt for multilateralism or neutrality at various stages of the Westphalian era. Indeed there are various, often conflicting interpretations of medieval history, and some of these interpretations hardly fit my neo-medieval description of present-day Europe. That said, the aim of this book is to show the unique features of the emerging Euro-polity and I would rather overemphasize than blur the existing contrasts between the two major paradigms.

One more qualification is due at the beginning of this chapter. Unlike in the fields of democracy and economics, the impact of enlargement on European foreign and security affairs is quite straightforward. There is no evidence to suggest that new members are willing or able to enhance the Westphalian scenario. The new member states are all pro-American and not very eager to engage in security projects that are purely European. This is not to deny that in the past new members have proved quite willing to adjust their foreign policies to the demands of the Union. For instance, Sweden, Austria, and Finland became active players in the CFSP field despite their initial preference for political non-alignment and neutrality.[6] Moreover, a pro-American stance has not prevented Great Britain from being one of the motors behind the ESDP project.[7] But the medieval scenario does not imply the abandonment of the CFSP/ESDP project: it only envisages a continuous existence of multiple centres of authority in this field. All this, however, has implications for the design and structure of the chapter, because the straightforward impact of enlargement in this particular field leaves me without a dilemma or puzzle to solve. So I will try to comprehend how the neo-medieval international system works in present-day Europe. The position of new member states is thus moved to the background. Of course, I will illustrate how enlargement reinforces the neo-medieval scenario, but I will not try to convince the reader of something that is quite obvious.

The EU as an international actor

A typical Westphalian state is clearly a different type of international actor than the current EU. To qualify as a state, the political actor in question must have clear and fixed borders and a central government in charge, first and foremost, of the military and police forces. The Westphalian state is premised on the absolute notion of sovereignty which emphasizes internal hierarchy and territorial demarcation.[8] The EU is not a fully sovereign actor within its own territory, and this territory is constantly in flux due to successive waves of enlargement. The EU also lacks other basic characteristics of a state in this field. Most notably it is not the prime actor in charge of defence of its territory. In fact, it has no military capability to do the job. Its nascent military forces are destined to perform small peacekeeping operations rather than territorial defence. And unlike a typical Westphalian state, the Union basically relies on civilian means to promote its international objectives. These international objectives also differ from the typical objectives of Westphalian states. The CFSP is not about securing the international balance of power and repelling foreign aggression. The CFSP is largely about identifying a common position for member states on certain issues—positions that often amount to the lowest common denominator. Of course, the Union is not a powerless international actor and we have seen many times that the Union's 'soft power' can be applied in a quite assertive manner.[9] However, the Union has always shown more interest in exporting its goods, laws, and norms than in imposing its direct rule on the external environment. In this sense it also differs from Westphalian states, especially those in existence after the eighteenth century.

It is rather easy to show that the enlarged EU does not look and behave like a state in the foreign policy field. But does this mean that it looks and acts like a medieval empire? In my view, the answer is positive, despite all problems and qualifications. As was the case in medieval Europe, the EU's borders are soft and in flux. The distinction between EU members and non-members is increasingly blurred and is being replaced by a typical neo-medieval cleavage between Europe's centre(s) and periphery.[10] As in medieval Europe, we see a multiplicity of various military and police institutions that are not governed by a single European centre. In fact, most of these institutions have members from non-EU countries and the Union as such can hardly shape them.[11] Like all empires the Union is more preoccupied with maintaining its internal cohesion than in solving external problems on the ground. The rulers of the Union, like medieval rulers, sometimes resort to violence, but like them they prefer to rely on civilian rather than military means and their imperial politics being justified in normative rather than power terms.

Table 6.1 shows what the Union should look like to resemble either the Westphalian or the neo-medieval model. The reality of today is closer to the latter model, but let me spell out my argument in more depth.

Let us start with the issue of borders, because borders are crucial to any foreign policy analysis. As Christopher Hill put it: 'The word "foreign" originally referred to that which is "outside," and where there is an outside there must not only be an inside but also a line of demarcation between the two.'[12] In medieval Europe power was not territorially bound and the geographical bases of each unit were almost as ill-defined as the political bases for government and administration.[13] In fact, borders as we know them did not exist. Instead of clear, sharp, and sealed lines on the ground, we had porous and vaguely defined border zones called *limes* or *marches*. The Treaties of Westphalia made rulers sovereign on a given territory and the exercise of this sovereignty required sharp and clear borders. Westphalian states thus became 'bordered power-containers', to use Anthony Giddens' expression.[14] The monopoly of violence within states' borders was recognized, but states were supposed to refrain from intervention in other states' 'internal affairs'. Since there were no sharp and clear borders in medieval Europe, internal and external war could not be clearly distinguished. Armies fought warlords, bandits, and rebels as well as other recognizable centres of power.[15] In the post-Westphalian era wars between states became the essence of security policy, while fighting bandits and rebels became a largely 'domestic' matter.

Table 6.1. The EU as an international actor

Major features	Neo-Westphalian state	Neo-medieval empire
Type of borders	Hard and fixed border lines	Soft border zones in flux
Institutional structure	Single European army and police governed from one centre	Multiplicity of various overlapping military and police institutions
Policy aims	Defence against external aggression and maintaining the balance of power	Diffusion of internal conflicts and pacification of the external environment
Policy means	Military–civilian	Civilian–military
Legitimizing strategies	Might makes right	Our norms are right

Progressive globalization has undermined states' capacities to maintain discrete political, cultural, and especially economic space within their administrative boundaries. Moreover, modern weapons technology has made the traditional concept of territorial defence largely obsolete. And yet, a central, hierarchical, and territorially bounded government is still in charge of modern states' foreign and security policies.[16] The situation is all the more complex when we consider the EU. Here we have external boundaries of member states, some of which serve also as the external boundaries of the Union. The internal boundaries are being partially abolished, especially in the economic field, but remain most crucial as demarcation lines of political order and cultural identity. Their military function is quite peculiar. There are no soldiers stationed to defend the internal boundaries of EU member states, but member states still have their own national territorial defence structures. Moreover, co-operation between national armies across internal borders is hardly ever a matter for the Union to provide and is always subject to the member states' approval.

The external boundaries of the Union are said to be hard, but this is often more a matter of rhetoric than reality.[17] Since the fall of the Soviet system, the hard and fixed border dividing the two parts of Europe is no longer there and one can hardly envisage a return to the *status quo ante* through the progressive implementation of the Schengen accords. Besides, one can hardly seal borders that are in flux due to successive waves of enlargement. Moreover, the Union exports its governance to neighbouring states thus further blurring the distinction between insiders and outsiders. (Obviously, borders are even more blurred when we look at relations between individual EU members.) In fact, it is difficult to establish what is foreign policy and what domestic policy within the EU. Enlargement is one of those crucial policy fields that shows the difficulty in applying the inside/outside dichotomy in the case of the Union. In short, EU borders resemble more a medieval than a Westphalian pattern. The same can be said about the Union's institutional structure for what is still called 'foreign' and security policy.

Medieval Europe was a patchwork of various quasi-sovereignties and overlapping hierarchies whose powers were defined in complicated contracts and oaths. Contemporary experts also talk about quasi-sovereignties and overlapping hierarchies within the EU. The EU is said to represent a multilayered polity that is constantly 'pooling' and 'mixing' sovereignty.[18] Its foreign and security policy is formed and executed at various governmental levels and within distinct legal pillars.[19] We do not have a central, hierarchical government of the EU but a kind of 'network governance' in which a variety of economic and political agents (both 'public' and 'private') interact in a relatively unstructured manner.[20] As Christopher Hill put it:

The EU's foreign policy system is not one of government because there is no consistent and comprehensive pattern of decision-making—one can never be sure from where the next decision is going to come. But its policy-making culture (for that is what 'governance' means, if anything) is certainly multilevel and mixed actor in character.[21]

Enlargement has obviously made it more difficult for the Union to acquire a centrally governed, let alone a single, foreign policy. The number of members has nearly doubled and the new members have quite different if not divergent international preoccupations and priorities. Of course, the Union's external economic policies are run in a more centralized manner, but even here the EU's sovereignty is constrained by its cumbersome decision-making system and the residual powers of the member states.[22]

Various empirical studies have shown how these overlapping and quasi-sovereign centres of power function in the present-day EU. For instance, Magnus Ekengren has looked at the way Sweden executed its six-month presidency of the EU in the first half of 2001. He discovered that the Swedish government functioned as an inter-European link between various levels of EU governance. Sweden tried to enhance its national goals through the EU presidency, but was embedded in the European multi-layered reality in which many different actors exercise pressure and demand action. As a result the Swedish 'national representation' to a large extent functioned as a 'co-administration' of the Union's own policy together with the EU bureaucracy in Brussels.[23]

The lack of centralized government is even more striking when we examine the variety of institutional modes of engagement by individual EU members in military operations. They range from unilateral military interventions by Britain or France to various forms of multilateral interventions with little input of the EU as such. Even the unprecedented 2003 EU intervention in the eastern Congo was under UN auspices and most of the EU soldiers came from one country, France.[24] Most military deployments by EU members have been headed by NATO and functioned under American command. When NATO failed to respond to a crisis on Europe's borders, like the 1997 collapse of order in Albania, the EU was unable to get its act together and the intervention was orchestrated and executed by practically one member state, Italy.[25] Enlargement is not likely to make the situation any more straightforward because the new members do not want to see the Union in charge of their diplomacy and defence.[26] In fact, they see NATO as the most important security organization in Europe, a position shared by the majority of the old EU member states.

The basic foreign policy aims of the EU are also closer to the medieval than the Westphalian pattern. The complexity of various institutional and territorial arrangements in the Middle Ages made it difficult to pursue any straightforward policy agenda. There was no equivalent to *raison d'état* or national interest in the Middle Ages. A similar situation exists in Europe today. The Union has its institutions but it is missing a sense of purpose. As Barry Buzan put it:

No consensus exists about what the Community [EU] should be doing, how it should be doing it, or what it should, as an evolving political entity, be striving to become. With states, we should expect to find a clearer sense of both purpose and form, a distinctive idea of some sort which lies at the heart of the state's political identity.[27]

In December 2003 the Union adopted its own 'European Security Strategy', but its vague and open-ended phrases only confirmed how difficult it is for the Union to spell out its own equivalent of *raison d'état*.[28] Commenting on the document, François Heisbourg concluded:

The EU cannot have a proper security strategy as long as decisions on the use of force rest in the hands of its member governments. The ESS [European Security Strategy] can capture at any given moment what appears to unite the EU25 in analytical and policy terms. But the security strategy does not emanate from a fully fledged strategic actor that can wield force on its own account.[29]

When we try to establish policy aims by looking at states' practice we see that defence against foreign aggression and maintenance of the balance of power were the key preoccupations in the Westphalian era. This is quite understandable. Since borders were fixed they had to be defended and the most effective way of preventing foreign invasion was to assure a balance of power between states and coalitions of states. In a medieval Europe without clear borders such policies and objectives made no sense. Stability, understood in a broader regional context, was more important, and diffusion of various internal conflicts within the empire was crucial for the well-being of the existing centres. In this sense, the Union is very similar. Although clear borders are still in place between EU members, they no longer have divisions of soldiers lined up along them ready to repel possible aggression. This does not mean that individual EU members have identical foreign policy aims. In fact addressing these differences in purpose and aims became the major preoccupation of the CFSP framework, and this has arguably been at the expense of the Union's ability to address external problems as such. For instance, those who criticized the EU's inability to orchestrate a sound policy towards Bosnia have often been reminded that unlike 1914 the Europeans did not go into war over Sarajevo a century later.[30] In other words, the CFSP framework of cooperation has become the important centre of debating, bargaining, and compromising on national policies of member states. It has become a platform where these various policies meet and part. Putting those laboriously elaborated common European positions into action is another matter. As Knud-Erik Jørgensen observed:

Many observers seem to take for granted that the EPC/CFSP exists solely to meet external challenges. Yet, when we move our attention from 'outside' to the 'inside' effects of ECP/CFSP, we see that there are legitimate reasons to doubt that assumption.... The CFSP may be less successful in solving problems outside the EU, it has been very successful as a shock-absorbing mechanism—protecting outside conflicts from causing problems internally.[31]

The recent accession of many countries with different policy agendas will press the CFSP to devote even more time and energy to the diffusion of internal conflicts with little space for the traditional Westphalian agenda. At the same time, the fuzzy character of the Union's new external borders will make the Union more exposed to external shocks, especially in the near abroad. The Union therefore has a vested interest in preserving peace and stability in broader European region. This is why the new waves of enlargement are envisaged with ever greater geostrategic than economic rationale. It is also why the EU invests its money and extends its system of governance onto unstable countries in Eastern Europe, the Balkans, and the Maghreb. Unlike Westphalian states, the Union does not send its soldiers to defend external borders and contain the enemy. The Union sends soldiers to enforce and keep internal peace in neighbouring states and tries to embrace them through a policy of conditional help and enlargement. In this sense the Union also resembles a medieval empire. A typical Westphalian state would be content with a policy of balancing and military containment.

This brings me to the issue of policy means. There was a great deal of predatory behaviour in medieval Europe, and there is no point in denying it. However, it would be wrong to assume that military means were the preferred tool of 'foreign' policy at the time. Medieval rulers preferred to use civilian means in pursuing their European objectives. For instance, the Habsburgs augmented their territories chiefly through marriage and inheritance. Other actors, especially major cities, pursued their objectives through trade. The Papacy relied on the Church's spiritual 'power' and well-organized taxation. Armed forces were used rather reluctantly in medieval Europe, because as shown by Paul Kennedy, they were not predictable and reliable instruments: 'Ragtag troops, potentially disloyal mercenaries, inadequate supplies, transport problems, unstandardized weapons, were the despair of most commanders. Even when sufficient monies were allocated to military purposes, corruption and waste took their toll.'[32]

According to Kennedy, 'war waging' was intimately connected with the birth of the 'nation state'.[33] The statistics assembled by K. J. Holsti confirm this claim: between the Treaty of Westphalia and the final defeat of Napoleon in 1814, there were fifty-eight wars in Europe, or one every 2.9 years.[34] All this suggests that the Union's preference for civilian rather than military means confirms its resemblance to the medieval rather than the Westphalian model. Although the Union has now acquired some rudimentary military capability its preferred (and most powerful) foreign policy tools are still civilian and range from preferential trade agreements and financial aid to institutional dialogue, and export of rules and governance models, to EU accession.[35]

The way the Union legitimizes its policies is also more medieval than Westphalian. Unlike Westphalian states, the Union does not argue that 'might is right', but tries to convince other actors that its norms and values are universal and superior and as such ought to be promoted abroad. The difference between the medieval and the Westphalian legitimizing principle was well described by Charles W. Kegley and Gregory A. Raymond:

Having made glorification of the state acceptable, Westphalia paved the way for the belief that 'the end justifies means' and 'might makes right' that were to later rationalize the use of war as a tool of foreign policy. What mattered was the expedient pursuit of egocentric interest, not lofty ideals, absolute moral values, or unbending religious principles. Realism substituted *raison d'état* for morality, secularized international affairs, and pushed it outside the realm of religion. *Raison d'état* and the doctrine of the balance of power were deeply offensive to the universalist tradition founded on the primacy of moral law since they cut foreign policy loose from all ethical moorings.[36]

Thus the medieval preoccupation with the question whether a war is just or unjust was no longer there in the post-Westphalian era, and with this all moral constraints in conducting foreign policies disappeared.

And a plethora of 'Westphalian' analysts, from Bodin and Hobbes to Kissinger and Waltz, strongly argued that moral rules do not apply to states.[37] The EU's insistence on the promotion of human rights, democracy, and social values in its foreign policy is obviously at odds with the Westphalian rationale. The Union's normative language is secular and not religious, and in this sense the parallel with the Middle Ages does not apply. Nevertheless, the Union, like medieval actors, tries to justify its policies in terms of values and norms and not in terms of power calculations.[38] Moreover, the Union does not seek any exemptions from the values and norms it preaches. Its simple message to other countries in the region is: follow our successful example of peaceful coexistence based on economic integration and eventually join the club. Increasingly even some Asian and Latin American countries are encouraged to follow the European model of integration and in return are being offered material incentives in terms of market access, legal and administrative expertise, and financial help.[39]

In summary, although the Union is gradually acquiring some of the typical diplomatic and even military instruments of a Westphalian state it does not really look like and behave as such. The recent enlargement has made the Westphalian scenario even less likely despite the ever more ambitious ESDP project. The ESDP will add another institutional layer to the governance system in this particular field, and only reinforce the neo-medieval setting in Europe.[40]

The emerging international system in Europe

The previous section showed the evolving nature of the Union as an international actor, but it has also revealed the dynamics by which EU member states are changing and progressively developing a different kind of mutual relationship with each other.[41] These states are no longer the sole actors in Europe, the distinction between domestic and international affairs is further blurred, and institutionalized forms of collective bargaining are becoming more crucial than the traditional balance-of-power politics.[42] Does this mean that a new international system is on the rise in Europe, and if so, what are its major features? Are we witnessing the end of the Westphalian international syndrome and do the new types of interstate relations resemble medieval Europe?

There is general agreement among specialists in the field of international relations that the emergence of sovereign, territorial states following the Peace of Westphalia largely determined the nature of the international system in Europe. Medieval Europe was not divided into separate states with clear borders; it was organized horizontally according to function.[43] Empires had no fixed geographic limits and the form and scope of their political control varied.[44] But the Peace of Westphalia sanctioned the division of Europe into territorial states and laid down two basic principles determining their mutual relations: the principles of equality and sovereignty of states.[45] From then on states were recognized as the key international actors that were entitled to exercise absolute power within their borders without external interference. The superior rights of two universal entities, the Papacy and the empire, were no longer accepted.[46]

Of course, in empirical terms states were hardly equal, and sovereignty was never absolute even in the case of the most powerful actors.[47] Nevertheless, the new normative arrangement had profound implications for the structure of the system as such and the behaviour of individual actors. A system of sovereign and formally equal states could not but be anarchic in the sense that no power could formally impose any solutions on individual states. The system was also geared to war and conflict. As Kenneth Waltz put it: 'With many sovereign states, with no system of law enforceable among them, with each state judging its grievances and ambitions according to the dictates of its own reason or desire—conflict, sometimes leading to war, is bound to occur.'[48] The key ways of avoiding the hegemony of the strongest states have been self-help and balance-of-power politics. Inviolability of borders and territorial defence became the greatest preoccupation. States formed alliances with each other in search of security, but they were often unable to prevent conflicts over real or imagined imbalances.

Throughout modern history there were numerous attempts to constrain the damaging effects of this mechanism through agreements on certain universal principles of morality and government. In the aftermath of the Napoleonic wars, for instance, the so-called 'Concert system' sought to establish equilibrium of power through the redistribution of people and territories and through a mechanism of regular meetings between great powers.[49] In the aftermath of the Second World War, the UN system also represented an effort to introduce a mechanism for solving international disputes by peaceful means and according to some clearly defined legal criteria. However, the two Westphalian principles were never questioned. States were still regarded as being equal and sovereign.[50]

The Westphalian principles were seriously compromised, however, in the course of European integration. The introduction of the principle of 'qualified majority voting' (based on a system of 'weighted' votes), and the granting of certain 'binding' powers to the ECJ implied that states could no longer be regarded as the sole, equal, and totally sovereign centre of power within their own borders.[51] The system subsequently became less anarchic, and less geared to balancing and self-help. Member states still try to pursue their individual and often selfish visions of national interest, but they usually utilize the EU institutional framework to bargain over their differences. (Although many other factors have also been identified as contributing to this change and the EU is only one among many institutional platforms used by European states[52]). Enlargement is likely to give another boost to this trend, because it will further erode the principle of territoriality and introduce more layers of sovereignty. This would make it virtually impossible for EU member states to act as typical Westphalian states, let alone practise Westphalian power politics à la Metternich and Bismarck. In a Europe resembling a neo-medieval empire, relations between post-Westphalian states simply cannot resemble the interstate pattern that we know from 1648. Table 6.2 shows how the future European system is likely to differ from the past.

Most features of this emerging international system have been described already, but let me underline some major points. The anarchical system has already been constrained by the coordination of member states' external economic relations in the early years of European integration. The Coal and Steel Community was in fact a major step away from the Westphalian prototype because the members of the Community were no longer free to make sovereign decisions in the field crucial for their readiness to fight wars. The 1957 Treaty of Rome created a common trade policy and gave the Community the power to initiate association agreements between the EC and third countries and to conclude international treaties. Setting up the European Political Cooperation project in the late 1970s represented an extension of common efforts directly into the field of 'high politics'. Since the 1992 Maastricht Treaty CFSP had become an EU objective, and since the late 1990s there is even a Common European Security and Defence Policy. The CFSP/ESDP project is intergovernmental, which means that member states remain principal foreign policy actors. But as we said, the CFSP/ESDP became an important centre of foreign policy and defence coordination at odds with the Westphalian logic of anarchy. Foreign and security policies of the member states are now firmly geared to the CFSP/ESDP governance centre even though this centre remains relatively weak. (One can argue that the Economic and Financial Committee (ECOFIN) became a similar centre for interstate coordination focusing on monetary policies.)

Table 6.2. Two types of international system in Europe

Westphalian international system	Neo-medieval international system
The system is basically anarchic without a clear power centre	The system is geared towards the empire's power centre(s), however weak and dispersed
All states are formally equal and their authority over a certain territory is absolute	States have formally unequal participatory rights in various functional fields and their authority over a certain territory is shared
Non-intervention in internal affairs of other states is the basic principle of interstate order	Intervention is recognized as legitimate either in support of certain moral norms (human rights, for instance) or in order to enforce compliance with agreed laws
National governments are prime international actors with little input other actors in the decision-making system	Various national, supranational, regional, and local governments participate in the decision-making system and their access varies depending on the functional field
Balancing, bandwagoning, and ganging up over territorial gains and spheres of political influence is the essence of interstate politics	Collective bargaining over laws, procedures, and the empire's institutional structure is the essence of interstate politics
Interests are basically about national security and are considered as given or even eternal	Interests are essentially matters of policy preference and burden sharing and change depending on political affiliations and ideological fashions
Conflicts are primarily about borders and jurisdiction over them	Conflicts are primarily about exclusion from the core and abuse of agreed procedures
States provide for their own security through a system of territorial defence and military forms of deterrence	Security within a broader empire is sought through the process of economic integration and 'soft' conflict prevention

It is obvious that EU member states no longer enjoy absolute sovereignty on their territory. It is less obvious whether their formal rights are still equal. Uniformity of rights and duties of all members was the declared principle of European integration from the early days. However, each time the Council of Ministers decides by qualified majority, the member states' representatives are provided with unequal numbers of weighted votes.[53] Various opt-outs negotiated in the field of monetary integration, justice and home affairs, and common defence also introduce an element of inequality. For instance, the EMU chapter of the EC Treaty provides for only partial participation in decision-making of member states who do not adopt the single currency. Enlargement makes the situation even more complex because the number of countries outside the 'Euro group', for instance, is now larger than that of the 'ins'. And it is far from being clear how transitional the various 'transitional' arrangements imposed on the new members will be, even with regard to the four basic economic freedoms. Finally, in anticipation of enlargement, the Treaty of Nice has allowed for so-called 'enhanced cooperation' initiatives to be launched by eight member states or more. This is likely to introduce even further differentiation in the legal status of individual members. In fact, the legal and institutional discourse in the Union has changed dramatically over the past few years from one of uniformity and harmonization to one of flexibility and differentiation.[54] Enlargement was clearly the major factor behind this change.

With growing differentiation in the legal status there has also been more assertive intervention in the internal affairs of member states. Since the Amsterdam Treaty the Union has the right to intervene not only if a member state violates its vast body of economic and administrative *acquis*, but also if it does not comply with the principles of democracy, human rights, and the rule of law proclaimed in Article 6(1) EU. The intrusive and open-ended nature of this intervention became clear in 2000 when Jörg Haider's FPÖ extremist party became part of the Austrian government and the EU decided to 'punish' Austria.[55] The Union does not have provisions for intervening in member states' foreign and defence policies, but these are provided by the Treaty on Conventional Forces in Europe (the CFE Treaty). Parties to this treaty have to report the location of their heavy weapons and allow their inspection. Under this treaty more than 50,000 items of heavy military equipment—artillery, helicopters, tanks, and so on—have been destroyed and the possession of the remaining arsenal has been limited and subject to verification.[56]

In sum, we have a system in which member states' budgets, administrative regulations, judicial decisions, and even the size of their military forces is subject to European scrutiny and possibly intervention. In this environment, to use Robert Cooper's expression, 'security, which was once based on walls, is now based on openness and transparency and mutual vulnerability'.[57] Of course, transparency and openness are relative rather than absolute concepts, and conflicts between EU members have not disappeared. But these conflicts are primarily about exclusion from the core and abuse of agreed procedures rather than about borders.

Both old and new EU members fear that cheating by other members will put them in a disadvantageous position. They fear, above all, losing control of decisions affecting their interests. Individual member states might opt out from certain fields of integration, but they still want a seat at the table when matters affecting their interests are being discussed and decided. However, inequality is an unavoidable result of greater differentiation. With the creation of European power centres there must also come the feeling of exclusion and marginalization. Enlargement has underlined the conflict between the large and small member states of the Union, as was vividly illustrated by disagreements about the new voting procedures proposed by the draft of the European Constitution.[58] Above all, enlargement has recreated a centre–periphery syndrome. This is because the new members are excluded from certain fields of integration not by their free choice, but by the need to catch up with old members in terms of legal adjustment and economic development. They obviously fear that this 'second rank' peripheral status will last indefinitely.

Ever stronger calls for a 'hard core' or a 'two-speed' Europe only reinforce this fear. For instance, the German Foreign Minister, Joschka Fischer, envisaged the creation of a 'centre of gravity' within the Union; an 'avant-garde, the driving force for the completion of political integration'.[59] In a similar spirit the French President, Jacques Chirac, called for a 'group pionnier' to foster further integration.[60] Some old member states such as Denmark and Great Britain fear that the threat of a core group is aimed at prodding them towards a more cooperative stance with regard to agendas set in Paris, Berlin, and Brussels. The new members fear that such calls are about perpetuating the division of Europe between an affluent and stable core, and an impoverished and unstable periphery.[61] After all, the concept of 'core' goes hand-in-hand with the concept of 'periphery'. They are two sides of the same coin. If the contrast between the core and the periphery is not to be significant, there is no need to create a core. If everybody can join the core group, there is no reason for having it.

Proponents of the core do not want to become hostage to the least developed and the least pro-integration EU members. Opponents of the core want to be full members of a Europe of equals, even if this Europe of equals can only represent the lowest common denominator. That kind of conflict between Europe's periphery and centre is quite medieval, and it is likely to be central to the enlarged EU.[62] The way of coping with this conflict is again not likely to be Westphalian. Collective bargaining over laws, procedures, and the empire's institutional structure already form the essence of interstate politics within the EU. In present-day Europe, one can hardly imagine any EU member(s) going to war against another member(s) over territorial gains and spheres of influence. Nor is it very conceivable to see EU members going to war with each other over abused common laws and procedures, as once envisaged by Martin Feldstein.[63] Individual member states will obviously form various coalitions supporting or opposing certain projects, but there is nothing to suggest that these coalitions will be stable and comprehensive enough to resemble the Westphalian balance-of-power syndrome. The cleavages of national interests within the enlarged EU are simply too diversified and complex for the emergence of any firm pattern of coalitions between either large and small, the relatively poor and rich, Baltic and Mediterranean, Atlantic and Continental, or Euro-enthusiastic and Euro-sceptic member states.

The complexity of the current and future bargaining process can be understood even better when we consider that member states are not the only actors taking part in the European bargaining process. Various supranational, regional, and local centres of governance also participate in the decision-making system of the EU and their access to decisions varies depending on the functional field, political stature, and legal arrangements. Clearly, even Metternich and Bismarck would find it difficult to apply their Westphalian recipes for coping with this very complex and interdependent European setting. This setting is truly medieval and it requires medieval or neo-medieval solutions.[64] Moreover, one of the reasons for embarking on the integration project was to escape from the Westphalian syndrome. As Joschka Fischer put it in his famous speech at Humboldt University: 'The core of the concept of Europe after 1945 was and still is a rejection of the European balance of power principle and the hegemonic ambitions of individual states that had emerged following the Peace of Westphalia in 1648'.[65] Member states have developed a new pattern of relations with each other and enlargement is likely to reinforce this pattern.

Competing universalistic claims: EU versus United States

There can be little doubt that EU member states have avoided the Westphalian syndrome for several decades. The question is whether the current system is durable considering the major strategic shocks of the last fifteen years. Some scholars argue that the successful European integration project has benefitted from the peculiar geostrategic circumstances of the cold war. As John J. Mearscheimer argued: 'The demise of the Cold War order is likely to increase the chances that war and major crises will occur in Europe . . . . the basic nature of states is to focus on maximizing relative power, not on bolstering stability.'[66] Other scholars point to the implications of 9/11. Can a 'civilized' Europe survive in a largely 'uncivilized' world? The answer depends on many different factors both internal and external. However, if I had to choose only one major factor determining the future of Europe's interstate relations, I would point to the United States. This is because the United States is the most important player shaping the global environment. Whether this environment becomes more 'civilized' or 'bellicose' largely depends on American use and misuse of its enormous power. Moreover, the United States is a European power *sui generis*. The United States was not only the post-Second World War pacifier of relations between the major European states, but also one of the engines behind the project of European integration.[67] Much has changed over the last fifteen years in Europe, but it is safe to assume that European leaders still keep the United States in mind when making any foreign policy decision. This has profound implications for our analysis, because the American omnipotent presence in Europe and the world changes the nature of Westphalian politics. The global implications have been well grasped by G. John Ikenberry:

In the classic Westphalian world order, states hold a monopoly on the use of force in their own territory while order at the international level is maintained through the diffusion of power among states. Today's unipolar world turns the Westphalian image on its head. The United States possesses a near-monopoly on the use of force internationally; on the domestic level, meanwhile the institutions and behaviors of states are increasingly open to global—that is, American—scrutiny. Since September 11, the Bush administration's assertion of 'contingent sovereignty' and the right of preemption have made this transformation abundantly clear.[68]

The implications of the American presence for Europe are equally profound, and they again point to the medieval setting. In the Middle Ages the highly fragmented and decentralized network of socio-political relationships was held together by the two competing universalistic claims of the Church and the Empire.[69] The former was ecclesiastical and the latter secular, but both were backed by vast institutional structures, legal arrangements, and cultural appeals. The EU may well resemble a medieval empire, as we argued, but the United States certainly does not resemble the medieval Church despite its strong moralist rhetoric.[70] However, the point here is not to argue that the EU and the United States resemble two chief medieval powers, but that Europe is confronted with two actors having competing claims to supremacy, however disguised. Both the EU and the United States would like to shape the international strategies, institutions, and policies of European states in various functional fields from defence to commerce and culture. (American efforts to shape purely 'domestic' affairs in EU member states are not discussed here.)[71]

157

This is most visible in the security field. Here the United States has the greatest leverage and a developed organizational structure to exercise this leverage; that is, NATO.[72] When the Union made an effort to create its independent defence structure following the St. Malo Agreement between Britain and France, the United States' reaction was to accuse Europeans of duplication, discrimination, and decoupling.[73] When the EU proved undeterred and continued its Rapid Reaction Force project, the United States responded by its own 'duplicating' move: a NATO Rapid Reaction Force consisting of a 9,000 strong combat-ready Response Force, able to be deployed anywhere and to reach 21,000 by 2006. This obviously put the European defence project under pressure and confronted EU member states with a double loyalty dilemma (in financial, organizational, and political terms). After all, NATO is seen by its European members as the most crucial European security pillar and a device to assure American involvement on the old continent.

But the United States does not only try to influence European external policies in the field of defence. It also tries to shape the commercial policies of European states either through formal EU–American dialogue (read bargaining) or through informal bilateral channels with individual EU members.[74] In the field of trade the EU is a more equal and coherent actor than in the security field. Nevertheless, the American economy remains an important if not the most important reference point for economic decisions made in the EU.[75] There is also no doubt that both the EU and the United States compete as international culture settlers and moral champions.[76]

In recent years there has been an unprecedented proliferation of literature discussing an alleged or apparent crisis in transatlantic relations. Most of this literature talks about Europe versus the United States and depicts the conflict in global terms. However, Europe has always been the American 'playing field' and various European states have regularly played in American rather than EU shirts, depending on the issue, the ruling governing party, and the circumstances of the day.[77] Quite often these are 'friendly matches' in a sense that divergence of views is not dramatic and the battle is relatively mild. But sometimes the division lines are sharp and both the United States and the EU play foul. This was most vivid in 2003 on the eve of the American-led invasion of Iraq when the Bush administration asked individual EU members (and prospective members) to declare their stance on a case that was largely based on manufactured intelligence reports.[78] The EU was unable to stand up to this challenge and left some of its largest members such as Germany and France battling the American position on their own. (The unanimous support for the United States of all new (by now) East European EU members has been discussed earlier.)

The motivations of those Europeans who side with the United States rather than the EU are complex and subject to change. Countries such as Britain, Ireland, Italy, and Poland have special historical and cultural ties with the United States. These ties often go hand-in-hand with more intense economic relations and special security arrangements. Power considerations seem, however, most crucial. The point is not that all countries naturally fear American 'hegemony', but that they see certain advantages in siding with the United States. Even the French political elite seem to believe that American military engagement in Europe offers a more sound security base than a nascent ESDP.[79] Despite all the problems, not one European country has sought to leave NATO since 1989, and many have queued up to join. Moreover, in open defiance of the CFSP/ESDP framework, France together with 'federalist' Germany is an active member of the Quint, a secretive consultation body consisting of the four largest European states plus the United States.[80] The most probable explanation of the French and German positions here is that they find the Quint a more useful and efficient body than a loose and 'overcrowded' cooperation framework such as the CFSP.

Similar reasoning extends to other international fields. A large part of the British, but also the Dutch and probably even the French and German, economic elite is not necessarily convinced that the EU regulatory model is superior to the American one.[81] A large part of the Irish, the Portuguese, and the Polish elite has more problems with the absence of God in EU policy than with the presence of God in American policy. And there are always those Europeans who would prefer to live under American domination than under the domination of a (large) European neighbour. This large neighbour is often Germany, but for Slovenia, for instance, the large neighbour viewed with suspicion is Italy.[82]

Power considerations are also important for opting for the EU, however. Even such a close American ally as Great Britain supports a common European defence project largely because it finds total dependence on the Unites States in this field to be unwise.[83] Pro-American Eastern European post-Communist states also support a common European endeavour because they know that when it comes to security they cannot totally defy geography. Economic arguments for opting for the EU framework are obvious to all EU members.[84] Last but not least, the cultural appeal of

Europe is still powerful, benefiting the EU whose own cultural appeal is rather mediocre.[85]

And so we have different countries in Europe practising a difficult balancing act between two distinct European powers, the EU and the United States. Even if they openly side with one power, they do not want to break with the other. Most countries try not to take any clear sides, and act as if both powers were complementary in both normative and political terms. There is some merit in their reasoning because despite all the recent geostrategic earthquakes, the United States and Europe have much in common and often share similar aims.[86] However, they also differ. To start with, the EU increasingly resembles a neo-medieval empire, while the United States is still a typical Westphalian state. When one looks at Table 6.1 it is obvious that the United States meets all the major characteristics of a Westphalian state from the type of borders to the institutional structure to the policy means and aims.[87]

In recent years more and more authors have begun to call the United States an empire.[88] However, they have in mind a global superstate resembling a nineteenth-century Great Britain.[89] But as underlined at the beginning of this book, there is a significant difference between a Westphalian and medieval type of empire. Concentration rather than dispersion of power and hierarchical order, and a tight military grip, characterize the former.

In fact, the EU and the United States exercise power politics in a different manner. The United States is prepared or even inclined to coerce other countries to obedience even in defiance of international institutions and law. Multilateralism, however inefficient, and UN legitimacy remains the Union's most favoured path.[90]

American and European perceptions and priorities also diverge, especially since 9/11.[91] The United States now views the world through the prism of the war on terror, while the EU views it through the prism of global commerce and diplomacy.[92] Washington is primarily concerned about rogue states, the EU about failed states.[93] The United States tries to export its own liberal and democratic values, while the EU exports its own successful model of regional integration.[94] In addition, there is always the question of burden sharing and leadership: the United States wants the allies to shoulder more burdens of its leadership while the EU wants its American ally to share more leadership.[95]

Differences concerning policy style or the order of priorities can certainly be bridged, as manifested by post-Second World War trans-Atlantic history. However, since the end of the cold war there is also a growing realization of the various structural asymmetries between the EU and the United States. These would be more difficult to bridge even through skilful statecraft and enlightened leadership (which now seems in short supply anyway).[96] Europeans will try to use the EU to constrain American power, and the Americans will try to resist that.[97] In this context, continuing support by the United States for the European integration project cannot be taken for granted. In fact, a growing body of literature suggests that the Bush administration is trying to split 'new' and 'old' Europe in order to fence off the possible European challenge and to marginalize supporters of the 'Gaullist' line in Europe.[98] In due time such a policy may result in a resurgence of the Westphalian pattern in European politics with balancing and ganging up over political spheres of influence replacing the current system of institutional bargaining over laws and procedures.[99] However, such a scenario is not inevitable. First of all, there is no evidence that the EU would be willing and able to challenge American global hegemony in any serious way. The EU is in a position to balance some American external economic policies and erode the international legitimacy of certain of the latter's security actions, but not much more.[100] Besides, some Europeans might come to the conclusion that the complex and uncertain medieval scenario requires more rather than less American involvement in European politics, even if that implies a considerable loss of European independence.

The United States for its part may also conclude that undermining the process of European integration will do more harm than good. A disintegrating Europe falling back upon Westphalian patterns would damage American commercial interests and would demand a greater American security engagement. In other words, a weak and divided Europe is likely to present more problems for the United States than a prosperous and integrated one. And we should also keep in mind that despite the challenge of international terrorism, the United States is still under the pressures of economic globalization, social modernization, and cultural interdependence. These latter pressures will demand from the United States more consensus-driven policies and the application of soft rather than hard power.[101] If so, we may see more convergence rather than divergence in the way the United States and EU engage in power politics, and the notion of liberal internationalism may once again bring together the two sides of the Atlantic.[102] The EU and the United States are both likely to seek loyalty from individual states in Europe, but there are various ways in which they can exercise their pressure and sort out their competing claims.

Conclusions

When in 1977 Hedley Bull speculated on a possible return to the medieval pattern of interstate politics he still considered such a prospect relatively unlikely.[103] This is because he saw too little regional integration of states and too little disintegration of states as such. For a medieval scenario to materialize, Bull also wanted to see more private international violence, further growth of transnational organizations, and the technological unification of the world. His scepticism is still justified in the global context despite the recent rise of private international violence in the form of terrorism and the ever greater spread of modern technologies to even the most remote corners of the world. Nevertheless, since the 1970s the situation in Europe has gradually developed according to the medieval scenario. Today we have in Europe the essence of the medieval politics identified by Bull, namely a complex 'system of overlapping authority and multiple loyalty'.[104] This system is held together by two universalistic powers, the EU and the United States; and the pacifying presence of these two powers largely explains why we have relatively little disorder in the post-medieval Europe of today.[105] Member states have not disintegrated, but integrated accepting significant erosion of their sovereignty in various fields. Member states have ceased fighting with each other about territorial acquisitions and have changed the ways of protecting their spheres of influence. Their present conflicts are primarily about exclusion from the European core and abuse of agreed procedures, and they are being sorted out through complex institutional bargaining over laws and procedures. Intervention in the internal affairs of member states is now accepted either in support of certain moral norms (human rights, for instance) or in order to enforce compliance with those agreed laws.

The Union as such has also evolved into a fully-fledged international actor, however peculiar. And it resembles more a medieval empire than a Westphalian superstate. The EU's borders are in constant flux and are soft rather than hard. The Union's prime international objective is not to defend these borders against foreign invasion, but to diffuse internal conflicts and to stabilize (or even pacify) the external environment through the export of laws and regulations, economic aid, and state-building efforts. There is no single European centre of government to handle foreign affairs and security. Instead we see a multiplicity of various overlapping military and police institutions with the emerging European army and police being only one of many institutional frameworks used by the member states. Here again, the role of the United States is most crucial, but diplomatic and security engagements in Europe take on many different forms depending on the circumstances of the day.

Enlargement has clearly reinforced the neo-medieval scenario. With so many new members the Union can hardly afford a single foreign and security policy. And the pro-American stance of new members makes sure that the 'medieval' duality of competing universalistic claims in Europe is not likely to disappear. Before enlargement one could speculate about getting away from a system of overlapping authority and multiple loyalties in European foreign affairs. Such speculations now seem futile.

Whether this new European medievalism can remain prosperous and stable depends on many internal and external factors. The EU is now in the process of re-examining the 'right' balance between deepening and widening and the temptation to create a European core is greater than ever, especially for disillusioned federalists. But as we argued, this may have destabilizing implications. The American use and misuse of its enormous power in Europe and elsewhere will also shape the future of the old continent. Were the United States to withdraw its support for the European integration project and try to divide individual EU members into a pro-French and a pro-American camp, this would have highly destabilizing implications.

The way the EU addresses problems of global violence will also determine Europe's fortunes. The EU's reliance on international law and multilateral diplomacy can only be partially effective (and it is sometimes altogether ineffective). This is why Robert Cooper's suggestion of applying 'double standards' seems quite tempting. As Cooper put it: 'Among ourselves, we keep the law, but when we are operating in the jungle, we must also use the laws of the jungle.'[106] The danger is, however, that the zone of law and the zone of jungle will become increasingly blurred. Today, terrorists can often be found in the EU's largest cities. Moreover, in a Europe with multiple identities and loyalties, it is not always easy to distinguish friends from foes. Certain heavy-handed policies applied after 9/11 have already transformed large sections of loyal and law-abiding European citizenry of Muslim origin into rebels or even terrorists.[107] Finding the right balance between principles and prudence in foreign and security policy will be the key to Europe's future in this field.

Conclusions: Implications of Neo-medievalism

The fall of Communism transformed Europe beyond recognition—and this could not but affect the integration project. The eastward enlargement was the Union's response to the ongoing rapid and fundamental changes. Maintaining peace and stability once again became the major preoccupation of European leaders. There were also important cultural and economic arguments for moving the EU's borders further east. However, the implications of eastern enlargement have only partly been grasped by policy-makers, public opinion, and even students of European integration. The statist paradigm remains dominant in European discourse, and the European constitution is seen as the key instrument in providing effective governance. In contrast, this book has tried to show that the enlarged Union resembles not a state but a neo-medieval empire, and one wonders whether such an empire can indeed benefit from a constitution. In referenda on the constitution held in 2005 many Europeans cast a negative vote. Some of them clearly contest the wisdom of the EU's (past and future) enlargements further south and east. Perhaps the more profound question is: what would be their reaction when confronted with the neo-medieval reality? Does a neo-medieval empire represent good or bad news for Europe and its people?

This concluding chapter identifies the implications of neo-medievalism for the Union's geostrategic position, its governance capacity, and its political legitimacy. The first issue is about the EU's fuzzy and ever moving borders. How does the evolution of territorial politics impact on the course of European integration? Does the EU's new geographic reach demand a new type of geopolitics? Can this empire survive any further enlargements and if so, where is the EU likely to end?

The second issue is about the efficiency of the neo-medieval system. How is order to be created and maintained in a highly complicated, differentiated, or even divided EU? Will the new empire become more effective by relying on a simple or complex governance structure? Is a neo-medieval Europe suited to postmodern modes of governance?

The third issue is about democracy, identity, and justice in the neo-medieval empire. The political legitimacy of any actor can hardly be only output driven. But how can this highly pluralistic empire generate consensus on what is seen as legitimate? Can the enlarged EU secure a minimum level of democratic participation and representation?

These are all very difficult questions that can often be addressed only in a normative (rather than empirical) manner. Nonetheless we need to start thinking about the various problems and opportunities created by the neo-medieval scenario and try to identify solutions for curbing the former and enhancing the latter. The assertion of neo-medievalism will have serious implications for the EU's institutions, political processes, and self-image. Major if not dramatic adjustments will be needed, and some of them will certainly be difficult and painful. In fact, some Europeans may well be scared by the prospect of a neo-medieval empire.

This chapter addresses those fears. The first challenge concerns the politics of enlargement. The 'imperial' Union is likely to enlarge ever further to keep its neighbours stable and friendly. However, this will stir up public resistance in individual member states and give populist politicians an opportunity to exploit protectionist and xenophobic sentiments across Europe. Further enlargements will also put extra pressure on Europe's cohesion and coordination mechanisms. In other words, keeping the prospect of further enlargements open can stabilize the external environment, but it can also destabilize the internal one. The Union will therefore need to perform a difficult balancing act. Further enlargements may take more time and involve more conditions. The Union will also have to learn to handle better protectionist instincts and cultural anxieties related to ever further enlargements. That said, further enlargements on strategic grounds can hardly be put on ice. Peace and security are the most basic prerequisites of any successful integration, and the policy of conditional inclusion of neighbours proved quite efficient in assuring that. In fact, the more backward and unstable the new neighbours are, the more urgency there is to embrace them.

Neo-medievalism will require major adjustments to the existing governance system, but the required changes are fortunately also in line with the demands of global competition. I would even go a step further and argue that governance is the field where the neo-medieval and postmodern paradigms meet, if not converge. Multilevel governance in concentric circles that relies on self-regulation and co-regulation rather than central steering and punishments can work well under the new circumstances. The Open Method of Coordination (OMC) is an interesting laboratory test for examining the viability of this 'plurilateral' governance system as applied to the neo-medieval EU.

The most difficult challenge will probably come from the field of democracy and identity. A pan-European cultural identity is likely to remain weak in neo-medieval Europe and traditional democratic institutions are unlikely to work as well as in the current nation states. This will create serious legitimacy problems even if the new governance system proves to be remarkably efficient. The aspect of citizens' participation in the neo-medieval setting is likely to be the most problematic, but there are also serious problems in assuring effective means of democratic control and accountability. Populism is the greatest threat in a Union unable to enjoy strong legitimacy, and the best way to cope with this populist threat is to enhance the capacity of citizens to contest European decisions in a democratic way.

I have no hesitation in concluding that Europe should embrace a neo-medieval EU. A neo-medieval empire would be in a good position to stabilize the external environment, manage the presence of overlapping structures of power, and facilitate the flow of goods, services, and people throughout the EU's borders. Of course, one can come to a different conclusion, but this book has tried to show that neo-medievalism is already the dominant pattern in the enlarged EU, one that it would be extremely hard to change. Let me first briefly recapitulate this argument.

What makes Europe neo-medieval

The admittance to the Union of post-Communist countries from Eastern Europe has always been seen as a formidable challenge with serious implications for the nature of European integration. This is why the idea was long resisted not only by politicians such as François Mitterrand, but also by analysts committed to the federalist project. The evidence presented by this book confirms many of these 'fears': the nature of the Union has changed dramatically with this enlargement and it is clear that electorates sense the gravity of this change. The book shows the unprecedented scope and form of diversity in the enlarged EU that is clearly reminiscent of medieval Europe. It shows that the policies of the new member states reinforce the medieval governance pattern. It also shows that the enlargement process as such has been implemented in a truly imperial fashion. I contrast this medieval paradigm with the only seriously spelled out alternative: Westphalian statism. (As shown in the introductory chapter, the mysterious 'unidentified political object' has never represented such a serious alternative.) The existing body of evidence leaves little doubt that the enlarged EU cannot become a Westphalian superstate. The Union is on its way to becoming a neo-medieval empire with soft borders in flux, cascading socio-economic discrepancies, multiple cultural identities, and a polycentric government. Some features of this model were present before the fall of the Berlin Wall, but enlargement represents a decisive step towards medievalism that prevents other possible solutions from emerging.

The first main reason for the emerging medievalism is the enormous increase in diversity prompted by the last wave of enlargement. This book compared in great depth the new member states with old ones, and also with other post-Communist countries. There is no doubt that over the past several years the new members have succeeded in reforming their economies and legal structures and are on their way to catching up with the wealthy democracies of Western Europe. That said, the new members from Eastern Europe do not (yet) look and act like the old members from Western Europe. The new members are still much poorer than the old ones and are unlikely to close this gap in wealth in less than three decades. Their democratic institutions are still relatively unstable and rather fragile. Their economic, legal, and administrative structures are undeveloped compared to those in the old members. New members also have their own distinct histories, societies, and cultures. For instance, in none of the Western European states is 'de-communisation' such a central political issue as it is in Eastern European states. Unlike Western Europe, Eastern Europe still has relatively few immigrants from Third World countries, but it is struggling to come to terms with its own diverse and often sizeable national minorities like Russians in Latvia and Estonia or Hungarians in Romania and Slovakia. New members also have different foreign and security preoccupations, especially vis-à-vis the United States and Russia.

The EU has thus become a much more diversified entity following this particular wave of enlargement. True, the map of unity and diversity in the enlarged EU is extremely complex, and does not simply correspond to the old East–West divide. Moreover, the division lines across the EU are constantly changing, with the enlargement process constituting an important factor inducing adaptation if not convergence. In the past, countries such as Portugal, Greece, Spain, Ireland, and even Finland also underwent significant modernization and adaptation after joining the European Communities/Union. That said, the current plurality of different forms of governance, legal structures, economic zones of transactions, and cultural identities is striking and bears a remarkable resemblance to the situation in medieval Europe. There can hardly be a greater contrast than the one between the Union of today and the classical Westphalian state, which is characterized by a low degree of economic, legal, and cultural divergence and a high degree of overlap between functional and territorial borders.

The second main reason for emerging medievalism is the impact of enlargement on the European system of governance. This system has already been under pressure because modernization and globalization could not be handled properly by a hierarchical and relatively rigid type of Westphalian governance. Enlargement has only served to accentuate this mismatch and the Union is now moving firmly in a medievalist direction. The book has tried to assess the impact of enlargement in three crucial fields of governance: economics, democracy, and foreign affairs. The neo-Westphalian and neo-medieval ideal types again served as benchmarks. In all three fields the evidence points to enlargement enhancing what we have identified as a neo-medieval mode of governance. The evidence shows that further liberalization and devolution aimed at stimulating growth is likely to be the Union's main response to economic discrepancies prompted by enlargement. The Westphalian solution amounting to centrally distributed help to poor countries is likely to be limited and aimed at promoting efficiency rather than convergence. This is not necessarily because the new member states are more neo-liberal than the old ones. However, flexibility and liberalization gives the new members comparative economic advantage, while the old members seem determined to prevent any major increase in the EU's central budget for redistribution.

Institutional differentiation through delegation, devolution, and decentralized experimentation is also likely to be the Union's response to growing competition from the United States, China, Japan, and India. This would imply abandoning or softening the Westphalian model of economic governance characterized by clear hierarchical institutional structure, rigid laws, and regular controls and penalties for disobedience. (Difficulties in the Euro zone also signal problems in relying on a hierarchical mode of economic governance.) When responding to economic instability outside the EU's borders the Union is also likely to abandon or water down the Westphalian policy of containment through hard borders for goods and labour. A major way of coping with this type of instability has been to export European laws and regulations to neighbours, leading to a gradual extension of European governance beyond the EU's official borders. Countries such as Bosnia and Kosovo are practically EU protectorates, and there is a long list of countries from Ukraine to Palestine which are following EU instructions on organizing economic governance.

In the field of democracy, enlargement also reinforces the neo-medieval pattern. The structure of democratic governance is likely to become increasingly multilevel and multicentred. The system will lack a clear allocation of competences and straightforward hierarchy. A single powerful centre of authority as exists in all Westphalian states is not going to emerge in the enlarged Union. Nor can we expect the European Parliament to be the main vehicle for democratic representation. Instead we are likely to see various non-majoritarian institutions dominating the weak European Parliament (but also the increasingly weak national parliaments). The public space in the enlarged EU is likely to remain fragmented and weak preventing the rise of a single and dominant European identity, ethos, and demos. Enlargement has further increased the plurality of civic cultures in the Union making it difficult to arrive at the fairly homogenous cultural pattern required by the Westphalian model of democratic governance.

In the field of foreign and security policy the neo-medieval pattern is also easy to detect. Foreign and security policy is largely in the hands of member states. They are not only helplessly divided on some crucial issues, but tend to use other than European frameworks for meeting international objectives. Not only NATO and the UN, but also various formal or informal coalitions of the willing represent the means of European foreign policy. The Westphalian-like bipartisan foreign policy run by the European centre is very weak because individual member states have a complex set of diplomatic relationships within and across EU borders and they pursue their security in a different manner depending on the case and circumstances. Enlargement has clearly reinforced the neo-medieval pattern because new members are sensitive about their sovereignty and have largely divergent foreign preoccupations.

The emerging international system in Europe also looks more medieval than Westphalian. The system is truly polycentric and split into multiple, overlapping arenas that are only loosely connected. Like in the Middle Ages the system is geared towards two major power centres. This time it is not the Empire and the Papacy, but the EU and the United States. Unlike the Westphalian system, the current system is not anarchic. Collective bargaining over laws, procedures, and the empire's institutional structure is the present essence of interstate politics. In the enlarged EU we are unlikely to see the typical Westphalian interstate politics of balancing and ganging up over territorial gains and spheres of influence. The principle that might is right is no longer seen as acceptable in European 'foreign' affairs. Instead the spread of freedom, law, democracy, and prosperity is used as a legitimizing device.[1]

This leads to the notion of empire. This book has shown that the Union is not just a loose amalgam of various political units linked merely by a variety of flexible arrangements. The Union is a distinct actor that exerts important pressure on its own members and the external environment. It increasingly looks and acts like an empire even though it is one of a peculiar type. European integration is largely about conflict resolution among diverse member states. Today not only various economic interests are mediated within the EU framework, but also individual countries' foreign and security policies. But the EU is not just about internal power diffusion, but also about external power projection with enlargement policy representing the most powerful tool for imposing political control on neighbours. This book has shown how the intrusive policy of conditionality has led post-Communist countries to adopt the EU's laws and institutions. The compliance of the candidate countries from Eastern Europe was largely voluntary, and based on incentives rather than punishments. Nevertheless, the scope and form of the EU's interference in the domestic affairs of candidate countries was enormous and backed by a vast asymmetry of power between the EU and the candidates. However, it would be wrong to confuse the Union with the empires of the last two centuries. The Union does not engage in military conquests, forced territorial annexations, and the colonial type of economic extraction. The Union is largely a civilian power enlarging its territory by consent and diplomatic bargaining. Although some poor countries, especially from the Third World, may find the Union's trade policies unduly discriminating, the Union is by and large seen as a vehicle of economic growth rather than economic exploitation. (In fact, the Union transfers large sums of money to the Third World and to its poor neighbours.) The policy of enlargement is clearly about extending the EU's influence over neighbours. However, at the end of the accession process these neighbours are offered access to the EU's decision-making instruments and resources.

Having described the origins and nature of the neo-medieval empire, the principal implications of this new European 'creature' should now be established. Does this new empire represent a curse or blessing for the old continent and its people? I will start with the geopolitical implications of the described development. My major finding is: the new empire is likely to enlarge further chiefly for strategic reasons. This will complicate European governance and stir up public resistance, but it will help the Union to maintain peace and security in Europe.

Integration through enlargement

The Union has enlarged several times prior to 2004. First the United Kingdom, Denmark, and Ireland joined the original six member states of the European Economic Community (EEC) in 1973. Greece joined in 1981 and Portugal and Spain in 1986. In 1995 Austria, Finland, and Sweden were admitted. German unification also moved EU borders further east. With each new enlargement there have been institutional and procedural changes to the EU system.[2] New members have brought their diverse cultures, political concerns, and legal procedures to the Union. Although scholars tend to emphasize functional progress in the European project (the so-called deepening) one can argue that widening through successive waves of enlargement was equally or even more crucial in shaping the integration process and the nature of the Union as such. This seems to be even truer when one considers the last wave of enlargement. The scope of diversity imported by the Union with this new wave of enlargement will clearly determine the kind of functional progress it is likely to make. As argued throughout successive chapters, the fit-all statist solutions would be inadequate in this much wider and more diversified Union.

The last wave of enlargement also seems to suggest that further enlargements on strategic grounds will follow. In other words, new states are likely to be admitted on geopolitical grounds despite their poor record in implementing the letter and spirit of the *acquis communautaire* and despite an ever greater public resistance in current member states. (This obviously would not apply were Norway, Switzerland, Iceland, or Lichtenstein to join the EU.)

All previous enlargements represented a formidable challenge to the Union's political, economic, and cultural cohesion. Nevertheless, these enlargements could still be seen as a marriage of convenience between like-minded and like-looking countries. The Iron Curtain made any further enlargements in the eastern direction impossible and the political, cultural, and poverty gaps separating Western Europe from the Middle East and the Maghreb made any further southern enlargements similarly inconceivable. Morocco's membership application to the European Communities was flatly rejected. Turkey was offered a vague associate membership status, but a fully-fledged Turkish membership had not been seriously considered before the eastward enlargement. Today the situation is very different. The eastern enlargement has challenged the principle that membership can only be offered to relatively rich, politically stable, and culturally postmodern (Western) European countries. Further enlargements are likely to be driven by crude geostrategic considerations and represent the European style of power politics described in Chapter 2.

In fact, only a few months after admitting ten new countries to the Union, Turkey was invited to start official accession negotiations, as was Croatia. It is expected that other former republics of Yugoslavia will soon follow the path of Slovenia and Croatia. Spectacular regime change in Ukraine and Georgia has prompted calls for embracing these countries too.[3] And if Ukraine is an EU member, why not under certain circumstances Moldova, Belarus, or even Russia?[4] Israel in many respects already resembles most advanced European states, and one day strategic reasons might emerge to make it a fully-fledged EU member, possibly together with Palestine and Jordan.[5] Even EU membership for North African countries is conceivable at present. Beirut is very close to Nicosia, and Lebanon is not only relatively rich, but also culturally close to Europe, France in particular. The wave of popular protests in 2005 aimed at reducing the Syrian influence and presence in Lebanon evoked a lot of sympathy across the entire EU.[6] (Even before this democratic awakening Lebanon was admitted to the Eurovision song contest.) Lebanon might be a special case in this region, but those who point to a striking poverty gap between the EU and North Africa should keep in mind that most of the new member states from Eastern Europe were even more backward before their EU accession process got off the ground. For instance, in the early 1990s only one Eastern European country, Hungary, had a higher GNP per capita than Algeria. Even Tunisia and Morocco seemed more advanced than Romania at the time. Today these North African countries frequently complain that EU investment and aid has since been diverted to Eastern Europe, condemning them to economic marginalization. And if radical Muslim politics are getting the upper hand in this region, is this not due to the failure of the EU to embrace economic development and democracy there? Would North African reformers not be more effective in promoting liberal values if their countries were offered the prospect of EU membership?

All this is not to say that Russia or Tunisia will (or should) soon become EU members. The group of current and future EU neighbours is extremely diversified, and only some of these neighbours will ever have the intention let alone the capability to meet the Union's tough economic and political entry conditions. That said, it seems plausible to argue that some further enlargements on largely strategic grounds are conceivable and even likely. To start with, the geostrategic environment of Europe has changed dramatically following the collapse of the Soviet empire, the wars in the Balkans, and the 9/11 terrorist attack on the United States. The Union has to respond to the mounting security, political, and economic threats resulting from persistent instability and conflict on the EU's borders and beyond. The idea that member states can continue to integrate their markets and institutions as if nothing dramatic has happened in the world over the last decade or so is simply naive. Without a viable policy to address these new threats the integration project will be in jeopardy, and the policy of conditional admittance to the Union has proved to be a powerful tool of stabilizing an external environment.

This brings us to another important reason for further enlargements on strategic grounds. Namely, the Union has no other equally effective foreign policy tool to shape its unstable external environment. In other words, it can hardly do without further enlargements. As mentioned in Chapter 2 alternative solutions to a fully-fledged EU membership for Central and Eastern European states were tried and failed in the early 1990s. Today, it is equally obvious that similar alternative solutions in the form of Strategic Partnerships or Neighbourhood Policy are inadequate to shape political and economic developments in the EU's unstable neighbours to the south and east. At the same time, the policy of conditional admission to the Union has clearly produced some 'wonders' not only in such countries as Poland or Hungary, but also in Romania, Bulgaria, Croatia, and Turkey. The last case is particularly illuminating. Although Turkey still has a long way to go in order to meet the entire package of EU entrance conditions, it has already made a number of historical concessions under the EU's insistence including abolition of the death penalty, the release of Kurdish parliamentarians imprisoned for their non-violent opinions, and the introduction of broadcasts in minority languages.[7] In other words, keeping the prospect of enlargement open provides the Union with effective international leverage. Many countries are willing to modify their behaviour in line with EU wishes in the hope of obtaining EU membership. Fixing its borders, on the other hand, will deprive the Union of part of its attraction and will demotivate or frustrate countries that are left out. This might be acceptable to some EU members, but not to those who happen to share borders with unstable and frustrated neighbours in Eastern Europe, the western Balkans, or the Mediterranean. This represents yet another reason for further enlargements on strategic grounds.

There is a certain path-dependency logic in the process of enlargement. Each enlargement brings the EU new neighbours and these new neighbours usually end up as candidates for EU accession. Two factors are at work here. One is the geopolitical concern of EU members exposed to instability outside EU borders. The other is the demonstration effect of the ever wider EU on its immediate neighbours. The case of Poland and Ukraine is very illustrative here. Poland's concerns about developments in Ukraine and its active engagement there is forcing the Union to adopt a much more inclusive attitude towards this unstable neighbour than most other EU member states would wish, especially those further west and south. Poland's former and present Presidents, Lech Walesa and Aleksander Kwasniewski, were present and active in Kiev during the 'Orange Revolution' and the latter delivered a passionate appeal for EU membership for Ukraine at the 2005 Davos Global Forum.[8] But Poland also serves as a model for reform-oriented politicians in Ukraine itself. Their reasoning is simple: if Poland can be a prosperous EU member why not Ukraine? These reformers would not expect their country to look like Germany or France, but post-Communist and culturally close Poland is another matter, and they want to follow Poland's European path.[9] The fact that these new EU neighbours are increasingly poor and unstable does not undermine but actually reinforces the pressure for further enlargement. This is because greater neighbourhood problems ask for greater commitments and more effective leverage, and the latter can only be provided by a conditional membership offer.

It is easy to see why the EU may be compelled to carry out further enlargements on strategic grounds. The question is: at what price? The negative implications of further enlargements are similar in nature to the ones associated with this last enlargement, but their scale is probably greater. For instance, if the Union were to admit only Turkey and Ukraine around 2015 this would add 125 million citizens (40 per cent) to the current number of citizens. But numbers seem less important than the nature of the diversity to be imported by the Union. Cultural diversity, understood in terms of both democratic orientations and religious patterns, will be particularly difficult to address. It is not only individual member states that find it increasingly difficult to handle the coexistence of different cultures within their borders; the Union itself is poorly equipped to address any possible manifestations of cultural conflicts.[10] But even if Europe were to avoid the 'black' scenario of the 'clash of civilizations' the increased cultural diversity is likely to make it even harder for the Union to acquire a minimum level of common European identity. And a certain degree of cultural identity is required for any political project to be seen as legitimate in the long term. Enlargement to countries that are evermore distant both culturally and politically is clearly resisted in most of the member states and undermines the legitimacy of the entire European project. In fact, there is ample evidence suggesting that the vote against the European Constitution was in part a vote against further EU enlargements, especially to Turkey.[11] One can go even further and argue that further enlargement would give extra ammunition to populist politicians exploiting the fear of other supposedly alien if not hostile cultures and cheap labour forces 'invading' the Union.

Managing interstate politics in the ever wider Union would also represent a challenge. With more new and poor members there would be a fresh incentive for some old and rich members to form a core of European decision-making. There is no reason to believe that the idea of creating a formal 'hard core', or a kind of *directoire* within the Union, is going to be any less divisive in the future than in the past. And there will also be a renewed challenge to the European mode of governance as increased diversity would demand new and innovative ways of stimulating economic growth, maintaining legal order, and assuring social cohesion.

These problems and challenges seem familiar to students of enlargement. All previous enlargements, especially the last one, have been opposed by some segments of the public and elite in member states. All previous enlargements have put pressure on European institutions and shaped the nature of European integration. And since the next envisaged waves of enlargement are about admitting to the Union even more 'poor', 'unstable', and 'premodern' countries than the previous enlargements, the challenge is proportionally greater. But the benefits of further enlargements on strategic grounds cannot be ignored either, especially if one considers the possible negative implications of not enlarging further. And there is little in the most recent history of Europe to suggest that the Union will have the comfort to think about the pros and cons of enlargement in purely theoretical terms. As Carl Bildt, a former prime minister of Sweden, put it in the aftermath of the French 'no' vote in the referendum on the European Constitution:

If Europe is seen as closing its door to Turkey, the Balkans and the Ukraine, it should know it is opening the door for other forces and risks creating instability on its very doorstep in the decades ahead. Different satellite arrangements, whatever glorious labels they are given, will do next to nothing to compensate as long as that door is closed.[12]

The Union is therefore unlikely to try to close its doors—but it will make the accession process longer and it will fill it with an ever longer list of membership conditions. The entrance to the Union of any new countries is likely to be partial, too, as was already the case with the last wave of enlargement. There are likely to be even more transitional arrangements and open-ended 'safeguard' clauses further blurring the distinction between members and non-members. As the European system of governance becomes less hierarchical and more benign, the implementation of the accession process is likely to be more fuzzy and ambivalent. The European Commission, in particular, might no longer be in a position to handle future enlargements in a largely top-down technocratic manner. This is not necessarily because its formal powers are likely to be weaker, but because further enlargements would be more sensitive in electoral terms and would therefore require more political intervention from member states. This brings us to the major issue related to further enlargements. Whether any further enlargements on strategic grounds will represent a failure or a success for the Union will very much depend on the way the Union adjusts its governance to the increasingly neo-medieval environment prompted by these enlargements. At issue is the efficiency and legitimacy of the entire European system of governance. This brings us to the next sections of this concluding chapter.

Governing the neo-medieval Europe

One does not even need to take into account any further enlargements to see that the Union is already extremely complex and diversified. Chapter 3 has shown the scale and nature of diversity resulting from the accession of post-Communist countries. The fact that the map of unity and diversity in the current EU does not simply correspond to the old East–West divide does not make the European setting any less complex. The question is: how to prevent chaos, if not anarchy, in this complex and diversified environment? What kind of governance mode can prove effective in the enlarged EU?[13] Can the process of integration be continued under these new circumstances?

The dominant reply to these questions is very much informed by the history of the state. Westphalian states prevailed over other units existing in the Middle Ages because they were able to harden their borders and constrain 'exit' options for political and economic actors.[14] This has helped them to reduce diversity and foster homogeneity within their respective borders. Westphalian states have also been effective in installing a central and hierarchical form of governance. Their strong bureaucracies were able to provide top-down administrative control and steering. The principle that rules should apply equally was predominant in most Westphalian states and this required uniformity and standardization of public action throughout the entire territory. Central goal setting was also essential to this notion of governance, and implementation of these goals required state intervention by either laws or policies. The 'basic' law, in the form of a constitution, has been essential in defining the rules of the political game and structuring institutions.

Friends of a modern European state are clearly in favour of a similar kind of governance to be applied in the enlarged EU. They argue for strict observance of the so called 'community method' that underlines the equal rights and duties of all member states.[15] They insist that the *acquis communautaire* has to be applied fully by all members without exception and call for an efficient system of monitoring and eventual sanctioning to ensure that member states comply. They want the central government of the Union to have ever broader powers and a visible 'face' in a form of a Union president and foreign minister, for instance. They want to strengthen the European bureaucratic branch to help the Commission to guard the treaties and to offer strategic steering and guidance. They want the adoption of a European Constitution that would clarify the rules of interstate bargaining and delineate the competencies of European institutions. They want greater economic, political, and cultural convergence among member states and insist on a strict distinction between EU members and non-members. Friends of a modern European state are also sceptical about or even hostile towards any kind of flexibility, subsidiarity, pillarization, devolution, and differentiation in the Union's law and policy. They argue that these solutions are not only vaguely defined but also quite dangerous because they disrupt the unitary nature of the EU institutional system and create unworkable procedures of decision-making. In fact, they often see greater flexibility and differentiation as a step towards disintegration.[16]

This book has tried to show that this reasoning is unduly negative if not wrong altogether. A hierarchical system of governance fostering greater discipline and convergence within the EU's borders should not be the aim of European integration, but as one among many possible means of enhancing peace, freedom, and prosperity for the member states and their citizens (which I see as the most essential aim of integration). The fact that this hierarchical system of governance has proved its virtues in the history of Westphalian states does not necessarily mean that it would bring about similar benefits for an EU that more closely resembles a neo-medieval empire. And finally, this hierarchical system of governance has proven to be less effective in coping with the current pressures of modernization and globalization. Integration of markets does not necessarily lead to the harmonization of societies' institutions. An effective economic regime must allow individuals and member states to organize themselves in a pattern of overlapping jurisdictions, with each jurisdiction responsible for the provision of a specific class of public goods.[17] I will scrutinize the aim of European integration somewhat later but will now concentrate on governance questions.

Modern studies of governance and organization identified several different systems and modes of governance.[18] There is little consensus on what represents the most effective way of governing complex and differentiated polities like the enlarged EU. What one person sees as a way of recognizing change and plurality, another sees as a recipe for disorder encouraging free riding.[19] Some argue that all social systems tend towards atomization and anarchy while others believe that even the most chaotic systems are able to generate a dynamic order.[20] There is not even a commonly agreed definition of governance.[21] Nevertheless, there is agreement on some basic findings by most experts in the field. To start with, an effective system of governance does not need to be state-based or state-centric.[22] (And the concept of state needs to be located socially, disaggregated institutionally, and reorganized into its various component policy networks.) An effective system of governance does not even need to be territorial or territorially fixed. (And the concept of territorial governance need not entail mutual exclusion.[23])

Moreover, an effective system of governance must be able to represent the basic types of variety found in the system to be governed.[24] This means that the more diverse the qualities to be governed, the more diverse the necessary governing measures and structures, and the more diverse the relationship between them.[25] As Tanja Börzel put it:

In an increasingly complex and dynamic environment, where hierarchical coordination is rendered difficult if not impossible and the potential for deregulation is limited because the problems of market failure, governance becomes only feasible within policy networks, providing a framework for an efficient horizontal coordination of the interests and actions of public and private corporate actors, mutually dependent on their resources.[26]

Finally, compliance in a highly complex, 'plurilateral' system of governance requires different measures than in a relatively simple hierarchical system of governance.[27] Where hierarchy is minimal, compliance derives more from shared aspirations and cooperative practices than from perceived obligations or coercive threats that foster the automatic acceptance of laws and directives.[28] Governance in the 'plurilateral' system is about enabling socio-political interactions and encouraging varied arrangements for coping with problems and distributing services among the numerous actors. The principal patterns of interaction are self- and co-regulation, public–private partnerships, co-operative management, and joint entrepreneurial ventures.

Two conclusions can be drawn from this analysis. First, the neo-medieval setting is not per se ungovernable, but effective governance in a complex and differentiated environment requires different solutions than the ones successfully applied by Westphalian states. In other words, a plurilateral rather than hierarchical mode of governance seems better suited to the enlarged EU.

The second conclusion is that the EU has already adopted many features of what we have identified as the 'plurilateral' system of governance. The EU's governance is increasingly non-territorial, multilevel, and multicentred. The governance is more about bargaining between different actors than about automatic implementation of commands from the centre. EU institutions, member states, and sub-states (cities and regions), public and private agents, transnational and supranational actors—all interact with each other in complex networks of varying horizontal and vertical density. Decision-making competencies are shared by actors at different levels rather than monopolized by European (or member states') executives. European law is more often 'soft' than 'hard'.[29] Compliance with laws and directives in the EU is often voluntary (or there are few sanctions for non-compliance). Encouragement of best practices, shaming, and persuasion are more in use than orders, commands, and administrative directives. Consider for instance the 2005 European Council's decision not impose fines on Germany and France for running an 'excessive' budget deficit as envisaged by the Stability and Growth Pact. The Council stated: '[T]he purpose of the excessive deficit procedure is to assist rather than to punish, and therefore to provide incentives [...] to pursue budgetary discipline, through enhanced surveillance, peer support and peer pressure.'[30]

Moreover, the Treaties of Maastricht, Amsterdam, and Nice have formalized the existence of overlapping orders within the EU and introduced provisions for greater flexibility and differentiation. As Gráinne de Búrca and Joanne Scott put it: 'The paradigm (however notional) of uniformity, homogeneity and one-directional integration is gradually being replaced by one of flexibility, mixity and differentiation.'[31]

The so-called Open Method of Coordination (OMC) is a good example of this new mode of governance. It was announced at the 2000 European Summit in Lisbon and defined as an experimental approach to EU governance based on benchmarking of national progress towards common European objectives and organized mutual learning.[32] The OMC obliges member states to pool information, compare themselves to one another, and reassess current policies and programmes in light of their relative performance. However, the OMC does not seek to homogenize member states' inherited policy regimes and institutional arrangements. The purpose is experimental learning and deliberative problem-solving across the EU rather than enforced convergence from the top. This type of benign disciplinary regime has been said to represent an 'advanced form of a liberal government', although this is not a view shared by all students of European integration.[33]

However, the 'plurilateral' system of governance is more often than not the result of actions taken by individual member states outside the official framework of European integration. Consider, for instance, the way individual European states have coped with the problems posed by conflicts of law in enforcing international contracts. While large trade flows demand certainty in contract enforcement, the solution has not been found in harmonizing national laws or even in guaranteeing the recognition of foreign courts' awards through official treaties. As Alessandra Casella and Jonathan S. Feldstein pointed out, private international traders have instead been encouraged to settle their disputes through specialized arbitration, deemed to be more responsible and more informed about the usages and customs of their specific transactions. In the classical hierarchical system, the private administration of law was not recognized by state powers. However, legal changes in countries such as France, Italy, the Netherlands, Portugal, and Spain have allowed international traders to opt out of the jurisdiction of the national courts, leading to the emergence of a new 'private' international jurisdiction.[34]

The fact is, however, that the 'plurilateral' system of governance is still widely contested, and there is strong pressure to inject more hierarchy and coercion into the European system.[35] Consider, for instance, the opposition to flexibility clauses in EU law (constitution), pressure to impose strict sanctions for non-compliance of the EMU Stability Pact rules, or the noted criticism of the OMC.[36] Of course, governance is not a zero-sum game; political bargaining requires compromises, and we are living in a period of change with many transitory arrangements. In fact, plurilateralism should not be seen as a pure model that represents a clear-cut opposite to pyramidal centralism based on coercion. Plurilaterism can envisage some mixture of flexibility and discipline, openness and secrecy, tradition and innovation. That said, some basic choices ought to be made. This book has argued that the emerging neo-medieval setting cannot be governed by a system that proved workable for a very different actor than the Union now is. The Union is more likely to benefit from a 'plurilateral' than a hierarchical system of governance and it is time to agree on this and try to make this 'plurilateral' system work. This is not an endorsement of total freedom or of anything-goes policies. Governance in its essence is about the maintenance of collective order, the achievement of collective goals, and the collective process of rule through which order and goals are sought.[37] But there are various ways of achieving that. The Union needs some kind of a central government, but it does not need a unitary government structured like a pyramid.[38] The Union needs a sort of constitutional order, but this order can leave room for a large degree of flexibility and differentiation.[39] The Union should make various actors comply with the agreed rules and prevent free riding, but incentives and shaming may offer the prospect of greater compliance than commands and sanctions.[40] The Union needs to provide some guidance and steering, but this does not need to prevent compromise and accommodation in the formulation and implementation of its policies.[41]

Of course, a 'plurilateral' system of governance will also create some problems. For instance, differentiation may imply discrimination against some actors.[42] Flexibility may encourage free riding. And it is not certain whether European self-organizing networks can deliver any tangible public goods.[43] However, even greater problems are to be expected if the hierarchical system of government were to continue to be applied in the enlarged EU. A 'plurilateral' system of governance is likely to work better provided that it is well thought through and put in practice in a consistent manner.

Legitimacy in the neo-medieval Europe

A 'plurilateral' system of governance may well prove relatively efficient in the enlarged EU, but can it also enjoy legitimacy? Most would agree that legitimacy is not only a function of efficiency, but also of democracy and affection.[44] (And some would argue that the lack of affective and democratic sources of legitimacy could prevent the Union from acquiring the utilitarian form of legitimacy based on effectiveness.) One day the EU may well have charismatic leaders admired if not loved by a broad spectrum of citizens across Europe. However, it is less likely to see trust and affection for the EU emanating from a strong cultural pan-European identity. A complex system of plurilateral governance with many flexible arrangements, fluid membership, variable purpose, and a net of concentric functional frames of cooperation is prone to generate multiple identities rather than homogenous cultural identity. Constitutional rather than national patriotism would therefore be the only available means of enhancing the legitimacy of the medieval system.[45] Put differently, democracy becomes the Union's basic 'legitimation principle'[46]. But how is this to be achieved? After all, the major criticism of the 'plurilateral' system of governance is that it is not democratic. As Deidre Curtin argued, the EU's growing fragmentation and power diffusion is a sign of 'democratic retrogression' because 'governmental decisions in international matters are only very weakly accountable in modern democracies'.[47] According to Neil Walker, accountability is a particularly serious problem in a 'crowded institutional context, where popular affinity is contested or diluted and lines of responsibility are blurred'.[48] According to Johan P. Olsen, citizens' involvement and participation is difficult in a large-scale and multilevel polity like the EU.[49] And Svein S. Andersen and Tom Burns pointed to the serious problems of representation in a Union governed by diffused networks and institutions: 'The "democracy of organizations" tends to replace the democracy of citizens and their territorial representatives, and expertise is strategically engaged in policy processes often at the expense of elected officials and government leadership.'[50]

Chapter 5 has confirmed that in a neo-medieval EU it would be difficult to make democracy work in a Westphalian fashion. The question is whether the neo-medieval empire can possibly find new ways for political participation, representation, and accountability that would be seen as legitimate. To answer this question we need again to compare the characteristics and quality of democracy in the neo-medieval and neo-Westphalian systems. Absolute normative judgements are of little help here. I expect that in a system with fuzzy borders and plurilateral govern-ance, democracy assumes different meanings and features. Some demo-cratic quality will surely be compromised, but there are also some obvious gains for democracy in the new Europe.

Let us start with the fundamental issue of 'voice' and 'exit'. This simple dichotomy has been elaborated by Albert Hirschman to describe alter-native mechanisms for an individual's reaction to the performance of various organizations and institutions he or she belongs to.[51] (This was later adopted by successive generations of political scientists to analyse complex organizations such as states or the EU itself.[52]) Exit is about escaping from a given regime and voice is about efforts to change a regime rather than escape from it. Constraining exit options through boundary building fosters the development of systemic structures for internal political negotiations. This is how democracy is born, it is argued. Those who are unable to exit will raise their voices and press for creating institutional channels to make themselves heard. When boundaries are soft and individuals can easily exit, voice becomes difficult to channel, organize, and discipline. There is less need to convince the rulers to change their policies and no complex procedural techniques develop to weight and combine the preferences of the affected. The 'full exit' world is therefore a world without voice and without democracy, by extension.[53]

Democratic theory often emphasizes the virtues of boundary building, but it tends to underemphasize the virtues of free exit.[54] Systems with soft borders and thus ample opportunities for exit may well have problems in developing structures of political negotiation, but there is also less need for such structures because individuals can seek fulfilment of their needs outside the borders of the system. This is not to argue that in a Europe with fuzzy borders democracy would be redundant, but to show that opportun-ities for exit may also became an important source of legitimacy. Westpha-lian states have indeed succeeded in giving 'voice' to their structures, but they have done this by constraining certain freedoms and liberties, that is, exit options. In a neo-medieval empire the opportunity for voice might be less organized and disciplined, but this would be compensated by greater opportunities for exit. And this time around exit does not need to be as dramatic and permanent as separation or exile.[55] Political and economic actors can simply move their activities to other parts of the Union with only few practical implications. The challenge for the Union is to make these opportunities for exit worthwhile for a broader strata of citizens. So far exit options are being chiefly utilized by chief executive officers (CEOs),

Eurocrats, professional soccer players, and academics. Most European cit-izens are unable or unwilling to cross borders in search of either material goods or spiritual values, and they often entertain populist if not xeno-phobic ideas. They are the party of territoriality, to use Charles Maier's expression.[56]

Another major critique of the complex system of plurilateral governance associated with the neo-medieval setting is that it lacks a clear division of power and a firm system of checks and balances. After all, various flexible informal arrangements, fluid membership, and variable purpose represent the major features of this plurilateral governance. They make it difficult to know who holds the real power, how decisions are being made, and whether all important arguments have been deliberated. Can a neo-medi-eval system of multilayered and multispeed arrangements run by an ever-changing group of unidentified people ever be seen to be legitimate?[57]

Such reasoning is only partly justified. To start with, the major objective behind the division-of-power principle and the system of checks and balances is to prevent the concentration of power in one institutional centre. But the neo-medieval setting with plurilateral governance does not have the problem of concentration of power. Power in this system is deconcentrated, dispersed, divided, fragmented, or even fused. There is no urgent need for special arrangements to put brakes on the centre. There is no clearly identified, hierarchical centre here. This causes some problems, but it can also be seen as an advantage. Legal checks and balances are certainly important. However, an in-built 'pluralism of authorities', to use Zygmunt Bauman's expression, can also prevent abuse of power quite effectively.[58]

The division-of-power principle and the system of checks and balances is also intended to force mutual deliberation between institutions repre-senting particular interests. As Stephen L. Elking pointed out, this was chiefly what James Madison had in mind when he proposed to fragment political power.[59] He wanted to oblige political factions to give reasons for their preferences and to make them compromise or even abandon parti-cularistic interests. One can say many bad things about plurilateral gov-ernance, but not that it obstructs deliberation. It is widely acknowledged that the multiactor and multirational bargaining process that is central to this system demands and generates much more self-reflection and colle-ctive deliberation than a hierarchical system of governance.[60] And if this indeed is the case, the neo-medieval Union may well enjoy what Erik Oddvar Eriksen and John Erik Fossum labeled 'legitimacy through deliberation'.[61]

Finally, the division-of-power principle and the system of checks and balances is aimed at providing greater democratic controls and accountability. The plurilateral governance associated with the neo-medieval setting is said to offer very little in this respect, but I am not sure whether this criticism is correct. True, complex networks notoriously escape formal democratic control, but they are subject to a variety of informal controls that are less present in hierarchical systems. Dispersion of power contributes to accountability because different centres watch each other's moves and publicize abuses of power. Enhanced deliberation also contributes to accountability because issues are considered in more depth by a variety of actors. True, parliaments find it difficult to gain insight into multicentred bargaining by networks, but this only underlines the growing inadequacy of traditional forms of democratic control. In other words, one should not idealize the system of democratic accountability used in Westphalian states. Elections represent a very crude means of controlling officials. Parliaments and their specialized committees have proved more efficient in exercising democratic control, but they also are under fire for failing to perform the controls, largely because they lack the adequate expertise and resources.[62] Of course, European networks are not subject to a direct electoral test, but most of them are not self-appointed either. The existing body of European treaties contains some pretty rigid rules defining the competences of individual actors and structuring the decision-making system.

Moreover, major actors involved in European multicentred bargaining are either nation states subject to direct electoral scrutiny or EU institutions subject to indirect electoral scrutiny. In other words, European plurilateral governance is not being exercised by self-appointed and largely unaccountable NGOs and it is not rule free. We see a combination of formal and informal decision-making practices with various actors involved in political bargaining, each of them enjoying different forms of legitimacy.

All this is not to say that democratic controls in a neo-medieval Europe are likely to be superior to those exercised in Westphalian states. Only that there are various ways of assuring accountability and that traditional forms of democratic control are not as effective as is often claimed, especially when exercised in the complex economic and political environment of today. The danger is, however, that informal rather than formal controls of complex rather than simple governance networks make it particularly difficult for ordinary citizens to feel in charge of daily policies. (And there is also growing evidence showing that national executives are able to escape from the scrutiny of their respective national parliaments when making deals within the EU.[63]) This is fertile ground for populist arguments accusing the EU of being isolated and insulated from ordinary people (and their elected representatives).[64] These arguments would only lose their credibility if European citizens were offered greater opportunities for political participation. But again, participation is seen as problematic in the European context. Will the neo-medieval EU offer a greater opportunity for participation?

Participation, representation, and contestation

A study of recent European documents suggests that citizen participation is currently the centre of attention, but serious doubts remain.[65] Few people bother to vote in the European elections largely because of the peculiar position of the European Parliament and the nature of European political representation described in Chapter 5. European referenda have proved an arena for populism rather than genuine participation. This is not surprising because a referendum forces politicians to present compli- cated international questions in simplistic black-and-white terms which rewards populist politics and demagoguery.[66] Even noble plans to involve the institutions of civil society in European decision-making may in the end constrain rather than enhance democratic participation. Civil society representatives are not elected by the people (and usually not even by their members), they do not offer equal access to decision-making, and they pursue parochial agendas.

All this has long been predicted by political theorists from Jean-Jacques Rousseau and Immanuel Kant to Robert Dahl. They argued that the larger the unit the more difficult it is to offer citizens valuable forms of partici- pation. The decision centre is further away in a larger unit and the power of a single vote is smaller with the increase in the size of the electorate.[67] This cannot but stimulate a feeling of apathy, alienation, banalization, and introversion. The legitimacy of the European project subsequently suffers and it is therefore likely that we will see the rise of non-conventional (populist) politics or even anti-politics in neo-medieval Europe.

The situation does not need to be desperate, however, provided that at least three basic measures are taken to address the problem of citizen participation. As Robert A. Dahl rightly argued: 'The larger scale of de- cisions need not lead inevitably to a widening sense of powerlessness, provided citizens can exercise significant control over decisions on the smaller scale of matters important to their daily lives: education, public health, town and city planning.'[68] In other words, the neo-medieval Union requires strengthening citizen participation at the local and nation state levels (which is not easy but presumably easier than at the European level). Moreover, it is important that certain domains remain outside EU competencies. The more the Union extends its functional competencies, the more pressure there is for enhancing citizen participation. But it is this type of participation that the enlarged EU will be unable to offer in an adequate way.

Second, various networks of European governance ought to provide greater access to organized groups of citizens.[69] In theory, a plurilateral system of governance through networks should be better able to reach to the grassroots than a hierarchical system. However in practice European networks are still often run by unelected committees of national civil servants and Commission officials with little oversight by European or national parliaments. Access to these networks by various regional, professional, and societal actors is screened on a rather arbitrary basis. It is therefore important to find a way of assuring broader and more equal participation not only by national administrations and the traditional social partner organizations representing business and labour, but also by other non-state and sub-national actors with relevant interests and expertise. Of course, this is easier said than done, but as Jonathan Zeitlin found out, the European 'Social Inclusion' process with the use of the Open Method of Coordination has already mobilized many relevant bodies in the fight against poverty and exclusion.[70] Networks of anti-poverty NGOs and local/regional authorities have been extremely active in drawing domestic information upwards from their national affiliates, commenting critically on official reports, mobilizing pressure on EU institutions, diffusing European information downwards to their affiliates, and linking them together horizontally through conferences and round tables, often supported financially by the Commission and Parliament. But if networks are to be a genuine means of enhancing participation, some basic Europe-wide rules for their engagement are needed.[71] On the one hand, we need to make mandatory the inclusion of social and local actors into some if not most European decision-making processes. On the other, we need to make these social and local actors observe the basic rules of openness and transparency.

Finally, the civic and political rights of EU citizens ought to be enforced.[72] A mere extension of the rights already enjoyed within the national framework will not do.[73] European citizens should be offered meaningful ways for contesting decisions directly affecting them. This is because within the

European framework the traditional forms of participation and representation are weaker or not available. This is also because networks are about organized groups of citizens rather than individual citizens who do not necessarily wish to join organizations, let alone engage in politics. Policy networks may well make a greater contribution to the promotion of the public interest than traditional democratic mechanisms.[74] However, agreements resulting from bargaining between insiders in networks can result in costs being externalized to outsiders. There ought to be a mechanism to protect individual citizens against this.[75] The EU offers some standard mechanisms of contestation. European citizens have the right to petition the European Parliament and the right to apply to the ombudsman in order to bring to his or her attention any case of poor administration by the Community institutions and bodies (with the exception of legal bodies, however).[76] They also have the right to access European documents and the right to apply to European institutions and to receive a reply. Although these means of contesting the decisions of various authorities at the European level have been increasingly utilized in recent years, they are not likely to compensate for the weakness of state-like means of popular participation and representation in European affairs.[77] And again, one wonders whether this will be exploited by populist politicians orchestrating campaigns against European decisions and projects.

Populism is certainly a very serious threat in the neo-medieval Europe, but I would argue that the Union should not be afraid of contentious politics.[78] In fact, it should encourage certain forms of popular contestation in the search for greater legitimacy. After all, throughout European history contentious politics has been practised by true democrats, not only by populists.[79] And there was always a vocal group of democratic theorists arguing that the sovereignty of people lay not so much in electoral authorization as in the right of resistance.[80] One can even go a step further and argue that the neo-medieval setting of the enlarged EU is more conducive to what Philip Pettit called the 'contestatory' type of democracy, as opposed to the traditional electoral variety.[81] As argued in Chapter 5, upgrading the powers of the European Parliament or engineering the European public space is not likely to enhance the Union's democratic legitimacy and may even damage it. But allowing or even stimulating democratic contestation may well diffuse public frustration about the way decisions are being taken at the European level. Citizens may well miss a genuine European parliamentary representation and feel alienated from the various European centres of decision-making.

However, enhancing citizens' opportunities for contesting the decisions they find unjust or harmful to their interests can represent a powerful means of legitimization. The Union cannot afford to ignore that.

True, various mass demonstrations and protests organized over the last decade or so by European farmers, fisherman, and truckers have resulted in populist and protectionist slogans or even outright violence. Although successive European referenda have given the electorate the opportunity to cast protest votes concerning major European projects, they have also fallen prey to populist slogans. This does not always need to be the case. Political contestation is an instrument that can also be used by liberal democrats utilizing the modern means of communication and organization for making their views heard.[82] We ought to make sure that contestation is practised in a political and institutional setting that is conducive to liberal democracy rather than to populism.[83] As Philip Pettit pointed out, for a 'contestatory' form of democracy to work well the polity must be deliberative, inclusive, and responsive.[84] There is certainly a long way to go before the Union is in a position fully to meet these criteria. It would also be wrong to reduce contestation to mass protests and actions. The Union can strengthen the institutional channels of contestation by broadening scope for private litigation in the ECJ or by strengthening the powers of the European Ombudsman.[85] European referenda can be redesigned in a way that enhances deliberation and informed (if not conscientious) choice.[86] Moreover, contestation should not only be seen in terms of individual resistance and non-cooperation. Individuals would be in a better position successfully to contest European decisions when acting through various social movements or public interest groups and forging workable alignments with national governmental actors, supranational institutions, and each other. That said, it is also plausible to conclude that the legitimacy of the new neo-medieval polity is more likely to emerge from the capacity of citizens to contest European decisions than from the predominance of any single channel of representation.[87]

The case for optimism

Friends of a modern European state believe that the EU should be in charge of increasing numbers of domains of public and private life. They want to engineer a European public with a positivist ethos. They want to copy state-like institutions on the European level. Ultimately, they hope that this will provide the Union with a similar kind of legitimacy to that which states possess. Their views have received harsh public treatment in a series of referenda on the draft of the European Constitution. Does Europe have any alternative? I do not believe that the Union can simply be dismantled and that we return to a system of completely sovereign nation states. If this is so, the integration project ought to be adjusted to the emerging neo-medieval reality. Europe needs, first of all, a different approach to governance and legitimacy. In my view, the EU can function as a sort of 'meta-governor': a governing body that distributes decision-making competence between multitudes of territorially and functionally defined self-governing actors. The EU should not try to impose tight hierarchical control but act as a mediator between various European networks and as a facilitator of continuous communication, cooperation, and compromise between such networks. It should guarantee free access to these networks and make sure that the ongoing bargaining process is transparent and open. The borders of the Union should be flexible and open to those neighbours who embrace the basic set of liberal values and accept the rules operating within the neo-medieval empire. A new constitution may help the Union to structure and organize the new polity. But the Union needs only a few simple, relatively short, and widely comprehensible constitutional rules. The comprehensive (and in parts incomprehensible) compilation of the existing body of European treaties that was put to the vote across the EU in 2005 does not meet these criteria.

Friends of a European state believe that medievalism will bring the European integration process to its end and represent a recipe for chaos and conflict. They may well be right, but it is too early to say. International bodies such as the EU do not collapse with a big bang. Consider the fate of the Western European Union that had a purely virtual existence for several decades. Many claim that NATO is no longer a functional organization despite appearances. The EU has also been under extraordinary pressure since 1989, but the prevailing Westphalian recipes are not likely to make it work better. In fact, I have tried to show that adjusting to a neo-medieval environment through a gradual extension of the plurilateral system of governance is the best remedy for coping with the current set of challenges. The rise of a neo-medieval empire does not need to herald the end of European integration. On the contrary, such an empire seems to be better suited than a Westphalian state to meeting some of the basic aims of integration. I have tried to show that a neo-medieval empire is in a good position to cope with the pressures of globalization because of its inbuilt flexibility and ability to learn. I have tried to show that a neo-medieval empire is in a good position to compete with the United States and other great powers, because it pulls together vast European resources without eliminating Europe's greatest strength: its pluralism and diversity. I have tried to show that a neo-medieval empire is in a good position to provide conflict prevention in its neighbourhood, because it is able to shape the behaviour of various actors through the EU membership conditionality. I have tried to show that a neo-medieval empire is in a good position to be seen as legitimate by its citizens, because it tries to bring governance structures closer to them, and relies on incentives rather than punishments.

I have not tried to hide the problems and difficulties that the neo-medieval empire is likely to encounter, but it is clear that this empire also possesses considerable advantages. Moreover, I have tried to show that the Westphalian solutions are largely inadequate for coping with an enlarged EU. It is time to recognize the neo-medieval reality and make it work.

Notes

Introduction: The Neo-medieval Paradigm

1. The term 'empire' has been used in many contexts and for many different purposes. I will define the major characteristics of the emerging European empire later in the book. At this point, however, it is important to mention that empire in this introduction is about a distinct way of organizing political space that is not based on the principle of territoriality and absolute sovereignty. This notion of empire draws from the later cited work of Fredrich Kratochwil, John Gerard Ruggie, Adam Watson, and Ole Wæver. In many other studies empire is largely about coercive impositions, and I will argue in Chapter 2 that the Union can also fit this definition, with certain important qualifications. It is also important to keep in mind that the degree of coercion applied by empires has seldom been uniform in terms of territory and policy field. As Barry Buzan and Richard Little pointed out, some empires have been remarkably flexible units: 'They had neither fixed geographic limits nor a uniform degree of internal political control. They can be seen in terms of concentric circles of control, ranging from complete absorption at the core, through varying degrees of control over foreign, military, and domestic policy in the middle zones, to mere hegemony at the outer margins.' See Barry Buzan and Richard Little, *International Systems in World History* (Oxford: Oxford University Press, 2000), p. 177. For different uses of the term empire, see especially Michael W. Doyle, *Empires* (Ithaca, NY: Cornell University Press, 1986), and Michael Hardt and Antonio Negri, *Empire* (Cambridge, MA: Harvard University Press, 2000). For an historical analysis of different types of empire, see S.N. Eisenstadt, *The Political Systems of Empires* (Glencoe, NY: Free Press, 1963), Paul Kennedy, *The Rise and Fall of the Great Powers* (New York: Vintage, 1987), Edward Gibbon, *Decline and Fall of the Roman Empire* (New York: Viking, 1952), Dominic Lieven, *Empire: The Russian Empire and its Rivals* (New Haven, CT: Yale University Press, 2001), or Eric Hobsbawn, *The Age of Empire, 1975–1914* (New York: Pantheon, 1987). See also Jack Snyder, *Myths of Empire. Domestic Politics and International Ambition* (Ithaca, NY: Cornell University Press, 1991).

2. For this particular concept of empire see Niall Ferguson, *Colossus: The Price of America's Empire* (New York: Penguin, 2004) or *Two Hegemonies: Britain 1846–1914 and the United States 1941–2001*, Patrick Karl O'Brien and Armand Clesse, eds. (Aldershot: Ashgate, 2002).
3. See Jan Zielonka, 'How New Enlarged Borders will reshape the European Union', *Journal of Common Market Studies*, 39:3 (2001), pp. 507–36 and 'Introduction: Boundary making by the European Union', in *Europe Unbound: Enlarging and Reshaping the Boundaries of the European Union*, Jan Zielonka, ed. (London: Routledge, 2002), pp. 1–16.
4. Although Demark has now opted into the Schengen Protocol. See Protocol on the Schengen Acquis. Available at: http://europa.eu.int/eur-lex/lex/LexUriServ/LexUriServ.do?uri=OJ:C:2004:310:0348:0350:EN:PDF. See also Protocol on position of Denmark. Available at: http://europa.eu.int/eur-lex/lex/LexUriServ/LexUriServ.do?uri=OJ:C:2004:310:0356:0360:EN:PDF. Britain and Ireland have resisted the pressure in the Convention to opt into the Schengen Acquis and formally remain outside this framework, but in practice they have 'opted-in' to a large part already. (See Protocol on the Schengen Acquis available as above.) This does not mean that member states are now eager to see the EU totally in charge of their borders. For instance, as this book goes to print several member states are fiercely resisting the European Commission's proposal to form a Common External Border Guard.
5. For instance, 80 per cent of 'illegal' immigration is due to the expiry of tourist visas, while only 20 per cent results from illegal frontier crossing. Moreover, a large segment of the migration movements in Europe derives from the ethnic conflicts that have taken place in the Balkans which have led to sizeable displacements of the resident populations. Another segment of migration involves ethnic Germans, Hungarians, Poles, Russians, Finns, Greeks, and Turks returning from other countries in the region. The former case creates demand for peacekeeping and economic-reconstruction efforts on behalf of the EU rather than merely a hard border separating the Balkans from the rest of the continent. Nor are hard borders usually seen as a means of dealing with the latter type of migration. See e.g. Didier Bigo, 'Frontiers and Security in the European Union: The Illusion of Migration Control', in *The Frontiers of Europe*, Malcolm Anderson and Eberhard Bort, eds. (London: Pinter, 1998), pp. 148–64.
6. See Giuliano Amato and Judy Batt, *Final Report of the Reflection Group on The Long-term Implications of EU Enlargement: The Nature of the New Border* (Florence: Robert Schuman Centre and Forward Studies Unit, EC, 1999), p. 42.
7. Thomas Christiansen and Knud Erik Jøregensen, 'Transnational Governance Above and Below the State: The Changing nature of Borders in the New Europe', *Regional & Federal Studies*, 10 (2000), p. 74. See also Lykke Friis and Anna Murphy, 'The European Union and Central and Eastern Europe: Governance and Boundaries', *Journal of Common Market Studies*, 37 (1999), p. 228.

8. This has been well argued in Pierre Hassner, 'Fixed borders or moving border-lands? A new type of border for a new type of entity', in *Europe Unbound*, op. cit., pp. 38–50.

9. Available at: http://www.notre-europe.asso.fr/article.php3?id_article=168 & lang=en. An academic version of the same reasoning is represented by, for instance, Neil MacCormick who views the Union as a *sui generis* institution. See Neil MacCormick, *Questioning Sovereignty* (Oxford: Oxford University Press, 1999)

10. Of course there were other reasons, such as the fear of Germany most notably, that were responsible for the EDC failure. For an in-depth analysis see Edward Furdson, *The European Defence Community: A History* (London: Macmillan, 1980), especially pp. 192–9.

11. See, for example, Leon N. Lindberg and Stuart A. Scheingold, *Europe's Would-be Polity. Patterns of Change in the European Community* (Englewood Cliffs, NJ: Prentice Hall, 1970), p. 21.

12. See, for example, Jo Shaw, 'Flexibility in a "Reorganized" and "Simplified" Treaty,' in Bruno de Witte (ed.), *Ten Reflections on the Constitutional Treaty for Europe* (Florence: European University Institute, 2003), pp. 187–206. Of course, it can be argued that the draft of the European Constitution does more than merely simplify and organize the body of existing European law.

13. See Ben Rosamond, *Theories of European Integration* (London: Macmillan, 2000), p. 7 and p. 87.

14. Ernst B. Haas, 'The Study of Regional Integration: Reflection on the Joy and Anguish of Pretheorizing', in *European Integration: Theory and Research*, L.N. Lindberg and S.A. Scheingold, eds. (Cambridge, MA: Harvard University Press, 1971), p. 27. Also Ernst B. Haas, 'The Obsolescence of Regional Integration Theory' (Berkeley, CA: Institute of International Studies Working Paper, 1975).

15. Donald J. Puchala, 'Of Blind Men, elephants and international integration', *Journal of Common Market Studies*, 10/3 (1972), pp. 267–8.

16. Helen Wallace and William Wallace, *Flying Together in a Larger and more Diverse European Union* (The Hague: Netherlands Scientific Council for Government Policy, 1995), pp. 28–9.

17. Wallace and Wallace, op. cit., p. 12.

18. Philippe C. Schmitter, 'Imagining the Future of the Euro-polity with the Help of New Concepts', in *Governance in the European Union*, Gary Marks et. al., eds. (London: Sage, 1996), pp. 132–6. For Schmitter's abstract models see Philippe C. Schmitter, 'A Revised Theory of Regional Integration', in *Europe's Would-be Polity. Patterns of Change in the European Community*, op. cit, pp. 232–63.

19. Jo Shaw and Antje Wiener, *The Paradox of the 'European Polity'* (Cambridge, MA: Harvard Jean Monnet Working Papers Series, 10/1999), p. 2.

20. Philippe C. Schmitter, 'Imagining the Future of the Euro-polity with the Help of New Concepts', in *Governance in the European Union*, op. cit. p. 132.

21. Walter Hallstein quoted in David Mitrany, *The Functional Theory of Politics* (London: Martin Robertson, 1975), p. 249. David Mitrany, 'The Prospect of European Integration: Federal or Functional', *Journal of Common Market Studies*, IV/2 (1965), pp. 119–49, particularly pp. 127 and 145. I should add here that using the state as a reference point or benchmark in the study of European integration does not necessarily imply any sympathy for a European state.

22. 'From Confederacy to Federation—Thoughts on the finality of European integration', Speech by Joschka Fischer at the Humboldt University in Berlin, 12 May 2000. Available at: http://www.auswaertiges-amt.de/_aktuel/index. htm. See also a pro-federalist statement from the Belgian Minister for Foreign Affairs reported in *De Volkskrant*, 5 September 2000. For a comprehensive analysis of the role of federalist ideas in the development of Europe's institutions from the Coal and Steel Community to the EU of today, see Michael Burgess, *Federalism and European Union: Building of Europe 1950–2000* (London: Routledge, 2000).

23. For a comprehensive elaboration of this argument, see Christopher Booker and Richard North, *The Great Deception: The Secret History of the European Union* (London: Continuum, 2003).

24. Although, the term United States of Europe was openly used by the President of the European Convention. See e.g. a speech by Valéry Giscard d'Estaing, Chairman of the European Convention, Opening of the academic year at the College of Europe, Bruges, 2 October 2002. Available at: http://european-convention. eu.int/?docs/speeches/3314.pdf. Max Kohnstamm and Wolfgang Hager used the term 'a nation writ large' in their book on the European Union. See *A Nation Writ Large? Foreign Policy Problems Before the European Community*, Max Kohnstamm and Wolfgang Hager, eds. (London: Macmillan, 1973). For the use of the term 'U.S. of Europe' see also Leon N. Lindberg and Stuart A. Scheingold, *Europe's Would-be Polity: Patterns of Change in the European Community* (Englewood Cliffs, NJ: Prentice Hall, 1970), p. 8. See also Johan Galtung, *Europe in the Making* (New York: Crane Russak, 1989).

25. See, for example, Volker Bornschier, 'Western Europe's move toward political union', in *State-building in Europe: The Revitalizing of Western European Integration*, Volker Bornschier, ed. (Cambridge: Cambridge University Press, 2000), pp. 3–37.

26. Françoise Duchêne, *Jean Monnet: The First Statesman of Interdependence* (New York: W. W. Norton, 1994), p. 401.

27. For a classical definition of a state see Max Weber, 'Politik als Beruf', in *Gesammelte politische Schriften* (Tübinge: J. C. Mohr, 1971), p. 506.

28. Charles S. Maier, 'Does Europe need a frontier? From territorial to distributive community', in *Europe Unbound*, Jan Zielonka, ed. (London: Routledge, 2002), p. 21.

29. Stephen D. Krasner, *Sovereignty, Organized Hypocrisy* (Princeton, NJ: Princeton University Press, 1999) and Andres Osiander, 'Sovereignty, International

Relations and The Westphalian Myth', *International Organization*, 55/2 (2001), pp. 251–87.

30. See, for example, Charles Tilly, *Coercion, Capital, and European States, A.D. 990–1990* (Oxford: Basil Blackwell, 1990) or Michael Keating, *Nations Against the State* (Basingstoke: Palgrave/Macmillan, 2001), pp. 30–3. For an analysis of contemporary Europe see e.g. John Loughlin, 'Regional Autonomy and State Paradigm Shifts in Western Europe', *Regional and Federal Studies*, 10/2 (2000), pp. 10–34.

31. Jean Dunbabin, 'Government', in *The Cambridge History of Medieval Thought c. 350–1450*, J. H. Burns, ed. (Cambridge: Cambridge University Press, 1988), p. 479. Before the fifteenth century authors were using such terms as *res publica, regnum*, or *civitas* that basically implied a different notion of territorial authority than the term *status*.

32. John Gerard Ruggie, 'Continuity and transformation in the world polity: Towards a neorealist synthesis', *World Politics*, 35 (1983), p. 274. See also Friedrich V. Kratochwil, 'Of Systems, Boundaries, and Territoriality: An Inquiry into the Formation of the State System', *World Politics*, 39/1 (1986), pp. 21–52.

33. Georges Duby, *La Société aux Xie et XIIe siécles dans la region mâconnaise* (Paris: Colin, 1953), pp. 170–1

34. The former concept, for instance, was known from the time of the Roman empire. According to Norman Davies, 'The *limes*, the "frontier line", was a vital feature of the Empire's defence. It was not, as is sometimes supposed, an impenetrable barrier. From the military point of view it was more of a cordon, or series of parallel cordons, which, whilst deterring casual incursions, would trigger active counter-measures as soon as it was seriously breached. It was a line which normally could only be crossed by paying *portaria* and by accepting the Empire's authority.' See Norman Davies, *Europe: A History* (Oxford: Oxford University Press, 1996), pp. 185–8.

35. See Walter Ullmann, *Principles of Government and Politics in the Middle Ages* (London: Methuen, 1966), pp. 215–30.

36. For a review of three basic modes of non-territorial organization in the Middle Ages, see e.g. Hendrik Spruyt, *The Sovereign State and Its Competitors* (Princeton, NJ: Princeton University Press, 1994), pp. 34–57. See also Figure 12.1 in Barry Buzan and Richard Little, *International Systems in World History*, op. cit., p. 245.

37. See Norman Davies, *Europe: A History* (Oxford: Oxford University Press, 1996), pp. 379–82.

38. Gianfranco Poggi, *The Development of the Modern State* (London: Hutchinson, 1978), p. 98.

39. See Alexander Motyl, 'Is Everything Empire? Is Empire Everything?', *Comparative Politics*, forthcoming.

40. For typologies of empires see e.g. S. N. Eisenstadt, *Political Systems of Empires* (New York: Free Press, 1963), p. 10–12, or Alexander J. Motyl, *Imperial Ends. The*

Decay, Collapse, and Revival of Empires (New York: Columbia University Press, 2001), pp. 18–20. It should be noted, however, that some authors argue that the relationship between the centre and periphery is not only about control and disharmony, but also about harmony and mutual dependency. See Johan Galtung, 'A Structural Theory of Imperialism', *Journal of Peace Research*, 8/2 (1971), pp. 82–3.

41. See, for example, Michael W. Doyle, *Empires* (Ithaca, NY: Cornell University Press, 1986), p. 19.

42. See John H. Kautsky, *The Politics of Aristocratic Empires* (Chapel Hill: University of North Carolina Press, 1982), p. 127 and p. 144. See also J. H. Burns, *The Cambridge History of Medieval Political Thought c. 350–c. 1450* (Cambridge: Cambridge University Press, 1988), p. 179.

43. See, for example, Yale H. Ferguson and Richard W. Mansbach, *Polities: Authority, Identities, and Change* (Columbia: University of South Carolina Press, 1996), pp. 355–71.

44. Ole Wæver, 'Imperial Metaphors: Emerging European Analogies to Pre-Nation-State Imperial Systems', in *Geopolitics in Post-Wall Europe: Security, Territory and Identity*, Ola Tunander, Pavel Baev, and Victoria Ingrid Einagel, eds. (London: Sage 1997), p. 65. See also chapters 2 and 5 by Tunander and Østergaard.

45. It must be stressed, however, that some definitions of empires exclude more-loosely organized polities. For instance, Watson distinguishes between independent states, hegemony, suzerainty, dominion, and empire. See Adam Watson, *The Evolution of International Society* (London: Routledge, 1992), pp. 14–16.

46. See Alexander J. Motyl, 'Thinking About Empire', in *After Empire: Multiethnic Societies and Nation Building*, Karen Barkley and Mark von Hagen, eds. (Boulder, CO: Westview, 1997), p. 25.

47. See, for example, the widely discussed book by Niall Ferguson, *Colossus: The Price of America's Empire* (London: Penguin, 2004), or Dominic Lieven, *Empire: the Russian Empire and its Rivals* (New Haven, CT: Yale University Press, 2001).

48. Erik Holm has in fact envisaged the future EU as a kind of Westphalian empire with 'clearly defined authority, legitimized by consent and equipped with power'. See Erik Holm, *The European Anarchy: Europe's Hard Road into High Politics* (Copenhagen: Copenhagen Business School Press, 2001), pp. 235–40.

49. In this book I argue that the EU has already acquired several important imperial characteristics, but I do not try to indicate any specific date for the imperial birth. Nor do I speculate on the possible lifespan and trajectory of this empire. For an effort to construct specific parabolas of imperial trajectories, see Rein Taagepera, 'Expansion and Contraction Patterns of Large Polities: Context for Russia', *International Studies Quarterly*, 41/3 (1997), pp. 481–4. For a more in-

depth analysis of the problem of the imperial birth and death, see Alexander J. Motyl, *Imperial Ends: The Decay, Collapse, and Revival of Empires* (New York: Columbia University Press, 2001).

50. This has been pointed out to me by Charles Maier, who also observed that he could hardly imagine Frederick Barbarossa and Philip Augustus jointly proposing to affiliate with the Polish monarchs. In his view the Crusader Kingdoms of Jerusalem and Acre with their 'condominized periphery' come closest to my imperial notion of the EU.

51. For more about the use of models in analysing the future of European integration, see Richard Münch, 'Between Nation-State, Regionalism and World Society: The European Integration Process', *Journal of Common Market Studies*, 34 (1996), p. 381.

52. James A. Caporaso, 'The European Union and Forms of State: Westphalian, Regulatory or Post-Modern?', *Journal of Common Market Studies*, 34 (1996), p. 31.

53. See Ole Wæver, 'Imperial Metaphors: Emerging European Analogies to Pre-Nation-State Imperial Systems', in *Geopolitics in Post-Wall Europe*, Ola Tunander, Pavel Baev, and Victoria Ingrid Einagel, eds. (London: Sage, 1997), p. 61.

54. 'From Confederacy to Federation—Thoughts on the finality of European integration', Speech by Joschka Fischer at the Humboldt University in Berlin, 12 May 2000. Available at: http://www.auswaertiges-amt.de/_aktuel/index.htm.

55. This has also been presented as a possible if not likely scenario by serious analysts. See e.g. Heather Grabbe, *The Constellations of Europe: How Enlargement will Transform the EU* (London: Centre for European Reform, 2004), p. 73.

56. See, for example, Stéphane Beulac, *The Power of Language in the Making of International Law: The Word Sovereignty in Bodin and Vattel and the Myth of Westphalia* (Leiden: Martinus Nijhoff, 2004).

57. Andreas Osiander, *The States System of Europe, 1640–1990: Peace-making and the Conditions of International Stability* (Oxford: Clarendon Press, 1994), especially p. 78.

58. See Rodney Bruce Hall and Friedrich V. Kratochwil, 'Medieval tales: Neorealist "science" and the abuse of history', *International Organization*, 47/3 (1993), pp. 479–91.

59. My neo-medieval model contains many typical postmodern characteristics such as 'disjoined' and 'fragmented' government or 'unbundling territoriality'. However, as Leszek Kolakowski puts it: 'Having no clear idea what *modernity* is, we have recently tried to escape forward from the issue by talking about *postmodernity*.... I do not know what postmodern is and how it differs from premodern.... And what might come after the postmodern?' See Leszek Kolakowski, *Modernity on Endless Trial* (Chicago: Chicago University Press, 1990), p. 6. For the use of the 'postmodern' term in describing the neo-medieval setting see, for example, John Gerard Ruggie, 'Territoriality and beyond: Problematizing modernity in international relations', *International Organization*,

47 (1993), p. 171, or Robert Cooper, *The Post-modern State and the World Order* (London: Demos, 2000).

60. See, for example, Deborah Cohen and Maura O'Conner, *Europe in Cross-national Perspective* (London: Routledge, 2004).

61. See Ole Wæver, 'Imperial Metaphors: Emerging European Analogies to Pre-Nation-State Imperial Systems', in *Geopolitics in Post-Wall Europe*, Ola Tunander, Pavel Baev, and Victoria Ingrid Einagel, eds. (Sage: London, 1997), especially p. 61, or Andrew Gamble, 'Regional Blocs, World Order and the New Medievalism', in *European Union and New Regionalism: Regional Actors and Global Governance in a Post-hegemonic Era* (Aldershot: Ashgate, 2001), pp. 21–38. The use of the term 'neo' makes sure that we are not applying any simplistic analogies in this book.

62. This was during our conversation on one of my earlier drafts of this book in 2003. For Wallace's own model of integration and convergence in the context of the EU's enlargement, see Helen Wallace, 'Coming to Terms with a Larger Europe: Options for Economic Integration', *SEI Working Paper*, 23 (1998), p. 21.

63. James A. Caporaso, 'The European Union and Forms of State: Westphalian, Regulatory or Postmodern?', *Journal of Common Market Studies*, 34 (1996), p. 31.

64. See Philippe C. Schmitter, 'Imagining the Future of the Euro-polity with the Help of New Concepts', in *Governance in the European Union*, op. cit., p. 132.

65. See Jan Zielonka, 'How New Enlarged Borders will Reshape the European Union', op. cit., p. 516.

66. As Sartori puts it: 'An undefined concept is, by the same token, a boundless concept'. The standard manner of delimiting a concept is to define it *a contrario*, that is, by establishing its opposite, contrary, or contradictory'. See Giovanni Sartori, *The Theory of Democracy Revisited* (Chatham, NJ: Chatham House 1987), p. 182.

67. By the same token I distance myself from all-encompassing definitions of empire such as the presented by Hardt and Negri. See Michael Hardt and Antonio Negri, *Empire* (Cambridge, MA: Harvard University Press, 2000), pp. xii and 166.

68. It is worth noting that the most successful efforts to develop a theory of European integration have usually come from American rather than European scholars. Recent examples include Mark Pollack, *The Engines of European Integration. Delegation, Agency and Agenda-Setting in the EU* (Oxford: Oxford University Press, 2003), Andrew Moravcsik, *The Choice for Europe: Social Purpose and State Power from Messina to Maastricht* (London: UCL Press, 1999), and *European Integration and Supranational Governance*, Wayne Sandholtz and Alec Stone Sweet, eds. (Oxford: Oxford University Press, 1998). For an effort to develop theoretical approaches to enlargement, see Frank Schimmelfennig and Ulrich Sedelmeier (eds.), *The Politics of European Union Enlargement: Theoretical Approaches* (London: Routledge, 2005).

69. For an interesting discussion on Europeanization see e.g. Héritier Adrienne et al., *Differential Europe: The European Union Impact on National Policymaking* (Lanham, MD: Rowman and Littlefield, 2001), or *Politics of Europeanization*, Claudio Radaelli and Kevin Featherstone, eds. (Oxford: Oxford University Press, 2003).

70. Complementarity between realism and liberalism was well illustrated in Joseph S. Ney, 'Neorealism and Neoliberalism', *World Politics*, 40/1 (1987), pp. 234–51. Vast areas of complementarity between realism and constructivism are enumerated in Alexander Wendt, 'Constructing International Politics', *International Security*, 20/1 (1995), pp. 71–81. See also Christopher Hill, '1939: The Origins of Liberal Realism', *Review of International Studies*, 15/4 (1989), pp. 319–28.

71. See, for example, Daniel Wincott, 'Institutional Interaction and European Integration: Towards an Everyday Critique of Liberal Intergovernmentalism', *Journal of Common Market Studies*, 33/4 (1995), pp. 597–609. See also an interesting exchange between Simon Hix, 'Approaches to the Study of the European Community: The Challenge to Comparative Politics', *West European Politics*, 17/1 (1994), pp. 1–30, and Andrew Hurrell and Anand Menon, 'Politics like any other? CP, IR and the Study of the EU', *West European Politics*, 19/2 (1996), pp. 386–402.

72. See, for example, Anne-Marie Burley and Walter Mattli, 'Europe before the Court: A Political Theory of Legal Integration', *International Organization*, 47/1 (1993), pp. 41–76; Paul Pierson, 'The Path to European Integration: A Historical Institutionalist Analysis', *Comparative Political Studies*, 29/2 (1996), pp. 123–63; *Building Postwar Europe: National Decision-Makers and European Institutions, 1948–1963*, Anne Deighton, ed. (Basingstoke: Macmillan, 1995); Jürgen Habermas, 'Constitutional Democracy: A Paradoxical Union of Contradictory Principles?', *Political Theory*, 29/6 (2001), pp. 766–81; and Thomas Christiansen, Knud Erik Jorgensen, and Antje Wiener, 'The Social Construction of Europe', *Journal of European Public Policy*, 6/4 (1999), pp. 528–44.

Chapter 1: Return to Europe

1. If we take into consideration all the ten accession countries (including Cyprus and Malta) that entered the EU in 2004, the population amounts to 20 per cent of the EU-15. The percentage of the EU population increases from 20 per cent up to 28 per cent if we also include Romania and Bulgaria in our calculations. The calculations are based on data from 'The candidate countries' in *Eurostat Yearbook 2002, The Statistical Guide to Europe: Data 1990–2000* (Luxembourg: Office for Official Publications of the EC, 2002), p. 3.

2. It is important to note that this was calculated taking into consideration annual GDP at current prices in PPS (Purchasing Power Standards). The percentage of GDP in PPS is the same for the ten new member states (including Cyprus and

Malta) as for the eight Central and Eastern European countries. However, if we include Romania and Bulgaria in the calculations, the percentage for all the twelve candidate countries (annual GDP in PPS) rises to 11 per cent of GDP for the current EU-15. All the calculations are based on the data from *Eurostat* and were made for the year 2001.

3. Linz and Stepan show well the various implications of prior regime type for transition paths towards democracy. See Juan J. Linz and Alfred Stepan, *Problems of Democratic Transition and Consolidation: Southern Europe, South America, and Post-Communist Europe* (Baltimore, MD: Johns Hopkins University Press, 1996), pp. 55–65.

4. For major characteristics of the Communist system see e.g. George Schöpflin, *Politics in Eastern Europe 1945–1992* (Oxford: Blackwell, 1993), or Zbigniew Brzeziński, *The Soviet Bloc* (New York: Preager, 1967).

5. As a leading Polish democratic politician put it on the eve of Eastern European transition: 'For now two roads lie open before my country and our newly freed neighbors... one road leads to nationalism and isolationism, the other to a return to our "native Europe".' Adam Michnik, *Letters from Prison* (Berkeley: California University Press, 1998), p. 150. See also Attila Ágh, *Emerging Democracies in East Central Europe and the Balkans* (Cheltenham: Edward Elgar, 1998), p. 4.

6. For instance, in his widely cited article published in 1991, Claus Offe feared that 'it is possible that the majority of the population finds neither democracy nor a market economy a desirable perspective', and he subsequently identified seven negative scenarios that might be prompted by the reforms undertaken by these countries: (*a*) Democratic politics may block or distort the road to privatization and hence marketization; (*b*) Privatization may succeed, but fail to lead to marketization and hence growth and prosperity; this could be due to the conservation of cartels and monopolistic structures which make the transition one that occurs not from 'plan to market' but 'from plan to clan'; (*c*) Privatization may succeed, but lead to the obstruction of democratic politics through powerful interferences originating from domestic or international owners of capital; (*d*) Democratic politics may evolve, but fail to lead to the peaceful resolution of social conflict as it is dominated by ethnic, territorial, and minority conflicts that do not lend themselves to democratic forms of compromise; (*e*) Marketization may succeed, but fail to generate the reality of (or even the widely perceived prospect for) an equitable distribution of its benefits; (*f*) Accumulated disappointments and frustrations with these failures may give rise to demands for a type of 'democracy' that is based on an institutional structure other than civil liberties and representative government, for example populist presidential dictatorship; (*g*) Conversely, frustrations with economic performance and distribution may also lead to demands for marketization without private property, for example a return to state ownership of productive assets. See Claus Offe, 'Capitalism by Democratic Design? Democratic Theory Facing the Triple

Transition in East Central Europe', *Social Research*, 58 (1991), pp. 886–7. It should also be noted that such pessimistic evaluations of Eastern European fortunes persisted for a long period of time. See e.g. 'An EEPS Round Table: The Revolutions of 1989: Lessons of the First Post-Communist Decade', *East European Politics and Societies*, 13/2 (1999).

7. See, for example, Leslie Holmes, *Post-Communism: An Introduction* (Oxford: Polity Press, 1977), p. 9; Geoffrey Pridham, 'Comparative reflections on democratization in East-Central Europe: a model of post-Communist transformation?' in *Prospects for Democratic Transformation in East-Central Europe*, Geoffrey Pridham and Attila Ágh, eds. (Manchester: Manchester University Press, 2001), pp. 13–19; *Politics, Power, and the Struggle for Democracy in South-East Europe*, Vol. 2, Karen Dawisha and Bruce Parrott, eds. (New York: Cambridge University Press, 1997), pp. 1–39; *The Consolidation of Democracy in East-Central Europe*, Vol. 1, Karen Dawisha and Bruce Parrott, eds. (New York: Cambridge University Press, 1997), pp. 1–39. Martha de Melo, 'A Comparative Analysis of Twenty-Eight Transition Economies in Europe and Asia', *Post-Soviet Geography and Economics*, 37/6 (1996), pp. 265–85.

8. For the most famous example of such optimistic determinism, see Francis Fukuyama, 'The End of History?' *The National Interest*, 16 (1989), pp. 3–18.

9. This has been well argued in Grzegorz Ekiert, 'Patterns of Postcommunist Transition in Central and Eastern Europe' in *Capitalism and Democracy in Central and Eastern Europe: Assessing the Legacy of Communist Rule*, Grzegorz Ekiert and Stephen E. Hanson, eds. (Cambridge: Cambridge University Press, 2003).

10. See, for example, Jon Elster, 'Constitution-Making in Eastern Europe: Rebuilding the Boat in the Open Sea', *Public Administration*, 71 (1993), pp. 169–217. Also Jon Elster, Claus Offe, and Ulrich K. Preuss, *Institutional Designs in Post-Communist Societies: Rebuilding the Ship at Sea* (Cambridge: Cambridge University Press, 1998).

11. At the eve of Eastern European transformation Bruce Ackerman argued, for instance, that a constitution, unlike normal legislation, needs to win a direct mandate from the people, but Wolfgang Merkel pointed out that the circumstances of Eastern Europe are 'miles away from that kind of conceptual structure of public discourse which lifts referendum out of manipulative ratification into the higher sphere of deliberative politics'. See Wolfgang Merkel, 'Institutions and Democratic Consolidation in East Central Europe', Estudio/Working Paper 86 (Madrid: Instituto Juan March de Estudios e Investigationes, 1996), p. 26. Also Bruce Ackerman, *The Future of Liberal Revolution* (New Haven, CT: Yale University Press, 1992), p. 53–4.

12. For instance, Juan Linz forcefully advanced the virtues of parliamentarism in contrast to the perils of presidentialism, whereas Shugart and Carey insisted that properly crafted presidential or premier–presidential forms of government can overcome the traditional disadvantages of presidential

regimes. See Juan J. Linz, 'The Perils of Presidentialism', *Journal of Democracy*, 1/1 (1990), pp. 51–69 and 'The Virtues of Parliamentarism', *Journal of Democracy*, 1/4 (1990), pp. 84–91. Also Matthew Soberg Shugart and John M. Carey, *Presidents and Assemblies: Constitutional Design and Electoral Dynamics* (Cambridge: Cambridge University Press, 1992), pp. 273–87. Also *Postcommunist Presidents*, Ray Taras, ed. (Cambridge: Cambridge University Press, 1997).

13. See, for example, S.E. Finer, Vernon Bogdanor, and Bernard Rudden, *Comparing Constitutions* (Oxford: Clarendon Press, 1995), or Istvan Pogany, 'Constitution Making or Constitutional Transformation in Post-communist Societies', *Political Studies*, 44/3 (1996) pp. 565–91.

14. See Robert Elgie and Jan Zielonka, 'Constitutions and Constitution-Building: Comparative Perspective', in *Democratic Consolidation in Eastern Europe. Vol.1: Institutional Engineering*, Jan Zielonka, ed. (Oxford: Oxford University Press, 2001), pp. 25–47, and Jan Zielonka, 'New Institutions in the Old East Bloc', *Journal of Democracy*, 5/2 (1994). See also Liborio Mattina, 'La riforma delle istituzioni', in *La sfida dell'allargamento. L'Unione europea e la democratizzazione dell'Europa centro-orientale*, Liboria Mattina, ed. (Bologna: Il Mulino, 2004), pp. 85–130.

15. See, for example, Laurence Whitehead, 'Three International Dimensions of Democratization', in *The International Dimensions of Democratization*, Laurence Whitehead, ed. (Oxford: Oxford University Press, 1996), p. 4, or Jan Aart Scholte, 'Globalization, Governance and Democracy in Post-Communist Romania', *Democratization*, 5/4 (1998), pp. 52–77.

16. See, for example, Jeffrey S. Kopstein and David A Reilly, 'Postcommunist Spaces: A Political Geography Approach to Explaining Postcommunist Outcomes', in *Capitalism and Democracy in Central and Eastern Europe*, Grzegorz Ekiert and Stephen E. Hanson, eds. (Cambridge: Cambridge University Press, 2003), pp. 121–3, or Hans Peter Schmitz and Karin Sell, 'International Factors in Processes of Political Democratization: Towards a Theoretical Integration', in *Democracy without Borders: Transnationalization and Conditionality in New Democracies*, Jean Gruel, ed. (London: Routledge, 1999), p. 39

17. For instance, Sachs and Warner argued that harmonizations with EU economic institutions, regulations, and policies will slow down economic growth in the region and Peter Mair asserted that 'little more than ten years after celebrating their escape from communist control and their return to, or discovery of, democracy, the accession polities are likely to find themselves becoming encased in a system in which popular democracy has little or no role.' See Peter Mair, 'Popular Democracy and EU Enlargement', *Eastern European Politics and Society*, 17/1 (2003), p. 63, and Jeffrey Sachs and Andrew Warner, 'Achieving Rapid Growth in the Transition Economies of Central Europe', Development Discussion Paper, No. 57, Harvard Institute for International Development, July 1996.

18. Frank Schimmelfenning, 'Democratic Conditionality and Democratic Consolidation in Eastern and Central Europe', paper presented at the Centre for European Studies conference, Harvard University, December 2003.

19. For a more in-depth analysis of this relationship see Jan Zielonka, 'Conclusions: Foreign Made Democracy', in *Democratic Consolidation in Eastern Europe. Vol. 2: International and Transnational Factors*, Jan Zielonka and Alex Pravda, eds. (Oxford: Oxford University Press, 2001), pp. 520–3.

20. See, for example, William Pfaff, *Barbarian Sentiments* (New York: Hill and Wang, 2000), pp. 166–8.

21. Alina Mungiu-Pippidi and Denisa Mindruta, 'Was Huntington Right? Testing Cultural Legacies and the Civilizational Border', *International Politics*, 39 (2002), pp. 193–213. Gabriel Bădescu's study focusing on Catholic Transylvania that previously belonged to the Habsburg empire and the rest of Orthodoxed and 'Ottomanised' Romania also refutes the existence of any clear 'civilization border'. The study was based on the 1995–9 World Values Survey and will soon appear in Hans-Dieter Klingemann, Dieter Fuchs, and Jan Zielonka, eds. *Democracy and Political Culture in Eastern Europe* (London: Routledge, 2006), forthcoming.

22. Moreover, although cultural and historical legacies may be unable to determine post-Communist paths, they nevertheless make it easier or harder for some countries to catch up with the western part of the continent. As Jacques Rupnik put it: 'When one looks at a prospective map based on the socio-economic criteria (industralization, urbanization, and communications) that identify the post-communist regions most likely to "reconnect" with Western Europe, one is struck by its similarity to Europe in 1914. The "Habsburg factor" seems to be an important ingredient in assessing the chances of the democratic and market-oriented transition and of a successful "reconnection" with the European Union countries. Another historical query for the future concerns the extent of German influence in this process knowing that East Prussia used to stretch to Kaliningrad, alias Köningsberg. If the Baltic states are added to Habsburg Central Europe, we come closer to another dividing line in the reconnection process; the line between Western and Eastern Christendom. One should be beware of historical or cultural determinism, but the correlations between the three maps are striking.' Jacques Rupnik, 'Europe's New Frontiers: Remapping Europe', *Daedalus*, 123 (1994), pp. 92–3.

23. Croatia's GDP growth for the year 2001 was 4.1 per cent and the net FDI has risen ten times, reaching 1,094 million USD, compared to the year 1994. Latest data available at: http://www.europa.eu.int/ comm/external_relations/see/croatia/index.htm, or *Transition Report Update* (London: European Bank for Reconstruction and Development, 2004).

24. This shows that the dividing line does not necessarily run between post-Communist and post-Soviet states or between Central and south-eastern European states (or the Balkans).

25. For an analysis of the relationship between economic and democratic reforms see e.g. Guilermo O'Donnell, 'Do economists know best?' in *The Global Resurgence of Democracy*, Larry Diamond and Marc F. Plattner, eds. (Baltimore, MD: Johns Hopkins University Press, 1996), pp. 336–42. See also Bela Greskovits, *The Political Economy of Protest and Patience* (Budapest: Central European University, 1997).

26. Ralf Dahrendorf, *Reflections on the Revolution in Europe* (London: Chatto and Windus, 1990), p. 99.

27. For instance, Adam Przeworski in his important book published on the eve of post-Communist transformation bluntly stated: 'Haggard argued that "democratic stalemate produces a zigzag or stop-go effort to adjust but need not lead to political destabilization, repression, or authoritarian installation". My view is different: In spite of these zigzags, [economic] reforms can advance quite far under democratic conditions, but they are politically destabilizing....Forget geography for a moment and put Poland in the place of Argentina, Hungary in place of Uruguay. You will see states weak as organizations; political parties and other associations that are ineffectual in representing and mobilizing; economics that are monopolistic, overprotected, and overregulated; agricultures that cannot feed their own people; public bureaucracies that are overgrown; welfare services that are fragmentary and rudimentary. And will you not conclude that such conditions breed governments vulnerable to pressure from large firms, populist movements of doubtful commitment to democratic institutions, armed forces that sit menacingly on the sidelines, church hierarchies torn between authoritarianism and social justice, nationalist sentiments vulnerable to xenophobia?' See Adam Przeworski, *Democracy and the Market. Political and Economic Reforms in Eastern Europe and Latin America* (Cambridge: Cambridge University Press, 1991), p. 180 and p. 190.

28. 'Things are bound to get worse before they get better', Dahrendorf argued, 'it is hard to tell how long the trek through the valley of tears will take, but certain that it will take longer than a lifetime of the first parliament and always likely that it will engender a degree of disillusionment which will threaten the new constitutional framework along with the economic reforms, which promised so much but could not deliver in time.' See Ralf Dahrendorf, *Reflections on the Revolution in Europe* (London: Chatto and Windus, 1990), pp. 77–8.

29. For basic economic data on the ten countries analyzed here, see http://www.evd.nl/main.asp or http://www.worldbank.org/eca/eu-enlargement/index.html

30. For a detailed analysis of the wage crisis in these countries, see *Paying the Price: The Wage Crisis in Central and Eastern Europe*, Daniel Vaughan-Whitehead, ed. (London: Macmillan, 1998).

31. Centrum Badanie Opinii Spolecznej (CBOS) data of May 1992 cited in Lena Kolarska-Bobińska, *Completed Transformation: Integration into the European Union* (Warsaw: Instytut Spraw Publicznych, 1999), pp. 3–4.

32. See data published by *Eurostat* in 2002. In fact, some economists argue that high rates of Eastern European unemployment are due to the significant EU trade surplus with these states rather than to market reforms as such. See John Eatwell et. al., *Not 'Just Another Accession'—The Political Economy of EU Enlargement in the East* (London: Institute for Public Policy, 1997), p. 47.

33. Elena A. Iankova, *Eastern European Capitalism in Making* (Cambridge: Cambridge University Press, 2002).

34. For a broader analysis of the patterns of institutionalization of contentious politics in Eastern Europe, see Grzegorz Ekiert and Jan Kubik, *Rebellious Civil Society: Popular Protest and Democratic Consolidation in Poland, 1989–1993* (Ann Arbor: University of Michigan Press, 1999).

35. Béla Greskovits, *The Political Economy of Protest and Patience. East European and Latin American Transformations Compared* (Budapest: Central European University Press, 1998), especially pp. 177–88.

36. See e.g. *Socialism, Capitalism, Transformation*, Leszek Balcerowicz, ed. (Budapest: Central European University Press, 1995); Salvatore Zecchini, 'The Role of International Financial Institutions in the Transition Process', in *Lessons from the Economic Transition: Central and Eastern Europe in the 1990s*, Salvatore Zecchini, ed. (Dordrecht: Kluwer, 1997); Steven M. Fish, 'The Determinants of Economic Reform in the Post-Communist World', *East European Politics and Societies*, 12/2 (1998), pp. 127–40; Susan Senior Nello and Karen E. Smith, *The European Union and Central and Eastern Europe: The Implications of Enlargement in stages* (Aldershot: Ashgate, 1998), pp. 39–54.

37. See, for example, Jeffrey S. Kopstein and David A. Reilly, 'Explaining the Why of the Why: A Comment on Fish's "Determinants of Economic Reform in the Post-Communist World" ', *East European Politics and Societies*, 13/3 (1999), pp. 613–26.

38. Calculation made on the basis of EBRD, *Transition Report Update 2002* (London: European Bank for Reconstruction and Development, 2002).

39. *Eurostat; Statistics for Economic and Monetary Union (eurozone) and European Union (EU-15)* (Luxembourg: Office for Official Publications of European Communities, 2002).

40. See especially Samuel P. Huntington, *Political Order in Changing Societies* (New Haven, CT: Yale University Press, 1968), pp. 192–262. See also Samuel P. Huntington, *The Third Way. Democratization in the Late Twentieth Century* (Norman: University of Oklahoma Press, 1991), pp. 231–57.

41. This fear has been articulated especially by scholars comparing South American and Eastern European transitions. See, for example, a quote from Adam Przeworski's *Democracy and the Market* in note 27, or Robert Kaufman, 'Approaches to the Study of State Reform in Latin America and Postcommunist Countries', *Comparative Politics*, 31 (1999), pp. 357–75. Also scholars studying the inter-war history of Eastern Europe feared a resurgence of praetorian politics in the region following the collapse of Communism. See e.g. Thomas

Ertman, 'Democracy and Dictatorship in Interwar Europe Revisited', *World Politics*, 50 (1999), pp. 475–505, or Vesna Pusic, 'Dictatorship with Democratic Legitimacy: Democracy versus Nation', *East European Politics and Society*, 8 (1994), pp. 383–401. Finally, it has been argued that some of the causes for the malfunctioning and possible failure of the newly established regimes in Eastern Europe could have been structural. See e.g. Herbert Kitscheld's review essay, 'Structure and Process-Driven Explanations of Political regime Change', *American Political Science Review*, 86 (1992), pp. 1028–34.

42. This point has been argued very convincingly by Ken Jowitt. See e.g. Ken Jowitt, 'The New World Disorder', in *The Global Resurgence of Democracy*, Larry Diamond and Marc F. Plattner, eds. (Baltimore, MD: Johns Hopkins University Press, 1996), pp. 27–35.

43. For a detailed analysis of the constitutional process in these countries see *Democratic Consolidation in Eastern Europe, Vol. 1: Institutional Engineering*, Jan Zielonka, ed. (Oxford: Oxford University Press, 2001).

44. This distinction has been made in Stephen Holmes, 'Constitutionalism', in *The Encyclopedia of Democracy*, Vol. I, Seymour Martin Lipset, ed. (Washington, DC: Congressional Quarterly, 1995), p. 300.

45. See, for example, *Strategic Survey 1992–1993* (London: Brassey's for the International Institute for Strategic Studies, 1993), pp. 103–8.

46. See Joseph Rothschild, *East-Central Europe between Two World Wars* (Seattle: University of Washington Press, 1990), pp. 9 ff.

47. Whether Russia's restrain was a deliberate choice is a matter of discussion. See e.g. *Gorbachev, Yeltsin and Putin: Political Leadership in Russia's Transition*, Archie Brown and Lilia Shevstova, eds. (Washington, DC: Carnegie Endowment for International Peace, 2001).

48. For a detailed analysis see especially Wade Jacoby, *The Enlargement of the European Union and NATO: Ordering from the Menu in Central Europe* (Cambridge: Cambridge University Press, 2004), and Zoltan Barany, *The Future of NATO Expansion: Four Case Studies* (Cambridge: Cambridge University Press, 2003).

49. The Pact for Stability was initially an initiative of the French Prime Minister, Edouard Balladur, presented in June 1993. See Mathias Jopp and Hanna Ojanen, eds., *European Security Integration: Implications for Non-alignment and Alliances* (Helsinki: Ulkopoliittinen instituutti; Bonn: Institut für Europäische Politik; Paris: WEU Institute for Security Studies, 1999)

50. EBRD, *Transition Report—Energy in Transition 2001* (London: European Bank for Reconstruction and Development), 2001, pp. 186–7.

51. See, for example, Chris Javis, 'Rise and Fall of the Pyramid Schemes in Albania', *IMF Working Paper*, WP/99/98, pp. 4–5.

52. Although as Ivan Krastev rightly pointed out, the relationship between reform and corruption is anything but simple. See Ivan Krastev, *Shifting Obsessions. Three Essays on the Politics of Anticorruption* (Budapest: Central European University Press, 2004), especially pp. 34–40.

53. For a comparative analysis of economic reforms in post-Communist countries, see Christian von Hirschhausen, *Modernizing Infrastructure in Transformation Economies: Paving the Way to European Enlargement* (Cheltenham: Edward Elgar, 2002), pp. 52–3.

54. See EBRD, *Transition Report—Energy in Transition 2001* (London: European Bank for Reconstruction and Development, 2001), pp. 186–7.

55. European Commission—Eurostat, *Towards an Enlarged European Union: Key indicators on Member States and Candidate Countries* (Luxembourg: Office of Official Publications for the European Communities, 2003).

56. The literature on democracy usually distinguishes between liberal and illiberal or merely 'electoral' types of democracy. See, for example, Guilermo O'Donnell, 'Illusions about Consolidation', *Journal of Democracy*, 7/2 (1996), pp. 34–51, and Fareed Zakaria, 'The Rise of Illiberal Democracy', *Foreign Affairs*, 76/6 (1997), pp. 22–43.

57. Dieter Fuchs and Hans-Dieter Klingemann, 'Eastward Enlargement of the European Union and the Identity of Europe', *West European Politics*, 25/Special Issue 2 (2002), p. 40. See also an interesting analysis of the evolution of political discourses in various post-Communist countries: John S. Dryzek and Leslie T. Holmes, *Post-Communist Democratization: Political Discourses across Thirteen Countries* (Cambridge: Cambridge University Press, 2002).

58. Data from The New Democracies Barometer cited in Christian W. Haerpfer, *Democracy and Enlargement in Post-Communist Europe: The Democratization of the General Public in Fifteen Central and Eastern European Countries, 1991–1998* (London: Routledge, 2002), p. 18. See also Sarah Oates, William L. Miller, and Åse Grødeland, 'Towards a Soviet Past or Socialist Future? Understanding Why Voters Choose Communist Parties in Ukraine, Russia, Bulgaria, Slovakia, and the Czech Republic', in *Party Development and Democratic Change in Post-Communist Europe*, Paul G. Lewis, ed. (London: Frank Cass, 2001), pp. 16–31.

59. USAID, *The 2001 NGO Sustainability Index for Central and Eastern Europe and Eurasia*, 5th edn. (United States Agency for International Development, Bureau for Europe and Asia, Office of Democracy and Governance, March 2002), p. 79 and p. 158. It is important to take into consideration the fact that there can be wide discrepancies between the number of registered and the number of active NGOs. For instance, in Latvia there are about 5,000 NGOs registered, however only about 1,500 are active, but of those barely 800 can be considered truly viable (p. 96). On the other hand, in some countries like Belarus there are as many unregistered NGOs active as registered ones, since numerous organizations choose not to register due to 'the burdensome nature of the registration process' (p. 40). The above factors contribute to the distortions and unreliability of the statistical data concerning the activity of the NGOs in Central and Eastern Europe and transition countries. For contrasting evaluations of the scale and impact of the civil society in the region, see Marc Morjé Howard, *The Weakness of Civil Society in Post-Communist Europe*, (Cambridge: Cambridge

University Press, 2003), and Grzegorz Ekiert and Jan Kubik, *Rebellious Civil Society. Popular Protest and Democratic Consolidation in Poland, 1989–1993* (Ann Arbor: University of Michigan Press, 1999).

60. See, for example, Taras Kuzio and Marc Nordberg, 'Nation and State Building, Historical Legacies and National Identities in Belarus and Ukraine: A Comparative Analysis', *Canadian Review of Studies in Nationalism*, 26 (1999), pp. 69–90.

61. See, example, Kataryna Wolczuk, *The Moulding of Ukraine: The Constitutional Politics of State Formation* (Budapest: Central European University, 2001), and Gwendolyn Sasse, 'The "New" Ukraine: A State of Regions', *Regional & Federal Studies*, 11/3 (2001), pp. 69–100.

Chapter 2: European Power Politics

1. This is what Andrew Moravcsik and Kalypso Nicolaides called in another context a 'Christmas tree effect'. This is when small concessions are made 'on issues that mattered enormously to some countries at a relatively small, if still extant, cost to others'. See Andrew Moravcsik and Kalypso Nicolaides, 'Explaining the Treaty of Amsterdam. Interest, Influence, Institutions', *Journal of Common Market Studies*, 37/1 (1999), p. 74. See also Richard E. Baldwin, Joseph F. Francois, and Richard Portes, 'EU enlargement. Small costs for the west, big gains for the east', *Economic Policy*, 12/24 (1997), pp. 127–76. After the conclusion of accession negotiations in Copenhagen in 2002, European Enlargement Commissioner, Günter Verheugen, told the European Parliament foreign affairs committee on 23 January 2003: 'We're getting enlargement cheaper than we thought we would', in European Commission, 'The Cost of Enlargement discussed in Parliament', *Enlargement Weekly*, 28 January 2003. Available at: http://europa.eu.int/comm/enlargement/docs/newsletter/latest_weekly.htm.

2. The overall enlargement package amounts to 40.85 billion euros, but experts point out that net transfers to the new member states would not exceed 10 billion euros. This is merely one-tenth of what West Germany committed to East Germany in the process of unification, which comes to DM 210 billion. For more details see Barbara Böttcher, 'Mission accomplished—accession on May 1, 2004', in *EU Enlargement Monitor Central and Eastern Europe*, Deutsche Bank Research, No. 20, 20 January 2003, and Hans-Werner Sinn, 'Germany's Economic Unification: An Assessment after Ten Years', *Review of International Economics*, 10/1 (2002), pp. 113–28.

3. Several weeks before concluding the accession negotiations, Anders Fogh Rasmussen, the Prime Minister of Denmark holding the Union's rotating presidency, argued: 'I feel confident that at the end of the day all EU leaders will realize that we are facing a historic moment, we're going to make a historic decision, and this should not be overshadowed by a detailed discussion on

budget and agriculture.' Internet source VOY Forums available at: http://www.voy.com/64474/230.html.

4. See, for example, Lawrence Freedman, 'World View: Widening the circle of Europe', *Independent*, 17 November 1989; Timothy Garton Ash, 'World View: Poor but clubbable', *Independent*, 19 January 1990; and Egbert Jahn 'The Future of Europe, Eastern Europe and Central Europe', in *Restructuring Eastern Europe: Towards a New European Order*, Ronald J. Hill and Jan Zielonka, eds. (Aldershot: E. Elgar, 1990), pp. 205–6.

5. For Hungary and Poland the accession negotiations lasted for four years ten months, while the overall process (from application to accession) took ten years one month. This is comparable to the southern enlargement: negotiations for Portugal and Spain took more than six years and the overall process nearly nine. It should be mentioned, however, that the accession of Austria, Finland, and Sweden was much shorter. See Graham Avery, 'The Enlargement on Negotiations', in *The Future of Europe: Enlargement and Integration*, Fraser Cammeron ed. (Clardan: Routledge), pp. 35–63.

6. For instance, Britain's first and second applications were rejected by the European Communities. See, for example, David Baker and David Seawright, eds., *Britain for and against Europe: British Politics and the Question of European Integration* (Oxford: Clarendon Press, 1998), pp. 16–17; and George Wilkes, ed., *Britain's Failure to Enter the European Community, 1961–6: The Enlargement Negotiations and Crises in European, Atlantic, and Commonwealth Relations* (London: Frank Cass, 1997).

7. For a somewhat different version of this argument, see Kjell Engelbrekt, 'Multiple Asymmetries: The European Union's Neo-Byzantine Approach to Eastern Enlargement', *International Politics*, 39 (2002), pp. 37–52.

8. In both cases I assume that both rational interest-based calculations as well as normative belief systems are crucial in forming the motivations. For a clash between the two opposite theoretical interpretations, see Jeffrey T. Checkel and Andrew Moravcsik, 'A Constructivist Research Program in EU Studies?' *European Union Politics*, 2/2 (2001), pp. 219–49. See also Andrew Moravcsik and Milada Vachudova, 'National Interests, State Power, and EU Enlargement', *Eastern European Politics and Society*, 17/1 (2003), pp. 42–57.

9. 'Address by Vaclav Havel, President of the Czech Republic before the Members of the European Parliament, Strasbourg, 16 February 2000, Available at http://www.hrad.cz/presinedt/ havel/speeches/2000/1602_uk.html.

10. Tony Blair, British Prime Minister, *PM: A Clear Course for Europe*, Cardiff, UK, 28 November 2002. Available at: http://www.pm.gov. uk/output/page6709.asp.

11. Romano Prodi, President of the European Commission, *Enlargement—the Final Lap*, Speech/02/463 (Brussels: European Parliament, 9 October 2002), European Access Plus available at: www.europeanaccessplus.co.uk.

12. European Commission, *Flash Eurobarometer 132/2, Enlargement of the European Union* (Brussels, European Commission, Directorate General, Enlargement:

November 2002), pp. 48 and 62. One should add that 80 per cent said that the EU will gain a stronger voice internationally as a result of enlargement.

13. See, for example, Daniel Vernet, 'The Dilemmas of French Foreign Policy', *International Affairs*, 68/4 (1992), pp. 655–64. EC Commissioner Frans Andrissen launched another widely discussed proposal for a European Political Area. See Andrissen's speech to the 69th Assembly of Eurochambers, Brussels, 19 April 1991. Alternatives to enlargement were also seriously discussed by academics. For instance, Richard Baldwin looked at future European integration in terms of a 'wedding cake', where all the CEECs with the EU Association Agreements would form an Association of Association Agreements based on the duty-free trade in industrial goods. Only the most-advanced Central and Eastern European Countries (CEECs) would form an organization of European Integration, which would be the similar to European Economic Area (EEA) Agreement but without migration. On the top of Baldwin's Integration 'wedding cake' would be the EU member states with full rights. See Richard E. Baldwin, *Towards an Integrated Europe* (London: Center for Economic Policy Research, 1994), pp. 221–3.

14. Of course, we will never know whether the Union could indeed have frozen the accession process for several decades the way it has done in the case of Turkey. In my view it could, and it therefore tried to keep all options open until the advanced stages of negotiations. For instance, as Lykke Friis has shown, the purpose of so-called Europe Agreements seemed to be to 'prevent further enlargement for the foreseeable future by providing the countries with a number of concessions, which would remove their immediate incentive of applying for EC membership'. Only later were the Europe Agreements officially presented as a means for preparing Central and Eastern European countries for EU membership. Lykke Friis, 'Approaching the "third half" of EU grand bargaining—the post-negotiation phase of the "Europe Agreement game" ', *Journal of European Public Policy*, 5/2 (1998), p. 322. See also Ulrich Sedelmeier, 'The European Union's association policy towards Central and Eastern Europe: Political and economic rationales in conflict', Working Papers in Contemporary European Studies (Sussex: Sussex European Institute, 1994).

15. See Malcolm Rifkind, 'A Wider Europe: Britain's Vision', *European Documents Series*, Institute of European Affairs, 14 (1996), p. 16 and ff. The assertion of national interests in EU policies towards Eastern Europe was well illustrated by José Ignacio Torreblanca Payá, *The European Community and Central Europe (1989–1993): Foreign Policy and Decision-Making* (Madrid: Centro de Estudios Avanzados en Ciencias Sociales, 1997), pp. 40–1.

16. Frank Schimmelfennig, 'The Community Trap: Liberal Norms, Rhetorical Action, and the Eastern Enlargement of the European Union', *International Organization*, 55 (2001), p. 72.

17. Helen Sjursen also argued that 'ethical-political arguments, which testify to a sense of kinship-based duty' have been behind the EU decision to enlarge. See

Helene Sjursen, 'Why Expand? The Question of Legitimacy and Justification in the EU's Enlargement Policy', *Journal of Common Market Studies*, 40/3 (2002), pp. 491–513.

18. Frank Schimmelfennig, op. cit., p. 66.

19. The key importance of geopolitical considerations behind the process of European integration has been confirmed by recent historical studies. See, for example, Robert H. Lieshout, Mathieu L.L. Sergers, and Anna M. van der Vleuten, 'De Gaulle, Moravcsik, and The Choice for Europe', *Journal of Cold War Studies*, 6/4 (2004), pp. 89–139. Also Adrian Smith, 'Imagining geographies of the "new Europe": geo-economic power and the new European architecture of integration', *Political Geography*, 21/5 (2002), pp. 647–70.

20. One could add that there were also fears in some European circles that widening of the Union would make deepening of the Union more difficult. As Jacque Delors put it: 'Reconciling an enlarged Europe with a deeper form of Union is a real dilemma, and it will not be achieved with a few optimistic declarations.' See, for example, Jacques Delors, *An 'Avant-garde' Driving the Europe Unification Process Forward*, Speech of Jacques Delors at the International Bertelsmann Forum, 2001, 'Europe without borders', Berlin, 19–20 January 2001. However, those in favour of deepening have in fact used enlargement as an argument for deepening European integration. For more detailed analysis of the widening versus deepening dilemma, see Markus Jachtenfuchs, 'Deepening and widening integration theory', *Journal of European Public Policy*, 9/4 (2002), pp. 650–7, or Josef M. Van Brabant, 'EU Widening and Deepening—Are these goals reconcilable?' *MOCT–MOST: Economic Policy in Transitional Economies*, Vol. 11/2 (2001), pp. 113–41, or Bruno de Witte, 'Anticipating the Institutional Consequences of Expanded Membership of the European Union', *International Political Science Review/Revue internationale de science politique*, 23/3 (2002), pp. 235–48.

21. Wim Kok, *Enlarging the European Union. Achievements and Challenges* (Florence: European University Institute, 2003), p. 2.

22. Anna Sher analysed speeches delivered by top EU officials on the future of Europe during the year 2000 and concluded: 'Without exception, in all speeches the prospect of enlargement is discussed in conjuncture with the issues of security and stability of Europe ... It is not enough for a given country, or a set of countries, of east-central Europe to establish democracy, the rule of law, human and minority rights to "guarantee" Europe as a whole with stability and peace. For those achievements must be locked in, secured through, unification [of Europe].' Anna Sher, 'A Di-Vision of Europe: The European Union Enlarged', in *Empire's New Clothes. Unveiling EU Enlargement*, József Böröcz and Melinda Kovács, eds., Central Europe Review, 2001. Available at: http://www.ce-review.org/, pp. 256–7.

23. For an earlier attempt to grasp this peculiar nature of the EU as an international actor, see Jan Zielonka, 'Constraints, Opportunities and Choices in European

Foreign Policy', in *Paradoxes of European Foreign Policy*, Jan Zielonka, ed. (The Hague: Kluwer Law International, 1998), pp. 10–13.

24. As I explained in my earlier work, all institutional arrangements concerning the EU have been the product of hard and delicate political bargaining that had to satisfy each of the diverse participants and their conflicting, if not eccentric, agendas. This could not but result in ambiguity, incoherence, and a lack of transparency. Moreover, the system has been constantly in flux, with new deals being negotiated and renegotiated with an ever growing number of actors in response to an ever changing international environment. See Jan Zielonka, *Explaining Euro-Paralysis* (London: Macmillan, 1998), p. 185.

25. Robert Cooper, 'The next empire', *Prospect*, October 2001, p. 26.

26. See, for example, David Baldwin, *Economic Statecraft* (Princeton, NJ: Princeton University Press, 1988), pp. 8–9, or Olav Stokke, ed., *Aid and Political Conditionality* (London: Frank Cass, 1995), pp. 11–13.

27. Intervention de M. Jacques Santer, Président de la Commission européenne devant le Parlement européen, Agenda 2000, Strasbourg, le 16 julliet 1997. Available at: http://europa.eu.int/comm/agenda2000/rapid/9716fr.htm. For a more modest final assessment of the enlargement package, see Chapter 2, n.2.

28. See e.g. Andrew C. Winner, 'The Baltic States: Heading West', *Washington Quarterly*, 25/1 (2002), pp. 207–19.

29. In Copenhagen the European Council decided that Eastern European applicants must meet three basic criteria for EU membership: (*a*) stability of institutions guaranteeing democracy, the rule of law, human rights, and the protection of minorities; (*b*) the existence of a functional market economy as well as the capacity to cope with the competitive pressures and market forces within the Union; and (*c*) the ability to take on the obligations of membership including adherence to the aims of political, economic, and monetary union. The first 'political' criterion was considered to be a precondition for the opening of accession negotiations, while the other criteria were to be fulfilled by the time of membership. See Council of the European Union, *Presidency Conclusions: Copenhagen European Council* (Brussels, 1993).

30. The accession negotiations were conducted under thirty-one chapters in the following functional fields: 1. Free movement of goods, 2. Freedom of movement of persons, 3. Freedom to provide services, 4. Free movement of capital, 5. Company law, 6. Competition policy, 7. Agriculture, 8. Fisheries, 9. Transport policy, 10. Taxation, 11. Economic and Monetary Unit (EMU), 12. Statistics, 13. Social policy, 14. Energy, 15. Industry, 16. SMEs (small and medium sized enterprises), 17. Science and research, 18. Education and training, 19. Telecommunications, 20. Culture and audiovisual, 21. Regional policy, 22. Environment, 23. Consumers and health protection, 24. Justice and home affairs, 25. Customs union, 26. External relations, 27. CFSP (Common Foreign and Security Policy), 28. Financial control, 29. Financial and budgetary provisions, 30. Institutions, 31. Other.

31. Melinda Kovács and Peter Kabachnik, 'The Shedding Light on the Qualitative Other: The EU's Discourse in the Commission Opinions of 1997', and Melinda Kovács, 'Putting Down and Putting Off: The EU's Discoursive Strategies in the 1998 and 1999 Follow-UP Reports', in *Empire's New Clothes. Unveiling EU Enlargement*, József Böröcz and Melinda Kovács, eds., Central Europe Review, 2001. Available at: http://www.ce-review.org/, p. 172 and p. 230.

32. The high level of economic dependence prompted much richer countries such as Switzerland and Norway to align their laws and regulations with the EU's *acquis communautaire* even in the face of their publics' reluctance to embrace fully-fledged EU membership. See Stephan Kux and Elf I. Sverdrup, 'Fuzzy Borders and Adaptive Outsiders, Norway, Switzerland and the EU', *Journal of European Integration*, 22/3 (2000), pp. 237–70.

33. According to this system the applicant states are placed on the same imagined start line and they must compete to reach the finishing line first. States that do not comply with the EU conditions simply fall behind or drop out of the running altogether. See, for example, Bernard Steunenberg, 'Enlargement and reform in the European Union', in *Widening the European Union: The Politics of Institutional Change*, Bernard Steunenberg, ed. (London: Routledge, 2002), pp. 6 and 44.

34. See, for example, Lykke Friis and Anna Murphy, 'The European Union and Central and Eastern Europe: Governance and Boundaries', *Journal of Common Market Studies*, 37/2 (1999), p. 213.

35. The structural theory of imperialism was elaborated in the early 1970s by Johan Galtung. But as the following passages will show, I am not thinking along Galtung's original line. See Johan Galtung, 'A Structural Theory of Imperialism', *Journal of Peace Research*, 8/2 (1971), pp. 81–117.

36. Melinda Kovács and Peter Kabachnik, 'The Shedding Light on the Qualitative Other: The EU's Discourse in the Commission Opinions of 1997', in *Empire's New Clothes: Unveiling EU Enlargement*, József Böröcz and Melinda Kovács, eds., Central Europe Review, 2001. Available at: http://www.ce-review.org/, p. 171

37. Edmund Burke spoke about a 'detached' empire in a somewhat different way. See *Speech of Edmund Burke Esq. On Moving his Resolution for Conciliation with the Colonies* (London, 22 March 1775).

38. In fact, it was often pointed out by experts that a too-harsh treatment of the candidates would produce the Spanish syndrome in the enlarged EU. After accession to the EU, Spain tried very hard to renegotiate all the concessions it had made under pressure in the pre-accession stage and this often led to paralysis of EU decision-making. See, for example, Lorena Ruano, 'Origins and implications of the European Union's enlargements negotiations procedures', *EUI Working Paper* (Florence: European University Institute, 2002), or Antje Hildebrandt, 'What is Special about Enlarging the European Union towards the East? A Comparison with the Southern Enlargement', *Institute for Economies in Transition, BOFIT*, 13 (2002) available at http://granum.uta.fi/granum/kirjantiedot.php?tuote_id=7785.

39. As a Special Report on Twinning pointed out: 'The interaction of the numerous public administrations involved in Twinning created administrative complexity, diminishing efficiency and effectiveness.' See EC—Court of Auditors, 'Twinning as the main instrument to support institution-building in Candidate Countries', European Communities Special Report, 6 (2003).

40. For a more detailed analysis of the EU accession conditions see, for example, Karen E. Smith, 'The Evolution and Application of EU Membership Conditionality', in *The Enlargement of the European Union*, Marise Cremona, ed. (Oxford: Oxford University Press, 2003), pp. 114–15.

41. See, for example, Phenon Nicolaides, 'Preparing for Accession to the European Union: How to establish Capacity for Effective and Credible Application of EU rules' in *The Enlargement of the European Union*, Marise Cremona, ed. (Oxford: Oxford University Press, 2003), p. 65.

42. See, for example, Anthony Pagden, *Lords of All the World, Ideologies of Empire in Spain, Britain and France c.1500–c.1800* (New Haven, CT: Yale University Press, 1995), p. 17.

43. Of course, there are historical examples of empires without true emperors. For instance, the Soviet empire was highly centralized, but even Stalin could not be seen as an equivalent of an emperor. Those who talk about the rise of the American empire do not consider the president to be a kind of emperor. See, for example, Peter Bender, 'America: The New Roman Empire?' *Orbis*, 41/1 (2003), pp. 145–59, or G. John Ikenberry, 'American power and the empire of capitalist democracy', in *Empires, Systems and States*, Michael Cox, Tim Dunne, and Ken Booth, eds. (Cambridge: Cambridge University Press, 2001), pp. 191–212.

44. See, for example, *The Transformation of Governance in the European Union*, Beate Kohler-Koch and Reiner Eising, eds. (London: Routledge, 1999).

45. For a detailed and sophisticated analysis of this problem see, for example, Simon Hix, *The Political System of the European Union* (London: Macmillan, 1999); John Peterson and Elizabeth Bomberg, *Decision-Making in the European Union* (London: Macmillan, 1999); and Fritz W. Scharpf, *Governing in Europe: Effective and Democratic?* (Oxford: Oxford University Press, 1999).

46. See, for example, an interview with the former EU Commissioner, Frans Andrissen, in *De Volkskrant* (16 March 1996), or Franklin Dehousse, 'In deciding to push east, the EU has signed its death warrant', *International Herald Tribune*, 29 December 1995.

47. 'We want to join Europe via Dublin, not Brussels', one of Poland's Euro-sceptics told me. He feared that EU accession would bring about relaxation of laws on divorce and abortion. For a review of Euro-sceptic arguments in Poland see Aleks Szczerbiak, 'After the election, nearing the endgame: the Polish euro-debate in the run up to the 2003 EU accession referendum', Sussex European Institute Working Paper (Brighton: University of Sussex, 2002). See also Paul Taggart and Aleks Szczerbiak, 'Parties, positions and Europe: Euroscepticism in

the EU candidate states of Central and Eastern Europe', Sussex European Institute Working Paper (Brighton: University of Sussex, 2001).

48. For a comprehensive analysis of this problem, see *Winners and Losers of EU Integration: Policy Issues for Central and Eastern Europe*, Helena Tang, ed. (Washington, DC: World Bank, 2000).

49. Earlier in the accession process the Mediterranean countries made sure that the eastward enlargement would go hand in hand with EU Mediterranean policy. See, for example, Esther Barbé, 'Balancing Europe's Eastern and Southern Dimensions', in *Paradoxes of European Foreign Policy*, Jan Zielonka, ed. (Dordrecht: Kluwer Law International, 1998), pp. 117–29.

50. These safeguard clauses allow for 'protective measures' to be taken in the five years following enlargement in the areas of economy, internal market, justice, and home affairs. These measures can be triggered by difficulties or failure to implement commitments in the new member states. See European Communities, *Enlargement of the European Union: An Historic Opportunity* (Brussels: European Commission, Enlargement Directorate-General, 2003), p. 29.

51. Slovakia and Poland have been mentioned in this context because of their low capacity to absorb EU structural funds. See, for example, Bengt O. Karlsson, *The Cost of EU Enlargement—Summary*, a report to the Expert Group on Public Finance, Ministry of Finance, Sweden, Stockholm, 2002, p. 78, or a Polish governmental report on costs and benefits of joining the EU: *Bilans korzyści i kosztów przystąpienia Polski do Unii Europejskiej. Prezentacja wyników prac polskich ośrodków badawczych* (Warsaw: UKIE, 2003).

52. The accession deal in candidate states had to be endorsed by national referenda. This was a tough assignment not only because individual governments had to cope with groups likely to lose from accession to the Union, but also because previously held referenda in these countries merely mobilized populist politicians rather than voters as such. (And most of these referenda to be valid required half the electorate to cast a vote.) For an analysis of the accession referenda and their implications for EU law and politics, see Anneli Albi, 'Referendums in Eastern Europe: The Effects on Reforming the EU Treaties and on the Candidate Countries' Positions in the Convention', EUI Working Paper (Florence: European University Institute, 2002).

53. See European Commission, *Report on the Results of the Negotiations on the Accession of Cyprus, Malta, Hungary, Poland, the Slovak Republic, Latvia, Estonia, Lithuania, the Czech Republic and Slovenia to the European Union prepared by the Commission's departments* (Brussels: European Commission, Enlargement Directorate-General, 2003)

54. The Commission started to play the leading role in the accession process as early as July 1989 when its president, Jacques Delors, accepted the task of coordinating aid for Eastern Europe from so called G-24 (group of 24 industrialized countries) consisting of the Western industrialized countries associated

with several international organizations. It then was put in charge of the Phare programme that channelled various types of assistance to the would-be candidate countries on the principle of strict conditionality monitored by the Commission. The Commission was also the architect of the Europe Agreements that provided a legal and institutional framework of further cooperation and gradual integration between the two parts of Europe. And it was also the Commission who prepared the blueprint for enlargement, the Agenda 2000.

55. Ulrich Sedelmeier and Helen Wallace, 'Eastern Enlargement: Strategy or Second Thoughts?' in *Policy Making in the European Union*, Helen Wallace and William Wallace, eds. (Oxford: Oxford University Press, 2000), p. 457.

56. This was the exemplification of a famous bicycle 'theory' attributed to Walter Hallstein, the first president of the European Commission: One must keep moving forward or fall. See, for example, Michael Emerson, '1992 and after— the bicycle theory rides again', *Political Quarterly*, 59/3 (1998), pp. 289–99. See also Walter Hallstein, *United Europe. Challenge and Opportunity* (Cambridge, MA: Harvard University Press, 1962), p. 56.

57. This has been confirmed to the author by Wim Kok, former Prime Minister of Holland. The term 'Leadership in disguise' is borrowed from a Ph.D. thesis by Remko Vahl, *Leadership in Disguise: The Role of the European Commission in EC Decision-Making on Agriculture in the Uruguay Round* (Leiden: Leiden University, 1996). See also Neil Nugent, 'The Leadership Capacity of the European Commission', *Journal of European Public Policy*, 4/2 (1995), pp. 603–23.

58. Certainly the selection of countries to open accession negotiations with the EU was one such controversial decision before both the Luxembourg and the Helsinki European Councils. Also the Commission's decision to support the German position on the restriction of the movement of labour was quite controversial, especially because the member of the Commission responsible for enlargement was German and coming from the ruling party in this country. For a more detailed analysis of the role of the European Commission in enlargement, see Joanna Przetakiewicz, *The Role of the Commission in the Process of Enlargement. To what Extent is the Commission an Actor in Its Own Right? A Case Study of the Enlargement Process Towards Central and Eastern Europe*, thesis presented at the College of Europe, Bruges, Department of European Political and Administrative Studies, 1997–8.

59. Graham Avery recalls Günter Verheugen declaring it to be 'the best day so far' in his job when the Council gave its agreement to the 'road map' in December 2000. See Graham Avery, 'The Enlargement Negotiations', in *The Future of Europe: Integration and Enlargement*, Fraser Cameron, ed. (New York: Routledge), pp. 35–63.

60. This included such diverse organizations as the International Monetary Fund (IMF) and the Open Society Institute. See Susan Senior-Nello, 'The Impact of

External Economic Factors: The Role of the IMF', in *Democratic Consolidation in Eastern Europe. Vol 2: International and Transnational Factors*, Jan Zielonka and Alex Pravda, eds. (Oxford: Oxford University Press, 2001), pp. 77–109. See also regular reports of the OSI, monitoring the EU's minority rights conditionality, available at: http://www.eumap.org.

61. For more details see Karen E. Smith, *The Making of EU Foreign Policy: The Case of Eastern Europe* (Basingstoke: Macmillan, 1999), particularly the chapter 'Explaining the Making of Foreign Policy Towards Eastern Europe', pp. 162–83.

62. This has become clear during the Dutch and French referenda on the draft of the European Constitution. Many those voting 'no' have expressed their protest against the last wave of the EU's enlargement. See, for example, Philippe Ricard, 'Le non souligne les difficultés de l'élargissement', in *Le Monde*, 31 May 2005.

63. Public resistance to further enlargements should not be underestimated, however. See e.g. Georges Marion, 'La droite allemande accuse la Turquie d'avoir contribué à la victoire du non français', in *Le Monde*, 1 June 2005, and Gamze Avci, 'Putting the Turkish EU Candidacy in Context', *European Foreign Affairs Review*, 7/1 (2002), pp. 91–110.

Chapter 3: Diversity and Adaptation

1. See, for example, Wolfgang Pott, 'NRW fürchtet den Osten', *Die Welt*, 31 March 2002; or Diethart Goos, 'Wer stoppt die Mafia-Banden aus Osteuropa?', *Die Welt*, 30 December 1996.

2. For instance the Dutch government commissioned a special report focusing on these kinds of questions and the subsequent report contained 400 pages of detailed analysis on the increased diversity within the EU as a result of the eastward enlargement. See *Towards a Pan-European Union* (The Hague: Scientific Council for Government Policy, 2001).

3. See Tanja A. Börzel and Thomas Risse, *When Europe Hits Home: Europeanization and Domestic Change*, EUI Working Paper, No. 2000/56 (Florence: European University Institute, 2000).

4. This section will draw from Jan Zielonka and Peter Mair, 'Introduction: Diversity and Adaptation in the Enlarged European Union', in *The Enlarged European Union. Diversity and Adaptation*, Peter Mair and Jan Zielonka, eds. (London: Frank Cass, 2002), pp. 1–19.

5. While diversity involves difference, divergence usually implies moving further apart. See also Christina Schäffner, Andreas Musolff, and Michael Towson, 'Diversity and Unity in European Debates', in *Conceiving of Europe: Diversity in Unity*, Andreas Musolff, Christina Schaffner, and Michael Townson, eds. (Aldershot: Dartmouth, 1996), pp. 1–14.

6. See, for example, Wolfgang Wessels, 'An Ever Closer Fusion? A Dynamic Macro-political View on Integration Process', *Journal of Common Market Studies*, 35/3 (1997), pp. 267–99; *Convergence in the Enlarged European Union*, Serena Giusti and Lucia Tajoli, eds. (Milan: Egea Edizioni, 2003); or Robert Leonardi, *Convergence, Cohesion and Integration in the European Union* (London: Macmillan, 1995), pp. 33–59.

7. This is despite the preamble to the Treaty on European Union that talks about 'creating an ever closer union'. See, for example, the 1989 address by Jacques Delors in Bruges, reprinted in *The European Union: Readings on the Theory and Practice of European Integration*, Brent F. Nelsen and Alexander C-G. Stubb, eds. (London: Lynne Rienner, 1994), pp. 51–64.

8. Those who insist that their aim is qualified rather than total unity need to make clear what mixture of diversity and unity they want to achieve. However, this is usually not the case even in otherwise very competent analyses. See, for example, Eric Philippart and Monika Sie Dhian Ho, 'From Uniformity to Flexibility: Management of Diversity and its Impact on the EU System of Governance', in *Constitutional Change in the EU: From Uniformity to Flexibility?*, Gráinne de Búrca and Joanne Scott, eds. (Oxford: Hart Publishing, 2000), pp. 299–336.

9. See T. Koopmans, 'The Quest for Subsidiarity', in *Institutional Dynamics of European Integration: Essays in Honor of Henry G. Schermers*, Deirdre Curtin and Ton Heukels, eds. (Dordrecht: Martinus Nijhoff, 1994), and Alexander C. G. Stubb, 'Negotiating Flexible Integration in the Amsterdam Treaty', in *European Integration After Amsterdam: Institutional Dynamics and Prospects for Democracy*, Karlheinz Neunreither and Antje Wiener, eds. (Oxford: Oxford University Press, 2000).

10. See Loukas Tsoukalis, *The European Community and its Mediterranean Enlargement* (London: Allen and Unwin, 1981).

11. Giuliano Amato and Judy Batt, *Final Report of the Reflection Group on the Long-term Implications of EU Enlargement: The Nature of the New Border* (Florence: Robert Schuman Centre and Forward Studies Unit, EC, 1999), p. 11.

12. Vaclav Havel, 'Overcoming the Division of Europe', Speech to the European Parliament, Strasbourg, February 16, 2000. Available at: http://www.hrad.cz.

13. Heather Grabbe, *A Partnership for Accession? The Implications of EU Conditionality for the Central and East European Applicants*, EUI Working Paper, No. 99/12 (Florence: European University Institute, 1999). See also Alina Mungiu-Pippidi, 'Facing the Desert of Tartars: the Eastern Border of Europe', in *Europe Unbound*, Jan Zielonka, ed. (London: Routledge, 2002).

14. See, for example, Helen Wallace, 'Whose Europe is it Anyway?', *European Journal of Political Research*, 35/3 (1999), pp. 287–306, and Helen Wallace, 'The Domestication of Europe: Contrasting experiences of EU membership and non-membership', Daalder Lecture, Leiden University, 1999.

15. For instance, a special report on enlargement by the Advisory Council to the Government of the Netherlands envisaged that the increased diversity caused by the next wave of enlargement may affect the entire set of the EU complex policy cycle consisting of preparation, decision-making, implementation, and persistence. If problems resulting from diversity are not addressed properly in one phase they return with force in subsequent phases. The result is a decrease in EU efficiency and subsequent legitimacy crisis. See *Naar een Europabrede Unie* (Sdu Uitgevers voor de Wetenschappelijke Raad voor het Regeringsbeleid: Den Haag, 2001), pp. 48–9. See also Keith Dowding, 'Rational choice and institutional change. An overview of current theories', in *Widening the European Union: The Politics of Institutional Change*, Bernard Steunenberg, ed. (London: Routledge, 2002), pp. 21–38.

16. Graham Avery and Fraser Cameron, *The Enlargement of the European Union* (Sheffield: Sheffield Academic Press, 1998).

17. Adrienne Héritier, 'Differential Europe: The European Union Impact on National Policymaking', in *Differential Europe. The European Union Impact on National Policymaking*, Adrienne Héritier et al. (Boston, MA: Rowman and Littlefield, 2001), p. 2.

18. See Helen Wallace and William Wallace, *Flying Together in a Larger and More Diverse European Union* (The Hague: Working Documents of the Netherlands Scientific Council for Government Policy, No. 87, 1995), and Jonathan Story, 'The Idea of the Core: The Dialectics of History and Space', in *The Politics of European Treaty Reform*, Geoffrey Edwards and Alfred Pijpers, eds. (London: Pinter, 1997), pp. 15–43.

19. This does not mean that the interpretation and application of the *acquis* is always rigid and inflexible. See Claus-Dieter Ehlermann, 'How Flexible is Community Law? An Unusual Approach to the Concept of Two Speeds', *Michigan Law Review*, 82/5 & 6 (1984), pp. 1274–93.

20. For a legal and economic case against trade harmonization, for instance, see Paul Krugman, 'What Should Trade Negotiators Negotiate About', *Journal of Economic Literature*, 35/1 (1997), pp. 113–20.

21. See William Wallace, 'Government without statehood: the unstable equilibrium' in *Policy-Making in the European Union*, 3rd ed., Helen Wallace and William Wallace, eds. (Oxford: Oxford University Press, 1996).

22. See Adrienne Héritier, *Policy-Making and Diversity in Europe: Escaping Deadlock* (Cambridge: Cambridge University Press, 1999), p. 2 and vv.

23. See Adrienne Héritier et al., *Ringing the Changes in Europe: Regulatory Competition and the Transformation of the State: Britain, France and Germany* (Berlin: de Gruyter, 1996).

24. A similar conclusion has been reached by Helen Wallace when writing about enlargement. In her view there are 'well-established techniques for adapting EU legislation to accommodate different circumstances in individual member states, whether by variation of substantive provisions or by delayed

implementation'. See Helen Wallace, 'EU Enlargement: A Neglected Subject', in *The State of the European Union: Risks, Reform, Resistance and Revival*, Maria Green Cowles and Michael Smith, eds. (Oxford: Oxford University Press, 2000), p. 162.

25. Héritier, *Policy-Making and Diversity in Europe*, op. cit., p. 8.

26. Lisa L. Martin, 'Heterogeneity, linkage and common problems', in *Local Commons and Global Interdependence*, Robert O. Keohane and Elinor Ostrom, eds. (London: Sage, 1995), pp. 79–91.

27. Note Nicholas Rescher's argument: 'Consensus is not a criterion of truth, is not a standard of value, is not an index of moral or ethical appropriateness, is not a requisite for co-operation, is not a communal imperative for a just social order, is not, in itself, an appropriate ideal.... Consensus is no more than one positive factor that has to be weighed on the scale along many others.' See Nicholas Rescher, *Pluralism: Against the Demand for Consensus* (Oxford: Clarendon Press, 1993), p. 199.

28. This was, for instance, attempted in *Towards a Pan-European Union* (The Hague: Scientific Council for Government Policy, 2001), p. 354.

29. For a catalogue of possible economic problems caused by this wave of enlargement see, for example, Roy Gardner, 'The Enlargement', in *The Economics of the European Union: Policy and Analysis*, Mike Artis and Frederick Nixson, eds. (Oxford: Oxford University Press, 2001), pp. 80–96. See e.g. Miroslav N. Jovanovic, 'Where are the Limits to the Enlargement of the European Union?', *Journal of Economic Integration*, 14/1 (1999), pp. 467–96.

30. However, many analysts warn against the risk of elevating manifestations of social differences between East and West to an almost mythical level, cautioning against a presentation of Eastern Europe simply as a region of abandoned children, street beggars, and tuberculosis patients that may spread its social diseases westward in the aftermath of enlargement. They also point out that most of the statistics indicating welfare gaps between Western and Eastern Europe fail to take account of the sizeable unregistered 'shadow' economy in the region. In fact, citizens in many of the new member states have long been accustomed to coping with social shortfalls through household production, the farming of small private plots, or work in the 'second' informal economy. For instance, Friedrich Schneider and Dominik H. Enste estimate that Hungary has the largest black economy with 31 %, followed by Bulgaria with 26 %, whereas the Slovakia and the Czech Republic have the smallest with 14 % and 13 %, respectively. In all the transition countries, the shadow economies have grown in the past years. See Friedrich Schneider and Dominik H. Enste, *The Shadow Economy: An International Survey* (Cambridge: Cambridge University Press, 2002), p. 33. See also Friedrich Schneider, 'What Do We Know About the Shadow Economy? Evidence from 21 OECD countries', *World Economics*, 2/4 (2001), pp. 19–32; and Rainer Neef and Manuela Stănculescu, eds., *The Social Impact of Informal Economies in Eastern Europe* (Burlington, VT: Ashgate, 2002).

31. For more details see Jean-Luc Dehaene and Ania Krok-Paszkowska, *The Political Dimension of EU Enlargement: Looking towards Post-accession; Report of the Reflection Group* (Florence: European University Institute, 2001), p. 33. See also Daniel Gros, 'Health not Wealth: Enlarging the EMU', *West European Politics*, 25/2 (2002), pp. 141–50.

32. The good health of some of the post-Communist economies is confirmed by the World Economic Forum's global competitiveness index. According to the 2003–4 ranking, for instance, Estonia scores better than Spain, Portugal, France, Belgium, Ireland, Greece, and Italy. See *The Global Competitiveness Report 2003–2004* (Oxford: Oxford University Press, 2003), Table 1, p. 15.

33. Long-run growth projections estimate a period of 15–30 years for the new members to catch up to the income levels of the old ones. See, for example, Stanley Fisher, Ratna Sahay, and Carlos A. Végh, *How Far is Eastern Europe from Brussels?* IMF Working Paper, WP 53, Washington, DC, 1998, p. 28.

34. See Robert Leonardi, *Convergence, Cohesion and Integration in the European Union* (London: Macmillan, 1995), p. 4, and Liesbet Hooghe, ed., *Cohesion Policy and European Integration* (Oxford: Oxford University Press, 1996), pp. 5–6.

35. See, for example, the 1989 Delors Report citied in Robert Leonardi, *Convergence, Cohesion and Integration in the European Union*, op. cit., p. 6

36. Fabio Sdogati, 'Introduction', in *EU Enlargement to the CEECs: Trade Competition, Delocalisation of Production, and Effects on the Economies of the Union*, Salvatore Baldone, Fabio Sdogati, and Lucia Tajoli, eds. (Milan: Franco Angeli, 2002), p. 17.

37. *European Voice*, 24 September 1998, p. 15. See also Parlement Européen, 'La politique de l'environnement et l'élargissement', *Fische Thématique*, 23/17 (1998), Luxembourg, p. 15.

38. Theories of economic integration that argue that labour which is free to migrate moves from low-wage to high-wage areas, fail to appreciate the many social and psychological factors inhibiting migration. They fail, for instance, to explain why migration from low-wage Greece and Portugal to richer countries of the Union is relatively low. See e.g. Willem Molle, *The Economics of European Integration: Theory, Practice, Policy* (Aldershot: Ashgate, 1997), pp. 189–213.

39. Migrants usually represent a relatively cheap solution for filling in seasonal or structural shortages of labour within the EU. These shortages will only get greater with the evolving demographic trends in Western Europe. For example, the population of Italy, currently 57 million, is projected to decline to 41 million by 2050. In the next five decades the proportion of the Italian population that is sixty five or older will rise from 18 per cent to 35 per cent. *Replacement Migration: Is it A Solution to Declining and Aging Populations?* Population Division, Department of Economic and Social Affairs, United Nations Secretariat, New York, 2000, ESA/P/WP.160, pp. 43–9. For data covering the entire EU, see pp. 85–92. See also Hans Korno Rasmussen, *No Entry: Immigration Policy in Europe* (Copenhagen: Copenhagen Business School Press, 1997).

40. As Daniel Vaughan-Whitehead pointed out, 'the fall in real wages and living standards, the disappearance of social services that previously were generously provided, and cuts in social protection could increase the risk of industrial relocations from the EU to Central and Eastern Europe', p. 33. Daniel Vaughan-Whitehead, *Economic and Social Gaps, New Hidden Borders in the Enlarged Europe?* EUI Working Paper, No. 2000/29 (Florence: European University Institute, 2000). Also see Bob Deacon, 'Eastern European welfare states: the impact of the politics of globalization', *Journal of European Social Policy*, 10/2 (2000), p. 156. Nevertheless, some authors demonstrate that social dumping in Eastern Europe is not necessarily present. 'The accusation of social dumping, which the less-developed European countries seem to have engaged in because their wages and social standards are low, is not justified. Low wages, low social standards, and high returns to capital are the necessary concomitants of a long-term adjustment process.', Hans-Werner Sinn, *Social Dumping in the Transformation Process?* CESinfo Working Paper, No. 508, June 2001, p. 34.

41. For more detailed debate on hard and soft power of the *acquis* see Brigid Laffan, 'The European Union polity: a union of regulative, normative and cognitive pillars', *Journal of European Public Policy*, 8/5 (2001), pp. 721–2.

42. Laszlo Bruszt, 'Making Markets and Eastern Enlargement: Diverging Convergence?', *West European Politics*, 25/2 (2002), p. 123.

43. For an in-depth analysis of corruption in Eastern Europe see Ivan Krastev, *Shifting Obsessions: Three Essays on the Politics of Anticorruption* (Budapest: Central European University Press, 2004).

44. Problems in assessing the implications of the empirical evidence concerning culture and democracy are well discussed in Herbert Kitschelt, 'Accounting for Postcommunist regime Diversity: What counts as a Good Cause?' in *Capitalism and Democracy in Central and Eastern Europe: Assessing the Legacy of Communist Rule*, Grzegorz Ekiert and Stephen E. Hanson, eds. (Cambridge: Cambridge University Press, 2003) pp. 49–88. See also Christian W. Haerpfer, *Democracy and Enlargement in Post-Communist Europe: The Democratization of the General Public in Fifteen Central and Eastern European Countries, 1991–1998* (London: Routledge, 2002), pp. 1–5.

45. For a comparison of media law in various countries of the EU and new member states, see Council of Europe, *Media Diversity in Europe*, Report Prepared by the AP-MD (Strasbourg, December 2002), and Alison Harcout, 'The regulation of media markets in selected accession states in Central and Eastern Europe', *European Law Journal*, 8/2 (2003), pp. 316–40.

46. For a detailed analysis of the party systems in some old and new member states see, for example, Geoffrey Pridham and Paul G. Lewis, eds., *Stabilizing Fragile Democracies: Comparing New Party Systems in Southern and Eastern Europe* (London: Routledge, 1996), particularly pp. 100–25.

47. For discussion on ethnic minorities in Central and Eastern Europe see Marcus Kreuzer and Vello Pettai, 'Patterns of Political Instability: Affiliation Patterns of

Politicians and Voters in Post-Communist Estonia, Latvia, and Lithuania', *Studies in Comparative International Development*, 38/2 (2003), pp. 76–98. Also see Vello Pettai and Klara Hallik, 'Understanding processes of ethnic control: Segmentation, dependency and co-optation in post-communist Estonia', *Nations and Nationalism*, 8/Special Issue 4 (2002), pp. 505–29, or Nida M. Gelazis, *The Effects of EU Conditionality on Citizenship Policies and Protection of National Minorities in the Baltic States*, EUI Working Paper, No. 2000/68 (Florence: European University Institute, 2000).

48. See, for example, Open Society Institute, *Monitoring the EU Accession Process: Minority Protection Vol. II, Case Studies in Selected Member states* (New York: OSI/ EU Accession Monitoring Program, 2002), particularly the chapter entitled 'The situation of Roma in Spain', pp. 281–359.

49. See, for example, Karen Kenkel, 'New Cultural Geographies', *New German Critique*, Special Issue on Minorities in German Culture, 46 (1989), pp. 181–90. Also Stephen Castles et al., *Here for Good: Western Europe's New Ethnic Minorities* (London: Pluto, 1984); and Stephen Castles and Mark J. Miller, *The Age of Migration: International Population Movements in the Modern World* (Basingstoke: Macmillan, 1993).

50. See for example the Freedom House Freedom in the World Data report available at: http://www.freedomhouse.org/ratings/allscore04.xl.

51. Dieter Fuchs and Hans-Dieter Klingemann, 'Eastward Enlargement of the European Union and the Identity of Europe', *West European Politics*, 25/2 (2002), pp. 19–54.

52. David D. Laitin, 'Culture and National Identity: "The East" and European Integration', *West European Politics*, 25/2 (2002), pp. 55–80.

53. Vladimir Tismaneanu, 'Discomforts of Victory: Democracy, Liberal Values and Nationalism in Post-Communist Europe', *West European Politics*, 25/2 (2002), p. 95. See also Ken Jowitt, *New World Disorder: The Leninist Extinction* (Berkeley: University of California Press, 1992), and Katherine Verdery, *What Was Socialism, and What Comes Next* (Princeton, NJ: Princeton University Press, 1996).

54. For a sophisticated analysis of various approaches to the study of the legacies in the post-Communist context, see Grzegorz Ekiert and Stephen E. Hanson, 'Time, Space and Institutional Change in Central and Eastern Europe', in *Capitalism and Democracy in Central and Eastern Europe: Assessing the Legacy of Communist Rule*, Grzegorz Ekiert and Stephen E. Hanson, eds. (Cambridge: Cambridge University Press, 2003), pp. 15–48.

55. See, for example, Ronald Inglehart and Wayne Baker, 'Modernization, Cultural Change and the Persistence of Traditional Values', *American Sociological Review*, 41/4 (1999), pp. 19–51.

56. See, for example, Geofrey Pridham, 'EU Enlargement and Consolidating democracy in Post-Communist States-Formality and Reality', *Journal of Common Market Studies*, 40/3 (2002), pp. 953–73, or Jan Zielonka, 'Foreign Made

Democracy', in *Democratic Consolidation in Eastern Europe, Vol. 2: International and Transnational Factors*, Jan Zielonka and Alex Pravda, eds. (Oxford: Oxford University Press, 2001), pp. 511–32.

57. See, for example, Peter Mair, 'Popular Democracy and EU Enlargement', *Eastern European Politics and Society*, 17/1 (2003), pp. 58–73. For a more general argument see Fritz W. Scharpf, *Governing in Europe: Effective and Democratic?* (Oxford: Oxford University Press, 1999), especially chapter 1.

58. See, for example, Darina Malová and Tim Haughton, 'Making Institutions in Central and Eastern Europe, and the Impact of Europe', *West European Politics*, 25/2 (2002), pp. 101–20, or Stephen Holmes, 'A European Doppelstaat?' *Eastern European Politics and Society*, 17/1 (2003), especially pp. 112–15.

59. See, for example, Alain Beuve-Mery and Serge Marti, 'Pourquoi l'Europe de l'Est vote George W. Bush: Le soutien des pays candidats aux Etats-Unis sur l'Iraq traduit leur adhesion au modele anglosaxon', *Le Monde*, 4 March 2003, and Editorial, 'Elargissement', *Le Monde*, 17 June 2003.

60. The so-called letter of eight entitled 'Europe and America Must Stand United' appeared in the *Wall Street Journal* on 30 January 2003. It was signed by five Western and three Eastern European leaders (Vaclav Havel, Leszek Miller, and Peter Medgyessy). This letter was followed by a letter of ten more Eastern European countries, all of them candidates to join NATO, that expressed even stronger support for American policy towards Iraq.

61. See, for example, Christophe Chatelot, 'Le gouvernement polonais accueille George Bush en allie sur de l'Amerique; Varsovie a un nouveau role international', *Le Monde*, 31 May 2003.

62. This regardless of some preliminary efforts to construct the European identity in contrast to the American one in the context of disagreements concerning the policy towards Iraq. See Jacques Derrida and Jürgen Habermas, 'Unsere Erneuerung nach dem Krieg: Europas Wiedergeburt', *Frankfurter Allgemeinen Zeitung*, 31 May 2003. See also a critique of this article by Timothy Garton Ash and Ralf Dahrendorf, 'Die Erneuerung Europas', *Süddeutsche Zeitung*, 5 July 2003.

63. Charles Hamden-Turner and Fons Trompenaars, *The Seven Cultures of Capitalism: Value Systems for Creating Wealth in the United States, Japan, Germany, France, Britain, Sweden and the Netherlands* (New York: Doubleday, 1993).

64. Michael Darmer and Laurens Kuyper, eds., *Industry and the European Union: Analysing Policies for Business*, (Northampton, MA: Edward Elgar, 2000).

65. For an analysis of the economic situation in the new member states see The Economist Intelligence Unit, *Europe Enlarged: Understanding The Impact* (Report prepared in cooperation with Accenture, Oracle, N M Rothschild & Sons, 2003); Economist Corporate Network, *European Union Accession: Practical Implications for Business in Central Europe* (Report prepared in cooperation with Ernst and Young, April 2002); and Antje Hildebrandt, 'What is Special about

Enlarging the European Union towards the East? A Comparison with the Southern Enlargement', *BOFIT Online*, No.13 (Bank of Finland, Institute for Economies in Transition, 2002).

66. János Mátyás Kovács, 'Approaching the EU and Reaching the US? Rival Narratives on Transforming Welfare Regimes in East-Central Europe', *West European Politics*, 25/2 (2002), pp. 175–204. For a recent assessment of the changing face of West European welfare regimes, see Maurizio Ferrera and Martin Rhodes eds., *Recasting European Welfare States* (London: Frank Cass, 2000).

67. Robert Kagan, *Of Paradise and Power: America and Europe in the New World Order* (New York: Alfred A. Knopf, 2003), pp. 3–4.

68. This has been reported by the *Financial Times*. See a special collection of articles published under the title 'The divided West' in connection with the G8 Summit in Evian in June 2003, p. 6.

69. Some of the latter are said actively to support the American design for the entire Europe in various functional fields. See, for example, Eugenio Scalfari, 'L'Europa americana che piace al Cavaliere', *La Repubblica*, 27 July 2003, p. 1 and p. 15.

70. For instance, for decades Germany and the Netherlands have been close American allies. Germany supported the first American-led intervention in Iraq and the military interventions in the former Yugoslavia and in Afghanistan. In fact, today Germany has more military and paramilitary personnel in Afghanistan than the United States. See, for example, Gerhard Schröder, 'Germany–U.S.: We can do more, but only all together', *International Herald Tribune*, 20 September 2003.

71. See the survey from April 2003 by CVVM (Czech polling organization). Available at: http://www.cvvm.cas.cz.

72. See the survey from February 2003 by CBOS (Polish polling organization). Available at: http://www.cbs.pl.

73. See Gallup International poll from February 2003. For more detailed description of attitudes in 'old' and 'new' Europe on the American intervention in Iraq, see William Horsley, 'Polls find Europeans oppose Iraq war', *BBC News*, 11 February 2003, and 'Europe and Iraq: Who stands where?' *BBC News*, 29 January 2003.

74. For a more detailed analysis of the differences in attitudes between Eastern and Western Europe towards possible security threats, see Jacques Rupnik, 'Europe. Les malentendus de l'élargissement', *En Temps Reel*, cahier 8 (Avril 2003), pp. 1–38, particularly pp. 10–11.

75. And the dividing lines run not only across individual European states, but also within them. For an in-depth analysis of European attitudes towards the United States see the *Economist*, 'Living with a super power', Special Report: American values, 4 January 2003, particularly the table entitled 'Suspicious minds'. Also Robert M. Worcester, *What Europeans Really Think about America—and the Future*

of the European Union, Margart Nally Memorial Lecture (IPR International Group and Greater London Group, House of Commons, 16 January 2003).

76. Timothy Garton Ash, 'Europe's Endangered Liberal Order', *Foreign Affairs*, 77/2 (1998), p. 61.

Chapter 4: Economic Governance

1. According to March and Olsen, governance involves 'affecting the frameworks within which citizens and officials act and politics occurs, and which shape the identities and institutions of civil society'. See James G. March and Johan Olsen, *Democratic Governance* (New York: Free Press, 1995), p. 6. It should be noted, however, that many economists apply a narrower notion of economic governance in the Union focusing on monitoring and enforcing the Stability Pact. In fact, R. A. W. Rhodes identified no less than six different meanings of the term governance. See R. A. W. Rhodes, 'The New Governance: Governing without Government', *Political Studies*, 44 (1996), pp. 652–67. For an analysis of the European type of governance see, for example, Beate Kohler-Koch, 'The Evolution and Transformation of European Governance', in *The Transformation of Governance in the European Union*, Beate Kohler-Koch and Reiner Eising, eds. (London: Routledge 1999), pp. 14–35. For an analysis of governance in the context of enlargement see, for example, Heather Grabbe, 'The governance of the EU. Facing the challenge of enlargement', *New Economy*, 8 (2002), pp. 113–17.
2. Literature on the subject often points to the fourth major challenge related to the EMU accession process: will the new members join the EMU relatively soon or will they be unwilling or unable? The former solution will obviously simplify the European economic governance system, while the latter will produce more variable geometry and concentric circles of a medieval nature. So far only some governments in the new member states want to join the EMU, and it is unclear when they will be ready. Moreover, several old member states are also unlikely to join the EMU in the foreseeable future. In other words, the variable geometry and concentric circles in this field are likely to be the order of the day for some years to come, preventing the creation of a single monetary governance system within the entire EU economic space. For more detailed analysis of the problem see, for example, Stefan Collignon, 'Is Europe going far enough? Reflections on the EU's economic governance', *Journal of European Public Policy*, 11/5 (2004), pp. 909–25, or David Cameron, 'The Challenges of Accession', *East European Politics and Societies*, 17/1 (2003), pp. 24–41.
3. Of course, these types of challenges are not mutually exclusive and some terms used have may be confusing. For instance, competition is forged not only between the EU and its external actors, but also among EU internal actors.

Moreover, many of these actors are multinationals that can hardly be classified as either European or extra-European. Similarly, the challenge of interdependence is both an internal and an external phenomenon from the EU perspective, and the former can hardly be applied only to the EU's immediate neighbours. Finally, I will show that the challenge of cohesion equally applies to EU members and non-members. In fact, the EU is sometimes more involved in economic governance in some neighbouring countries such as Bosnia than in its own members like Estonia. Nevertheless, I hope that this typology identifies three general types of economic challenge that confront the enlarged EU as such and that should be comprehended and tackled by EU decision-makers.

4. See, for example, Paul Krugman, *Geography and Trade* (Cambridge, MA: MIT Press, 1991), or Walter Mattli, *The Logic of Regional Integration: Europe and Beyond* (Cambridge: Cambridge University Press, 1999).

5. For a more-elaborate argument see especially Alessandra Casella and Jonathan S. Feinstein, 'Public Goods in Trade: On the Formation of Markets and Jurisdictions', *International Economic Review*, 43/2 (2002), pp. 437–56, or Alessandra Casella and Bruno Frey, 'Federalism and clubs. Towards an economic theory of overlapping political jurisdictions', *European Economic Review*, 36 (1992), pp. 639–46.

6. Giulio Tremonti, 'Il futuro del fisco' in *Nazioni sense ricchezza, ricchezza sensa nazioni*, Francesco Galgano, Sabino Cassese, Gulio Tremonti, and Tiziano Treu, eds. (Bologna: Il Mulino, 1993), p. 36. See also Allesandra Casella, 'Trade as an Engine of Political Change: A Parable', *Economica*, 61 (1994), p. 268.

7. However, as Roger Gough argues, the currencies of the new members are undervalued on a Purchasing Power Parity (PPP) basis—i.e. they are below the levels that would on average bring domestic prices in line with those abroad. Moreover, the size of the 'shadow' or 'black' economy should also be taken into consideration. This is estimated at 28 per cent of GDP, or some €100 billion. See Roger Gough, 'Stars in the East? New Europe and the EU Economy', in *The Perfect Union? New Europe and the EU*, Roger Gough and Anna Reid, eds. (London: Policy Exchange, 2004), p. 124.

8. Even the most enthusiastic Western European supporters of enlargement expected the new members to opt for greater redistribution from Brussels. As Malcolm Chalmers put it, for instance, 'The new members will have considerable powers within the EU, and will be able, in particular, to argue that financial transfers within the EU (through regional aid and agricultural budgets) should reflect their relative poverty. The result, at the 2006 budget review, is almost certain to be a big increase in net EU budget contributions from existing member states.' See Malcolm Chalmers, 'An Equal Partner: Europe's Role in the World Order', in *Reordering the World: The Long-term Implications of 11 September*, Mark Leonard, ed. (London: Foreign Policy Centre, 2002), p. 84.

9. Results of the accession negotiations available at: http://europa.eu.int/comm/enlargement/faq/faq2.htm. Spain has tried hard to renegotiate some of the

initial terms of its membership that were allegedly forced upon it in the process of accession. The frequently pronounced fear was that some of the new members from Eastern Europe would become equally tough or even awkward EU partners. See, for example, Robert-C. Hine, 'Customs union, enlargement and adjustment—Spain's accession to the European Community', *Journal of Common Market Studies*, XXVIII/1 (1989), pp. 1–27.

10. See *Gazeta Wyborcza*, 9 October 2003, p. 1. It should be noted, however, that some Polish officials expressed a more cautious opinion about the Commission's proposal. For instance, Jarosław Pietras, Poland's Under-Secretary for European Integration, told *Gazeta Wyborcza* (9 October 2003) that his government supports the Lisbon Agenda and would like to see the EU promoting both infrastructure (through structural and cohesion funds) and competitiveness. See also Tomasz Grzegorz Grosse and Jan Olbrycht, 'Debate on the New EU Cohesion Policy: Recommendations for the Polish Position', *Analyses & Opinions*, 10 (June 2003), p. 8.

11. Many scholars find the ability to extract and reallocate to be one of the major features of a state-building process and, in fact, the crucial pillar of any stateness. See, for example, Gabriel Ardant, 'Fiscal Policy and Economic Infrastructure of Modern States and Nations', in *The Formation of National States in Western Europe*, Charles Tilly, ed. (Princeton, NJ: Princeton University Press, 1975), pp. 164–242. See also Aaron Wildavsky, *Budgeting and Governing* (New Brunswick, NJ: Transaction, 2001).

12. For comparative data on state finances see IMF, *Global Financial Stability Report September 2004* (World Economic and Financial Surveys, September 2004). See also World Development Report 2000–01, World Bank (2001), pp, 306–7, Table 17.

13. As Quentin Peel rightly noted in the *Financial Times* (22 January 2004) this implies a serious cut in the EU's spending power just as the demands on the EU budget are set to rise disproportionately.

14. One can argue that originally the Cohesion Funds were agreed not so much to help new southern EU members, but to find ways of channelling back some EU money to Britain. Eastern European fears that financing the Lisbon Agenda at the expense of structural and cohesion funds represents an effort to save some common EU funds for the rich EU members are based on similar reasoning. For the former argument see Lisbeth Hooghe's Introduction or chapter 1 in *Cohesion Policy and European Integration: Building Multi-Level Governance* (Oxford: Oxford University Press, 1996), pp. 3–5. For the latter see Robert Sołtyk, 'Zabrać biednym, oddać bogatym', *Gazeta Wyborcza*, Gospodarka, 9 October 2003, p. 17.

15. See, for example, Kostantinos Mattas and Vangelis Tzouvelekas, 'The impact of EU membership: Lessons from the Greek experience', *Economia Internazionale*, 11/2 (1999), pp. 173–90.

16. See, for example, Johannes Stephan and Lothar Funk, 'Economic transition in Hungary and East Germany: Gradualism and shock therapy in catch-up development', *German Politics*, 9/3 (2000), pp. 217–18, or Claus Offe and Wade Jacoby, 'Varieties of transition: The East European and East German experience', *Governance*, 12/4 (1999), pp. 455–78

17. See Marta Petrusewicz, 'The Mezzogiorno: A bias for hope?', *Modern Italy*, 6/1 (2001), pp. 63–7, or Andrea Boltho, Wendy Carlin, and Pasquale Scaramozzino, 'Will East Germany Become a New Mezzogiorno?', *Journal of Comparative Economics*, 24/3 (1997), pp. 241–64. Although one should keep in mind that in the new member states, unlike in the Italian *Mezzogiorno* and East Germany, prices have not been artificially set.

18. As Jacques Pelkmans has put it: 'Net transfers have little to do with the costs and benefits of club membership for countries which pay, and can lead to addiction and lethargy rather than growth if market integration, macroeconomic stability and domestic reforms are not taken seriously.' See Jacques Pelkmans, 'Economic implications of Enlargement', *BEEP briefing*, 1, Bruges, 2002, p. 2.

19. It was agreed that all member states (the fifteen 'old' and the ten 'new' member states) will finance the budget according to the same rules. About €3.2 billion will be contributed by the new member states. All twenty-five will pay €98.9 billion. The breakdown between member states is subsequently calculated according to the precise rules of the own resources system. The traditional own resources will include €1,219 billion agricultural duties and sugar levies, €10,155 billion customs duties, and €14,324 billion from the VAT based resource, and €73,221 billion from the GNI resources. See RAPID, 'Enlargement and the EU Budget: Commission proposes expenditure for the 10 new Member states', *RAPID—The Press and Communication Department of the European Commission*, IP/04/161, Brussels, 4 February 2004. See also RAPID, 'Enlargement and the EU Budget: Commission proposes expenditure for the 10 new Member states', *RAPID—The Press and Communication Department of the European Commission*, IP/04/161, Brussels, 4 February 2004.

20. For a catalogue of these protectionist rules and growth hampering regulations, see Marian L. Tupy, 'EU Enlargement: Costs, Benefits and Strategies for Central and Eastern European Countries', *Policy Analysis*, 489, 18 September 2003, pp. 1–20.

21. See, for example, Burson-Marsteller, 'Enlargement 2004', *Big Bang and Aftershocks: Policy Implications for Business*, Brussels 2004, p. 10–13.

22. Václav Klaus, *Renaissance: The Rebirth of Liberty in the Heart of Europe* (Washington, DC: Cato Institute, 1997), p. 113.

23. See Benjamin Powell, 'Economic Freedom and Growth: The case of the Celtic Tiger', *Cato Journal*, 22,3 (2003), pp. 436–7. It should be emphasized here that countries such as Estonia or Slovakia offer very attractive tax rates. See, for example, the OECD report on income tax available at: http://www.oecd.org/

document /49/0,2340,en_2649_34597_30481201_1_1_1_1, 00.html or the world wide tax rate available at: http://www.worldwide-tax.com/index.asp# partthree.

24. See, for example, Helmut Wagner, 'Pitfalls in EMU-enlargement', available at: http://www.aicgs.org/c/wagnerc.shtml, or Likka Korhonen, 'Some implications of EU membership on Baltic monetary and exchange rate policies', in *The Road to the European Union: Estonia, Latvia and Lithuania*, Vello Pettai and Jan Zielonka, eds. (Manchester: Manchester University Press, 2003), pp. 255–81.

25. See Magnus Feldmann and Razeen Sally, 'From the Soviet Union to the European Union: Estonian Trade Policy, 1991–2000', *The World Economy*, 25/1 (2002), pp. 79–106; or Razeen Sally, 'Free Trade in Practice, Estonia in the 1990s', *Central Europe Review*, 10 July 2000. Available at: http://www.ce-review.org/00/27/sally27.html.

26. See, for example, Michael Dauderstädt, 'Cohesive Growth in the Enlarging Euroland: Patterns, Problems and Policies', in *Cohesive Growth in the Enlarging Euroland*, Michael Dauderstädt and Lothar Witte, eds. (Bonn: Friedrich-Ebert-Stiftung, 2001), pp. 7–24.

27. The absolute economic value of the latter is relatively small. EU transfers to the new members in the period of 2004–6 amounting to euro 49 billion could, for instance, be compared with euro 104 billion of the old members' trade surplus with the would-be new members in the period 1995–2000. Many economists believe that a large part of this surplus was caused by distorted competition between the Western and Eastern European states. More relevant data available at: http://europa.eu.int/comm/enlargement/faq2.htm

28. See European Commission, *The Modernization of Social Protection in Candidate Countries: New Opportunities and Challenges for the European Union*, Brussels 2002, Synthesis report, p. 27.

29. For instance, several reports the World Bank argued that even though certain segments of the Eastern European population suffer from the ongoing economic transition, it is highly inappropriate to speak about overall impoverishment or pauperization in this region. See, for example, World Bank, *Making Transition Work for Everyone: Poverty and Inequality in Europe and Central Asia*, Washington, DC, 2000.

30. See János Mátyás Kovács, 'Approaching the EU and Reaching the US? Rival Narratives on Transforming Welfare Regimes in East-Central Europe', *West European Politics*, 25/2 (2002), p. 190.

31. Martin Mácha, 'Le système de sécurité sociale en République tchèque', *Revue Belge de Sécurité Sociale*, 43 (2001) available at http//socialsecurity.fgov.be/bib/frames/fr/rbss_1_2001_macha.htm..

32. Speech of the Prime Minister in the House of Commons, 23 February 1999. See also Tony Blair and José-Maria Aznar, 'The Euro Is Changing the Face of Europe', *Financial Times*, 13 June 2000, and Tony Blair's speech to the European Parliement on 23 June 2005. Available at: http://www.number-10.gov.uk/output/Page7714.asp.

33. See Daniel C. Vaughan-Whitehead, *EU Enlargement versus Social Europe? The Uncertain Future of the European Social Model* (Cheltenham: Edward Elgar, 2003), p. 22.
34. Anthony Black, *Guilds and Civil Society in European Political thought from the Twelfth Century to the Present* (London: Methuen, 1984), p. 46.
35. See George Renard, *Guilds in the Middle Ages* (London: G. Bell and Sons, 1919), p. 44
36. According to Loukas Tsoukalis this is already the case. See Loukas Tsoukalis, *What Kind of Europe?* (Oxford: Oxford University Press, 2003).
37. European Competitiveness Report 2001 (Brussels: European Communities, 2001), p. 9
38. European Competitiveness Report 2002 (Brussels: European Communities, 2002), p. 9. Performance of individual countries is analysed on page 21.
39. See the report of the 2537th Council meeting, Economic and Financial Affairs, Brussels, 4 November 2003, C/03/306, 13689/03 (Presse 306), p. 7. The average dependency ratio (defined as the number of persons aged 60+ years per 100 persons aged 15–59 years) is expected to reach 47 in 2020 and 70 in 2050. See United Nations Population Division (2002), *World Population Prospects: The 2002 Revision*. Available at: http://www.un.org/esa/population/unpop.htm.
40. See European Commission, *The EU Economy: 2002 review* (Brussels: European Communities, 2003), p. 12.
41. Ibid.
42. World Economic Forum, *Global Competitiveness Report 2003–2004* (New York: Oxford University Press, 2003); on Finland, see pp. 56–7; on the United States, see pp. 194–5.
43. For a systematic comparison of various EU member states see Alasdair Murray, 'The Lisbon Scorecard IV. The status of economic reform in the enlarging EU', Centre for European Reform Working Paper, March 2004, especially pp. 74–5.
44. For a more-elaborated argument see David P. Calleo, *Rethinking Europe's Future* (Princeton, NJ: Princeton University Press, 2001), pp. 365–6.
45. For instance, two Dutch professors of economics have recently argued that the United States needs higher economic growth because of higher population growth, but there is no reason for the Union to imitate American growth promotion policies at the expense of social provisions that according to the authors represent value in themselves. See Henriëtte Massen van den Brink and Wim Groot, 'Economische groei is ook niet alles', *De Volkskrant*, 27 March 2004, p. 7.
46. See, for example, Table 4.16 on the distribution of income and consumption in Ali M. El-Agraa, *The European Union: Economics & Policies*, sixth edn. (Harlow: Prentice Hall, 2001), p. 95.
47. See European Commission, *The EU Economy: 2002 Review* (Brussels: European Communities, 2003), p. 36, especially Table 3. Although the EU has an equal score to the United States when one looks at GDP per hour worked

(in purchasing power standards), it scores much worse on GDP per employee or GDP per capita (both in purchasing power standards). See also Mary O'Mahony and Bart van Ark, eds., *EU Productivity and Competitiveness: An Industry Perspective: Can Europe Resume the Catching-up Process?* (Luxembourg: Office for Official Publications of the European Communities, 2003).

48. Lisbon European Council: Presidency Conclusions available at: http://europa.eu.it/comm/off/index-en.htm.

49. Cynics may argue that the Lisbon declaration resembles Nikita Khrushchev's claim to catch and surpass the economies of the capitalist West before the end of the twentieth century. As we know, by the end of the 20th century the Soviet Union was no longer there.

50. One of the most impressive and persuasive analyses of the problem is *An Agenda for a Growing Europe. Making the EU Economic System Deliver*, Report of an Independent High-Level Study Group established on the initiative of the President of the European Commission chaired by André Sapir. See André Sapir et al., *An Agenda for a Growing Europe: The Sapir Report* (Oxford: Oxford University Press, 2004). See also Michèle Debonneuil and Lionel Fontagné, *Compétitivité, Conseil d'Analyse Economique*, Report No. 40, La Documentation Française, Paris, 2003, and European Commission, 'Choosing to Grow: Knowledge, Innovation and Jobs in a Cohesive Society', Report to the Spring European Council, 21 March 2003 on the Lisbon Strategy of Economic, Social, and Environmental Renewal, COM(2003) 5 final, Brussels, January 2003. For more academic analyses of the problem see Loukas Tsoukalis, ed., *Competitiveness and Cohesion* (Oxford: Oxford University Press, 2000), and Maria João Rodrigues, ed., *The New Knowledge Economy in Europe: A Strategy for International Competiveness and Social Cohesion* (Cheltenham: Edward Elgar, 2002).

51. Paolo Guerrieri, 'Europe and the Challenge of the Global Economy', in *Europe 2020: Adopting to a Changing World*, Otto von der Gablentz et al, eds. (Baden-Baden: Nomos, 2000), p. 68.

52. Fritz W. Scharpf, 'Notes Toward a Theory of Multilevel Governing in Europe', MPIfG Discussion Paper 00/5, November 2000, p. 8

53. *An Agenda for a Growing Europe*, op.cit., pp. 129–55.

54. Ibid., pp. 136–42.

55. For instance, as the Estonian Prime Minister, Juhan Parts, put it in his remarks at the opening of Inter-Governmental Conference in Rome on 4 October 2004: 'Estonia views any move to QMV on tax and social security as not acceptable. We want a comprehensive Europe and a competitive Europe is a Europe, which considers competition and diversity of member states as an asset not a liability.' These remarks are available at: http://europa.eu.int/futurum/documents/other/oth041003_2_en.pdf.

56. The distinction between internal readjustments and external shocks is quite fuzzy. As Fritz Breauss argues: 'Because of the different macroeconomic impact

in the EU member countries (real GDP, prices, real exchange rates, current account), enlargement can also be interpreted as a potential external shock hitting the widely harmonized EU asymmetrically and hence introducing new disturbances into the EU.' See Fritz Breauss, 'Macroeconomic Effects of EU Enlargement for Old and New Members', WIFO Working Paper, No. 143/2001, Vienna, p. 2.

57. See Commission of the European Communities, Wider Europe—Neighbourhood: A New Framework for Relations with our Eastern and Southern Neighbours, COM(2003) 104 final, Brussels, 11 March 2003.

58. For basic statistical data on this region see United Nations Development Programme, *Arab Human Development Report 2003: Building a Knowledge Society* (United Nations Development Programme, Regional Bureau for Arab States (RBAS), New York, 2003).

59. See the 2003 EBRD transition report. According to the report Russia would be able to sustain its overall growth rate only if it would manage to foster growth outside the core natural resources sector and introduce a series of structural economic and legal reforms that would offer economic actors incentives, and security to carry on normal economic transactions. See EBRD, *Transition Report Update* (London: European Bank for Reconstruction and Development, 2003).

60. As Table 1.2 shows, Belarus has registered a relatively impressive GDP cumulative growth since 1989. Ukraine has registered more impressive economic growth only in recent years. For instance, in 2004 the *Economist* predicted 8.5 per cent growth in GDP for Ukraine; available at: http://www.economist.com/countries/Ukraine/PrinterFriendly.cfm?Story_ID=2570448.

61. The growth rates in the region vary by country. In 2001, the economy of Kosovo grew by 11 per cent, Albania by 6.5 per cent, Serbia and Montenegro by 5.5 per cent, and Bosnia-Hercegovina by 2.3 per cent. However the Macedonian economy shrank by 4.1 per cent in 2001. For more updated information see Commission of the European Communities, *The Stabilisation and Association process for South East Europe*, Third Annual Report, COM(2004) 202/2 final, Brussels, 30 March 2004.

62. See European Commission, Directorate-General for Economic and Financial Affairs, 'The Western Balkans in Transition', Occasional Paper, 1 (2003), pp. 1–2.

63. For more details see Economist Intelligence Unit, *Country Report: Croatia* (London: Economist Intelligence Unit, June 2004), p. 8.

64. For the opinion on Croatia's prospects of EU membership see Günter Verheugen, *Vorstellung der Meinung der Kommission zu Kroatien vor dem europäischen Parlament*, SPEECH/04/186, Strassburg, den 20. April 2004.

65. After the EU decision to open accession negotiations with Turkey, the French President, Jacques Chirac, said: 'Will [Turkey] succeed? I don't know, what is clear, is that she will need time, a lot of time, 10–15 years at least'. See http://eurobserver.com/9/20012.

66. For an analysis of the economic situation in Turkey see, for example, Jürgen von Hagen and Iulia Traistaru, *The South-East Europe Review 2002–2003*, World

Economic Forum, May 2003. Available at: http://www.weforum.org/pdf/SEEurope/SEEM_Review.pdf or European Round Table (ERT), Turkey—a new corporate world for Europe. An evaluation of the implications of potential Turkish membership of the European Union, Turkish–EU Enlargement Council of the European Round Table of Industrialists, July 2004. Available at: http://www.abig.org.tr/images/ERT%20Rapport.pdf.

67. For instance, nearly 1.2 million migrants from the former Yugoslavia reside in Germany, while Austria hosts 75,600. Greece hosts 131,600 legal migrants from Albania, while Italy has 31,000. See OECD, *Main Trends in International Migration, ANNUAL REPORT 2002*, SOPEMI OECD, Paris, 2003, pp. 79–80.

68. I will elaborate on the distinction between the Westphalian and neo-medieval types of international relations in the next chapter.

69. I will devote more attention to the hard border concept envisaged by Schengen in Chapter 5. For now suffice to say that the EU's efforts to seal its external border is largely a symbolic exercise: most experts agree that the utility of hard borders to handle migratory flows and transnational crime can easily be questioned. For an earlier version of this argument see Jan Zielonka, 'How new Enlarged Borders will Reshape the European Union' *Journal of Common Market Studies*, 39 (2001), pp. 519–23.

70. *Wider Europe—Neighbourhood: A New Framework for Relations with our Eastern and Southern Neighbours*, Communication from the Commission to the Council and the European Parliament (Brussels, 11 March 2003), COM(2003) 104 final. See also Council conclusions, '*Wider Europe—Neighbourhood*.' Available at: http://europa.eu.int/comm/external_relations/we/doc/cc06_03.pdf (18 June 2003).

71. Ibid.

72. See Commission of the European Communities, General Secretariat, *Copenhagen European Council*, 12 and 13 December 2002, *Presidency Conclusions*, DOC/02/15, December 2002. Available at: http://europa.eu.int/futurum/documents/other/oth121202_en.pdf.

73. *Wider Europe—Neighbourhood: A New Framework for Relations with our Eastern and Southern Neighbours*, cited in note 65.

74. Ibid.

75. Because these countries are so different from the current EU members it is probably rather bizarre to see them adopting EU rules and regulations. Nevertheless, leaders of these countries are quite prepared to follow EU advice and argue that special treatment for Central and Eastern European countries was guided by political and cultural prejudices rather than economic rationale. See, for example, and interview with King Hassan in the *Financial Times*, 28 October 1994.

76. See *Bosnia and Herzegovina Country Strategy Paper 2002–2006*. (Brussels: European Commission, External Relations Directorate General, 2002), Annex 1: Multiannual indicative Programme for the Period 2002–2004, pp. 4–5.

77. As reported by the *Financial Times*, 11 November 2003.
78. For a more detailed analysis of this issue see e.g. 'The Ottoman Dilemma. Power and Property Relations under the United Nations Mission in Kosovo', Lessons Learned and Analysis, Unit of the EU Pillar in Kosovo, Pristina, 8 August 2002. Available at European Stability: Initiative: www.esiweb.org-esiweb@t-online.de.
79. See Gerhard Knaus and Felix Martin, 'Travails of The European Raj', *Journal of Democracy*, 14/3 (2003), pp. 60–74.
80. For instance, in 2005 the European Commission has made a proposal for the introduction of special local visas at the borders of the EU. See COM (2005) 56, Proposal for a Regulation of the European Parliament and of the Council laying down rules on local border traffic at the external land borders of the member states and amending the Schengen Convention and the Common Consular Instructions (23 February 2005).
81. See James G. March and Johan Olsen, 'Organizing Political Life: What Administrative Reorganization Tells Us About Government', *American Political Science Review*, 77 (1983), pp. 196–281.
82. See, for example, Vincent Ostrom and Elinor Ostrom, 'Public Goods and Public Choices', in *Polycentricity and Local Public Economies: Readings from the Workshop in Political Theory and Policy Analysis*, Michael McGinnis, ed. (Ann Arbor: Michigan University Press, 1999), pp. 75–105.
83. See, for example, Barry Weingast, 'The Economic Role of Political Institutions: Market-Preserving Federalism and Economic Development', *Journal of Law and Economic Organization*, 11(1995), pp. 1–31.
84. Romano Prodi, 'After the Reform: A Future Strategy for Europe as a Whole', Speech at the International Bertelsmann Forum, Europe without Borders, Berlin, 2001. See also the European Commission's *White Paper on Governance in the European Union*, Brussels, 2001. Available at: http//europa.eu.int/comm./governance/index_en.htm.
85. Liesbet Hooghe and Gary Marks, 'Unravelling the Central State, but How? Types of Multi-level Governance', *American Political Science Review*, 97 (2003), pp. 233–43.

Chapter 5: Democratic Governance

1. The democratic orientations of European citizens are evidenced by numerous empirical studies. See, for example, a comparative set of data from the World Values Survey discussed in Ronald Inglehart, 'Postmodernization Erodes Respect for Authority, but Increases Support for democracy', in *Critical Citizens: Global Support for Democratic Government*, Pippa Norris, ed. (Oxford: Oxford University Press, 1999), pp. 236–56. See also Larry Siedentop, *Democracy in Europe* (London: Penguin Press, 2001).

2. See, for example, Neil Walker, 'The EU as a Constitutional Project', *Federal Trust Constitutional Online Papers*, 19/04, 2004. Available at: http://www.fedtrust.-co.uk/uploads/constitution/19_04.pdf. Also Andrew Moravcsik, 'Is there a "Democratic Deficit" in World Politics? A Framework for Analysis', *Government and Opposition* (2004), p. 350.

3. This has been spelled out in more details in J. H. H. Weiler, *The Constitution of Europe* (Cambridge: Cambridge University Press, 1999), p. 336.

4. See, for example, Daniel Wincott, 'Does the European Union Pervert democracy? Questions of Democracy in New Constitutionalist Thought on the Future of Europe', *European Law Journal*, 4/4 (1998), pp. 411–28.

5. See, for example, Brigid Laffan, Rory O'Donnell, and Michael Smith, *Europe's Experimental Union: Rethinking Integration* (London: Routledge, 2000), pp. 74–87, or Jeremy Richardson, 'Policy-making in the EU: Interests, ideas and garbage cans of primeval soup', in *European Union: Power and Policy-making*, Jeremy Richardson, ed. (London: Routledge, 2001), pp. 4–5.

6. The notion of a Westphalian state is hardly ever used in the study of democracy. The literature in this field often talks about a 'nation state' and since modern nations crystallized later than the Peace of Westphalia, it is not entirely correct to use the terms 'nation states' and 'Westphalian states' as synonyms. However, for the sake of simplicity and consistency, I am talking here about 'Westphalian nation states'. After all, nation states were all Westphalian states and a demise of Westphalian states goes hand in hand with a demise of nation states. See, for example, *Continuity and Change in the Westphalian Order*, James A. Caporaso, ed. (Oxford: Blackwell, 2000).

7. For a definition of democracy see, for example, Robert Dahl, *Democracy and its Critics* (New Haven, CT: Yale University Press, 1989), p. 221; or Joseph Schumpeter, *Capitalism, Socialism and Democracy*, 2nd ed. (New York: Harper, 1947), p. 269. See also David Collier and Steven Levitsky, 'Democracy "with Adjectives": Finding Conceptual Order in Recent Comparative Literature', *World Politics*, 49/3 (1997), p. 430.

8. Ralf Dahrendorf, 'The Challenge for democracy', *Journal of Democracy*, 14/4 (2003), p. 107. See also Pierre Manent, 'Current problems of European democracy', *Modern Age*, 45/2 (2003). Available at: http://www.findarticles.com/p/articles/mi_m0354/is_1_45/ai_99699586.

9. Jürgen Habermas, 'Toward a Cosmopolitan Europe', *Journal of Democracy*, 14/4 (2003), p. 97–8.

10. See Robert Dahl, *Democracy and its Critics* (New Haven, CT: Yale University Press 1989), Part 1, pp. 13–36.

11. Some authors envisage democracy at a global level, while others believe that democracy can only flourish at a local level. In fact, local regional devolution has been promoted precisely as a way of extending and deepening democracy. For the latter argument see Michael Keating, 'Europe's Changing Political landscape. Territorial restructuring and new forms of government', in

Convergence and Divergence in European Law, Paul Beaumont, Carole Lyons, and Neil Walker, eds. (Oxford: Hart, 2002), pp. 3–18. The former vision is elaborated in David Held, 'Democracy: From City-States to a Cosmopolitan Order?' in *Prospects for Democracy*, David Held, ed. (Oxford: Polity Press, 1993), pp. 13–52. See also a special 2004 issue of *Government and Politics* edited by David Held and Mathias Koenig-Archibugi.

12. See Robert Dahl, op.cit., ch. 17.

13. The former include not only classical intergovernmental organizations such as the United Nations (UN), but also international standard setting bodies such as the World Health Organization (WHO) or global regulatory agencies such as the World Trade Organization (WTO). Anne-Marie Slaughter has also pointed to the increase in influence of global (often informal) networks of government officials—police investigators, financial regulators, even judges and legislators. See Anne-Marie Slaughter, *A New World Order* (Princeton, NJ: Princeton University Press, 2004).

14. Jacques Thomassen, 'Support for Democratic Values', in *Citizens and the State: A Relationship Transformed*, Dieter Fuchs and Hans-Dieter Klingemann, eds. (Oxford: Oxford University Press, 1995), p. 413.

15. For normative evaluations of European democratic governance see Neil Mac-Cormick, 'Democracy, Subsidiarity and Citizenship in the Context of the European Union', *Law and Philosophy*, 16 (1997), pp. 331–56, or Yves Mény, 'De la démocratie en Europe: Old Concepts and New Challenges', *Journal of Common Market Studies*, 41/1 (2002), pp. 1–13.

16. See William Wallace, 'Conclusions . . . ', in *Policy-making in the EU*, Helen Wallace and William Wallace, eds. (Oxford: Oxford University Press, 2000), p. 530–1. See also S. Rokkan, D. Urwin, F. H. Aerebot, P. Malaba, and T. Sandle, *Centre–Periphery Structure in Europe* (Frankfurt: Campus Verlag, 1987), pp. 17–18.

17. See Beate Kohler-Koch, 'Network Governance within an Enlarged European Union', in Amy Verdun and Osvaldo Croci, *Institutional and Policy-making Challenges to the European Union in the Wake of Eastern Enlargement* (Manchester: Manchester University Press, 2004) and Liesbet Hooghe and Gary Marks, 'Unraveling the Central State, but how? Types of Multi-Level Governance', *American Political Science Review*, 97/2 (2003), pp. 233–4.

18. Perry Anderson, *Lineages of the Absolute State* (London: NLB, 1974), pp. 37–8. See also Joseph Reese Strayer, *On the Medieval Origins of the Modern State* (Princeton, NJ: Princeton University Press, 1970), pp. 26–36.

19. Daniel Philpott, *Revolutions in Sovereignty—How Ideas Shaped Modern International Relations* (Princeton, NJ: Princeton University Press, 2001), p. 79.

20. Helen Wallace, 'The Institutional Setting', in *Policy-Making in the European Union*, op. cit., p. 36.

21. Jeremy Richardson, ed., *European Union Power and Policy-Making* (London: Routledge, 2001), pp. 12–15, and Christopher Hood, 'The Garbage Can Model of Organization: Describing a Condition or a Perspective Design Principle?' in

Organizing Political Institutions, Morten Egeberg and Per Lægreid, eds. (Oslo: Scandinavia University Press, 1999), pp. 59–78.

22. Liesbet Hooghe and Gary Marks, 'Unraveling the Central State, but How? Types of Multi-level Governance', *American Political Science Review*, 97/2 (2003), p. 234.

23. Commission of the European Communities, *European Governance—A White Paper*, COM(2001)428 final (2001). Available at: http://europa.eu.int/cgi-bin/ eur-lex/udl.pl?REQUEST=Seek-Deliver & COLLECTION = com & SERVICE = all & LANGUAGE=en&DOCID= 501PC0428.

24. The initial idea was not to draft a European Constitution but to review the treaties and make the institutions fit for enlargement. The European Summit in Laeken in December 2002 published a Declaration on the Future of Europe (http://european-convention.eu.int/pdf/LKNEN.pdf), which set up the Convention on the Future of Europe. Its initial task was to prepare the 2004 Intergovernmental Conference (IGC) by presenting possible answers to the (mainly) institutional dilemmas the Union was facing, and which were listed in the Laeken Declaration. The Convention took up its work in February 2003 and very soon after that it became clear that its aim was not to produce a list of suggestions for the 2004 IGC but in fact to draft a new constitutional treaty. The Convention worked for eighteen months and finally drew up the Draft Treaty establishing a Constitution for Europe (http://european-convention.eu.int/DraftTreaty.asp?lang=EN). The 2004 IGC was brought forward and took up its work under the Italian presidency (http://www.ueitalia2003.it/EN/) in the second half of 2003. However, the final negotiations failed and the conference was prolonged into the Irish EU presidency (http://www.eu2004.ie/) during the first half of 2004. Under the Irish leadership the twenty-five member states' governments agreed to the new constitutional treaty, but the satification process has been stalled by the negative votes in the French and Dutch referenda. See Olivier Duhamel, Des Raisans du 'Non' (Paris: Seriel, 2005). See also John Temple Lang, *The Convention on the Future of Europe—So far*, Federal Trust Online Papers (2003). Available at: http:// www.fedtrust.co.uk/uploads/constitution/18_03.pdf; Jo Shaw et al., *The Convention on the Future of Europe: Working towards a EU Constitution* (London: Kogan Page, 2003); John Erik Fossum, 'Still a Union of Deep Diversity? The Convention and the Constitution for Europe', ARENA Working Paper (2003), available at: http://www.arena.uio.no/publications/wp03_21_abstract.htm.

25. Oral report to the European Council by Valéry Giscard D'Estaing, Chairman of the Constitutional Convention, published in *Journal of Democracy*, 14/4 (2003), p. 60.

26. A draft of the European constitutions was adopted on 18 June 2004 by the European Summit in Brussels and is available at http://ue.eu.int/uedocs/ cms_Data/docs/pressdata/en/misc/81243.pdf.

27. Stéphane Beulac, 'Constitutio Westphalica: Europe's First Constitution?', Paper presented at the 2004 Biennial Conference of the European Community Studies Association in Canada, Montreal, 29 May 2004. Beulac notes that the Treaties of Osnabrück and Münster that laid the foundations for the Peace of Westphalia were also called the 'Charte constitutionnnelle de l'Europe'. See Stéphane Beulac, *The Power of Language in the Making of International Law* (Leiden: Martinus Nijhoff, 2004), p. 83.

28. As Yves Mény rightly argued, 'The separation of powers principle has never been implemented in the EU in the same way it has been in national democratic systems. In fact, powers of the EU were often distributed in an ad hoc fashion, characterized by overlaps and mixtures rather than separation. The spheres of legislative and executive bodies were blurred and confused'. And according to Mény the draft of the European Constitution has clarified the situation only slightly. For instance, no clear answer has been given to the question 'Who is the Executive of the EU?' See Yves Mény, 'Making Sense of the EU: The Achievements of the Convention', *Journal of Democracy*, 14/4 (2003), pp. 68–9.

29. Kirsty Hughes, 'A Dynamic and Democratic EU or Muddling Through Again? Assessing the EU's Draft Constitution', Federal Trust Online Papers (2003). Available at: http://www.fedtrust.co.uk/uploads/constitution/25_03.pdf; Paul Craig, 'The Constitutional Treaty: Legislative and Executive Power in the Emerging Constitutional Order', EUI Working Papers (2003), available at: http://www.iue.it/PUB/law04-7.pdf; John Erik Fossum, 'Still a Union of Deep Diversity? The Convention and the Constitution for Europe', ARENA Working Papers (2003), available at: http://www.arena.uio.no/publications/wp03_21_abstract.htm.

30. 'The CER guide to the EU's constitutional treaty', Centre for European Reform, Policy Brief, London, July 2004. Available at: www.cer.org.uk.

31. 'European Integration: New Opportunities and Challenges', address by Vaira Vike-Freiberga, President of Latvia, at the Institute of European Affairs in Dublin, 4 June 2002. Available at: http://europa.eu.int/futurum/documents/speech/sp040602_en.htm.

32. Dimitrij Rupel, 'The Future of Europe-Debate', Ljubljana, 3 July 2001. Paper available at: http://europa.eu.int/futurum/documents/other/oth030701_en.pdf.

33. Currently, the legal basis of the EU consists of two treaties, amended many times. See Jo Shaw, *Law of the European Union* (Basingstoke: Palgrave, 2000) p. 10.

34. These are words used by Peter Hain, British government representative at the Convention on the Future of Europe, former British Minister for Europe, and now Secretary of State for Northern and Wales Ireland. Available at: http://www.publications.parliament.uk/pa/cm200203/cmhansrd/vo030617/debtext/30617-13.htm.

35. My argument here is largely based on the work of Michael Keating. See especially Michael Keating, 'Europe's Changing Political Landscape. Territorial restructuring and new forms of government', in *Convergence and Divergence in European Law*, Paul Beaumont, Carole Lyons, and Neil Walker, eds. (Oxford: Hart, 2002), pp. 3–18, and Michael Keating, *The New Regionalism in Western Europe: Territorial Restructuring and Political Change* (Aldershot: Edward Elgar, 1998). See also James Hughes, Gwendolyn Sasse, and Claire Gordon, 'EU Enlargement, Europeanization and the Dynamics of Regionalization in CEECs', in *The Regional Challenge in Central and Eastern Europe: Territorial Restructuring and European Integration*, Michael Keating and James Hughes, eds. (Brussels: Presses interuniversitaires europeènnes/Peter Lang, 2003), pp 69–88.

36. It has been estimated that some 70 to 80 per cent of Community programmes are managed by local and regional authorities and national governments can no longer monopolize the contacts between their country and the EU levels of policy-making. See Peter Norman, *The Accidental Constitution* (Brussels: Eurocomment, 2003), p. 133, citing the Lamassoure report on competences. Entire Lamassoure Report is available at: http://www.europarl.eu.int/meet-docs/committees/afco/20020326/443686en.pdf.

37. According to a study by the World Bank, 67 per cent of Eastern Europe's population is living in cities, which makes this region as urbanized as the leader in this field, Latin America. However, cities in Eastern Europe are not always as competitive as their Western European counterparts and contain a large percentage of poor. See Robert M. Buckley and Frederico Mini, 'From Commissars to Mayors: Cities in the Transition Economies' (2000). Available at: http://wbln0018.worldbank.org/eca/eca.nsf/0/b80a1486ce739a-ba852569640076306f?OpenDocument. See also John Agnew, 'How Many Europes? The European Union, Eastern Enlargement and Uneven Development', *European Urban and Regional Studies*, 8/1 (2001), pp. 29–38.

38. Michael Keating, 'Europe's Changing Political Landscape. Territorial restructuring and new forms of government', in *Convergence and Divergence in European Law*, Paul Beaumont, Carole Lyons, and Neil Walker, eds. (Oxford: Hart, 2002), p. 12.

39. For an overview of this literature see Liesbet Hooghe and Gary Marks, 'Unraveling the Central State, but How? Types of Multi-level Governance', *American Political Science Review*, 97/2 (2003), p. 234; see also Philippe Schmitter, *How to Democratise the European Union and why Bother?* (Boston: Rowman, and Littlefield, 2000). The virtue of multilevel governance in Europe has also been recognized by the European Commission's White Paper on Governance; see Commission of the European Communities, *European Governance—A White Paper*, COM(2001)428 final (2001). Available at: http://europa.eu.int/cgi-bin/eur-lex/udl.pl?REQUEST=Seek-Deliver&COLLECTION=com&SERVICE= all&-LANGUAGE=en&DOCID=501PC0428.

40. For instance, the model of representative government was formulated only in the eighteenth century. See Robert A. Dahl, *Polyarchy: Participation and Opposition* (New Haven, CT: Yale University Press, 1979), p. 169.

41. Juan J. Linz and Alfred Stepan, *Problems of Democratic Transition and Consolidation* (Baltimore, MD: Johns Hopkins University Press, 1996), p. 17.

42. Although in some cases it is the popular vote rather than parliament that elects a country's president, who is often but not always head of the executive. Legislative prerogatives of parliaments also vary. For a more in-depth analysis of the scope of parliamentary powers see, for example, Gerhard Loewenberg and Samuel C. Patterson, *Comparing Legislatures* (Lanham, MD: University of America Press, 1979), pp. 43–67.

43. Alec Stone Sweet, *Governing with Judges: Constitutional Politics in Europe* (Oxford: Oxford University Press, 2000).

44. See, for example, Giandomenico Majone, 'Delegation of Regulatory Powers in a Mixed Polity', *European Law Journal*, 8/3 (2002), pp. 319–39.

45. There are at present cross-national party groups in the European Parliament and since the treaty requires large majorities for taking decisions, it forces these groups to form large alliances and coalitions. However, the respective electorates are usually not aware of these alliances and are not asked to 'ratify' them. Euro-parties organize the infrastructure of the European Parliament, but they do not bring up, channel, and aggregate citizen's demands. In fact, they hardly ever compete with each other the way national parties do. Splits and mergers of these parties are frequent, individual members' mobility is high, and MEPs often switch their party affiliation. For a more in-depth analysis see Luciano Bardi, 'Transnational Party Federations, European Parliamentary Party Groups and the Building of Europarties', in *How Parties Organize: Change and Adaptation in Party Organizations in Western Democracies*, Richard Katz and Peter Mair, eds. (London: Sage, 1995); also Amie Kreppel, *The European Parliament and Supranational Party System: A Study in Institutional Development* (New York: Cambridge University Press, 2002).

46. The European Parliament, first directly elected in 1979, has significantly increased its powers over the past two decades. The Single European Act introduced the cooperation procedure, the first step in making the EP a co-legislator with the European Council. The Maastricht Treaty then introduced the co-decision procedure (which was modified in the Amsterdam Treaty) which makes the EP a de facto co-legislator in policy areas in which it applies. This means that neither the European Council nor the European Parliament (EP) can adopt any legislation without the support of the other. See Andreas Maurer, 'The Legislative Powers and Impact of the European Parliament', *Journal of Common Market Studies*, 41/2 (2003), pp. 227–47. As far as other traditional legislative tasks are concerned, especially the selection of the executive and the judiciary, the EP has far less power. Although incoming European Commissioners have to undergo hearings in the EP, the Parliament

can only refuse the nomination of the Commission as a whole and not simply of individual Commissioners. This weakens the EP's influence considerably. (Although in October 2004 the incoming President of the European Commission was forced to reconsider the proposed list of his Commissioners under the EP's pressure.) Judges at the European Court of Justice and the Court of First Instance are all appointed in the member states without any approval from the EP being necessary.

47. The European Court of Justice (ECJ) consists of twenty-five judges (one from each member state) and is assisted by nine Advocate Generals. The ECJ's judgments have had major influence on the development of European law and the course of European integration. Benchmark judgments such as Costa v. ENEL, ECJ Case 6/64, established the supremacy of EU law. The court also established with its ruling in Les Vertes v. European Parliament, ECJ Case 294/83, that the European Community's founding treaties are a 'constitutional charter' paving the way for the still ongoing European constitutional debate. See, for example, Jo Shaw, *Law of the European Union* (Basingstoke: Palgrave, 2000), p. 26, p. 49, pp. 152–9. For an analysis of the European Central Bank in the democratic context see Nicolas Jabko, 'Democracy in the age of the Euro', *Journal of European Public Policy*, 10/5 (2003), pp. 710–39.

48. The European Council and Council of Ministers is composed of member states' governmental representatives whose positions depend on national elections. The voting system in the Council has developed over recent years and the Treaty of Nice (currently applicable) allocates weighted votes to the different member states. This system favours smaller member states which are given relatively more votes (in relation to their population) compared with larger member states. The Draft Treaty establishing a European Constitution got rid of the weighted votes and (if the Treaty is ever ratified) the qualified majority voting system will depend only on the number of member states and the percentage of the EU population they represent. For the Nice procedure see Wolfgang Wessels, 'Nice Results', *Journal of Common Market Studies*, 39/2 (2001); for the Draft Treaty see Giovanni Greve, 'Light and Shade of a quasi-Constitution: an assessment', *Federal Trust Constitutional Online Papers*, 08/04 (2004); available at: http://www.fedtrust.co.uk/uploads/constitution/08_04.pdf.

49. Even though governments might be willing to listen to the opinion of their national parliaments, they could still be outvoted on the European level, if the policy in question falls under qualified majority voting which denies member states' governments a national veto. And since the ruling of the ECJ in Costa v. ENEL, ECJ Case 6/64, the doctrine of supremacy has been established. This means that in case of conflict between European and national law (as adopted by national legislatures), European law prevails. See also Karen J. Alter, *Establishing the Supremacy of European Law: The Making of an International Rule of Law in Europe* (Oxford: Oxford University Press, 2001).

50. See R. Daniel Kelemen, 'The Politics of "Eurocratic" Structure and the New European Agencies', *West European Politics*, 25/4 (2002), pp. 93–118.

51. See, for example, Giandomenico Majone, 'Temporary Consistency and Policy Credibility: Why Democracies Need Non-Majoritarian Institutions', *RSC Working Paper*, No. 96/57 (Florence: European University Institute, 1996).

52. As Adrienne Heritier pointed out, 4,500 lobbies and 650 consultancy firms and lawyers' offices specialize in EU affairs and have disproportionate access to and influence over EU decisions. See Adrienne Heritier, 'Composite democracy in Europe: the role of transparency and access to information', *Journal of European Public Policy*, 9/5 (2003), p. 816.

53. See Martin Shapiro, 'The Problems of Independent Agencies in the United States and the European Union', *Journal of European Public Policy*, 4/2 (1997), pp. 276–91. Majone argues that American experience shows that independent regulatory bodies can be kept politically accountable by a combination of control instruments: clear statutory objectives, oversight by specialized legislative committees, strict procedural requirements, judicial review, appointments of key personnel, budgetary controls, reorganizations, professionalism, public participation, monitoring by interest groups, and even interagency rivalry. See Giandomenico Majone, 'The new European agencies: Regulation by information', *Journal of European Public Policy*, 4/2 (1997), pp. 262–75.

54. William Wallace and Julie Smith, 'Democracy or Technocracy? European Integration and the Problem of Popular Consent', in *The Crisis of Representation in Europe*, Jack Hayward, ed. (London: Frank Cass, 1995), p. 143.

55. Yves Mény, 'De la démocratie en Europe: Old Concepts and New Challenges', *Journal of Common Market Studies*, 41/1 (2003), p. 4.

56. As Marc F. Plattner rightly observed, the European Parliament is the only directly elected and most open of the major EU institutions, but it is also the least powerful. See Marc F. Plattner, 'Making Sense of the EU: Competing Goals, Conflicting Perspectives', *Journal of Democracy*, 14/4 (2003), p. 49.

57. Andrzej Rapaczyński, 'Constitutional Politics in Poland: A Report on the Constitutional Committee of the Polish Parliament', in *Constitution Making in Eastern Europe*, A. E. Dick Howard, ed. (Washington, DC: Woodrow Wilson Center Press, 1993), p. 118. For Rapaczyński this quest for the absolute and unconstrained power of the people is characteristic of societies that 'fought hard for freedom to air their true convictions', but Wiktor Osiatyński also adds: 'Poland has never had a strong tradition of constitutionalism that limited parliamentary authority.' See Wiktor Osiatyński, 'Perspectives on the Current Constitutional Situation in Poland', in *Constitutionalism and Democracy: Transitions in the Contemporary World*, Douglas Greenberg et al., eds. (Oxford: Oxford University Press, 1993), p. 319. Similar views were expressed in other Eastern European countries. See, for example, András Sajó, 'The Roundtable Talks in Hungary', in *The Roundtable Talks and the Breakdown of Communism*, Jon Elster, ed. (Chicago: Chicago University Press, 1996), p. 92.

58. 'Constructing a New Europe', Lecture by Toomas Hendrik Ilves, Minister of Foreign Affairs of Estonia, at Humboldt University, Berlin, 5 February 2001. Available at: http://europa.eu.int/futurum/documentsspeech/sp050201_en. htm.

59. And one should add that the EU has demanded from the candidate states ever further 'depoliticization' of their respective civil services and judiciary, in particular. This was a very plausible demand considering that these bodies were under Communist control in the past, but after the initial years of democratic consolidation the issue was no longer de-communization, but the extent of 'political' control by the parliamentary majority of the day, however democratically elected.

60. As Alec Stone Sweet rightly observed: 'When the court annuls a bill on rights grounds, it substitutes its own reading of rights, and its own policy goals, for those of the parliamentary majority'; see Alec Stone Sweet, *Governing with Judges* (Oxford: Oxford University Press, 2000), p. 105.

61. For a comprehensive review of the first years of constitutional courts in Eastern Europe see Herman Schwartz, 'The New Eastern European Constitutional Courts', *Michigan Journal of International Law*, 13 (1992), pp. 741–85.

62. See Wojciech Sadurski, *Rights before Courts: A Study of Constitutional Courts in Postcommunist States of Central and Eastern Europe* (Dordrecht: Kluwer Law International, 2005), especially the concluding chapter pp. 289–99.

63. See Wojciech Sadurski, 'Postcommunist Constitutional Courts in Search of Political Legitimacy', *EUI Working Paper*, Law 2001/11, 2001.

64. Ibid. See also Spencer Zifcak, 'Hungary's Remarkable, Radical, Constitutional Court', *Journal of Constitutional Law in Eastern and Central Europe*, 3 (1996), p. 26.

65. The data taken from Gábor Halmai and Kim Lane Schepple, 'Living Well is the Best Revenge: The Hungarian Approach to Judging the Past', in *Transitional Justice in New Democracies*, A. James McAdams, ed. (Notre Dam, IN: University of Notre Dame Press, 1996), pp. 155–84 and p. 181, Figure 1. Similar data, with respect to Czech Republic and Slovakia, are given by Herman Schwartz, *The Struggle for Constitutional Justice in Post-Communist Europe* (Chicago: University of Chicago Press, 2000) p. 320, n. 22. See also the 2004 *Eurobarometer* poll showing that people in the EU-25 trust the ECJ more than they trust any other European institution and this 'trust gap' is particularly evident in new member states. European Commission, *Eurobaromter 2004* (Brussels, 2004).

66. See, for example, Susanne Rentzow, 'The Power of Ideas: How Bundesbank Ideas Have Influenced the Reconstruction of the National Bank of Poland', *German Politics*, 11/1 (2002), pp. 173–90; Bilin Neyapti, 'Central bank independence and economic performance in eastern Europe', *Economic Systems*, 25/4 (2001), pp. 381–99; Dan Exeter, 'Legal Reforms of the Polish Health Care System in View of Accessing the European Union', *European Journal of Health Law*, 8/1 (2001), pp. 5–25.

67. See, for example, a speech by Jan Kavan, Deputy Prime Minister and Minister of Foreign Affairs of the Czech Republic, at the Centre for European Policy Studies, Brussels, 19 March 2001. Available at: http://europa.eu.int/futurum/documents/speech/sp190301_en.htm.
68. See R. Daniel Kelemen, op.cit., pp. 109–11.
69. See, for example, Address by Ms Kristiina Ojuland, Estonian Foreign Minister, 'An EU of 25 and Estonia's Role in it', at the European Policy Centre's lecture series 'Meet the New Member States', 23 October 2002, Brussels. Available at: http://www.vm.ee/eng/kat_140/2961.html?arhiiv_kuup=kuup_2002; or a contribution by Prime Minister Milos Zeman of the Czech Republic to 'The Debate on the Future of Europe', 14 June 2001, available at: http://www.europa.eu.int/futurum/documents/contrib/cont140601_en.htm.
70. See, for example, an interview of Slovenian Foreign Minister, Dimitrij Rupel, on 13 March 2003; available at: www.eu.2003.gr; or comments of Lithuanian Foreign Minister, Antanas Valionis, on 14 June 2004; available at www.urm.it.
71. See 'Poles raise stake in EU summit', *Financial Times* (10 December 2003) and 'Battle ahead on Polish voting Right', *Financial Times* (10 December 2003). For more information see also the Polish Ministry for Foreign Affairs at http://www.msz.gov.pl/start.php?page=1040000001 as well as http://www.vote-2004.com/mediacentre/display.asp?IDNO=1436.
72. The overall turnout at the 2004 European Parliament election was 45.7 per cent. The individual turnout numbers for all member states, new and then old, lowest turnout first, were as follows: Slovakia 16.96 per cent, Poland 20.87 per cent, Estonia 26.83 per cent, Slovenia 28.3 per cent, Czech Republic 28.32 per cent, Hungary 38.5 per cent, Latvia 41.34 per cent, Lithuania 48.43 per cent, Cyprus 71.19 per cent, Malta 82.37 per cent, Sweden 37.8 per cent, Portugal 38.6 per cent, Great Britain 38.83 per cent, Netherlands 39.3 per cent, Finland 39.4 per cent, Austria 42.43 per cent, France 42.76 per cent, Germany 43 per cent, Spain 45.1 per cent, Denmark 47.9 per cent, Ireland 58.8 per cent, Greece 63.4 per cent, Italy 73.1 per cent, Luxembourg 89 per cent, Belgium, 90.81 per cent (compulsory voting); data available at: http://www.elections2004.eu.int/ep-election/sites/en/results1306/turnout_ep/index.html.
73. Interestingly, the country with the lowest turnout at the European elections, Slovakia, had the highest turnout of all membership referenda and the new member state with the highest turnout for the EP elections, Malta, had the lowest in its membership referendum. The turnout for membership referenda, highest first, was as follows: Slovakia 92 per cent Lithuania 90 per cent, Slovenia 90 per cent, Hungary 84 per cent, Czech Republic 77 per cent, Poland 77 per cent, Estonia 67 per cent, Latvia 67 per cent, Malta 54 per cent, Cyprus no referendum held. Available at: http://news.bbc.co.uk/1/hi/world/europe/2266385.stm.

74. Renauld Dehousse, 'Constitutional Reform in the European Community. Are there Alternatives to the Majority Avenue?' in *The Crisis of Representation in Europe*, Jack Hayward, ed. (London: Frank Cass, 1995), p. 134.

75. Dehousse points out that James Madison was well aware of this problem when drafting the American Constitution. See *The Federalist Papers*, No. 10, Garry Wills, ed. (New York: Bantam, 1982), p. 45.

76. See Gabriel A. Almond and Sidney Verba, *The Civic Culture* (Princeton, NJ: Princeton University Press, 1963). Also Gabriel A. Almond, 'The Intellectual History of the Civic Culture Concept', in *The Civic Culture Revisited*, Gabriel A. Almond and Sidney Verba, eds. (Boston: Little, Brown and Company, 1980), p. 1–36.

77. The latter has well been argued in J. H. H. Weiler, *The Constitution of Europe*, op.cit., p. 337.

78. Of course this is not to ignore the experiences of multinational states that have managed to sustain multiple identities. See, for example, Michael Keating, 'Europe's Changing Political Landscape: Territorial Restructuring and New Forms of Government', in *Convergence and Divergence in European Public Law*, Paul Beaumont, Carole Lyons, and Neil Walker, eds. (London: Hart, 2002), p. 7.

79. Mathew J. Gabel and Christopher J Anderson, 'The Structure Of Citizen Attitudes and the European Political Space', *Comparative Political Studies*, 25/8 (2003), pp. 893–913; Philip Schlesinger, 'The Changing Spaces of Political Communication: The Case of the European Union', *Political Communication*, 16/3 (1999) pp. 263–79; Hans-Jörg Trenz and Klaus Eder, 'The Democratizing Dynamics of a European Public Sphere: Towards a Theory of Democratic Functionalism', *European Journal of Social Theory*, 7/1 (2004), pp. 5–25.

80. See, for example, Simon Hix et al., 'The Party System in the European Parliament: Collusive or Competitive?', *Journal of Common Market Studies*, 41/2 (2003), pp. 309–31. Also Luciano Bardi, 'Transnational Party Federations, European Parliamentary Party Groups and the Building of Europarties', in *How Parties Organize: Change and Adaptation in Party Organizations in Western Democracies*, Richard Katz and Peter Mair, eds. (London: Sage, 1995); David Scott Bell and Christopher Lord, *Transnational Parties in the European Union* (Aldershot: Dartmouth, 1998).

81. During the European Summit in Göteborg some 25,000 people demonstrated and there were several dozens injured and hundreds of arrests as protestors clashed with the police. See e.g. *Time* magazine online: www.time.com/time/world/article/0,8599,168274,00.html.

82. For a more in-depth analysis of the European public space see Philip Schlesinger and Diedre Kevin, 'Can the European Union Become a Sphere of Publics?' in *Democracy in the European Union*, Erik Oddvar Eriksen and John Erik Fossum, eds. (London: Routledge), pp. 222–8.

83. As Michael Keating rightly argued, 'The fact that these values are universal ones shared elsewhere in the world no more disqualifies Europe than it

disqualifies the United States, which is also an ethnically heterogeneous society built on universal values.' See Michael Keating, 'Europe's Changing Political Landscape: Territorial Restructuring and New Forms of Government', op.cit., p. 7

84. For instance, Brigid Laffan went as far as to argue that a European identity can be shaped successfully only if it is of a civic nature; that is, centred on values enshrined at the core of the political system and envisaged as a means by which individuals elect and collaborate, despite their differences, as a result of these shared values. See Brigid Laffan, *Constitution-building in the European Union* (Dublin: Institute for European Affairs, 1996).

85. The notion of 'constitutional patriotism' is usually associated with the work of Jürgen Habermas. See, for example, Jürgen Habermas, 'Yet again: German identity—a unified nation of angry DM Burghers?', *New German Critique*, 52 (1991), pp. 84–101; or Jürgen Habermas, *The Philosophical Discourse of Modernity: Twelve Lectures* (Cambridge, MA: MIT Press, 1987), pp. 11–16. For a comprehensive analysis of the origin of the concept and Habermas' interpretation of it, see Jan-Werner Müller, *Another Country: German Intellectuals, Unification and National Identity* (New Haven, CT: Yale University Press, 2000), pp. 90–119.

86. Kalypso Nicolaïdis, 'The Constitution as European Demoi-cracy?', *Federal Trust European Online Papers*, 38/03, 2003, p. 6. Available at: http://www.fedtrust.-co.uk/uploads/constitution/38_03.pdf.

87. Paul Howe, 'A Community of European: The Requisite Underpinnings', *Journal of Common Market Studies*, 33/1 (1995), pp. 27–46. Also Alex Warleigh, *Democracy and the European Union* (London: Sage, 2003), p. 11–12.

88. Jacques Rupnik, 'Joining Europe together or separately? The implications of the Czecho-Slovak divorce for EU enlargement', in *The Road to the European Union: The Czech and Slovak Republics*, Jacques Rupnik and Jan Zielonka, eds. (Manchester: Manchester University Press, 2003), p. 26.

89. Václav Klaus, *Česká cesta* (Prague: Profile, 1994), p. 136. It must be noted, however, that Václav Havel's views were quite the opposite. He repeatedly stressed the Czech obligation to prepare for EU membership not only in economic and legal terms, but also by cultivating 'Europeanness'. He argued that 'An open international environment and advanced democratic culture of our neighbors, friends and allies constitute the best ground for the advancement of our own uniqueness.' See his speech on the Czech national holiday, 28 October 2000. Available at: www.hrad.cz/president/Havel/speeches/2000/2810_uk.html.

90. *Eurobarometer*, June 2004, p. 182. Available at: http://europa.eu.int/comm/public_opinion/archives/eb/eb61/eb61_en.pdf.

91. This data are presented and analysed in Dieter Fuchs and Hans-Dieter Klingemann, 'Eastward Enlargement of the European Union and the Identity of Europe', *West European Politics*, 25/2 (2002), pp. 19–54.

92. According to June 2004 *Eurobarometer*, only 27 per cent of respondents in the new member states trust their legal system as opposed to 48 per cent in the old ones. Only 42 per cent of respondents in the new member states trust their police as opposed to 65 per cent in the old member states. Op. cit., p. 19.

93. For an in-depth analysis of a rich set of comparative data on civil society in the new member states, see especially Joerg Forbrig, *Civil Society: Theory and Practice in East-Central Europe*, Ph.D. thesis, Florence, European University Institute, 2004 (unpublished). See also *Think Tanks in Central and Eastern Europe* (Washington, DC: Freedom House, 1999); and Katherine Gaskin and Justin Davis Smith, *A New Civic Europe? A Study of the Extent and Role of Volunteering* (London: National Centre for Volunteering, 1997). For an in-depth analysis of local democracy in Eastern Europe, see Catherine Perron, *Les pionniers de la démocratie* (Paris: Presses Universitaires de France, 2004).

94. Klaus von Beyme, 'Parties in the process of consolidation in East-Central Europe', in *Prospects for Democratic Consolidation in East-Central Europe*, Geoffrey Pridham and Attila Ágh, eds. (Manchester: Manchester University Press, 2001), p. 146 and p. 154.

95. As one of the major studies on the Eastern European party systems observed: 'Whereas in Western Europe in the 1980s and 1990s economic social protectionism typically goes with libertarian political-cultural positions, the relationship between the two dimensions is less deterministic in Eastern Europe where it varies cross-nationally. In democracies succeeding bureaucratic-authoritarian or patrimonial communism, the overriding competitive dimension tends to combine economic market liberalism with socio-cultural libertarian individualism at one pole, and social protectionism with traditional collectivism, if not authoritarianism, at the other.' See Herbert Kitschelt et al, *Post-Communist Party Systems: Competition, Representation, and Inter-Party Cooperation* (Cambridge: Cambridge University Press, 1999), p. 402. See also Anna M. Grzymała-Busse, *Redeeming the Communist Past: The Regeneration of Communist Parties in East Central Europe* (Cambridge: Cambridge University Press, 2002), especially pp. 123–74.

96. See http://euobserver.com/?aid=16766; and http://www.guardian.co.uk/guardianpolitics/story/0,,1238317,00.html.

97. See, for example, Helena Luczywo, *Media Market Development Privatisation and Ownership Patterns in SEE and New EU Member Countries*, conference paper, June 2004. Available at: http://www.mirovni-institut.si/media_ownership/conference/pdf/Luczywo.pdf. Also Mihaly Galik, *Concentration of Media Ownership and its impact on Media Freedom and Pluralism*, conference paper, June 2004. Available at: http://www.mirovni-institut.si/media_ownership/conference/pdf/Galik.pdf; Michal Klima, *Czech Media Market* 1992–2004, conference paper, June 2004. Council of Europe, *Media Diversity in Europe, Strasburg, 2002*. Available at: http://www.mirovni-institut.si/media_ownership/conference/http://

www.coe.int/T/E/Human_Rights/media/5_Documentary_Resources/2_Thematic_ documentation/Media_pluralism/PDF_H_APMD_2003_001%20E%20 Media%20 Diversity.pdf.

98. David Marquand, *Parliament for Europe* (London: Jonathan Cape, 1979); Andrew Moravcsik, 'Is there a "Democratic Deficit" in World Politics? A Framework for Analysis', *Government and Opposition*, 39/2 (2004), pp. 336–63; Andrew Moravcsik, 'Reassessing Legitimacy in the European Union', *Journal of Common Market Studies*, 40/4 (2002), pp. 603–24. Giandomenico Majone, 'Europe's 'Democratic Deficit: The Question of Standards', *European Law Journal*, 4/1 (1998), pp. 5–28; Frank Decker, 'Governance beyond the nation-state. Reflections on the democratic deficit of the European Union', *Journal of European Public Policy*, 9/2 (2002), pp. 256–72; Paul Magnette, 'European Governance and Civic Participation: Beyond Elitist Citizenship?' *Political Studies*, 51/1 (2003), pp. 144–60.

99. Yves Mény, 'De La Démocratie en Europe: Old Concepts and New Challenges', *Journal of Common Market Studies*, 41/1 (2003), p. 11.

100. Phillipp Schmitter, *How to Democratize the European Union and Why Bother?* (Oxford: Rowman and Littlefield, 2000), pp. 17–18; condominio is only one of the four possible categories envisaged by Schmitter. The other three are *confederation, stato/federation, and consortio.* For the original typology see Schmitter in Gary Marks et al., eds., *Governance in the European Union* (London: Sage, 1996).

101. Ibid.

Chapter 6: Governance Beyond Borders

1. This is envisaged by the European Constitution adopted by the European Council in Brussels in June 2004 but not ratified by all member states. Available at: http://ue.eu.int/cms3_fo/ showPage.asp?id=251&lang=en&mode=g.

2. Data for 2004, available at: http://europa.eu.int/ comm/external_relations/delegations/intro/.

3. Initially the intention was to have these forces ready by the end of 2003, but the deadline has been shifted to 2005. For more detailed information see Gustav Lindstrom, *The Headline Goal.* Available at: http://www.iss-eu.org/esdp/05-gl.pdf.

4. Sebastian Princen and Michèle Knodt, 'Introduction: Puzzles and prospects in theorizing the EU', in *Understanding the European Union's External Relations*, Sebastian Princen and Michèle Knodt, eds. (London: Routledge, 2003), p. 204.

5. Andreas Osiander, *The States System of Europe, 1640–1990: Peace-making and the Conditions of International Stability* (Oxford: Clarendon Press, 1994), p. 78.

6. See, for example, Johanna Polvi-Lohikoski, *Changing Security Policy in Finland and Sweden*, Ph.D. thesis, European University Institute, Florence, 2003, p. 438

7. See, for example, the text of the British–French joint declaration at St. Malo. Available at: http:// www.iss-eu.org/chaillot/chai47e.html#3.

8. See Hendrik Spruyt, *The Sovereign State and Its Competitors* (Princeton, NJ: Princeton University Press, 1994), p. 56.

9. The concept of 'soft power' has been spelled out in Joseph S. Nye, *Soft Power: The Means to Success in World Politics* (New York: Perseus Books, 2004). For Europe's application of soft power through 'passive aggression' see, for example, Mark Leonard, *Why Europe will Run the 21st Century* (London: Fourth Estate, 2005), pp. 49–56.

10. See S. N. Eisenstadt, *The Political Systems of Empires* (New York: Free Press, 1969), p. x.

11. Consider especially NATO and OSCE. However, even organizations such as the Council of Europe include non-EU states. See S. Victor Papacosma, Sean Kay, and Mark R. Rubin, eds., *NATO after Fifty Years* (Wilmington, DE: SR Books, 2001; Council of Europe, *Council of Europe—Achievements and Activities* (Strasbourg: Council of Europe Publishing, 1996); Michael Bothe, Natalino Ronzitti, and Allan Rosas, eds., *The OSCE in the Maintenance of Peace and Security: Conflict Prevention, Crisis Management and Peaceful Settlement of Disputes* (London: Kluwer Law International, 1997).

12. Christopher Hill, 'The geopolitical implications of enlargement' in *Europe Unbound: Enlarging and Reshaping the Boundaries of the European Union*, Jan Zielonka, ed. (London: Routledge, 2002), p. 95.

13. See Federico Chabot, 'Was There a Renaissance State?' in *The Development of the Modern State*, Heinz Lubasz, ed. (New York: Macmillan, 1964), p. 30.

14. Anthony Giddens, *The Nation-state and Violence* (Cambridge: Polity Press, 1995), p. 120.

15. See Martin Shaw, *Theory of the Global State: Globality as Unfinished Revolution* (Cambridge: Cambridge University Press, 2000), p. 44.

16. As Gianfranco Poggi put it: 'To qualify as a state, the organization in question must be a unitary one; all political activities must originate from it or refer to it.... Federal states represent a major exception to this rule, because they systematically divide governmental powers not just between different organs of the central state but between the latter and other political entities (sometimes called states). Historically, however, centralization applies to them too, as a trend in the actual relations between the two levels.' We may add that even in federal states, foreign and security affairs are usually in the hands of the central federal government. See Gianfranco Poggi, *The State: Its Nature, Development and Prospects* (Oxford: Polity Press, 1990), pp. 22–3.

17. For instance, under the pressure of new member states concerned about their unstable neighbours further south and east, the European Commission has proposed the introduction of special local visas at the borders of the Union. This is to facilitate transborder economic transactions and the movement of people. See COM (2005) 56, Proposal for a regulation of the European

Parliament and of the Council laying down the rules on local border traffic at the external land borders of the member states and amending the Schengen Convention and the Common Consular Instructions (23 February 2005). I spelled out the argument for soft rather than hard borders in Jan Zielonka, 'How New Enlarged Borders will Reshape the European Union', *Journal of Common Market Studies*, 39/3 (2001), pp. 507–36. See also Eberhard Bort, 'Illegal migration and cross-border crime: Challenges at the eastern frontier of the European Union', in *Europe Unbound*, Jan Zielonka, ed. (London: Routledge, 2002), pp. 191–212.

18. See Emil Kirchner, *Decision-Making in the European Community: The Council Presidency and European Integration* (Manchester: Manchester University Press, 1992), pp. 10–14 and 114–15.

19. Sebastian Princen and Michèle Knodt talk about multipillar and multilevel processes in the Union's external relations. op.cit., p. 205.

20. See Beate Kohler-Koch, 'The Evolution and Transformation of European Governance', in *The Transformation of Governance in the European Union* (London: Routledge, 1999), p. 23; or Michael Smith, 'Negotiating New Europe: the roles of the European Union', *Journal of European Public Policy*, 7/5 (2000), pp. 806–22.

21. Christopher Hill, 'Convergence, Divergence and Dialectics: National Foreign Policies and the CFSP', in *Paradoxes of European Foreign Policy*, Jan Zielonka, ed. (The Hague: Kluwer Law International, 1998), p. 43.

22. See Michael Smith, 'Foreign Economic Policy', in *Contemporary European Foreign Policy*, Walter Carlsnaes, Helene Sjursen, and Brian White, eds. (London: Sage, 2004), pp. 75–90; or Sarah Collinson, ' "Issue-systems", "multi-level games", and the analysis of the EU's external commercial and associated policies: A research agenda', *Journal of European Public Policy*, 6/2 (1999), pp. 206–24.

23. Magnus Ekengren, 'National Foreign Policy Co-ordination: The Swedish EU Presidency', in *Contemporary European Foreign Policy*, Walter Carlsnaes, Helene Sjursen, and Brian White, eds. (London: Sage, 2004), pp. 211–26.

24. France was the 'Framework' country for the operation, and it had most troops there. Available at: http://www.stimson.org/fopo/?SN=FP20040406632.

25. Denmark, France, and Greece together with Italy supported a military intervention in Albania, but Sweden, Great Britain, and Germany opposed it. For more details of Operation Alba in Albania see, for example, Paolo Tripodi, 'Operation Alba: A Necessary and Successful Preventive Deployment', *International Peacekeeping*, 9/4 (2002), p. 89–104. See also analyses available at: http://www.basicint.org/pubs/Papers/BP21.htm; http://www.isn.ethz.ch/securityforum/Online_Publications/WS4/Tanner.htm and http://www.aim-press.ch/dyn/trae/archive/ data/199704/70420–007-trae-tir.htm.

26. See, for example, Grzegorz Gromadzki and Olaf Osica, 'Pro-European Atlantists: Poland and Other Countries of Central and Eastern Europe After Accession to the European Union', *Batory Foundation's Policy Papers*, 3 (2001), p. 11; or Antonio Missiroli, ed., 'Bigger EU, wider CFSP, stronger ESDP? The view from

Central Europe', *Institute for Security Studies Occasional Paper*, 34 (2002), p. 20. See also a speech by Poland's Minister for Foreign Affairs, Bronislaw Bartoszewski, 'Polska polityka bezpieczenstwa. Polski punkt widzenia', delivered at Warsaw University, 11 May 2001. Available from the Polish Foreign Ministry's website at: www.msz.gov.pl.

27. Barry Buzan, *People, States and Fear: The National Security Problem in International Relations* (Brighton: Harvest-Wheatsheaf, 1983), p. 44. See also Jean-Marie Guéhenno, 'A Foreign Policy in Search of a Polity', *Paradoxes of European Foreign Policy*, op.cit., pp. 25–34.

28. 'A secure Europe in a better world—European Security Strategy', European Council, Brussels, 12 December 2003.

29. François Heisbourg, 'The "European Security Strategy" is not a security strategy', in Steven Everts et al., *A European Way of War* (London: Centre for European Reform, 2004), p. 28. It must be stressed, however, that the ESS looks better than the earlier so-called 'Asolo list' trying to draw a list of common European interests. See e.g. Simon J. Nutall's *European Foreign Policy* (Oxford: Oxford University Press, 2000), p. 123.

30. This also applies to bilateral relations in Europe. For instance, Jean-Marie Guéhenno, discussing the French and German policies towards the Yugoslav crisis, concluded: 'The only strong interest, which was common to the two nations, was to prevent the crisis jeopardizing the quality of Franco-German relations.' See Jean-Marie Guéhenno, 'A Foreign Policy in Search of a Polity', *Paradoxes of European Foreign Policy*, op. cit., p. 28.

31. Knud Erik Jørgensen, 'The European Union's Performance in World Politics: How Should We Measure Success?', *Paradoxes of European Foreign Policy*, op.cit., pp. 90–1.

32. Paul Kennedy, *The Rise and Fall of the Great Powers: Economic Change and Military Conflict from 1500 to 2000* (London: Unwin and Hyman, 1988), p. 71.

33. Ibid. p. 70.

34. K. J. Holsti, *International Politics: A Framework for Analysis*, sixth edn. (London: Prentice Hall International, 1992), p. 39. Unfortunately, we do not have similar statistics for the pre-1648 period.

35. See Karen E. Smith, 'The Instruments of European Union Foreign Policy', *Paradoxes of European Foreign Policy*, op. cit., pp. 67–85.

36. Charles W. Kegley and Gregory A. Raymond, *Exorcising the Ghost of Westphalia: Building World Order in the New Millennium* (Upper Saddle River NJ: Prentice-Hall, 2002), p. 135. See also Gianfranco Poggi, *The Development of the Modern State: A Sociological Introduction* (London: Hutchinson, 1978), p. 90.

37. Works of Bodin obviously preceded the Treaties of Westphalia. In fact, Jean Bodin's influential work *De La République* published in 1576 elaborated the concept of sovereignty and inspired the Westphalian arrangement. See, for example, Preston King, *The Ideology of Order: A Comparative Analysis of Jean Bodin and Thomas Hobbes* (London: Frank Cass, 1999), or Yves Charles Zarka,

Jean Bodin: Nature, Histoire, Droit et Politique (Paris: Presses universitaires de France, 1996). Also John Stoessinger, 'The nation-state and the nature of power', in *Perspectives on World Politics*, second edn., Richard Little and Michael Smith, eds. (London: Routledge, 1991), p. 24.

38. Because the Union's promotion of values is not consistent enough (and at times even hypocritical), I would not go as far as Ian Manners and argue that the Union is a 'normative power' that principally acts to 'extend its norms into the international system'. However, I also disagree with Rober Kagan's assertion that, 'Europe does not see a mission for itself that requires power. Its mission, if it has a mission beyond the confines of Europe, is to oppose power.' In my view, the Union simply practices a different type of power politics than typical Westphalian states, and also justifies the uses and misuses of this power in a different manner. See Ian Manners, 'Normative Power Europe: A Contradiction in Terms?', *Journal of Common Market Studies*, 40/2 (2002), pp. 235–58, and Robert Kagan, *Paradise and Power: America and Europe in the New World Order* (London: Atlantic Books, 2003), p. 68. For the EU's inconsistent promotion of its values see, for example, Catherine Gegout, *An Evaluation of the Making and Functioning of the European Union's Common Foreign and Security Policy (CFSP) System*, Ph.D. thesis, European University Institute, 2004.

39. This has been well illustrated in Claire Burgio, *The European Union's Promotion of 'Deep Integration' at the Regional Level: The Commercial Imperative*, M.Phil. thesis in European Politics and Society, Lincoln College, Oxford, 2004, pp. 22–4. See also Speech by Romano Prodi, President of the European Commission, 'Europe and Global Governance', Brussels, 31 March 2000.

40. For an in-depth legal and institutional analysis of the problem see Marise Cremona, 'The Impact of Enlargement: External Policy and External Relations', in *The Enlargement of the European Union*, Marise Cremona, ed. (Oxford: Oxford University Press, 2003), pp. 161–208.

41. As Alexander Motyl observed: 'As a polity that is simultaneously an international actor and a peculiarly structured political system with a core and peripheries, empire fits awkwardly in research agendas. IR theorists can easily accommodate empires as great powers but not as systems. Some, such as Yale Ferguson and Richard Mansbach, subsume empires under the category of "polities," thereby transforming them into but one species of a huge genus. Comparativists have an even harder nut to crack, as international relations are traditionally outside their field of interest, whereas hybrid entities with a core and peripheries appear to be both more and less than the systems or states the comparativists usually study.' See Alexander J. Motyl, *Imperial Ends: The Decay, Collapse, and Revival of Empires* (New York: Columbia University Press, 2001), pp. 1–2.

42. As Barry Buzan and Richard Little put it: '[I]t is change in the structure of the dominant units . . . .that represents the most fundamental, era-defining type of

transformation in international systems.' See Barry Buzan and Richard Little, *International Systems in World History* (Oxford: Oxford University Press, 2000), p. 7.

43. See, for example, Adam Watson, *The Evolution of International Society* (London: Routledge, 1992), pp. 138–51.

44. Scholars often talk about concentric circles of political control in the pre-Westphalian era, ranging from complete absorption at the core to mere hegemony at the outer margins. See Barry Buzan and Richard Little, op.cit., pp. 176–82, and Adam Watson, *The Evolution of International Society* (London: Routledge, 1992), pp. 14–16.

45. The peace resulting from a series of treaties negotiated in two Westphalian towns, Münster and Osnabrück, formally dealt with German internal affairs only. However, since most of the larger European actors were involved in the Thirty Years, War, the peace had a broader long-term significance. See E. A. Beller, 'Thirty Years War', in J.P. Cooper *The New Cambridge Modern History* Vol. IV: The Decline of Spam and the Thirty Years War: 1609–1659 (Cambridge: Cambridge University Press, 1970), pp. 306–58.

46. As Kalevi Holsti put it, the Peace of Westphalia represented 'an order created by states for states'. See Kalevi Holsti, *Peace and War: Armed Conflicts and International Order, 1648–1989* (Cambridge: Cambridge University Press, 1991), p. 25.

47. See, for example, Stephen D. Krasner, *Sovereignty, Organized Hypocrisy* (Princeton, NJ: Princeton University Press, 1999). David Held makes a useful distinction between the concepts of sovereignty and autonomy. The former refers to the entitlement of a state to rule over a bounded territory, while latter denotes the actual power a nation state possesses to articulate and achieve policy goals independently. See David Held, *Democracy and the Global Order* (Oxford: Polity Press, 1995), p. 100.

48. Kenneth N. Waltz, *Man, the State and War: A Theoretical Analysis* (New York: Columbia University Press, 2001), p. 159.

49. Burke called this 'the diplomatic republic of Europe' as quoted in Hedley Bull and Adam Watson, *The Expansion of International Society* (Oxford: Clarendon Press, 1984), p. 1.

50. As David Held put it: 'the UN Charter model, despite its good intentions, failed effectively to generate a new principle of organization in the international order—a principle which might break fundamentally with the logic of Westphalia ... ' See David Held, op.cit., p. 88. The realist school of international relations is obviously much more sceptical about the constraining effects of ethical ideas and good government. See, for example, Kenneth N. Waltz, op.cit., pp. 80–5.

51. This is so even if qualified majority voting (QMV) is hardly applied in practice, and especially in foreign affairs. For a more elaborate argument see, for example, James A. Caporaso, 'Changes in the Westphalian Order: Territory, Public Authority, and Sovereignty', in *Continuity and Change in the Westphalian Order*, James A. Caporaso, ed. (Oxford: Blackwell, 2000), pp. 15–21.

52. I discussed these factors in more detail in *Explaining Euro-paralysis* (London: Macmillan/Palgrave, 1998), pp. 39–43.

53. The system of weighted votes was originally introduced for the European Economic Community (EEC) with only six member states, and gradually adjusted up to the latest treaty in force, agreed in Nice. This system violates the formal equality of member states although it may be seen as an effort to introduce a substantive equality of states. See Jan Wouters, 'Constitutional Limits of Differentiation: The Principle of Equality', in *The Many Faces of Differentiation in EU Law*, B. de Witte, D. Hanf, and E. Vos, eds. (Antwerp: Intersentia, 2001), p. 301.

54. Bruno De Witte, 'Enlargement and the EU Constitution', in *The Enlargement of the European Union*, op.cit., p. 241. See also Gráinne de Búrca and Joanne Scott, eds., *Constitutional Change in the EU—From Uniformity to Flexibility?* (London: Hart, 2000).

55. This exercise of the Union's power to intervene in the domestic affairs of its member states has proved controversial and only partially successful, but has set an important precedent. See Per Cramér and Pål Wrange, 'The Heider Affair, Law and European Integration', *Europarättslig tidskrift* 28 (2000) or Matthew Happold, 'Fourteen against One: The EU Member states' Response to Freedom Party Participation in the Austrian Government', *ICLQ*, 49 (2000), p. 953.

56. See, for example, Catherine McArdle Kelleher, Jane M. O. Sharp, and Lawrence Freedman, eds., *The Treaty on Conventional Armed Forces in Europe: The Politics of Post-Wall Arms Control* (Baden-Baden: Nomos, 1996), or Pál Dunay, Gábor Kardos, and Andrew J. Williams, eds., *New Forms of Security: Views from Central, Eastern and Western Europe* (Aldershot: Dartmouth, 1995).

57. Robert Cooper, *The Breaking of Nations* (London: Atlantic Books, 2003) p. 55.

58. As the Latvian President, Vaira Vike-Freiberga, put it: 'I believe that most Latvians see the Europe of the future as a united continent of equal and sovereign partners, where relationships between member-states are based on partnership and mutual respect, and where the interests of all members are taken into account. This has been one of the European Union's main strengths to date. It will not bode well for Europe's future if this principle is changed, and if some of the EU's larger countries obtain a disproportionate say in important decision-making processes at the expense of their smaller neighbours.' See 'European Integration: New Opportunities and challenges', address by Vaira Vike-Freiberga, President of Latvia, at the Institute of European Affairs in Dublin, 4 June 2002. Available at: http:// europa.eu.int/futurum/documents/speech/sp040602_en.htm.

59. Joschka Fischer's speech at the Humboldt University in Berlin, 12 May 2000. Available at: http:// www.auswaertiges-amt.de/www/en/ ausgabe_archiv?archiv _id=1027.

60. See Jacques Chirac's speech at the German Bundestag in Berlin, 27 June 2000. Available at: http://www.bundesregierung.de/dokumente/Rede/ix_ 12732.htm.

61. This is well illustrated by Eastern European reactions to Joschka Fischer's speech at the Humboldt University. See, for example, a commentary of Poland's Foreign Minister, Bronislaw Geremek, quoted by PAP (Polska Agencja Prasowa). Available at: http://euro.pap.pl/cgi-bin/europap.pl?grupa=1&ID=81, and an interview with the Hungarian Prime Minister, Victor Orbán, for the Austrian newspaper, *Standard*, 18 June 2000.

62. See Jonathan Story, 'The Idea of the Core: The Dialectics of History and Space', in *The Politics of European Treaty Reform*, Geoffrey Edwards and Alfred Pijpers, eds. (London: Pinter, 1997), pp. 23–4.

63. See Martin Feldstein, 'EMU and International Conflict', *Foreign Affairs*, 76/6 (1997), pp. 60–73.

64. The term neo-medieval makes clear that we are not in the business of applying simplistic historical analogies. Global capitalism, new technologies (nuclear weapons among them), and democracy make it difficult for the EU to return to medieval behaviour. Today, the European social structure and its belief system are also quite different. Rodney Bruce Hall and Friedrich V. Kratochwil have shown well how medieval history could be abused in the field of international relations. See Rodney Bruce Hall and Friedrich V. Kratochwil, 'Medieval tales: neorealist "science" and the abuse of history', *International Organization*, 47/3 (1993), pp. 479–91.

65. Joschka Fischer, see note 55. The implicit assumption in the Fischer argument is that the balance-of-power politics in the cold war period was unworkable in the long term and quite dangerous. I cannot but agree with such reasoning.

66. John J. Mearsheimer, 'Back to the Future. Instability in Europe After the Cold War', *International Security*, 15/1 (1990), p. 52 and p. 5. See also John J. Mearsheimer, *The Tragedy of Great Power Politics* (New York: Norton, 2001).

67. Josef Joffe, 'Europe's American Pacifier', *Foreign Policy*, 54 (1984), pp. 64–82.

68. G. John Ikenberry, 'Illusions of Empire. Defining the New American Order', *Foreign Affairs*, 83/2 (2004), pp. 145–6.

69. This has been well illustrated and applied to the contemporary global setting by Jörg Friedrichs, 'The Meaning of New Medievalism', *European Journal of International Relations*, 7/4 (2001), pp. 475–502. See also Hendrick Spruyt, op.cit., pp. 54–5.

70. As Samuel Huntington put it: 'religiosity distinguishes America from most other Western societies. Americans are also overwhelmingly Christian, which distinguishes them from many non-Western peoples. Their religiosity leads Americans to see the world in terms of good and evil to a much greater extent than most other peoples. The leaders of other societies often find this religiosity not only extraordinary but also exasperating for the deep moralism it engenders, in the consideration of political, economic and social issues.' Samuel P. Huntington, 'Dead Souls. The Denationalization of the American Elite', *The National Interest* (2004), p. 18.

71. A growing body of literature on Americanization suggest that this is also the case.
72. See, for example, Stale Ulriksen, 'Requirements for future European military strategies and force structures', *International Peacekeeping*, 11/3 (2004), pp. 457–73, or Neil Winn, 'Towards a Common European Security and Defence Policy? The Debate on NATO, the European Army and Transatlantic Security', *Geopolitics*, 8/2 (2003), pp. 47–68.
73. See Madeleine K. Albright, 'The Right Balance Will Secure NATO's Future', in *Financial Times*, 7 December 1998. Available at: http://www.iss-eu.org/chaillot/chai47e.html#4.
74. See, for example, American economic assistance in Europe, available at: http://www.state.gov/p/eur/rls/rm/2003/19203.htm. See also H. Houweling and M. P. Amineh, 'The Geopolitics of Power Projection in US Foreign Policy: From Colonization to Globalization', *Perspectives on Global Development and Technology*, 2/3–4 (2003), pp. 339–89.
75. See, for example, the Commission's Trade web page available at: http://europa.eu.int/comm/trade/bilateral/usa/index_en.htm.
76. See, for example, Timothy Garton Ash, *Free World* (London: Allen Lane, 2004) and Diana Crane, Nobuko Kawashima, and Kenichi Kawasaki, *Global Culture: Media, Arts, Policy, and Globalization* (London: Routledge, 2002).
77. See, for example, John Peterson, 'America as a European Power: The end of empire by integration?', *International Affairs*, 80/4 (2004), pp. 613–29.
78. See, for example, Lawrence Freedman, 'War in Iraq: Selling the Threat', *Survival*, 46/2 (2004), pp. 7–50.
79. Michael Brenner, 'The CFSP Factor: A Comparison of United States and French Strategies', *Cooperation and Conflict*, 38/3 (2003), pp. 187–209. Or Michèle Alliot-Marie, 'France Is Ready to Play its Role in Global Security', *European Affairs*, 4/1 (2003). Available at: http://www.europeanaffairs.org/archive/2003_winter/2003_winter_58.php4.
80. See Catherine Gegout, 'The Quint: Acknowledging the Existence of a Big Four-US Directoire at the Heart of the European Union's Foreign Policy Decision-Making Process', *Journal of Common Market Studies*, 40/2 (2002), pp. 331–44.
81. See, for example, Alicia Adsera and Carles Boix, 'Must we choose? European unemployment, American inequality, and the impact of education and labor market institutions', *European Journal of Political Economy*, 16/4 (2000), pp. 611–38.
82. See, for example, Bojko Bučar and Irena Brinar, 'Slovenian Foreign Policy', in *Civil Society, Political Society, Democracy*, Adolf Bibič and Gigi Graziano, eds. (Ljubljana: Slovenian Political Science Association, 1994), p. 442.
83. See, for example, Joylon Howorth, 'Discourse, Ideas, and Epistemic Communities in European Security and Defence Policy', *West European Politics*, 27/2 (2004), pp. 211–34.

84. See, for example, Dan Hamilton and Joseph Quinlan, *Partners in Prosperity: The Changing Geography of the Transatlantic Economy* (Washington, DC: SAIS, 2004), or David P. Calleo, *Rethinking Europe's Future* (Princeton, NJ: Princeton University Press, 2001), especially 'Globalism and the case for a European Bloc', pp. 207–49. For EMU as a unifying factor see Loukas Tsoukalis, *What Kind of Europe?* (Oxford: Oxford University Press, 2004), pp. 142–66.

85. See, for example, David D. Laitin, 'Culture and National Identity: "The East" and European Integration', *West European Politics*, 25/2 (2002), pp. 55–80.

86. This has been well argued by, for example, Philip H. Gordon, 'Bridging the Atlantic Divide', *Foreign Affairs*, 82/1 (2003), pp. 70–83. For a set of data illustrating a convergence of public values across the Atlantic, see Anthony J. Blinken, 'The False Crisis Over the Atlantic', *Foreign Affairs*, 80/3 (2001), pp. 35–48.

87. The issue of borders can be controversial. Unlike the EU, the United States certainly has fixed borders, but one may argue that its borders are equally porous and thus relatively soft. However, careful comparisons reveal that border regions in Europe are developing into a soft and comprehensive institutional layer within the European multilevel polity, while neither on the American–Mexican, nor on the American–Canadian border is such an encompassing territorially defined cross-border polity emerging. See Joachim K. Blatter, 'Debordering the World of States: Towards a Multi-Level System in Europe and a Multi-Polity System in North America? Insights from Border regions', *European Journal of International Relations*, 7/2 (2001), pp. 175–209.

88. See, for example, Michael Mann, *Incoherent Empire* (New York: Verso, 2003), or Chalmers Johnson, *The Sorrows of Empire: Militarism, Secrecy and the End of the Republic* (New York: Metropolitan Books, 2004). See also Jack Snyder, 'Imperial Temptations', *The National Interest* (2003), pp. 29–40.

89. See, for example, Niall Ferguson, *Colossus: The Price of America's Empire* (New York: Penguin Books, 2004), or Patrick Karl O'Brien and Armand Clesse, *Two Hegemonies: Britain 1846–1914 and the United States 1941–2001* (Aldershot: Ashgate, 2002). For other types of analogies see e.g. Andrew J. Bacevich, *American Empire: The Realities and Consequences of U.S. Diplomacy* (Cambridge, MA: Harvard University Press, 2002).

90. A comparison of the latest American and European official security strategies makes this difference plainly clear. See 'A secure Europe in a better world— European Security Strategy', European Council, Brussels, 12 December 2003, and the National Security Strategy of the United States. Available at: http://www.whitehouse.gov/nsc/nssall.html.

91. For a comprehensive list of foreign policy differences before 9/11 see e.g. Steven Everts, 'Unilateral America, Lightweight Europe?' CER Working Paper, London, February 2001, pp. 5–8.

92. As Claire Burgio showed, even when the EU exports its model of European integration into Latin America or Asia, it is not so much to balance the American strategic position in these regions (as the French would like to), but to pursue commercial interests. Commercial rather than strategic interests seem to be behind even the EU's controversial plans to lift its ban on arms sales to China. For the former argument see Claire Burgio, 'The European Union's Promotion of "Deep Integration" at the Regional Level: the Commercial Imperative', M.Phil. thesis, Oxford University, 2004, especially pp. 21–31. The French strategic vision of global multilateralism based on trading regions is discussed in 'M. Chirac exhorte les Européens à soutenir l'ONU en Irak', *Le Monde*, 30 August 2003. For the EU's arms sales policy shift see Reginald Dale, 'Trans-Atlantic dispute over arming China', *International Herald Tribune*, 15 July 2004.

93. See, for example, Andrew Moravcsik, 'Striking a New Transatlantic Bargain', *Foreign Affairs*, 82/4 (2003), pp. 74–89, or 'Isolation vs. engagement in the 21st century', a Special Issue of the *Journal of International Affairs* on Rogue States Isolation vs. Engagement in the 21st Century 54/2 (2001).

94. As Pascal Lamy, European Trade Commissioner, put it: 'European integration has always been about projecting a model of multilateral reconciliation, which recalls Kant's Utopian, federal (if I may use that term) association of free republics, on the rest of the world.... The EU has long experience, far more than most regional entities, of seeking an appropriate balance between trade liberalization and market integration, on the one hand, and policy integration and solidarity, on the other.' See Pascal Lamy, 'Europe and the Future of Economic Governance', *Journal of Common Market Studies*, 42/1 (2004), p. 15. See also Speech by Romano Prodi, President of the European Commission, 'Europe and Global Governance', Brussels, 31 March 2000.

95. See, for example, William Wallace, 'Europe the necessary Partner', *Foreign Affairs*, 80/3 (2001), pp. 20–1.

96. As Ivan Krastev put it: 'At present Europe and America are allies divided by common values and common interests.' See Ivan Krastev, 'The Anti-American Century?', *Journal of Democracy*, 13/2 (2004), p. 12.

97. This has been well argued by Stephen M. Walt, presenting his 'additional view' to a special report on the Trans-Atlantic Partnership prepared by the Council on Foreign Relations. See *Reviewing the Atlantic Partnership*, Report of an Independent Task Force co-chaired by Henry A. Kissinger and Lawrence H. Summers and directed by Charles A. Kupchan (New York: Council on Foreign Relations, 2004), p. 29.

98. See, for example, Ronald D. Asmus, 'Rebuilding the Atlantic Alliance', *Foreign Affairs*, 82/5 (2003), pp. 28–30.

99. One can well envisage a scenario of increased secrecy, suspicion, and outright hostility among individual EU members. Some member states may stop

bargaining over their interests through the EU and resort to unilateral measures. Some may even decide to leave the EU altogether. See John J. Mearsheimer, *The Tragedy of Great Power Politics* (New York: Norton, 2001).

100. In my view, at present the only actor who is able to effectively contain American power is the American electorate.

101. This has been well argued in Joseph S. Nye, Jr., *The Paradox of American Power: Why the World's Only Superpower Can't Go It Alone* (Oxford: Oxford University Press, 2002).

102. Joseph S. Nye, 'U.S. Power and Strategy after Iraq', *Foreign Affairs*, 82/4 (2003), pp. 72–3. See also his 'The Decline of America's Soft Power', *Foreign Affairs*, 83/3 (2004), pp. 16–21.

103. Hedley Bull, *The Anarchical Society: A Study of Order in World Politics* (London: Macmillan, 1977), especially pp. 254–5 and 264–76.

104. Ibid., p. 254.

105. For some authors medievalism is a synonym of disorder and fragmentation. See, for example, Alain Minc, *Le Nouveau Moyen Âge* (Paris: Gallimard, 1993), p. 67.

106. Robert Cooper, 'Why we still need Empires', in *The Observer*, 7 April 2002. Available at: http://observer.guardian.co.uk/worldview/story/ 0,11581,680117,00 .html.

107. See, for example, Olivier Roy, 'EuroIslam: The Jihad Within?', *The National Interest*, 71 (2003), pp. 63–74.

Conclusions: Implications of Neo-medievalism

1. This has well been illustrated in Timothy Garton Ash, *Free World* (London: Penguin, 2005), pp. 209–24. See also Mark Leonard, *Why Europe Will Run the 21st Century* (London: Fourth Estate, 2005), pp. 35–48.

2. German unification did not prompt formal changes in the EU institutional system, but indirectly it has had an enormous impact on the integration process. For instance, the Stability Pact rules have been modified in 2005 with direct reference to the costs of German unification. See, for example, Deutsche Welle report from 21 March 2005. Available at: http://www.deutsche-welle.de/dw/article/ 0,1564,1524386,00.html; and Euractiv from 21 March 2005, available at http:// www.euractiv.com/Article?tcmuri=tcm:29-137047-16&type=News.

3. This has even been envisaged by members of the European Commission, Danuta Hübner and Margot Wallström, as reported by *Euobserver* on 28 February 2005. Available at: http://euobserver.com/?aid=18519.

4. On the EU's relations with Russia see, for example, Ania Krok-Paszkowska and Jan Zielonka, 'The European Union's Policies Toward Russia', in *Russia's Engagement with the West. Transformation and Integration in the Twenty-First*

Century, Alexander J. Motyl, Blair A. Ruble, and Lilia Shevtsova, eds. (Armonk, NY: M. E. Sharpe, 2005), pp. 151–69.

5. This has, for instance, been suggested by former Israeli Prime Minister Shimon Peres. Speaking to the Foreign Press Association in Jerusalem in February 2004, Peres said that if the Palestinians, Israelis, and Jordanians sign a peace agreement, they should be offered membership of the EU. He also said that EU Foreign Policy Chief Javier Solana and German Foreign Minister Joschka Fischer were 'rather positive' about the idea. See 'EU membership Touted for Israel, Palestine, Jordan', CBC News, 11 February 2004. Available at: http://www.globalpolicy.org/nations/sovereign/integrate/2004/0211touted.htm.

6. An overview of the EU's relations with Lebanon, available at: http://europa.eu.int/comm/external_relations/lebanon/intro/.

7. See, for example, 'Turkey: EU Bid Hinges on Further Rights Reforms', Human Rights Watch, 15 June 2004; available at http://hrw.org/english/docs/2004/06/15/turkey8816.htm.

8. For more details see, for example, Timothy Garton Ash and Timothy Snyder, 'Ukraine: The Orange Revolution', *New York Review of Books*, LII/7 (2005), p. 30. For a much less enthusiastic reception of Ukraine's quest for EU membership, see an interview with the French President, Jacques Chirac, in *Gazeta Wyborcza*, 28 February 2005, p. 28.

9. See, for example, Kataryna Wolczuk and Roman Wolczuk, *Poland and Ukraine: A Strategic Partnership in a Changing Europe?* (London: Royal Institute of International Affairs, 2002), pp. 45–7. Also *Droga do Europy: Opinie ukraińskich elit*, (Warsaw: Fundacja im. Stefana Batorego & Miedzynarodowa Fundacja 'Odrodzenie', 2004), p. 239.

10. For instance, according to Article I-17 of the draft of the European Constitution, culture is mentioned alongside tourism and administrative cooperation (among others) as an area of supporting, coordinating, or complementary action in the EU. In Part II the Constitution refers to the EU's task to '[respect] the diversity of the cultures and traditions of the peoples of Europe as well as the national identities of the Member States'. However, there is no mention of ethnic grouping below the nation-state level. Finally, Article III-280 deals with culture but only does so in a rather superficial and unspecific way. In the entire Constitution, the Union only once refers to national minorities, in Article I-2, stating that 'The Union is founded on the values of respect for human dignity, freedom, democracy, equality, the rule of law and respect for human rights, including the rights of persons belonging to minorities.' However, no reference is made to ethnic minorities and when the Treaty talks about non-discrimination in ethnic origin no specific ethnic minority in individual member states is mentioned—see Articles II-81, III-118, and III-124.

11. See, for example, Philippe Ricard, 'Le non souligne les difficultés de l'élargissement', *Le Monde*, 31 May 2005; and Georges Marion, 'La droite allemande

accuse la Turquie d'avoir contribué à la victoire du non français', *Le Monde*, 1 June 2005.

12. Carl Bildt, 'Europe must keep its "soft power" ', *Financial Times*, 1 June 2005, p. 17.

13. Governance is largely about 'sustaining co-ordination and coherence among a wide variety of actors with different purposes and objectives such as political actors and institutions, corporate interests, civil society, and transnational governments'. See Jon Pierre, 'Introduction: Understanding Governance', in *Debating Governance: Authority, Steering and Democracy*, Jon Pierre, ed. (Oxford: Oxford University Press, 2000), pp. 3–4.

14. As Albert Hirschman argued, the availability of exit options prevents the formation of states which rest on the limitations of those exits. See, for example, Albert O. Hirschman, 'Exit, Voice and the State', *World Politics*, 31/1 (1978), pp. 90–107.

15. Yuri Devuyst, 'The Community Method after Amsterdam', *Journal of Common Market Studies*, 37/1 (1999), pp. 109–20. See also interview with Jonathan Faull, Commission Director General for Justice and Home Affairs, on the Euractiv website in February 2004; available at: http://www.euractiv.com/Article?tc-muri=tcm:29-111966-16&type=News.

16. This especially applies to lawyers who tend to see the legal order as a harmonious and systematic whole and view differentiation and flexibility with suspicion. See, for example, Thomas Wilhelmsson, 'Legal Integration as Disintegration of National law' in *Legal Polycentricity: Consequences of Pluralism in Law*, H. Petersen and H. Zahle, eds. (Aldershot: Dartmouth, 1995), p. 125. See also R. Harmsen, 'A European Union of Variable Geometry: Problems and Perspectives', *Northern Ireland Legal Quarterly*, 45/(1994), pp. 109–31. However, similar criticism of flexibility and differentiation has also been expressed by historians and political scientists, including those rather sceptical about federal Europe. For instance, Tony Judt has argued that a more flexible, multispeed Europe will end up as a new League of Nations in which states opt out of those decisions that do not like and go along only with those that serve their partisan interests. See Tony Judt, 'The Grand Illusion', *New York Review of Books*, 11/7, (1996). For an overview of the arguments concerning subsidiarity and the Open Method of Coordination see, for example, Kees van Kersbergen and Bertjan Verbeek, 'Subsidiarity as a Principle of Governance in the European Union', *Comparative European Politics*, 2/2 (2004), pp. 142–62.

17. See references in Chapter 4 to the work of Casella, Mattli, and Krugman.

18. For instance, Jan Kooiman distinguished between self-governance, co-governance, and hierarchical governance. See Jan Kooiman, *Governing as Governance* (London: Sage, 2003), pp. 77–132.

19. As Herman van Gunsteren put it: 'Where one person sees plurality, the other one sees rubbish. Where one person sees variety, another sees disorder. Where the one sees monsters (unacceptable combinations such as centaurs), the other

sees fascinating novelties.' See Herman van Gunsteren, *A Theory of Citizenship* (Boulder, CO: Westview Press, 1998), p. 116.

20. For the former view see Amitai Etzoni, *The Active Society* (New York: Free Press, 1968). For the latter, see Ilya Prigogine and Isabelle Stengers, *Order out of Chaos* (New York: Bantam, 1984).

21. For instance, Richard Rhodes has identified no less than seven definitions of governance. See R. A. W. Rhodes, 'Governance and Public Administration,' in *Debating Governance: Authority, Steering and Democracy*, Jon Pierre, ed., (Oxford: Oxford University Press, 2000), pp. 55–63.

22. See, for example, Guy Peters, 'Globalization, Institutions and Governance', in *Governance in the Twenty-first Century: Revitalizing Public Service*, B. Guy Peters and Donald J. Savoie, eds. (Montreal: McGill-Queen's University Press, 2000), pp. 30–1.

23. John Gerard Ruggie, 'Territoriality and Beyond: Problematizing Modernity in International Relations', *International Organization*, 47/1 (1993), p. 148.

24. Anthony Wilden, *The Rules are no Game* (London: Routledge and Kegan Paul, 1987), p. 192.

25. See Jan Kooiman, op.cit., p. 194.

26. Tanja J. Börzel, 'Organizing Babylon: On the Different Conceptions of Policy Networks', *Public Administration*, 76/2 (1998), pp. 262–3. See also Ash Amin and Jerzy Hausner, 'Interactive governance and social complexity' in *Beyond Market and Hierarchy*, Ash Amin and Jerzy Hausner, eds. (Cheltenham: Edward Elgar, 1997), pp. 15–18.

27. The term 'plurilateralism' was first used by Philip G. Cerny in the early 1990s to describe the shift in the world order from a 'hierarchy of holistic actors, states, which impose order through power and hegemony, to a more complex, and diffuse set of interactive self-regulatory mechanisms or webs of power'. See Philip G. Cerny, 'Plurilateralism: Structural Differentiation and Functional Conflict in the Post-Cold War World Order', *Millenium*, 22/1 (1993), p. 31.

28. See James N. Rosenau, 'Change, Complexity, and Governance in Globalizing Space', in *Debating Governance: Authority, Steering and Democracy*, Jon Pierre, ed. (Oxford: Oxford University Press, 2000), p. 189. See also James N. Rosenau, *Along the Domestic–Foreign Frontier: Exploring Governance in a Turbulent World* (Cambridge: Cambridge University Press, 1997).

29. Soft law privileges, informal gentlemen's agreements, contracts instead of top-down regulation, and information or persuasion instead of repression. See, for example, Francis Snyder, 'Soft law and Institutional Practice in the European Community', in *The Construction of Europe: Essays in Honor of Emile Noël*, Stephen Martin, ed. (Deventer: Kluwer Law Academic, 1994), pp. 197–227.

30. The Presidency Conclusions of the European Council meeting held in Brussels on 22 and 23 March 2005, 7619/05 ANNEX II.

31. Gráinne de Búrca and Joanne Scott, *Constitutional Change in the EU: From Uniformity to Flexibility?* (Oxford: Hart, 2000), p. 2. See also Samantha Besson, 'From European Integration to European Integrity: Should European Law Speak with Just One Voice?', *European Law Journal*, 10/3 (2004), pp. 257–81.

32. See European Council, *Lisbon European Council Presidency Conclusions* (23–24 March 2000), para. 37. For a comprehensive treatment see Jonathan Zeitlin and Philippe Pochet, eds., with Lars Magnussen, *The Open Method of Co-ordination in Action* (Oxford: Peter Lang, 2005).

33. Jens Henrik Haar, 'Open co-ordination as Advanced Liberal Government', *Journal of European Public Policy*, 11/2 (2004), pp. 209–30. For a more critical evaluation of the OMC see Adrienne Héritier, 'New Modes of Governance in Europe: Policy-making without Legislating?' in *Common Goods: Reinventing European and International Governance*, Adrienne Héritier, ed. (Lanham, MD: Rowman and Littlefield, 2002), pp. 185–206.

34. Alessandra Casella and Jonathan S. Feinstein, 'Public Goods in Trade: On the Formation of Markets and Jurisdictions', *International Economic Review*, 43/2 (2002), p. 438.

35. Or, as Alex Warleigh put it: 'The practice of governance in the EU has been brought into line with many of those attached to the à la carte model, but its structures and "frame" have not.' He calls for 'the acceptance of the normative "frame" of à la carte flexibility, and choosing to consider it worthwhile in its own right rather than an expedient tool for diversity management which should ultimately be discarded.' See Alex Warleigh, *Flexible Integration: Which Model for the European Union?* (London: Sheffield Academic Press, 2002), pp. 88–9.

36. For the critique of the flexibility clauses in the Treaty of Amsterdam see the editorial comments in the *Common Market Law Review*, 34/4 (1997), pp. 767–72. See also The Bruges Group at: http://www.brugesgroup.com/mediacentre/euconstitution.live; and Danish Convention Member Jens-Peter Bonde at: http://www.bonde.com/index.phtml?aid=11714; on the stability pact see the speech by Professor Franz-Christoph Zeitler, Member of the Executive Board of the Deutsche Bundesbank, at the Forum for discussion of the Friends of Europe, the Hanns Seidel Foundation and the Konrad Adenauer Foundation, Brussels, 16 February 2004, available at: http://www.bis.org/review/r040223e.pdf; on the open method of coordination see, for example, Åse Gornitzka, *Coordinating Policies for a 'Europe of Knowledge'—Emerging practices of the 'Open Method of Coordination' in Education and Research*, ARENA Working Paper, 2005, available at: http://www.arena.uio.no/publications/working-papers2005/papers/05_16.xml; and Christoph Knill and Andrea Lenschow, *Modes of Regulation in the Governance of the European Union: Towards a Comprehensive Evaluation*, European Integration Online Papers (EIoP), 2003, available at: http://eiop.or.at/eiop/texte/2003-001.htm.

37. This has been stressed even by those opposing the state-centred, hierarchical notion of governance. See James N. Rosenau, op.cit., p. 175.
38. See Walter Kickert, 'Complexity, Governance and Dynamics: Conceptual Explorations of Public Network Management', in *Modern Governance*, Jan Kooiman, ed. (London: Sage, 1993), pp. 191–204.
39. As Marlene Wind rightly observed: 'The entire idea of unity, hierarchy, and coherence in law is an inherently modern one that did not exist in the Holy Roman Empire. The "unity" of Roman law was, in other words, very different from what we understand by unity and coherence today. The Roman Empire was highly polycentric and consisted of many layers and interlocking compartments of legal norms and rules. These coexisted side by side, linked together in a common norm system, yet semi-autonomous and self-defining.' See Marlene Wind, 'The European Union as a polycentric polity: returning to a neo-medieval Europe?' in *European Constitutionalism Beyond the State*, J. H. H. Weiler and Marlene Wind, eds. (Cambridge: Cambridge University Press, 2003), p. 126.
40. For instance, as Christopher Hood showed, for highly technical and discretional activities such as regulation, a more appropriate notion of control is one of 'interpolable balance' based on the idea of self-policing and overlapping checking mechanisms that do not assume control from a fixed place in the governance system. See Christopher Hood, 'Concepts and Control over Public Bureaucracies: "Comptrol" and "Interpolable Balance" ', in *The Public Sector*, Franz-Xaver Kaufmann, ed. (Berlin: Walter de Gruyer, 1991), pp. 347–66.
41. See Pierre Calame, 'Active Subsidiariaty: Reconciling Unity and Diversity', in *Governance in the European Union*, Olivier De Schutter, Notis Lebessis, and John Paterson, eds. (Brussels: European Commission, 2001), 226–40.
42. See Filip Tuytschaever, *Differentiation in European Law* (Oxford: Hart, 1999), pp. 105–15.
43. Networks are often being accused of pursuing their selfish and usually narrow interests and ignoring broader pan-European concerns. Nor can cooperation between networks for broader social purposes be assumed. See, for example, Fritz W. Scharpf, 'The Political Calculus of Inflation and Unemployment in Western Europe. A Game-Theoretical Interpretation', in *Governance and Generalized Exchange*, Bernd Marin, ed. (Frankfurt: Campus, 1990), pp. 117–46; or Fritz W. Scharpf, 'Coordination in Hierarchies and Networks', in *Games and Hierarchies in Networks*, Fritz W. Scharpf, ed. (Frankfurt: Campus, 1993), pp. 125–67.
44. Richard Bellamy and Dario Castiglione identified four dimensions of legitimacy relevant to the EU. According to them, legitimacy can be defined as 'the normatively conditioned and voluntary acceptance by the ruled of the government of their rulers'. Richard Bellamy and Dario Castiglione, 'Legitimizing the Euro-"Polity" and its "Regime"', *European Journal of Political Theory*, 2/1 (2003), pp. 10–11. See also *Accountability and Legitimacy in the European Union*,

Anthony Arnull and Daniel Wincott, eds. (Oxford: Oxford University Press, 2002).

45. As Franz C. Mayer and Jan Palmowski argued: 'A meaningful common European historical identification barely exists, [and] European identities have come to be expressed first and foremost through EU institutions and EU law.' Franz C. Mayer and Jan Palmowski, 'European identities and the EU: the Ties that Bind the Peoples of Europe', *Journal of Common Market Studies*, 42/3 (2004), p. 573.

46. See Erik Oddvar Eriksen, 'Deliberative supranationalism in the EU', in *Democracy in the European Union: Integration through Deliberation?*, Erik Oddvar Eriksen and John Erik Fossum, eds. (London: Routledge, 2000), p. 48.

47. Deidre Curtin, 'The Constitutional Structure of the Union: A Europe of Bits and Pieces', *Common Market Law Review*, 30/1 (1993), p. 20.

48. Neil Walker, 'Flexibility within a Metaconstitutional Frame', in *Constitutional Change in the EU: From Uniformity to Flexibility?* (Oxford: Hart, 2000), op.cit., p. 11.

49. Johan P. Olsen, 'What is a Legitimate Role for Euro-citizens?', *Comparative European Politics*, 1/1 (2003), pp. 91–108.

50. Svein S. Andersen and Tom Burns, 'The European Union and the Erosion of Parliamentary Democracy: A Study of Post-parliamentary Governance', in *The European Union: How Democratic Is It?*, Svein S. Andersen and Kjell A. Alliassen, eds. (London: Sage, 1996), p. 230.

51. See Albert O. Hirschman, *Exit, Voice, and Loyalty: Responses to Decline in Firms, Organizations, and States,* (Cambridge, MA: Harvard University Press, 1970). Also Albert O. Hirschman, 'Exit, Voice and the State', *World Politics*, 31/1 (1978), pp. 90–107.

52. See especially *State Formation, Nation Building, and Mass Politics in Europe: The Theory of Stein Rokkan*, Peter Flora with Stein Kuhnle and Derek Urwin, eds. (Oxford: Oxford University Press, 1999). The exit–voice dichotomy is analysed in the context of the democratization of Europe on pages 227–43.

53. This has been forcefully argued by Stefano Bartolini. See Stefano Bartolini, 'Exit Options, Boundary Building, Political Restructuring', European University Institute Working Paper, SPS, No. 1, Florence, 1998, pp. 6–22. See also Fritz W. Scharpf, *Governing in Europe: Effective and Democratic?* (Oxford: Oxford University Press, 1999), p. 27; and Jean-Marie Guéhenno, *La fin de la démocratie* (Paris: Flammarion, 1993).

54. And as students of Eastern Europe know, hard borders do not always guarantee voice. Both exit and voice were constrained under communist regimes in the region.

55. This has been pointed out in a slightly different context in Stefano Bartolini, 'Old and New Peripheries in the Process of European Territorial Integration', in *Restructuring Territoriality: Europe and North America*, Chris Ansell and Giuseppe di Palma, eds. (Cambridge: Cambridge University Press, 2004), pp. 19–44. See also Stefano Bartolini, *Restructuring Europe. Centre Formation,*

System Building, and Political Structuring between the Nation State and the European Union (Oxford: Oxford University Press, 2005).

56. Charles S. Maier, 'Territorialisten und Globalizten. Die beiden neuen "Parteien" in der Heutingen Demokratie', *Transit*, 14 (1997), pp. 5–14.

57. As Yannis Papadopoulos argued: 'The presence of actors' networks, often established according to *ad hoc* criteria, the prevalence of procedures where bargaining plays a non-negligible role; the deformalisation of legal instruments; the particulars of each policy subsystem that make it difficult to enter a pre-established pattern of role division and of actor behaviour.... These factors are likely to generate feelings of alienation.' See Yannis Papadopoulos, 'Cooperative Forms of Governance: Problems of Democratic Accountability in Complex Environments', *European Journal of Public Research*, 42/4 (2003), p. 482.

58. See Zygmunt Bauman, 'A Sociological Theory of Postmodernity', in *Between Totalitarianism and Postmodernity: A Thesis Eleven Reader*, Peter Beilharz, Gillian Robinson, and John Rundell, eds. (Cambridge, MA: MIT Press, 1992), p. 160.

59. Stephen L. Elkin, 'Madison and After: The American Model of Political Constitution', *Political Studies*, 44, Special Issue: Constitutionalism in Transformation: European and Theoretical Perspectives (1996), pp. 592–604; see pp. 593–4.

60. See Walter Kickert, 'Complexity, Governance and Dynamics: Conceptual Explorations of Public Network Management', op.cit., pp. 191–2, and Erik Oddvar Eriksen, 'Deliberative supranationalism in the EU', op.cit., pp. 58–9.

61. Erik Oddvar Eriksen and John Erik Fossum, 'Legitimation Through Deliberation', in *Democracy in the European Union: Integration through Deliberation?*, Erik Oddvar Eriksen and John Erik Fossum, eds. (London: Routledge, 2000), pp. 256–69.

62. See Claire Vandevivere, 'The Federal Parliament in Belgium: Between Wishes, Rules, and Practice', in *National Parliaments on their Ways to Europe. Losers or Latecomers?*, Andreas Maurer and Wolfgang Wessels, eds. (Baden-Baden: Nomos, 2001), pp. 77–98. Available at: http://aei.pitt.edu/archive/00001476/01/National_Parliaments_Losers_or_Latecomers.pdf.

63. Andreas Maurer, 'National Parliaments in the European Architecture: From Latecomers' Adaptation to Permanent Institutional Change?', *National Parliaments on their Ways to Europe. Losers or Latecomers?*, Andreas Maurer and Wolfgang Wessels, eds. (Baden-Baden: Nomos, 2001), pp. 27–76. Available at: http://aei.pitt.edu/archive/00001476/01/National_Parliaments_Losers_or_Latecomers.pdf.

64. See Yves Mény and Yves Surel, *Par le peuple, pour le people* (Paris: Fayard, 2000).

65. Already the 1996 European Council in Turin declared its prime ambition to bring 'the Union closer to its citizens'. See European Council, Turin, 29 March 1996, Conclusions of the Presidency, in Bulletin 3-1996. See also European Commission, *European Governance, A White Paper* (Luxembourg: Office for Official Publications of the European Communities, 2001), p. 28 and p. 40; and European Parliament, Committee on Constitutional Affairs, *Report on the*

Commission White paper on European Governance (Rapporteur Sylvia-Yvonne Kaufman), Brussels, A5-0399/2001, 2001. Available at: http://www2.europar-l.eu.int/omk/sipade2?PUBREF=-//EP//NONSGML+REPORT+A5-2001-0399+0 +DOC+PDF+V0//EN&L=EN&LEVEL=3&NAV=S&LSTDOC=Y.

66. As Giovanni Sartori so accurately put it: 'Referendum democracy represents not only perfect but also the most unintelligent incarnation of a systematic majority tyranny' based on 'an outright zero-sum mechanism of decision making: the winning majority takes all, the minority loses all.' We should add that such a zero-sum mechanism is particularly poorly suited a highly diversified neo-medieval setting with multiple large minorities. See Giovanni Sartori, *The Theory of Democracy Revisited*, Part I: *The Contemporary Debate* (Chatham, NJ: Chatham House, 1987), p. 115.

67. As Robert A. Dahl pointed out, the argument over the optimal unit goes in circles, as with a set of Chinese boxes: any unit you chose smaller than the globe itself can be shown to be smaller than the boundaries of an urgent problem. Yet the larger the unit the greater the cost of uniform rules, the larger the minorities who cannot prevail, and the more watered down the control of the individual citizen. See Robert A. Dahl, 'Democracy and the Chinese Boxes', in *Frontiers of Democratic Theory*, H.S. Kariel, ed. (New York: Random House, 1970), pp. 372–3.

68. Robert A. Dahl, 'A Democratic Dilemma: System Effectiveness versus Citizen Participation', *Political Science Quarterly*, 109/1 (1994), p. 33.

69. This is not such high toll as applied by the normative models of deliberative democracy that require all citizens to have an equal opportunity to contribute to public deliberation on matters of common concern. See Maeve Cooke, 'Five arguments for deliberative democracy', *Political Studies*, 48/5 (2000), p. 956.

70. See Jonathan Zeitlin, 'Social Europe and Experimental Governance: Towards a New Constitutional Compromise?' in *EU Law and the Welfare State: In Search of Solidarity*, Gráinne de Búrca, ed. (Oxford: Oxford University Press, 2005).

71. Flexibility and informality are at the roots of networks' engagement, but as Fritz W. Scharpf rightly argued, we need to know when networks are allowed to make decisions affecting broader strata of citizens and when they are only allowed to prepare decisions to be formally taken by the European Council and other traditional EU institutions. See Fritz W. Scharpf, *Governing in Europe: Effective and Democratic?*, op. cit., p. 20.

72. One of the implications of the rejection of the Constitutional Treaty is that the Charter of Basic Rights is not enforceable; but it is expected that the Court will make reference to it sooner rather than later if the Constitution does not come into force.

73. Commenting on the European citizenship provisions in the Treaty of Maastricht, J. H. H. Weiler observed: 'The citizenship chapter seemed to bestow

precious few rights, hardly any that were new, and some explicitly directed to all residents and not confined to citizens.' See J. H. H. Weiler, *The Constitution of Europe* (Cambridge: Cambridge University Press, 1999), pp. 325–6.

74. This has been argued, for example, in Robert E. Goodin, 'Institutionalizing the Public Interest: The Defence of Deadlock, and Beyond', *American Political Science Review*, 90/2 (1996), p. 340. See also Robert E. Goodin, 'Representing Diversity', *British Journal of Political Science*, 34/3 (2004), pp. 453–68.

75. This has been particularly well argued by Yannis Papadopolous, op. cit., p. 493.

76. Article 21 of the EC Treaty.

77. See European Ombudsman, *Annual Report* (Brussels, 2004). Available at: http://www.euro-ombudsman.eu.int/report04/pdf/en/rap04_en.pdf. Also Paul Magnette, 'Between Parliamentary Control and the Rule of Law: the Political Role of the Ombudsman in the European Union', *Journal of European Public Policy*, 10/5 (2003), pp. 677–94.

78. For an insightful analysis of the populist turn in Europe, see Cas Mudde, 'The Populist Zeitgeist', *Government and Opposition*, 39/4 (2004), pp. 542–63.

79. The new member states from Eastern Europe have a particularly rich history of political contention, as recently manifested by the resistance to communist rule by such grass-roots democratic movements as Poland's Solidarity or the Czechoslovak Charter 77. See Grzegorz Ekiert and Jan Rubik, *Rebellious Civil Society: Popular Protest and Democratic Consolidation in Poland, 1989–1993* (Ann Arbor: University of Michigan Press, 1999). For a Western case of contentious politics see, for example, Charles Tilly, *Popular Contention in Great Britain, 1758–1834* (Cambridge, MA: Harvard University Press, 1995).

80. See, for example, John Locke, *Two Treatises of Government*, Peter Laslett, ed. (New York: Metor, 1965), and Pasquale Pasquino, *Popular Sovereignty: What Does It Mean?* (Paris: CREA, Ecole Polytechnique, 1996).

81. See Philip Pettit, *Republicanism* (Oxford: Oxford University Press, 1999), especially pp. 183–205.

82. See Dough Imig and Sidney Tarrow, 'Political Contention in a Europeanising Polity', *West European Politics*, 23/4 (2000), pp. 73–93. Also Doug McAdam, Sidney Tarrow, and Charles Tilly, *Dynamics of Contention* (Cambridge: Cambridge University Press, 2001).

83. Many democratic theories pointed to a rather intimate connection between democracy and populism. See, for example, Yves Mény and Yves Surel, *Par le peuple, pour le peuple,* (Paris: Librairie Arhème, 2000), or Gianfranco Pasquino, *Populism and Democracy* (Bologna: Johns Hopkins University, Bologna Center, 2005), especially pp. 10–13. See also Petr Kopecky and Cas Mudde, *Uncivil Society?: Contentious Politics in Post-communist Europe* (London: Routledge, 2003).

84. According to Philip Pettit decisions can be effectively contestable if a democracy 'follows deliberative patterns of decision-making, that includes all the major voices of difference within the community and that responds

appropriately to the contestations raised against them'. See Philip Pettit, *Republicanism* (Oxford: Oxford University Press, 1999), p. 200.

85. The European Ombudsman's task is to allow EU citizens to contest actions of the European institutions if they feel that they have suffered from maladministration, such as administrative irregularities, unfairness, discrimination, abuse of power, failure to reply, refusal of information, or unnecessary delay. Allowing the Ombudsman to take complaints, if proven justified, to the ECJ, would clearly further strengthen his/her position and thereby widen channels of contestation. In addition it would be desirable to ensure the Ombudsman's independence by disconnecting the position from the European Parliament (which currently elects the Ombudsman), as the EP itself is a potential source for citizens' complaints. In this context, the European Court of Human Rights would be a good example of an additional channel of contestation, as citizens are allowed to appeal directly to the Court without having have to be referred to it via a national court (as is the case with the ECJ). These practices could potentially be extended to the ECJ in order to allow citizens better access to judicial contestation in the EU. See, for example, Adam Cygan, 'Protecting the Interests of Civil Society in Community Decision-Making—The Limits of Article 230 EC', *International and Comparative Law Quarterly*, 52/4 (2003), pp. 955–1012.

86. The Swiss and Italian experiences suggest that the space for populist politics is reduced if referenda tackle very specific projects that are not of a fundamental and very complex nature like the European Treaty or Constitution. See Thomas Christin, Simon Hug, and Pascal Sciarini, 'Interests and Information in Referendum Voting: An Analysis of Swiss Voters', *European Journal of Political Research*, 41/6 (2002), pp. 759–76: and Pier Vincenzo Uleri, 'On Referendum Voting in Italy: YES, NO or Non-vote? How Italian Parties Learned to Control Referendums', *European Journal of Political Research*, 41/6 (2002), pp. 863–83.

87. For a similar line of argumentation see Sidney Tarrow, 'Center–Periphery Alignments and Political Contestation in Late-Modern Europe', in *Restructuring Territoriality: Europe and North America*, Chris Ansell and Giuseppe di Palma, eds. (Cambridge: Cambridge University Press, 2004), p. 64.

Bibliography

Almond, G. and Verba, S., *The Civic Culture* (Princeton, NJ: Princeton University Press, 1963).

—— —— eds., *The Civic Culture Revisited* (Boston: Little, Brown and Company, 1980).

Alter, K. J., *Establishing the Supremacy of European Law: The Making of an International Rule of Law in Europe* (Oxford: Oxford University Press, 2001).

Amato, G. and Batt, J., *Final Report of the Reflection Group on The Long-term Implications of EU Enlargement: The Nature of the New Border* (Florence: Robert Schuman Centre and Forward Studies Unit, EC, 1999).

Amin, A. and Hausner, J., eds., *Beyond Market and Hierarchy* (Cheltenham: Edward Elgar, 1997).

Andersen, S. S. and Alliassen, K. A., eds., *The European Union: How Democratic Is It?* (London: Sage, 1996).

Anderson, M. and Bort, E., eds., *The Frontiers of Europe* (London: Pinter, 1998).

Anderson, P., *Lineages of the Absolute State* (London: NLB, 1974).

Andréani, G., Bertram, C., and Grant, C., *Europe's Military Revolution* (London: Centre for European Reform, 2001)

Ansell, C. and di Palma, G., eds., *Restructuring Territoriality: Europe and North America* (Cambridge: Cambridge University Press, 2004).

Arnull, A. and Wincott, D., eds., *Accountability and Legitimacy in the European Union* (Oxford: Oxford University Press, 2002).

Artis, M. and Nixson, F., eds., *The Economics of the European Union: Policy and Analysis* (Oxford: Oxford University Press, 2001).

Avery, G. and Cameron, F., *The Enlargement of the European Union* (Sheffield: Sheffield University Press, 1998).

Baker, D. and Seawright, D., eds., *Britain for and against Europe: British Politics and the Question of European Integration* (Oxford: Clarendon Press, 1998).

Baldone, S., Sdogati, F., and Tajoli, L., eds., *EU Enlargement to the CEECs: Trade Competition, Delocalisation of Production, and Effects on the Economies of the Union* (Milan: Franco Angeli, 2002).

Bartolini, S., *Restructuring Europe: Centre Formation, System Building, and Political Structuring between the Nation State and the European Union* (Oxford: Oxford University Press, 2005).

Beaulac, S., *The Power of Language in the Making of International Law: The Word Sovereignty in Bodin and Vattel and the Myth of Westphalia* (Leiden: Martinus Nijhoff, 2004).

Beaumont, P., Lyons, C., and Walker, N., eds., *Convergence and Divergence in European Law* (Oxford: Hart, 2002).

Beilharz, P., Robinson, G., and Rundell, J., eds., *Between Totalitarianism and Postmodernity: A Thesis Eleven Reader* (Cambridge, MA: MIT Press, 1992).

von Beyme, K., *Transition to Democracy in Eastern Europe* (Basingstoke: Macmillan, 1996)

Bibic, A. and Graziano, G., eds., *Civil Society, Political Society, Democracy* (Ljubliana: Slovenian Political Science Association, 1994).

Black, A., *Guilds and Civil Society in European Political Thought from the Twelfth Century to the Present* (London: Methuen, 1984).

Blondel, J. and Müller-Rommel, R., eds., *Cabinets in Eastern Europe* (Basingstoke: Palgrave, 2001).

Bothe, M., Ronzitti., N., and Rosas, A., eds., *The OSCE in the Maintenance of Peace and Security: Conflict Prevention, Crisis Management and Peaceful Settlement of Disputes* (London: Kluwer Law International, 1997).

Bradley, J., Petrakos, G., and Traistaru, I., *Integration, Growth and Cohesion in an Enlarged European Union* (New York: Springer, 2005).

Brown, A., *The Demise of Marxism-Leninism in Russia* (Basingstoke: Palgrave/Macmillan, 2004).

Bull, H., *The Anarchical Society: A Study of Order in World Politics* (London: Macmillan, 1977).

—— and Watson, A., *The Expansion of International Society* (Oxford: Clarendon Press, 1984).

de Búrca, G., ed., *EU Law and the Welfare State: In Search of Solidarity* (Oxford: Oxford University Press, 2005).

—— and Scott, J., eds., *Constitutional Change in the EU: From Uniformity to Flexibility?* (Oxford: Hart, 2000).

—— —— eds., *New Governance and Constitutionalism in Europe and the US* (Oxford: Hart, 2005).

Burgess, M., *Federalism and European Union: Building of Europe 1950–2000* (London: Routledge, 2000).

Burn, H. H., ed., *The Cambridge History of Medieval Thought c.350–c.1450* (Cambridge: Cambridge University Press, 1988).

Buzan, B. and Little, R., *International Systems in World History* (Oxford: Oxford University Press, 2000).

Calleo, D. W., *Rethinking Europe's Future* (Princeton, NJ: Princeton University Press, 2001).

Bibliography

Cameron, F., ed., *The Future of Europe: Integration and Enlargement* (London: Routledge, 2004).

Caporaso, J., ed., *Continuity and Change in the Westphalian Order* (Oxford: Blackwell, 2000).

Castles, S. and Miller, M. J., *The Age of Migration: International Population Movements in the Modern World* (Basingstoke: Macmillan, 1993).

Cerutti, F. and Rudolph, E., *A Soul For Europe* (Leuven: Peeters, 2001).

Cohen, D. and O'Conner, M., *Europe in Cross-national Perspective* (London: Routledge, 2004).

Cooper, R., *The Breaking of Nations* (London: Atlantic Books, 2003).

—— *The Post-modern State and the World Order* (London: Demos, 2000).

Cowles, M. G. and Smith, M., eds., *The State of the European Union: Risks, Reform, Resistance and Revival* (Oxford: Oxford University Press, 2000),

Cox, M., Dunne, T., and Booth, K., eds., *Empires, Systems and States* (Cambridge: Cambridge University Press, 2001).

Cremona, M., ed., *The Enlargement of the European Union* (Oxford: Oxford University Press, 2003).

Curtin, D. and Heukels, T., eds., *Institutional Dynamics of European Integration: Essays in Honor of Henry G. Schermers* (Dordrecht: Martinus Nijhoff, 1994).

Dahl, R., *Polyarchy: Participation and Opposition* (New Haven, CT: Yale University Press, 1979).

—— *Democracy and its Critics* (New Haven, CT: Yale University Press, 1989).

Dannreuter, R., ed., *European Union Foreign and Security Policy: Towards a Neighborhood Strategy* (London: Routledge, 2004).

Darmer, M. and Kuyper, L., eds., *Industry and the European Union: Analysing Policies for Business* (Cheltenham: Edward Elgar, 2000).

Davies, N., *Europe: A History* (Oxford: Oxford University Press, 1996).

Deighton, A., ed., *Building Postwar Europe: National Decision-Makers and European Institutions, 1948–1963* (Basingstoke: Macmillan, 1995).

De Schutter, O., Lebessis, N., and Paterson, J., eds., *Governance in the European Union* (Brussels: European Commission, 2001).

Doyle, M., *Empires* (Ithaca, NY: Cornell University Press, 1986).

Dryzek, J. S. and Holmes, L., *Post-Communist Democratization: Political Discourses Across Thirteen Countries* (Cambridge: Cambridge University Press, 2002).

Drulak, P., ed., *National and European Identities in EU Enlargement: Views from Central and Eastern Europe* (Prague: Institute of International Relations, 2001).

Duchêne, F., *Jean Monnet: The First Statesman of Interdependence* (New York: W. W. Norton, 1994).

Dunay, P., Kardos, G., and Williams, A. J., eds. *New Forms of Security: Views from Central, Eastern and Western Europe* (Aldershot: Dartmouth, 1995).

Edwards, G. and Pijpers, A., eds., *The Politics of European Treaty Reform* (London: Pinter, 1997).

Eisenstadt, S. N., *The Political Systems of Empires* (Glencoe, NY: Free Press, 1963).

Ekiert, G. and Hanson, S. E., eds., *Capitalism and Democracy in Central and Eastern Europe: Assessing the Legacy of Communist Rule* (Cambridge: Cambridge University Press, 2003).

—— Kubik, J., *Rebellious Civil Society: Popular Protest and Democratic Consolidation in Poland, 1989–1993* (Ann Arbor: University of Michigan Press, 1999).

Enste, D. H., *The Shadow Economy: An International Survey* (Cambridge: Cambridge University Press, 2002).

Eriksen, E. O. and Fossum, J. F., eds., *Democracy in the European Union: Integration Through Deliberation?* (London: Routledge, 2000).

Etzioni, A., *The Active Society* (New York: Free Press, 1968).

—— *Political Unification Revisited: On Building Supranational Communities* (New York: Lexington Books, 2001).

Farmer, D. J., *To Kill the King: Post-traditional Governance and Bureaucracy* (Armonk, NY: M. E. Sharpe, 2005).

Ferguson, N., *Colossus: The Price of America's Empire* (New York: Penguin, 2004).

Ferrera, M. and Rhodes, M., eds., *Recasting European Welfare States* (London: Frank Cass, 2000).

Flora, P., Kunhle, S., and Urwin, D., eds., *State Formation, Nation Building, and Mass Politics in Europe: The Theory of Stein Rokkan* (Oxford: Oxford University Press, 1999).

Fuchs, D. and Klingemann, H. D., eds., *Citizens and the State: A Relationship Transformed* (Oxford: Oxford University Press, 1995)

Furdson, E., *The European Defence Community: A History* (London: Macmillan, 1980).

von der Gablentz et al., eds., *Europe 2020: Adopting to a Changing World* (Baden-Baden: Nomos, 2000).

Galtung, J., *Europe in the Making* (New York: Crane Russak, 1989).

Garton Ash, T., *Free World* (London: Penguin Books, 2005).

Gaskin, K. and Smith, J. D., *A New Civic Europe? A Study of the Extent and Role of Volunteering* (London: National Centre for Volunteering, 1997).

van Gerven, W., *The European Union: A Polity of States and Peoples* (Stanford, CA: Stanford University Press, 2005).

Gibbon, E., *Decline and Fall of the Roman Empire* (New York: Viking, 1952).

Giddens, A., *The Nation-state and Violence* (Cambridge: Polity Press, 1995).

Giusti, S. and Tajoli, L., eds., *Convergence in the Enlarged European Union* (Milan: Egea Edizioni, 2003).

Gourgh, R. and Reid, A., eds., *The Perfect Union? New Europe and the EU* (London: Policy Exchange, 2004).

Grabbe, H., *The Constellations of Europe: How Enlargement will Transform the EU* (London: Centre for European Reform, 2004).

Greenbert, D. et al., eds., *Constitutionalism and Democracy: Transitions in the Contemporary World* (Oxford: Oxford University Press, 1993).

Grzymała-Busse, A. M., *Redeeming the Communist Past: The Regeneration of Communist Parties in East Central Europe* (Cambridge: Cambridge University Press, 2002).

Guéhenno, J., *La fin de la démocratie* (Paris: Flammarion, 1993).

van Gunsteren, H., *A Theory of Citizenship* (Boulder, CO: Westview, 1998).

Habermas, J., *The Philosophical Discourse of Modernity: Twelve Lectures* (Cambridge, MA: MIT Press, 1987).

Haerpfer, C. W., *Democracy and Enlargement in Post-Communist Europe: The Democratization of the General Public in Fifteen Central and Eastern European Countries, 1991–1998* (London: Routledge, 2002).

Hallstein, W., *United Europe: Challenge and Opportunity* (Cambridge, MA: Harvard University Press, 1962).

Hamden-Turner, C. and Trompenaars, F., *The Seven Cultures of Capitalism: Value Systems for Creating Wealth in the United States, Japan, Germany, France, Britain, Sweden and the Netherlands* (New York: Doubleday, 1993).

Hardt, M. and Negri, A., *Empire* (Cambridge, MA: Harvard University Press, 2000).

Hayward, J., ed., *The Crisis of Representation in Europe* (London: Frank Cass, 1995).

—— and Menon, A., eds., *Governing Europe* (Oxford: Oxford University Press, 2003).

Held, D., ed., *Prospects for Democracy* (Oxford: Polity Press, 1993).

Henderson, K., ed., *Back to Europe: Central and Eastern Europe and the European Union* (London: UCL Press, 1999).

—— ed., *The Area of Freedom, Security and Justice in the Enlarged Europe* (Basingstoke: Palgrave, 2005).

Héritier, A., *Policy-Making and Diversity in Europe: Escaping Deadlock* (Cambridge: Cambridge University Press, 1999).

—— ed., *Common Goods: Reinventing European and International Governance* (Lanham, MD: Rowman and Littlefield, 2002).

—— et al, *Ringing the Changes in Europe: Regulatory Competition and the Transformation of the State: Britain, France and Germany* (Berlin: de Gruyter, 1996).

—— A., Kerwer, D., Knill, C., Lehmkuhl, D., Teutsch, M., and Douillet A., *Differential Europe: The European Union Impact on National Policymaking* (Lanham, MD: Rowman and Littlefield, 2001).

Hill, C., *The Changing Politics of Foreign Policy* (Basingstoke: Palgrave/Macmillan, 2003).

—— Smith K. E., eds., *European Foreign Policy: Key Documents* (New York: Routledge, 2000).

Hill, R. J. and Zielonka, J., eds., *Restructuring Eastern Europe: Towards a New European Order* (Aldershot: Edward Elgar, 1990).

Hirschman, A. O., *Exit, Voice, and Loyalty: Responses to Decline in Firms, Organizations, and States* (Cambridge, MA: Harvard University Press, 1970).

Hix, S., *The Political System of the European Union* (New York: Palgrave/Macmillan, 2005).

Hobsbawn, E., *The Age of Empire, 1975–1914* (New York: Pantheon, 1987).

Holsti, K., *Peace and War: Armed Conflicts and International Order, 1648–1989* (Cambridge: Cambridge University Press, 1991).

—— *International Politics: A Framework for Analysis* (London: Prentice Hall, 1992.

Hooghe, L., ed., *Cohesion Policy and European Integration: Building Multi-level Governance* (Oxford: Oxford University Press, 1996).

—— Marks, G., *Multi-level Governance and European Integration* (Lanham, MD: Rowman and Littlefield, 2001).

Howarth, D. and Torfing, J., eds., *Discourse Theory in European Politics: Identity, Policy, and Governance* (Basingstoke: Palgrave, 2005).

Hughes, J., Sasse, G., and Gordon, C., *Europeanization and Regionalization in the EU's Enlargement to Central and Eastern Europe: The Myth of Conditionality* (New York: Palgrave/Macmillan, 2004).

Innes, A., *Czechoslovakia: The Short Goodbye* (New Haven, CT: Yale University Press, 2001).

Johnson, C., *The Sorrows of Empire: Militarism, Secrecy and the End of the Republic* (New York: Metropolitan Books, 2004).

Jowitt, K., *New World Disorder: The Leninist Extinction* (Berkeley: University of California Press, 1992).

Judson, P. M. and Rozenblit, M. L., eds., *Constructing Nationalities in East Central Europe* (New York: Berghahn Books, 2005).

Kagan, R., *Of Paradise and Power: America and Europe in the New World Order* (New York: Alfred A. Knopf, 2003).

Kaiser, W. and Starie, P., eds., *Transnational European Union: Towards a Common Political Space* (Abingdon: Routledge, 2005).

Kaplan, R., *International Governance of War-Torn Territories* (Oxford: Oxford University Press, 2005).

Katz, R. and Mair, P., *How Parties Organize: Change and Adaptation in Party Organizations in Western Democracies* (London: Sage, 1995).

Kaufmann, F., ed., *The Public Sector* (Berlin: de Gruyter, 1991).

Kawasaki, K., *Global Culture: Media, Arts, Policy, and Globalization* (London: Routledge, 2002).

Kazmer, D. R. and Konrad, M., *Economic Lessons from the Transition: The Basic Theory Re-examined* (Armonk, NY: M. E. Sharpe, 2004).

Keating, M. and Hughes, J., eds., *The Regional Challenge in Central and Eastern Europe: Territorial Restructuring and European Integration* (Brussels: Presses interuniversitaires européennes/Peter Lang, 2003).

Kegley, C. and Raymond, G. A., *Exorcising the Ghost of Westphalia: Building World Order in the New Millennium* (Englewood Cliffs, NJ: Prentice Hall, 2002).

Kelemen, D., *The Rules of Federalism: Institutions and Regulatory Politics in the EU* (Cambridge, MA: Harvard University Press, 2004).

Kennedy, P., *The Rise and Fall of the Great Powers* (New York: Vintage, 1987).

Kitschelt, H., Mansfeldova, Z., Markowski, R., and Tóka, G., *Post-Communist Party Systems: Competition, Representation, and Inter-Party Cooperation* (Cambridge: Cambridge University Press, 1999).

Klaus, V., *Renaissance: The Rebirth of Liberty in the Heart of Europe* (Washington, DC: Cato Institute, 1997).

Kohler-Koch, B., *Linking EU and National Governance* (Oxford: Oxford University Press, 2003)

—— and Eising, R., eds., *The Transformation of Governance in the European Union* (London: Routledge, 1999).

Kohnstamm, M. and Hager, W., eds., *A Nation Writ large? Foreign Policy Problems Before the European Community* (London: Macmillan, 1973).

Kok, W., *Enlarging the European Union: Achievements and Challenges* (Florence: European University Institute, 2003).

Kolakowski, L., *Modernity on Endless Trial* (Chicago: Chicago University Press, 1990).

Kooiman, J., ed., *Modern Governance* (London: Sage, 1993).

Kopeckỳ, P., and Mudde, C., *Uncivil Society? Contentious Politics in Post-communist Europe* (London: Routledge, 2003).

Krasner, S., *Sovereignty, Organized Hypocrisy* (Princeton, NJ: Princeton University Press, 1999).

Krastev, I., *Shifting Obsessions: Three Essays on the Politics of Anticorruption* (Budapest: Central European University Press, 2004).

Kreppel, A., *The European Parliament and Supranational Party System: A Study in Institutional Development* (New York: Cambridge University Press, 2002).

Krugman, P., *Geography and Trade* (Cambridge, MA: MIT Press, 1991).

Laffan, B., O'Donnell, R., and Smith, M., *Europe's Experimental Union: Rethinking Integration* (London: Routledge, 2000).

Leonard, M., *Re-Ordering the World: The Long-term Implications of 11 September* (London: Foreign Policy Centre, 2002).

—— *Why Europe will Run the 21st Century* (London: Fourth Estate, 2005).

Leonardi, R., *Convergence, Cohesion and Integration in the European Union* (London: Macmillan, 1995).

—— *Cohesion Policy in the European Union: The Building of Europe* (New York: Palgrave/Macmillan, 2005).

Liebich, A., *Les minorités nationales en Europe Centrale et orientale* (Geneva: George, 1997).

Lieven, D., *Empire: The Russian Empire and its Rivals* (New Haven, CT: Yale University Press, 2001).

Lindberg, L. N., and Scheingold, S. A., *Europe's Would-be Polity: Patterns of Change in the European Community* (Englewood Cliffs, NJ: Prentice Hall, 1970).

Linz, J. J., and Stepan, A., *Problems of Democratic Transition and Consolidation* (Baltimore, MD: Johns Hopkins University Press, 1996).

Longhurst, K. and Zaborowski, M., eds., *Old Europe, New Europe and the Transatlantic Security Agenda* (London: Routledge, 2005).

Lubasz, H., ed., *The Development of the Modern State* (New York: Macmillan, 1964).

MacCormick, N., *Questioning Sovereignty* (Oxford: Oxford University Press, 1999).

Mair, P. and Zielonka, J., eds., *The Enlarged European Union: Diversity and Adaptation* (London: Frank Cass, 2002).

Manea, J. and Pearce, R., *Multinationals and Transition: Business Strategies, Technology, and Transformation in Central and Eastern Europe* (Basingstoke: Palgrave, 2004).

Mann, M., *Incoherent Empire* (New York: Verso, 2003).

March, J. G. and Olsen, J., *Democratic Governance* (New York: Free Press, 1995).

Marks, G. et al., eds., *Governance in the European Union* (London: Sage, 1996).

Marquand, D., *Parliament for Europe* (London: Jonathan Cape, 1979).

Martin, S., ed., *The Construction of Europe: Essays in Honor of Emile Noël* (Deventer: Kluwer Law Academic, 1994).

Mattina, L., ed., *La Sfida dell'allargamento: L'Unione europea e la democratizziazione dell'Europa centro-orientale* (Bologna: Il Mulino, 2004).

Mattli, W., *The Logic of Regional Integration: Europe and Beyond* (Cambridge: Cambridge University Press, 1999).

Maurer, A. and Wessels, W., eds., *National Parliaments on their Ways to Europe: Losers or Latecomers?* (Baden-Baden: Nomos, 2001).

Mayhew, A., *Recreating Europe: The European Union's Policy towards Central and Eastern Europe* (Cambridge: Cambridge University Press, 1998).

McAdams, J., ed., *Transitional Justice in New Democracies* (Notre Dame, IN: University of Notre Dame Press, 1996).

Mearsheimer, J., *The Tragedy of Great Power Politics* (New York: W. W. Norton, 2001).

Menon, A. and Wright, V., eds., *From the Nation State to Europe: Essays in Honour of Jack Hayward* (Oxford: Oxford University Press, 2001).

Mény, Y. and Surel, Y., *Par le peuple, pour le peuple* (Paris: Librairie Arhème Fayard, 2000).

Merkl, P. H., *The Rift Between America and old Europe: The Distracted Eagle* (London: Frank Cass, 2005).

Milward, A., *The European Rescue of the Nation State* (London: Routledge, 2000).

Mitrany, D., *The Functional Theory of Politics* (London: Martin Robertson, 1975).

Molle, W., *The Economics of European Integration: Theory, Practice, Policy* (Aldershot: Ashgate, 1997).

Moravcsik, A., *The Choice for Europe: Social Purpose and State Power from Messina to Maastricht* (London: UCL Press, 1999).

Motyl, A. J., *Imperial Ends: The Decay, Collapse, and Revival of Empires* (New York: Columbia University Press, 2001).

—— Blair, A. R., and Shevtsova, L., eds., *Russia's Engagement with the West. Transformation and Integration in the Twenty-First Century* (Armonk, NY: M. E. Sharpe, 2005).

Müller, J. W., *Another Country: German Intellectuals, Unification and National Identity* (New Haven, CT: Yale University Press, 2000).

Musolff, A., Schaffner, C., and Townson, M., eds., *Conceiving of Europe: Diversity in Unity* (Aldershot: Dartmouth, 1996).

Neef, R. and Stănculescu, M., eds., *The Social Impact of Informal Economies in Eastern Europe* (Aldershot: Ashgate, 2002).

Nelsen, B. F. and Stubb, A., eds., *The European Union: Readings on the Theory and Practice of European Integration* (London: Lynne Rienner, 1994).

Neunreither, K. and Wiener, A., eds., *European Integration after Amsterdam: Institutional Dynamics and Prospects for Democracy* (Oxford: Oxford University Press, 2000).

Nicolaidis, K. and Howse, R., *The Federal Vision: Legitimacy and Levels of Governance in the United States and the European Union* (Oxford: Oxford University Press, 2001)

—— and Weatherill, eds., *Whose Europe? National Models and the Constitution of the European Union* (Oxford: Oxford University Press, 2003).

Norris, P., ed., *Critical Citizens. Global Support for Democratic Government* (Oxford: Oxford University Press, 1999).

O'Brien, P. K., and Clesse, A., eds., *Two Hegemonies: Britain 1846–1914 and the United States 1941–2001* (Aldershot: Ashgate, 2002).

Osiander, A., *The States System of Europe, 1640–1990: Peace-making and the Conditions of International Stability* (Oxford: Clarendon Press, 1994).

Ostrom, E. and Keohane, R., eds., *Local Commons and Global Interdependence* (London: Sage, 1995).

Pagden, A., *Lords of All the World, Ideologies of Empire in Spain, Britain and France c. c.1500–c.1800* (London: Yale University Press, 1995).

Pasquino, G., *Populism and Democracy* (Bologna: Johns Hopkins University, Bologna Center, 2005).

Payá, J. I. T., *The European Community and Central Europe (1989–1993): Foreign Policy and Decision-Making* (Madrid: Centro de Estudios Avanzados en Ciencias Sociales, 1997).

Perron, C., *Les pionniers de la démocratie* (Paris: Presses Universitaires de France, 2004).

Peter, B. G., and Savoie, D. J., eds., *Governance in the Twenty-first Century: Revitalizing Public Service* (Montreal: McGill-Queen's University Press, 2000).

Petersen, H. and Zahle, H., eds., *Legal Polycentricity: Consequences of Pluralism in Law* (Aldershot: Dartmouth, 1995).

Peterson, J. and Bomberg, E., *Decision-Making in the European Union* (London: Macmillan, 1999).

Pettai, V. and Zielonka, J., eds., *The Road to the European Union: Estonia, Latvia and Lithuania* (Manchester: Manchester University Press, 2003).

Pettit, P., *Republicanism* (Oxford: Oxford University Press, 1999).

Philpott, D., *Revolutions in Sovereignty—How Ideas Shaped Modern International Relations* (Princeton, NJ: Princeton University Press, 2001).

Pierre, J., ed., *Debating Governance: Authority, Steering and Democracy* (Oxford: Oxford University Press, 2000).

Poggi, G., *The Development of the Modern State* (London: Hutchinson, 1978).

—— *The State: Its Nature, Development and Prospects* (Oxford: Polity Press, 1990).

Pollack, M., *The Engines of European Integration: Delegation, Agency and Agenda-Setting in the EU* (Oxford: Oxford University Press, 2003).

Pridham, G. and Ágh, A., eds., *Prospects for Democratic Consolidation in East-Central Europe*. (Manchester: Manchester University Press, 2001).

—— Lewis, P. G., eds., *Stabilizing Fragile Democracies: Comparing New Party Systems in Southern and Eastern Europe* (London: Routledge, 1996).

Prigogine, I. and Stengers, I., *Order out of Chaos* (New York: Bantam, 1984).

Princen, S., and Knodt, M., eds., *Understanding the European Union's External Relations* (London: Routledge 2003).

Radaelli, C., and Featherstone, K., eds., *Politics of Europeanization* (Oxford: Oxford University Press, 2003).

Rasmussen, H. K., *No Entry: Immigration Policy in Europe* (Copenhagen: Copenhagen Business School Press, 1997).

Renard, G., *Guilds in the Middle Ages* (London: G. Bell and Sons, 1919).

Rescher, N., *Pluralism: Against the Demand for Consensus* (Oxford: Clarendon Press, 1993).

Richardson, J., ed., *European Union: Power and Policy-making* (London: Routledge, 2001).

Rodrigues, M. J., ed, *The New Knowledge Economy in Europe: A Strategy for International Competiveness and Social Cohesion* (Cheltenham: Edward Elgar, 2002).

Rosamond, B., *Theories of European Integration* (London: Macmillan, 2000).

Rose, R., Mishler, W., and Haerpfer, C., *Democracy and its Alternatives: Understanding Post-Communist Societies* (Oxford: Polity Press, 1998).

Rosenau, J., *Along the Domestic–Foreign Frontier: Exploring Governance in a Turbulent World* (Cambridge: Cambridge University Press, 1997).

Rupnik, J. and Zielonka, J., eds., *The Road to the European Union: The Czech and Slovak Republics* (Manchester: Manchester University Press, 2003).

Sadurski, W., *Rights before Courts: A Study of Constitutional Courts in Postcommunist States of Central and Eastern Europe* (Dordrecht: Kluwer Law International, 2005).

Sandholtz, W. and Stone Sweet, A., eds., *European Integration and Supranational Governance* (Oxford: Oxford University Press, 1998).

Sartori, G., *The Theory of Democracy Revisited* (Chatham, NJ: Chatham House, 1987).

Scharpf, F. W., ed., *Games and Hierarchies in Networks* (Frankfurt: Campus, 1993).

—— *Governing in Europe: Effective and Democratic?* (Oxford: Oxford University Press, 1999).

Schimmelfennig, F. and Sedelmeier, U., eds., *The Politics of European Union Enlargement: Theoretical Approaches* (London: Routledge, 2005).

Schmitter P., *How to Democratize the European Union and Why Bother?* (Oxford: Rowman and Littlefield, 2000).

Schwartz, H., *The Struggle for Constitutional Justice in Post-Communist Europe* (Chicago: Chicago University Press, 2000).

Seidelmann, R., ed., *EU, NATO and the Relationship Between Transformation and External Behavior in Post-Socialist Eastern Europe* (Baden-Baden: Nomos, 2002).

Senior Nello, S. and Smith, K. E., *The European Union and Central and Eastern Europe: The Implications of Enlargement in Stages* (Aldershot: Ashgate, 1998).

Sergi, B. S. and Bagatelas, W. T., eds., *Ethical Implications of Post-communist Transition Economics and Politics in Europe* (Bratislava: Iura Edition, 2005).

Shaw, J., *Law of the European Union* (Basingstoke: Palgrave, 2000).

Shaw, M., *Theory of the Global State: Globality as Unfinished Revolution* (Cambridge: Cambridge University Press, 2000).

Siedentop, L., *Democracy in Europe* (London: Penguin Press, 2001).

Slaughter, A., *A New World Order* (Princeton, NJ: Princeton University Press, 2004).

Smith, K. E., *The Making of EU Foreign Policy* (New York: Palgrave/Macmillan, 2004).

Smith, M. E., *Europe's Foreign and Security Policy: The Institutionalism of Governance* (Cambridge: Cambridge University Press, 2004).

Snyder, J., *Myths of Empire: Domestic Politics and International Ambition* (Ithaca, NY: Cornell University Press, 1991).

Sperling, J. and Kirchner, E., *Recasting the European Order: Security Architectures and Economic Cooperation* (Manchester: Manchester University Press, 1997).

Spruyt, H., *The Sovereign State and its Competitors* (Princeton, NJ: Princeton University Press, 1994).

Stark, D. and Bruszt, L., *Postsocialist Pathways: Transforming Politics and Property in East Central Europe* (Cambridge: Cambridge University Press, 1998).

Steunenberg, B., ed., *Widening the European Union: The Politics of Institutional Change* (London: Routledge, 2002).

Stokke, O., ed., *Aid and Political Conditionality* (London: Frank Cass, 1995).

Stone Sweet., A., *Governing with Judges* (Oxford: Oxford University Press, 2000).

Sweeney, S., *Europe, the State and Globalisation* (Harlow: Longman, 2005).

Tilly, C., ed., *The Formation of National States in Western Europe* (Princeton, NJ: Princeton University Press, 1975).

—— *Coercion, Capital, and European States, A.D. 990–1990* (Oxford: Basil Blackwell, 1990).

—— *Popular Contention in Great Britain, 1758–1834* (Cambridge, MA: Harvard University Press, 1995).

Tsoukalis, L., *The European Community and its Mediterranean Enlargement* (London: Allen and Unwin, 1981).

—— ed., *Competitiveness and Cohesion* (Oxford: Oxford University Press, 2000).

—— *What Kind of Europe?* (Oxford: Oxford University Press, 2003).

Tunander, O., Baev, P., and Einagel, V. I., eds., *Geopolitics in Post-Wall Europe* (London: Sage, 1997).

Tuytschaever, F., *Differentiation in European Law* (Oxford: Hart, 1999).

Ullmann, W., *Principles of Government and Politics in the Middle Ages* (London: Methuen, 1966).

Vachudova, M. A., *Europe Undivided: Democracy, Leverage, and Integration after Communism* (Oxford: Oxford University Press, 2005).

Vaughan-Whitehead, D. C., *EU Enlargement versus Social Europe? The Uncertain Future of the European Social Model* (Cheltenham: Edward Elgar, 2003).

Verdery, K., *What Was Socialism, and What Comes Next* (Princeton, NJ: Princeton University Press, 1996).

Verdun, A. and Croci, O., *Institutional and Policy-making Challenges to the European Union in the Wake of Eastern Enlargement* (Manchester: Manchester University Press, 2004).

Wallace, H., Wallace, W., and Pollack, M., eds., *Policy-Making in the European Union* (Oxford: Oxford University Press, 2005).

Wallace, W., *The Transformation of Western Europe* (London: Royal Institute of International Affairs 1990).

Walters, W. and Haahr, J. H., *Governing Europe: Discourse, Governmentality and European Integration* (New York: Routledge, 2005).

Waltz, K., *Man, the State and War: A Theoretical Analysis* (New York: Columbia University Press, 2001).

Warleigh, A., *Flexible Integration: Which Model for the European Union?* (London: Sheffield Academic Press, 2002).

—— *Democracy and the European Union* (London: Sage, 2003).

Weatherill, S. and Bernitz, U., eds., *The Role of Regions and Sub-national Actors in Europe* (Oxford: Hart, 2005).

Weiler, J. H. H., *The Constitution of Europe* (Cambridge: Cambridge University Press, 1999).

—— Wind, M., eds., *European Constitutionalism Beyond the State* (Cambridge: Cambridge University Press, 2003).

Wildavsky, A., *Budgeting and Governing* (New Brunswick, NJ: Transaction, 2001).

de Witte, B., ed., *Ten Reflections on the Constitutional Treaty for Europe* (Florence: European University Institute, 2003).

—— Hanf, D., and Vos E., eds., *The Many Faces of Differentiation in EU Law* (Antwerp: Intersentia, 2001).

Wolczuk, K., and Wolczuk, R., *Poland and Ukraine: A Strategic Partnership in a Changing Europe?* (London: Royal Institute of International Affairs, 2002).

Zeitlin, J. and Philippe P., eds., with Magnussen, L., *The Open Method of Co-ordination in Action* (Oxford: Peter Lang, 2005).

Bibliography

Zielonka, J., *Explaining Euro-paralysis* (London: Macmillan, 1998).

—— ed., *Paradoxes of European Foreign Policy* (The Hague: Kluwer Law International, 1998).

—— ed., *Europe Unbound: Enlarging and Reshaping the Boundaries of the European Union* (London: Routledge, 2002).

—— Pravda, A., eds., *Democratic Consolidation in Eastern Europe*, Vol 2: *International and Transnational Factors* (Oxford: Oxford University Press, 2001).

Zürn, M. and Joerges, C., *Law and Governance in Postnational Europe: Compliance Beyond the Nation-state* (Cambridge: Cambridge University Press, 2005).

Index